The New Global Politics of the Asia-Pacific

The New Global Politics of the Asia-Pacific presents a coherent framework for understanding the complex international and global politics of the Asia-Pacific. It is an introductory guide to the main frameworks needed to understand the region (realism, liberalism, critical theory), which is reader friendly, while still offering sophisticated competing interpretations. A highly topical account, which provides an overview of the main actors, institutions and contemporary issues such as security and transnational actors, it is required reading for undergraduate students of Asian Studies, International Politics and anyone interested in the region.

Key content includes:

* The US in the Asia-Pacific
* China and Japan in the Asia-Pacific
* Southeast Asia in the Asia-Pacific
* Australia in the Asia-Pacific
* Europe and the Asia-Pacific
* Globalization, regionalism and political economy
* Asian values, democracy and human rights
* Transnational actors
* Regional security order

Michael K. Connors lectures in Politics and Developmental Studies at La Trobe University. **Rémy Davison** is currently lecturer in Government at the University of Tasmania. **Jörn Dosch** is both senior lecturer in, and Head of, Asia Pacific Studies at the Department of East Asian Studies, University of Leeds.

The New Global Politics of the Asia-Pacific

Michael K. Connors, Rémy Davison and Jörn Dosch

RoutledgeCurzon
Taylor & Francis Group
LONDON AND NEW YORK

First published 2004
by RoutledgeCurzon
2 Park Square, Milton Park, Abingdon, Oxfordshire, OX14 4RN

Simultaneously published in the USA and Canada
by RoutledgeCurzon
270 Madison Avenue, New York, NY 10016

RoutledgeCurzon is an imprint of the Taylor & Francis Group

© 2004 Michael K. Connors, Rémy Davison and Jörn Dosch

Typeset in Baskerville by RefineCatch Ltd, Bungay, Suffolk
Printed and bound in Great Britain by TJ International Ltd, Padstow, Cornwall

British Library Cataloguing in Publication Data
A catalogue record for this book is available from the British Library

Library of Congress Cataloging in Publication Data
A catalog record for this book has been requested

ISBN 0–415–28562–3 (hbk)
ISBN 0–415–28563–1 (pbk)

Contents

Illustrations

Figures

Tables

Boxes

Preface

This book was written by three observers and teachers of the international politics of the Asia-Pacific. We each brought to the book our different political and theoretical perspectives. By luck, rather than design, we were happy to discover that our respective orientations cover the spectrum of approaches to international relations. This, we hope, has enabled us to produce a book that presents a balanced account of competing theoretical perspectives. While each chapter has a principal author, the final product is a result of a long dialogue between all of us.

We have attempted to write a book that is useful for those new to the study of Asia-Pacific international politics, and for those relatively new to international relations theory. We also believe the book will be of interest to the more general and scholarly reader seeking a concise and theoretically accessible account of select aspects of the new global politics of the Asia-Pacific, as well as fresh accounts of seemingly familiar material. As with any book there are topics here that have been given sparse treatment or no treatment at all. This is the cost of any attempt at closure! However, the book has been fashioned out of a concern to give broad coverage of two broad areas. The first half of the book takes a somewhat state-centric approach which might be seen as being quite traditional in an age when the state is being challenged. Without such a grounded understanding of the major state players in the international politics of the region, we believe it would be difficult to make sense of the so-called 'New Agenda' in international relations theory. The second half of the book attempts to present a select coverage of new agenda issues and, as such, balances the state-centric biases of the first half of the book. It goes without saying that a comprehensive introductory understanding of the Asia-Pacific is impossible without this dual approach. While there are some who would prefer one area or the other, we believe the two to be mutually enhancing. The book, we hope, will lead readers to search out the vast and rich literature that excitement about the Asia-Pacific has generated in the last few years.

A number of friends and colleagues have supported us in endeavouring to complete this book. The Politics Program at La Trobe University, Melbourne, kindly provided sufficient funds for us to employ an able research assistant, Ms Kathy Heba, to give the full manuscript a final eye before we sent it off to the able folk at Routledge. Most especially, we would like to thank Associate Professor Derek McDougall from the University of Melbourne for his comments on a draft of this book. Those comments helped us to focus our efforts and bring the project to completion. Derek's assistance was especially kind since we have, in some ways, stepped onto his own 'academic turf': Derek is the author of a widely read introductory book on the Asia-Pacific. Such generosity of spirit reminds us that there is still much left of the old university spirit, despite what seems to be the relentless commercialization of tertiary institutions.

Michael would like to thank John and Jak who kindly offered him refuge in their home several times during 2003, allowing him to work without distraction. After a hard day's work (most real workers would dispute this), he immensely enjoyed their company and friendship. As well as friendship, Szu-yao Fang offered constantly challenging perspectives on the politics of the Asia-Pacific. Meg Gurry is owed a heavy debt for sharing her understanding of Australia's international politics – some of which has made it into the Australian chapter. Michael would also like to make a special mention of Angela Gosling who, by changing his life many years ago, taught him that teachers can make a difference.

Rémy Davison would like to thank his best appointments: his life partner, defamation adviser, and general solicitor-in-charge, Josephine Swiney, for her boundless support and encouragement throughout the writing of this book, as well as for enduring having chapters read out to her. He would also like to thank Associate Professor Peter Shearman, his life tennis partner, for being (alternately) friend, supervisor, employer and editor.

Jörn Dosch would like to thank his wife Ana-Lucia, and his children Nils-Mateo and Amelie for their continued love and support in all that he does.

Michael Kelly Connors, La Trobe University, Australia
Rémy Davison, University of Tasmania, Australia
Jörn Dosch, University of Leeds, United Kingdom
December 2003

1 Introduction: the new global politics of the Asia-Pacific

Rémy Davison

'Why is there no NATO in Asia?' ask Christopher Hemmer and Peter Katzenstein (2002: 575) in *International Organization*. The answer is deceptively simple: in Europe, the United States built institutions; in East Asia, it did not.

The seductiveness of this answer fails to capture the complexity, uncertainty and instability of the Cold War era in the Asia-Pacific region. In 1949, none could have predicted the endurance of the Beijing and Taipei regimes, the Sino-Soviet split, or America's ignominious withdrawal from Vietnam. Equally, few could have anticipated the rapid marketization of the People's Republic of China (PRC) economy after 1979, the extraordinary growth of the East Asian newly industrializing countries (NICs), or the equally extraordinary collapse of many of them in 1997–98.

The Asia-Pacific is such a fluid and dynamic region that it demands continual reappraisal and reconsideration. Only a decade ago, it was the hub of global economic growth, as it accounted for 31 per cent of world output, more than either the European Union or the US. Yet, just a few years later, its economic miracle was in tatters and, at the dawn of the twenty-first century, politico-economic instability, terrorism and security threats emerged as the key issues confronting the nations of East Asia. In parts of the region, the Cold War is far from over, evidenced by the re-emergence of a forceful North Korean regime which embarked upon an aggressive ballistic missile programme in the 1990s. Although Pyongyang's position appeared to soften following *rapprochement* with South Korea, and certain diplomatic guarantees from the US, tensions flared up once more during 2002–03, as the communist regime posed a new threat to its immediate neighbours, South Korea and Japan.

The Asia-Pacific has emerged as a region of global significance. It houses the world's two biggest economies, the world's largest military power and the world's most populous nation. The region is also home to eight of the world's ten largest military forces. Communist, democratic and authoritarian regimes cohabit and coexist within the region, if not always peacefully. Although the Yalta system, which divided the post-war world into US and Soviet spheres of influence has disappeared, many Cold War relics remain scattered throughout the Asia-Pacific. Taiwan remains a point of friction between the US and China; the PRC remains a communist state, albeit one with many of the trappings of a capitalist market economy; the 1953 division of the two Koreas at the 38th parallel is still intact; Japan remains a military client state of the US, and US hegemony in the region persists.

In this chapter, we commence with a brief discussion of key developments in the Asia-Pacific during the Cold War. This is followed by an examination of the major paradigms in international relations – realism, liberalism, neo-Marxism and constructivism – which have been highly influential prisms through which both academic analyses, as well as policy makers, have viewed international relations in the Asia-Pacific. We provide an overview of the book in the final section of this chapter.

Locating the Asia-Pacific region

As Hemmer and Katzenstein note, there is a great deal of confusion over what constitutes 'Asia', the 'Asia-Pacific' and the 'Pacific'. In this volume, India, Pakistan and Russia are not the subject of case studies, although they can each claim to play important roles as Asian powers. However, important, albeit artificial, geographical divisions are frequently drawn between East, South and Central Asia. For example, Palmer (1991: 21) asks whether the Asia-Pacific can be described as a region, due to its diffuse geography, ethnicity and culture. This book focuses predominantly upon what former Australian foreign minister Gareth Evans describes as the 'East Asian hemisphere', comprising Northeast Asia (China, Japan, the two Koreas and Taiwan), Southeast Asia (the ASEAN 10), Australia and New Zealand. The breadth of both Asia and the Pacific Ocean means that Russia, Mongolia and Chile can rightfully claim membership of Asia-Pacific Economic Co-operation (APEC), but this book necessarily limits its discussion to two of the Pacific's key actors outside Asia: the US and Australia. Due to their respective strategic and economic interests, both countries are heavily enmeshed with the East Asian region; however, due to their geographical locations and cultural backgrounds, they are not of the East Asian region. Implicitly, APEC's very nomenclature recognizes this fact in that it broadens the notion of Asian economic co-operation to encompass the Asia-*Pacific*, a form of transcontinental regionalism Keohane and Nye (2001: 2) term 'multicontinental interdependence'.

Similarly, the definitional minefield which students of international politics confront when attempting to determine the geographical extent of 'Asia' or the 'Asia-Pacific' is rendered all the more difficult by notions of 'Asian' versus 'Western' values. This encompasses a wide range of issues and models, a number of which we consider in Chapter 12: authoritarianism *v.* democracy; communitarianism *v.* human rights; and the capitalist development state *v. laissez-faire* capitalism.

APEC proves the exception, rather than the rule, in studies of East Asia. No other Asian economic organization includes states from outside Northeast or Southeast Asia. ASEAN, the ASEAN Free Trade Area (AFTA), ASEAN Plus Three (APT) and Malaysia's 1990 East Asian Economic Caucus (EAEC) proposal comprise East Asian states exclusively. Conversely, security and dialogue forums, such as the Asia–Europe Meeting (ASEM) and the ASEAN Regional Forum (ARF), co-opt other states and regional actors, including the EU, Australia and the US, within a broad framework of mutual interests. However, it is notable that neither the ARF nor ASEM has developed the complex institutional framework of ASEAN, which has survived since 1967, while none of the other East Asian regional organizations, including the Southeast Asia Treaty Organization (SEATO), and the Asian and Pacific Council (ASPAC), remain.

This book evaluates the many changes and continuities in the new global politics of the Asia-Pacific region. That the region is of global significance both strategically and economically is beyond contestation. Of equal importance is the fact that both the US and Europe have developed such a level of interconnectedness with the Asia-Pacific that it arguably ranks foremost in the minds of American and European policy makers, ahead of other potential flashpoints, such as the Middle East and Central Asian regions.

The making of the Cold War in East Asia

The Cold War may have been a battle between the US and Soviet Union, but its battlefields were to be found in East Asia: in China, Korea and Vietnam. In this respect, conflict, confrontation and co-operation in East Asia have provided rich empirical data for analyses of the region. In the immediate post-war period, international relations theory was dominated by realism, which monopolized national foreign policy agendas throughout most of the world.

Historians have debated the causes of the Cold War incessantly, but all agree that the Korean War was a pivotal moment in this emergent 'tripolar' international system. Gaddis (1982: 110–15) argues that Korea was fundamentally an error of US foreign policy, driven by two imperatives: first, to atone for its early Cold War failures in Greece, Iran and Berlin; and, second, to restore US 'credibility' against the perceived threat of Soviet and Chinese communist expansionism. Gaddis asserts that despite US Secretary of State Acheson's assurances to Beijing that US interests extended only to preventing Soviet imperialism in China, in reality US policy was directed towards 'preventing the basis of a durable alliance between the Soviet Union and China'.

However, it was the Soviet Union's own diplomacy which destroyed the Sino-Soviet *entente cordiale* and divided the 'monolithic' communist bloc. Stalin's China policy in the 1940s was essentially motivated by realism, not international communism. Moscow sought to avoid a powerful communist state on its borders which might not only exhibit independence, but could also ultimately pose a challenge to the leading and guiding role of the Communist Party of the Soviet Union. In response, Mao's forces recommenced their insurrections against the Nationalists, leading to the virtual disintegration of the Nationalist government by 1948. Mao's suspicions of the Soviets deepened as Stalin urged him to concentrate his forces in northern China, leaving the south to the Nationalists. The damage to Sino-Soviet relations was permanent: in 1950, Stalin secured Mao's agreement that Mongolia would remain 'independent', albeit as a Soviet satellite. In return for some nominal financial and material assistance, Mao was also forced to cede some mining rights in Manchuria and Xinjiang to the Soviets.

If China could win concessions from the Americans while remaining in the Soviet camp, US Secretary of State John Dulles wrote in 1952, 'then there is little reason for her to change' (Gaddis 1992: 75). However, the Eisenhower Administration was uncertain about how to divide the communist bloc. Truman had viewed vigorous action in Korea as the only means by which to restore US credibility in the region, in an attempt to combat the perception that the US had 'lost' China. Conservative George Kennan had warned in 1947 that Soviet communist expansion had occurred much more quickly and successfully than the imperialist acquisitions of the Fascist and Nazi regimes in the 1930s. Therefore, Kennan (1947) argued, both communist China and the USSR needed to be contained, while the PRC could also be isolated from international affairs by continuing US support for the Nationalist regime in Taipei.

In East Asia, as well as Europe, Kennan's doctrine of the need to 'contain' the USSR became the linchpin of American policy. In Europe, the Soviet thrust was halted eighty miles west of Berlin; but in East Asia, the fall of the Nationalist Chinese government to Mao's communists in 1949 indicated that the US had underestimated the power of international socialism's 'second front'. Under a joint Soviet–American agreement, the two sides withdrew from the Korean Peninsula in 1949. However, North Korean forces' invasion of South Korea in 1950 provided the Truman Administration with the justification for military re-engagement with the region. The US deployed the Seventh Fleet to Formosa in June, ostensibly to protect the South Korean regime, as the Rhee government in the South had been quickly driven out of Seoul by North Korean forces by September 1950. The US's response was a United Nations Security Council (UNSC) resolution in October, calling for the establishment of UN-sponsored forces to restore stability in Korea. As the Chinese Nationalist government, now based in Taipei, was a permanent member of the UNSC, the PRC had no vote on the issue. The Soviet delegation absented itself, and the three other Permanent Members – the US, Britain and France – voted in favour of the resolution.

The US, Britain and Australia thus entered the war on the South's side with UN support for the intervention. In response, the PRC 'volunteers' covertly assisted the North. It has recently become apparent that the USSR also played a major covert role in the conflict. Although this was unclear at the time, the Korean War was the first armed conflict staged between nuclear powers. Despite the cessation of hostilities in 1953 with no decisive victory, the division of Korea, with a communist-dominated North, persists as one of the last remnants of the Cold War.

Throughout the Korean War, the American conservatives' view – that Mao's China and Stalin's USSR would form a communist bloc – appeared correct. The Soviets supplied China with over US$250 million in material assistance during the conflict, and relations were co-operative on issues such as Port Arthur and mineral resources in Manchuria and Xinjiang, which the Soviets returned to the PRC. Khrushchev's emergence as Soviet leader in 1957 initially maintained conciliatory policies towards China. However, the Soviets were disbursing a greater proportion of their foreign aid to satellites such as Egypt and, simultaneously, demanded China repay Korean War loans. Khrushchev also offered Soviet nuclear technology to Mao in return for virtually complete control over Chinese foreign policy. Mao, having witnessed the ruthlessness of the 1956 Soviet invasion of Hungary, rejected the overture. In 1959, Khrushchev abruptly cancelled nuclear co-operation with the PRC. However, China persisted with nuclear weapons development and exploded its first device in 1964.

During Khrushchev's leadership, the Sino-Soviet relationship moved from uneasy protagonism to Cold War, exemplified by military skirmishes on their common border (Bazhanov 1995: 160). In an attempt to counter Soviet hegemony, Mao began to look westward for allies. In 1964, France established diplomatic relations with the PRC when China was diplomatically isolated by American non-recognition and the Sino-Soviet split. Nevertheless, US administrations from Kennedy to Johnson continued to view the PRC as part of a contiguous communist bloc, a perspective which only underwent radical change with the election of President Nixon in 1968.

Unlike their predecessors, Nixon and, later, Kissinger, viewed Sino-Soviet relations through the prism of realism, not conservatism. Both had seen the Sino-Soviet split as a potentially fundamental change in the balance of power. Equally, they saw no US national interest in continuing to sacrifice money and troops in Vietnam. Nixon's Guam Doctrine, announced in 1969, indicated that the US would no longer deploy ground troops in support of East Asian governments, a move which presaged the gradual withdrawal of the US from the Vietnam War.

After Guam: from Cold War to Asian regional security

Throughout the 1950s and 1960s, a number of regional agreements were established in Southeast Asia designed to ensure security and stability in the region. The Southeast Asia

Treaty Organization (SEATO) was formed in Manila in 1954. SEATO was an American-inspired creation, rather than an endogenous form of regional integration, following the defeat of French forces in Indo-China. SEATO broadly provided for the security of Southeast Asia, although its only members from the region were Thailand and the Philippines. The majority of its members were Atlantic and Pacific powers: the US, Britain, France, Australia and New Zealand, although newly independent Pakistan was also included. SEATO was designed to defend Southeast Asia from armed attack, which provided justification for future interventions by member states in Vietnam. In 1962, the US narrowed its interpretation of SEATO to provide specific commitments to Thailand, which was related to the crisis in Laos. US policy makers argued that these commitments served to prevent communist aggression only, a clear indication that US foreign policy was primarily directed against PRC and Vietnamese influence in the region.

Following the failure of the Association of Southeast Asia (ASA) (1962), and the abortive South Korean-led Asian and Pacific Council (ASPAC) (1966), a key initiative was the formation of the Association of Southeast Asian Nations (ASEAN) in 1967. Its original members – Indonesia, Thailand, Singapore, the Philippines and Malaysia – eschewed the structure of a traditional military alliance, preferring instead to develop a set of principles aimed at ensuring non-interference in the internal affairs of ASEAN countries. Exemplifying 'old regionalism', ASEAN adopted many cues from the European Community (EC), establishing a large number of committees dealing with common interests such as banking, financial affairs, jurisprudence, shipping and employer organizations, as well as cultural organizations. From 1976 – notably, following the fall of Saigon – the Treaty of Amity and Co-operation provided a forum for the peaceful resolution of disputes between ASEAN member countries. However, unlike their EC counterparts, the ASEAN states did not introduce stringent regulatory frameworks; in fact, the 'ASEAN way' was the reverse of the European integration experience. ASEAN remained essentially a forum for regional dialogue, rather than an attempt at supranational institutionalism.

ASEAN has proven an enduring body, which has developed as an umbrella group for a wide range of important regional economic and security initiatives. These include the 1992 ASEAN Free Trade Agreement (AFTA); the Asia–Europe Meeting (ASEM) (1996); and the ASEAN Regional Forum (ARF) (1994). ASEAN has also expanded considerably, encompassing Brunei (1984), Vietnam (1995), Laos and Myanmar (1997) and Cambodia (1999). More recently, it has developed closer links with Japan, China and South Korea separately, with dialogue meetings under the auspices of ASEAN Plus One, as well as ASEAN Plus Three (APT), comprising ASEAN meeting with Japan, China and South Korea collectively. All of the original ASEAN-6, as well as Vietnam, are also members of Asia-Pacific Economic Co-operation (APEC) (1989).

Outside ASEAN, an important initiative of the early 1970s was the Five-Power Defence Arrangements (FPDA) (1971), comprising Malaysia, Singapore, Britain, Australia and New Zealand. The FPDA was primarily designed to ensure stability in Malaysia–Singapore relations, particularly following Singapore's expulsion from the Federation of Malaysia in 1965. As a strategic base during times of conflict, and as an important commercial centre in peacetime, Britain and Australia in particular saw the preservation of Singapore's autonomy from Malaysia – or any other state – as intrinsic to defence in the region, a posture explained partially by the successful Japanese invasion of the British fortress of Singapore in 1942.

For much of the Cold War, Europe was viewed as the geostrategic centre of superpower conflict; however, war took place in the East Asian theatre, not Europe, with both the US and USSR fighting proxy wars in the region. Soviet–American intervention in the region from 1945 divided the East Asian hemisphere into allies of either the capitalist West or the socialist East. Revolution in China in 1949 meant there were effectively 'four Chinas': the People's Republic of China; the Republic of China; British Hong Kong; and Portuguese Macao. Self-determination movements created newly independent states in the form of Indonesia, Malaysia and Singapore from old European colonial empires.

War has not been an uncommon occurrence in the region. The victory of Mao Zedong over the Kuomintang Nationalist Government itself sparked a conflict between American and British and Sino-Soviet forces on the Korean Peninsula in 1950, culminating in a bloody stalemate which left Korea bifurcated into North and South by 1953, a geographical and national division which remains today. French defeat at Dien Buen Phu in 1954 led to increased US intervention in Indo-China, resulting in the Vietnam quagmire that only ended with the fall of Saigon in 1975. Revolution, coups and conflict in Cambodia, Indonesia, Singapore and Malaya demonstrated the volatility of the region in the Cold War climate. The story of post-1945 East Asia appeared to suggest that states in the region had conflict and proximity in common, but little else.

Yet, from the 1960s, both exogenous and endogenous factors contributed to a gradual stabilization of the international politics of the Asia-Pacific. The reasons for this were manifold, but the emergence of a number of security regimes, such as the Association of Southeast Asian Nations (ASEAN) (1967); the Five-Power Defence Arrangements (FPDA) (1971); and the ASEAN Regional Forum (ARF) (1994) suggests that co-operative security, which envisages international consensus developed and managed through multilateral institutions and regimes, is becoming embedded in Southeast Asian diplomacy (Leifer 1998; Conetta 2002). Sino-American *rapprochement* from 1971, following the 1957–61 Sino-Soviet split, indicated that the US, the most powerful military actor in the region, was prepared to countenance a much less confrontational role in East Asia, particularly in light of the Vietnam débâcle. President Nixon's articulation of the Guam Doctrine in 1969 meant that the US was no longer prepared to commit ground forces to the defence of allies and satellites in the region. Sino-American reconciliation also paved the way for the emergence of the PRC as a regionally significant, and potentially globally significant, power, evidenced by the seating of Mao's China as a permanent member of the United Nations Security Council (UNSC).

The Asia-Pacific is highly dynamic and fluid – economically, politically and culturally – particularly given the development of a Chinese diaspora throughout many parts of the region. During the 1980s and 1990s, it became the hub of global economic growth, and a key destination for foreign direct investment (FDI). The emergence of the 'four tigers' (South Korea, Taiwan, Hong Kong and Singapore) and the 'little dragons' (Indonesia, the Philippines, Thailand and Malaysia) as first- and second-tier 'newly-industrialized countries' (NICs), respectively, suggested that the 'East Asian' capitalist-development state had succeeded, while 'Anglo-Saxon', 'Colbertist' and 'Third Way' Western models of capitalism were floundering.

However, the enormous development gains made by the 'little dragons' were damaged badly by the Asian economic crisis of 1997–98, which wiped billions of dollars from East Asian stock markets, decimated currencies and shattered savings. The prescription of harsh medicine, administered largely by the US and its Western IMF partners, imposed heavy burdens upon Indonesia, Thailand and South Korea in particular, from which they have yet to fully recover. Indeed, Waldon Bello (2002: 1) asks whether East Asia's future involves 'strategic economic co-operation or marginalization'. East Asian states have been forced to endure this form of Western interventionism for the best part of 500 years, represented most recently by the IMF and World Bank structural adjustment programmes.

The Asia-Pacific region is home to a number of potential flashpoints, many of which are discussed in this book, including the PRC-Taiwan; North Korea; separatist movements; and terrorism in Indonesia and the Philippines. Given the legacy of political and economic instability in the region, one of the key questions in this book is: how are international relations (IR) in the Asia-Pacific to be understood? Broadly speaking, three main paradigms can be identified as relevant to both scholarly research into IR and foreign policy. These are realism, liberalism and radicalism. The latter can be said to encompass a wide range of theories, including varieties of Marxism, constructivism and world order/global governance studies. As Peou (2002: 119) notes, 'The post-Cold War debate among positivist and post-positivist theorists of international security – particularly realists, liberals and constructivists – has not diminished'.

Approaches from international relations: realism, liberalism, neo-Marxism and constructivism

Realism and neo-realism

Realism was the dominant paradigm in international relations for most of the twentieth century, and it arguably remains the guiding logic in foreign policy decision making. For realists, a key attribute of the international system is war, which they argue is a natural condition. The central actor in international relations is the state, which is a unitary, rational, utilitarian entity, that has relative autonomy in decision making, within the constraints imposed by other states within the international system. Realists argue that the international system is essentially anarchic, in that there is an absence of central authority. They assert that whereas domestic systems are centralized and hierarchic, international systems are *de*centralized and anarchic (Waltz 1979). As central authority is lacking, states in the system are forced to provide for their own survival and security. Thus, the realist conception of the international system is one of self-help. Within this self-help system, states interact strategically, with each vying to maximize both their own security and interests.

Power is also central to the realist conception of international relations. According to realists, the structure of the international system is determined by the distribution of capabilities. A state's capabilities are measured by the extent to which it can project its power and influence. For Waltz, the only thing one need know about a state is the extent of its military power. According to Morgenthau (1948), power depends upon a state's access to resources – financial, natural, human – and these will determine the extent of a state's capabilities. The only constraints placed upon a state are imposed by the capabilities of the state itself, together with the structure of the system; i.e., the relative power of other states within the system.

Order in an anarchical system is a third key realist concern. How is order maintained? Hedley Bull (1977: 53) asks. The answer is via a balance of power. To avert the onset of general war, states will act militarily, often in coalition with others, in order to prevent the rise of a hegemonic power. Therefore, the general rule of balance of power theory is that should an individual state have the potential to overwhelm all the rest (Napoleon's France; Hitler's Germany), then states will form a counter-hegemonic coalition in order to restore the power balance.

In realist international theory, states seek only one goal: the maximization of their security. For neo-realists, such as Waltz, at a minimum states seek security and, at a maximum, global domination. All means available to the state are directed towards one end: relative power gains at the expense of other actors in the system. The realist conception of world order regards international economic transactions as subordinate to the political interactions which take place between states. Although realists accept the importance of economic power and trade linkages between states, these are viewed as ancillary adjuncts to politico-military power. Naturally economic strength is crucial to state power. But economic power is a means, not an end, to military power. To this extent, the realist paradigm suggested that states were relatively autonomous units, with exclusive sovereignty within their own national borders. Sovereignty itself has had formal status in international law since 1648, and the 1945 United Nations Charter confirmed the legal principle of state sovereignty. Consequently, both national sovereignty and the balance of power system have coexisted and developed symbiotically over 350 years.

The Cold War introduced a new balance of power structure. Whereas the multipolar European balance of power system (1648–1945) comprised a number of major powers, roughly equal in their capacities, the emergence of two superpowers – the USSR and US – after the Second World War introduced a *bipolar* structure, with the UK, France, West Germany, China and Japan relegated to the status of second-order powers, due to their vastly inferior military capabilities compared with the superpowers.

The extent to which the US and USSR could project their power was truly global. As a result, there was no continent which the Cold War left untouched. Although the military and financial dominance of the US was not seriously challenged by the USSR in the 1945–48 period, the emergence of Communist China in 1949 threatened to tip the power balance in the favour of the communist states. Although both China and the Soviet Union claimed to practise 'socialist' foreign policy, both exhibited realism in foreign policy, exemplified by the Sino-Soviet split of 1957–61, as the USSR sought to gain control of the overall direction of Chinese foreign policy, a feat it had already achieved throughout Eastern Europe. As a great power, China was able to resist Soviet attempts to transform the PRC into a client state.

What compels states to form regional security alliances? Why do they break down? How has ASEAN survived? Realists argue that regional co-operation takes place because of common external threats. Relative weakness is also an important precondition of co-operation, as weakness tends invite control. According to Waltz (1979: 201), 'The perils of weakness are matched by the temptations of power'. From a realist perspective, it would be impossible to leave South Korea or Taiwan without a credible defensive capability, as this could provide North Korea or China with the opportunity to annex these territories.

As *realpolitik* depends upon the credibility of a serious military deterrence capability, the trend throughout most of the Cold War was an escalation in the level of military capabilities among the major powers of the region, although this was not restricted to the superpowers, Japan and China. Even within ASEAN, the growth of Singapore's military capabilities in the 1990s vastly outpaced that of its rival, Malaysia. Due to the realist emphasis upon the importance of military power, critics argue that the search for military invulnerability has led to a *security dilemma*. This thesis asserts that security is relative; because states compete for power and influence, this competition ultimately results in arms races. At the height of the Cold War, the Soviets and the Americans each possessed well over 20,000 nuclear warheads. More recently, the US commitment to the development of theatre missile defence (TMD), a strategy which the PRC claims is designed to 'encircle' China, has led the PRC to implement new countermeasures, such as the rapid development of multiple independently-targeted re-entry vehicles (MIRVs), in response to US policy. The security dilemma emerges when it is impossible to distinguish between defensive and offensive capabilities, and states are arguably no less vulnerable with massive arsenals at their disposal than they are without them. However, realists argue that this is an oversimplified view of defence doctrine; they assert that counterforce and massive retaliation, two key doctrines of Cold War strategic thinking, provided stability in Soviet–US relations and rendered Chinese nuclear capabilities irrelevant (Glaser 1990: 302). For realists, conventional and nuclear deterrence has kept the peace in Korea and Taiwan, and even prevented the war in Vietnam escalating into conflicts between the US and the USSR/China, due to the overwhelming dangers of nuclear confrontation.

Realists also differ considerably from liberals in their approach to co-operation. For realists, the incentive to co-operate is weak, and will usually be confined to 'low politics' areas, such as trade and investment. In realist theory, co-operation also denotes relative weakness; states seek co-operative security (for example, the ARF) because they are unable to provide adequately for their own security. This is clearly the case for Japan, South Korea and Taiwan, and explains why they have sought and accepted regional security under an American military umbrella. In this respect, realists are fundamentally at variance with liberals; whereas liberals argue the incentives for regional and international co-operation and interdependence are strong, realists counter that states co-operate only because they are weak, and cannot guarantee their own security in the face of external threats.

Interdependence: liberal perspectives

Interdependence theory, a widely cited explanatory logic in an era of widespread industrial and technological modernization in the 1960s and 1970s, emerged as a challenge to the realist orthodoxy in the 1970s, primarily as an explanation of the failure of US military power to achieve its objectives in the Vietnam War. While Cooper's (1968) model of interdependence focused primarily upon macroeconomic integration between states, Keohane and Nye (1977) argued that linkages across a range of issue areas reflected a growing 'web' of interdependence between states. For liberal theorists, interdependence existed at the level of the firm, between economies, through military coalitions and even in cultural linkages between states. For Keohane and Nye, interdependence meant a growing level of *mutual dependence*; the greater the level of interdependence, the higher the propensity for international co-operation.

Keohane and Nye argued that international interdependence had developed such complexity that it was impossible for states to ignore the potential impact of their domestic and foreign policies upon other states. As a result, Keohane and Nye asserted that under conditions of complex interdependence, there was no longer any clear hierarchy of issues. Issues such as foreign *economic* policy were arguably of equal or greater importance than traditional foreign policy diplomacy. Moreover, as states developed enhanced levels of interdependence (for example, in areas such as trade and investment), they would be less likely to come into conflict, and more likely to identify common policy interests.

However, Keohane and Nye concede that interdependence is unlikely to be symmetrical; more often, relationships – such as trade, security or investment – are generally asymmetrical. For example, Southeast Asian states need Japanese investment, but Japanese firms also need Southeast Asia as a manufacturing base and a source of inexpensive labour. Thus, despite the inequalities in the relationship – Japanese corporations own many of the ASEAN states' productive assets, while ASEAN firms have few investments in Japan – ASEAN and Japan have achieved a certain level of interdependence, albeit asymmetrical. The incentive for increased co-operation between these two interdependent actors, Keohane and Nye argue, is high, as mutual benefits accrue if levels of interdependence increase. Therefore, complex interdependence is not merely a liberal theory of international integration, but also an explanation of international political co-operation.

Neoliberal institutionalism

Neoliberalism retains the key features of liberalism. For example, Grieco (1995) distinguishes between forms of *liberal* and *neoliberal* forms of institutionalism. The original liberal thesis was in diametric opposition to realism's central propositions. Liberals rejected realist claims that the state was a unitary and rational agent. It also rejected the key tenet of realist thought: that the international system was an anarchic and decentralized realm where power was measured by the distribution of capabilities. In orthodox liberal theory, states were merely one of many actors in world politics, with non-state actors such as firms and international organizations playing at least an equal, if not more important, role than states.

Neoliberal institutionalism has its basis in regime theory, which points to the proliferation of institutions in the post-war world. In international politics, institutions were frequently, but not exclusively, the product of US hegemony which provided the international public goods (security, financial, trading systems) necessary for the establishment of regimes. After 1944, the US sponsored the Bretton Woods system (the GATT, IMF, World Bank), as well as NATO, the UN and SEATO. For neoliberals, regimes establish the institutions, frameworks and norms, the so-called 'rules of the game'. These are reflected in East Asian regimes, such as the institutional structure of ASEAN, and the ARF's objectives, which include promotion of confidence-building measures (CBMs), preventative diplomacy mechanisms and conflict resolution mechanisms (Ball 2000: 35).

Neoliberal institutionalist approaches essentially accept many of realism's key premises (the state as the central unit in the international system; the state as rational actor). However, despite this, neoliberals argue that co-operation between states is not only possible due to the existence and capabilities of international organizations, but also more likely. In realist theory, international co-operation *is* possible under conditions of anarchy, but only if states conclude that their national interests are served by engaging in co-operation.

From a realist perspective, complex interdependence does not necessarily result in increased international co-operation, but quite the reverse. Due to the increased sensitivity associated with close bilateral relationships, realists argue that interdependence creates 'a mutuality of suspicion' (Waltz 1970: 220). States with vital interests beyond their borders watch the activities of others warily, as variations in policy may affect their firms, their trade or their investments. However, as an analytical framework, the ascendancy of realism has diminished; as McDougall (1998: 132) notes, 'there has been a shift from realist preoccupations to emphases that highlight "complex interdependence" and the role of culture in international politics'.

Interdependence and globalization appeared to be the dominant logics governing the East Asian region throughout the 1980s, and for most of the 1990s, as it became the hub of global economic activity. For proponents of interdependence, the exponential growth experienced by the first- and second-tier NICs for almost two decades demonstrated the dominance of transnational forces, such as production and finance, over traditional realist concerns, such as security and military power. The enmeshment of the potentially enormous Chinese economy with the post-Cold War global economy of the 1990s appeared to demonstrate the ascendancy of market forces, which, to some extent, relegated regional security to a second-order issue.

Dominance and dependence: neo-Marxist perspectives

Whereas liberals argue that interdependencies between states may be asymmetrical, dependency theorists claim that asymmetries reflect not interdependence, but *dominance* and *dependence*. Frank (1967; 1975) and Wallerstein (1979) posit that the structure of global capitalism creates international stratification between states of the developed industrial core and the underdeveloped periphery. Between the two lies a partially developed semi-periphery. For Frank, economic relations between states can never be in a state of mutual dependence, as inter-state relations are fluid and capitalist forces perennially readjust to altered market conditions. To this extent, any form of symmetry can exist only in a theoretical vacuum and without reference to a broader range of conditions which determines the structure of inter-state relations. Frank criticized capitalist-development theories and argued that comprador elites formed a nexus with core elites producing a structure of dependent underdevelopment. States' relations, therefore, reflect dominance and dependence and, in a number of instances, dependent underdevelopment and capital accumulation by the core at the expense of the periphery. Wallerstein's world-systems analysis takes this core–periphery relationship a stage further by suggesting that dependent underdevelopment is reflective of a world capitalist economy which is characterized by an international division of labour. Yoshihara (1988) develops the Frank–Wallerstein dependency thesis further in his study of Southeast Asia. Yoshihara argues that the form of capitalism developed in Southeast Asia represents 'ersatz' (or inferior), replacement capitalism, exemplified by growth without economic development. For Yoshihara, Southeast Asia will be unable to break out of its dependency upon foreign capital and technology as core firms (from Japan, the US and Europe) continue to control the key factors of production. Alternative neo-Marxist approaches employ Antonio Gramsci's critique of capitalism, which argues that hegemony is created by a ruling capitalist class. The overthrow of capitalism depends upon a successful counter-hegemonic struggle.

Although dependency and neo-Marxist theories were largely discounted in the early 1990s, due to East Asia's explosive growth and the dramatic increase in living standards in the region, dependency theory developed renewed momentum in the wake of the 1997 Asian economic crisis which appeared to empirically validate many radical critiques of economic interdependence and globalization. However, some liberal economists have also emphasized the importance of the international division of labour. For Krugman (1979), the 'new economic geography' of the global political economy determines why clustering or agglomeration among states occurs. In his 'new trade' thesis formed during the 1980s, Krugman argued that states sought to perpetuate the international division of labour through 'strategic trade policy'; i.e., protectionist trade policies. Dependency and liberal theorists agree broadly on the power of transnational forces in international relations which can affect and constrain states' national policy preferences. Where they diverge is how to counter the power of major states. For liberals, the answer lies in increased levels of inter-dependence and regional and global governance via institutions; for neo-Marxists, the answer is much more radical in that nothing less than the overthrow of the capitalist world economy will result in the destruction of the structure of dependency.

Constructivism

Realism, liberalism and neo-Marxism are viewed by many theorists as unsatisfactory accounts of international relations. No single theory appears to provide an adequate account of the complexities of the international system; nor do they pay sufficient attention to the influence of subnational and transnational actors in the policy-making process. Constructivism is a relatively recent approach to international relations which rejects the transaction cost approaches inherent in realism and liberalism. Liberals and realists ask 'what will be the benefits?' or 'who will gain more?' from transactions between states; conversely, constructivists explore subnational phenomena in order to explain dissonance in the behaviour of peoples, states and markets.

Constructivists have sought to apply alternative explanations to developments in international relations which they consider are treated inadequately by the dominant paradigms. With their focus upon military power and economics, realism, liberalism and neo-Marxism exclude issues such as culture, nationalism, identity, ideology and religion. Constructivists argue that these are critical issues which can at least partially determine states' policy responses.

Given that realists and neoliberals view the state as a unitary construct, traditional international relations theories cannot account for the influence of transnational ethnic groups, such as the Chinese diaspora in both Northeast and Southeast Asia. Islam is represented strongly throughout much of the East Asian region, and its impact upon decision making in Indonesia, Malaysia and the Philippines can have profound implications for states' foreign policies.

Social constructivists view the construction of common identities – whether cultural, religious or ethnic – as under-studied elements of international relations which nevertheless have an important and diffuse impact upon a range of issue areas. Similarly, the social construction of nationalism is considered an avenue of research which is largely disregarded by realist and neoliberal analyses. Constructivists can claim considerable empirical validity for their assertion that ideational constructs dominate traditional international relations theory. The social construction of terrorism and liberation movements provides a good example: who is a terrorist and who is a freedom fighter? How are these conclusions reached? Why are some religions intolerant of others? How are civilizational identities, such as 'Asia' and 'the West' constructed?

Institutionalism in East Asia is particularly apposite to a constructivist analysis. According to Acharya (1999: 3):

> Constructivists argue that through incremental interactions and socialization, states redefine their interests and develop a 'collective identity' that may enable them to overcome power politics and the security dilemma. In this respect, Constructivists take a sociological, rather than 'strategic interaction', view of co-operation in which collective identity is deemed to be constitutive of state interests. From a Constructivist standpoint, conditions such as anarchy, security dilemma and power politics are not permanent or 'organic' features of international relations, but are socially constructed. International relations are shaped not just by material forces, such as power and wealth, but also by inter-subjective factors, including ideas, culture and identity.

Constructivism has been viewed as a particularly useful prism through which to view regional organizations such as ASEAN and the ARF, which do not necessarily conform with realist or liberal explanations of state interaction. For example, ASEAN's employment of dialogue forums and confidence-building measures (CBMs) does not appear congruent with the realist conception of balances of power and defensive positionality. The relative lack of international integration between the ASEAN partners over almost forty years also suggests that liberal conceptions of interdependence and co-operation are not particularly applicable to ASEAN either. As Peou (2002: 136) argues, 'constructivism is closer to the truth than balance-of-power realism in that it seeks to explain regional security by looking at a wide range of ideational, inter-subjective as well as material factors'. Nevertheless, constructivism is not without its critics. Michael Leifer, the most influential realist on the Southeast Asian region, argues that institutions, such as the ARF, far from being predicated upon the 'ASEAN way' described by constructivists, merely represent 'lowest common denominator' international bargaining; a 'limited' and 'minimalist' structure which is limited to CBMs (Leifer 1998: 11–13). In Chapter 5, we provide a discussion of the comparative strengths and weaknesses of social constructivist, realist and liberal explanations of the 'ASEAN way'.

Structure of the book

Chapter 2 considers the impact of the United States upon the Asia-Pacific region. Arguably, the US has had the most influence upon the strategic environment and economic construction of the region over the past sixty years. Indeed, US troops have been stationed in the region since the 1940s, fighting major wars against Japan (1941–45), North Korea (1950–53) and North Vietnam (1965–73). Hot wars aside, the Asia-Pacific became the central geostrategic focus for the Cold War, with the region divided between American allies (ASEAN, Japan, South Korea, Taiwan) and the Communist quadrangle comprising the Soviet Union, the People's Republic of China, North Korea and Vietnam. Unlike Europe, where nuclear weapons kept the temperature of the Cold War cool (Waltz 1988), hot wars, and the precarious structure of the balance of power in the Asia-Pacific, saw the US presence become a permanent one.

Japan performed a significant *volte-face* in the 1990s, from client state of the US to cautious military power. As we argue in Chapter 3, the transformation of Japan from Cold War ally into a key politico-strategic partner of the US may not occur rapidly; the Diet has taken a piecemeal approach to legislative reform, which permits Japan to play a greater role in both regional and global security. Its constitution – which renounces war as an instrument of policy and commits Japan to a purely 'defensive' posture – has been largely circumvented by recent legislative initiatives, that are likely to make Japan a much more potent military force in the region. The end of the Cold War meant the end of Soviet containment of Japan, while the simultaneous emergence of China as a rival power and the US's gradual military disengagement with the region indicated that a major power would need to fill the power vacuum. However, realist perspectives suggest that the US has not resiled from its dominant military role in East Asia; more accurately, the US has sought since the 1991 Gulf War to end 'free riding' on the US's global defence system, of which Japan has been a beneficiary since 1945. As this chapter argues, it is difficult to predict how Japan will react strategically to the dramatically altered security environment of the Asia-Pacific, given its proximity to an emergent China and a newly aggressive North Korea, although Japanese anti-terrorism legislation and co-operation with the US on ballistic missile defence (BMD) give some indication.

The post-Cold War period has also seen China emerge as a regional actor of global significance, partly as a result of the collapse of the USSR, and partly due to the relative economic decline of Japan. At present, China is merely a regional power due to its relatively limited military capabilities, but it is a state of global significance given its potential market power, and its growing role as a centre for global manufacturing, augmented by its rapid integration with the economies of Hong Kong and Taiwan. In Chapter 4, we examine the PRC's relations with its regional neighbours, with particular reference to its relations with Taiwan, Hong Kong, Japan, North Korea and ASEAN. The chapter also discusses China's development of its 'new security concept', and the implications this may have for the conduct of the PRC's diplomacy.

In Southeast Asia, ASEAN is one of the few remaining examples of Cold War 'old regionalism' which has survived into the twenty-first century. Unlike its EU counterpart, ASEAN eschews major treaties and rigid institutional and jurisprudential frameworks, preferring an evolutionary, consensual and confidence-building approach to regional organization and security. The success of this approach over almost forty years has meant that ASEAN has not only expanded its membership, but can also claim to be the hub of Southeast Asian integration. As Chapter 5 notes, ASEAN represents a serious challenge to realist and liberal analyses of international relations in terms of its approach to institution building, which was not under the auspices of a hegemonic power, a characteristic of EU and global institutions. In this chapter, we consider the possibility that 'identity politics' has been at least as strong an influence on the construction of ASEAN as national self-interest and interdependence.

No state outside Asia has attempted to integrate with the region as persistently as Australia. While the Soviet Union and the US fought a Cold War of ideological and economic rivalry over Asia, neither showed any inclination to be anything other than hegemonic actors in the region. Conversely, Australia has employed 'middle power' diplomacy (Cooper *et al.* 1993) to reach accommodations with both Northeast and Southeast Asia. In 1989, Australia's most important accomplishment in the region was the APEC initiative, which encompassed not only ASEAN countries, but also Japan, China, Taiwan, Hong Kong, South Korea and the US. In doing so, Australia attempted to portray itself not only as a Pacific country, but as an integral member of the 'East Asian hemisphere'. However, as Chapter 6 notes, Australia staged a dramatic policy U-turn in 1996, directing its foreign policy initiatives towards a closer strategic and economic partnership with the US. Signs that Australia had moved from 'engagement' with Asia to 'national interest diplomacy' in its foreign policy orientation were exemplified by Australia's role in the independence ballot on East Timor in 1999, and its subsequent leadership of UN forces in that country. In doing so, Australia tore up over thirty years of appeasement policy towards Indonesia. As we argue in this chapter, Australia may have redefined its place in the region, but at considerable diplomatic cost in some respects.

Europe – particularly the EU – was slow initially to recognize the importance of East Asia. Despite the region's rapid economic growth during the 1980s, the EU was inwardly focused upon the completion of its internal market programme by 1993. In some respects, there were connections between the development of East Asian regionalism and the completion of the single market in the EU. Due to fears of 'Fortress Europe' (i.e., a protectionist trade bloc), APEC and AFTA were, to varying degrees, examples of 'reactionary regionalism', which were designed to buffer Asia-Pacific states from some of the negative implications of a more insular EU market.

The Asia–Europe meeting, founded in 1996, signalled that East Asia was a key priority for the EU, given growing trade and investment links between the EU and both Northeast and Southeast Asia. Individual EU states, such as France, not only initiated over ninety ministerial visits to the Asian region after 1995, but also signed 'global partnership' agreements with China and Japan (Davison 2004). ASEM is an inter-regional dialogue process, which has experienced some difficulties, notably over human rights in Myanmar. However, with the conclusion of four ASEM meetings, it transformed the EU from marginal player to strategic actor in East Asian affairs. As Chapter 7 notes, ASEM may offer the greatest potential for security-related interaction between the two regions.

In Chapter 8, the discussion shifts to issues of intra-regional security, with particular reference to potential flashpoints in the region. Case studies such as the PRC-Taiwan conflict, the Korean Peninsula, the South China Sea, radical Islam and local insurgencies are discussed in the context of weak states, the lack of a regional security network and unresolved Cold War conflicts. The chapter concludes with a brief discussion of how institutions such as the ARF may be able to build consensus on questions of mutual security.

The final four chapters of the book are concerned with transnational forces and their impact upon the region. In Chapter 9, the influence of globalization and the growth of regionalism are viewed as concomitant forces which have produced outcomes such as 'reactionary regionalism' and 'open regionalism'. Regionalism and globalization have also raised new questions concerning linkages between Northeast and Southeast Asia, as well as the role of the capitalist development state. These issues are discussed in Chapter 10, which considers the political economy of the 1997 Asian economic crisis.

The influence of transnational actors upon national, regional and global politics is a strongly contested area in international relations. Chapter 11 assesses the significance of non-state actors in the Asia-Pacific region, with specific reference to transnational corporations (TNCs) and non-government organizations (NGOs). The chapter concludes that although it is difficult to quantify 'influence', it presents a number of case studies which suggest that some transnational actors have had an important impact upon the direction of national policy.

The liberalizing influences associated with globalization are clearly not restricted to the economic realm. Asia's 'economic miracle' created a new and growing middle class in both Northeast and Southeast Asia. Although relatively few East Asian states can claim to be liberal democracies, the debate over 'Western democracy' and 'Asian democracy' persists, particularly as corruption (the Philippines in 1986; South Korea in 1988) and political instability (Thailand in 1992; Indonesia in 1998) led to the downfall of long-established authoritarian regimes, which were replaced by transitional democracies. As Chee (1993: 24) argues, Asia may simply present different variations on the notion of 'democracy'. In Chapter 12, we consider a number of the theoretical debates concerning the 'Western tradition' of liberalism, versus the concept of 'Asian values'.

References

Acharya, A. (1999) 'Realism, institutionalism, and the Asian economic crisis', *Contemporary Southeast Asia*, 21: 1–17.

Ball, D. (2000) *The Council for Security Co-operation in the Asia-Pacific: Its Record and its Prospects*, Canberra Papers on Strategy and Defence No. 139, Canberra: Australian National University.

Bazhanov, E. (1995) 'Russian policy toward China', in P. Shearman (ed.) *Russian Foreign Policy Since 1990*, Boulder, CO: Westview, pp. 159–80.

Bello, W. (2002) 'East Asia's future: strategic economic co-operation or marginalization?', Transnational Institute, September. Online. Available HTTP: <http://www.tni.org/reports/asia/crosspoints/paper6.htm> (accessed 26 January 2003).

Bull, H. (1977) *The Anarchical Society*, London: Macmillan.

Chee, C. H. (1993) 'Democracy: evolution and implementation, an asian perspective', in R. Bartley, C. H. Chee and S. P. Huntington (eds) *Democracy and Capitalism: Asian and American Perspectives*, Singapore: Institute of Southeast Asian Studies, pp. 1–26.

Conetta, C. (2002) 'World order, and cooperative security: a research and policy development agenda', Project on Defense Alternatives, *Briefing Memo*, 24, 9 September.

Cooper, A., Higgott, R. and Nossal, K. (1993) *Relocating Middle Powers: Australia and Canada in a Changing World Order*, Vancouver: University of British Columbia.

Cooper, R. (1968) *The Economics of Interdependence*, New York: McGraw-Hill.

Davison, R. (2004) 'French Security after September 11: Franco-American Discord', in P. Shearman and M. Sussex (eds) *European Security after 9/11*, Aldershot: Ashgate.

Frank, A. G. (1967) *Capitalism and Underdevelopment in Latin America*, New York: Monthly Review Press.

Frank, A. G. (1975) *On Capitalist Underdevelopment*, Oxford: Oxford University Press.

Gaddis, J. L. (1982) *Strategies of Containment: A Critical Appraisal of Post-war American National Security Policy*, Oxford: Oxford University Press.

Gaddis, J. L. (1992) *The United States and the End of the Cold War*, Oxford: Oxford University Press.

Glaser, C. L. (1990) *Analyzing Strategic Nuclear Policy*, Princeton, NJ: Princeton University Press.

Grieco, J. M. (1995) 'Anarchy and the limits of co-operation: a realist critique of the newest liberal institutionalism', in C. W. Kegley (ed.) *Controversies in International Relations Theory: Realism and the Neoliberal Challenge*, New York: St Martin's Press, pp. 151–72.

Hemmer, C. and Katzenstein, P. (2002) 'Why is there no NATO in Asia? Collective identity, regionalism, and the origins of multilateralism', *International Organization*, 56: 575–607.

Kennan, G. F. (1947) 'The sources of Soviet conduct', *Foreign Affairs*, 25: 566–82.

Keohane, R. and Nye, J. (1977) *Power and Interdependence: World Politics in Transition*, Boston, MA: Little, Brown.

Keohane, R. and Nye, J. (2001) 'Introduction', in J. Nye and J. D. Donahue (eds) *Governance in a Globalizing World*, Washington, DC: Brookings Institution Press, pp. 1–41.

Krugman, P. (1979) 'A model of innovation, technology transfer, and the world distribution of income', *Journal of Political Economy*, 87: 253–66.

Leifer, M. (1998) 'The ASEAN Regional Forum: a model for cooperative security in the Middle East', Department of International Relations Working Paper No. 1998/1, Australian National University, Canberra.

McDougall, D. (1998) *Australia's Foreign Relations: Contemporary Perspectives*, Melbourne: Addison-Wesley.

Morgenthau, M. J. (1948) *Politics Among Nations*, New York: Knopf.

Palmer, N. (1991) *The New Regionalism in Asia and the Pacific*, Toronto: Lexington Books.

Peou, S. (2002) 'Realism and constructivism in Southeast Asian security studies today: a review essay', *The Pacific Review*, 15: 119–38.

Wallerstein, I. (1979) *The Capitalist World Economy*, Cambridge: Cambridge University Press.

Waltz, K. (1970) 'The myth of national interdependence', in C. P. Kindleberger (ed.) *The International Corporation*, New York: MIT Press, pp. 205–23.

Waltz, K. (1979) *Theory of International Politics*, Reading, MA: Addison-Wesley.

Waltz, K. (1988) 'The origins of war in neo-realist theory', *Journal of Interdisciplinary History*, 18: 615–28.

Yoshihara, K. (1988) *The Rise of Ersatz Capitalism in South-East Asia*, Oxford: Oxford University Press.

2 The United States in the Asia-Pacific

Jörn Dosch

At the most basic level, United States objectives in East Asia have remained consistent over the last five decades: prevent the emergence of a regional hegemon; keep open the sea and air routes that transit the area; maintain commercial access to the economics of the region and the peace and stability that commerce requires; and preserve and strengthen security ties with allies and friends in the region.

(Marvin Ott 2001: 152)

The history of US–East Asia relations

When the Cold War came to an end, many observers predicted that the Pacific was about to replace Europe as the main focus and top priority of US foreign policy. The pundits, however, told only part of the story. The United States had been a Pacific Power long before it became an Atlantic one. The first American trade activities date back to 1784 when the *Empress of China* set anchor in the Chinese port of Canton. The *Empress* was the first American merchant ship ever to cross the Pacific. In the early 1840s the US intensified their commercial engagement in East Asia. Under the terms of the Treaty of Wanghia (1844), the US gained the right to trade in Chinese ports. More decisively, in 1853 Commodore Matthew Perry terminated Japan's self-imposed isolation and forced the country to enter into trade with the US. Both events paved the way for America's later colonial involvement in the region which took shape with the takeover of the former Spanish colonies in the Philippines and Guam in 1898. Within only a few decades the US had experienced a metamorphosis from a colony to a colonial power. Since the late nineteenth century the United States has held onto a pre-eminent position in the Asia-Pacific, only briefly interrupted by Japan's imperialistic attempts to establish a 'Greater East Asia Co-Prosperity Sphere' during the Pacific War.

In this chapter we will outline the major events in US–East Asia relations and Washington's policy priorities towards the region from the end of the Second World War until the morning of the twenty-first century. We will then highlight, firstly, three key variables that have formed the structure of America's involvement in the Asia-Pacific, and, secondly, explain why the United States has been able to hold on to its pre-eminent power position in the Asia-Pacific for more than a century.

The Cold War in the Asia-Pacific

The defeat of Japan in August 1945 was followed by the emergence of an Asia-Pacific Pax Americana in the post-Second World War era. Although the Cold War in the Asia-Pacific was characterized by a tripolar structure with the US, China and Russia as its poles and shifting power relativities within this triangular order, its central element was nevertheless American primacy or, as some argue, hegemony. Unlike Western Europe where the United States' leading security role was embedded in a multilateral structure centred on NATO, a system of bilateral alliances served as the backbone of security relations in the Asia-Pacific. The only attempt at multilateral alliance building during the Cold War failed: the Southeast Asia Treaty Organization (SEATO) was founded in 1954 and comprised Australia, Great Britain, France, New Zealand, Pakistan (until 1973), the Philippines, Thailand and the USA. Co-operation never really worked due to the high degree of diversity among the members. SEATO was finally dissolved in 1977. The system of bilateral security treaties that the United States initiated with its key allies in the Asia-Pacific, Japan, South Korea, Taiwan and the Philippines after the Second World War has proved to be the more promising alternative to multilateralism. Among these alliances, the US–Japan axis emerged as the most important. In 1951 the United States and Japan signed the San Francisco Peace Treaty and the highly unequal Mutual Security Treaty. While the first formally ended the American occupation of Japan, the second enshrined Japan's position as Washington's military satellite. In 1960 a bilateral defence pact between the two nations increased Japan's profile because it eliminated earlier provisions allowing the United States to intervene in Japanese politics, provided a nuclear umbrella and obliged the US to defend Japan if attacked. The pact also required Washington to consult Tokyo for using military bases in Japan. At the same time the defence pact further integrated Japan as a key player on the chessboard of America's global Cold War security and defence strategy (see Umbach 2000 for a comprehensive overview and analysis).

The Cold War security architecture of the Asia-Pacific was strikingly different from the one in Europe, not only in terms of its structure but even more with regard to the implications. While the American–Soviet balance of power kept Europe relatively secure and stable, the ideological–political antagonism between the two superpowers resulted in armed conflict in the Asia-Pacific. In fact, the two 'hot wars' of the Cold War were fought in East Asia, in Korea (1950–53) and Vietnam (1965–73).

From about 1949 to 1975, the American presence in the Asia-Pacific region was dominated by its overall global anti-communist strategy. Maintaining military superiority over the Soviet Union and China was the highest priority. A first attempt to do this was the support given to the Nationalist Kuomintang (KMT) in the Chinese Civil War, which ended in bitter failure and recriminations. The US was again involved in military action in Korea, where it came to a stalemate in 1953. These failures persuaded both Democrats and Republicans in the US of the need for massive military strength, and subsequent administrations all authorized huge investment in submarines, aircraft carriers, nuclear and conventional weapons, and the maintenance of over 100,000 US troops in Asia, mostly based in Japan and Korea.

Another aspect of the strategy of containment was to support almost any regime that was perceived as anti-Communist. This was promoted in the early 1950s by Secretary of State John Foster Dulles among others. Firstly, anti-Communist governments were supposed to prevent the spread of communism by clamping down on communist political movements in their territories. Secondly, US aid would make them prosperous, democratic countries which would have a 'demonstration effect' on neighbours, and also on the populations of communist countries themselves. The key countries that benefited from US support in this context were Japan, South Korea, Taiwan, the Philippines, and several countries in Southeast Asia. The results were mixed. The Philippines degenerated into the extremes of political decadence and corruption under President Ferdinand Marcos, who none the less received steadfast US support. Other states guilty of abuse of human rights and with few democratic freedoms were also beneficiaries of US aid, and the US exposed itself as simply supporting totalitarian regimes provided they were anti-Soviet. On the other hand, it may be argued that Japan and some other countries evolved into successful, prosperous, democratic states under US tutelage.

The greatest disaster of US policy was the war in Vietnam. By the early 1960s, US Asian policy was extremely rigid, doctrinaire and probably ill-informed. Ignoring the great diversity of the Asia-Pacific region, the military appeared to believe in a 'domino theory' whereby a successful communist movement (for example, in North Vietnam) would inevitably spread and overthrow pro-US governments in the whole region. This was the pretext for the massive bombing of Hanoi in 1965, leading to a ten-year war that devastated much of Indo-China, and finally ended in humiliating defeat.

However, there was a third player in the situation: the People's Republic of China (PRC). The trilateral relationship tended to work in a 'two-against-one formation' and all three powers utilized the structure to their own advantage. The US manoeuvred between the PRC and USSR by strengthening or neglecting bilateral alliances in response to perceived shifts in relative power. Similarly, the Chinese utilized the conflict between the other two powers quite skilfully. Briefly, the Chinese were allies of the Soviet Union during the 1950s, and gained economic and military assistance from them. However, relations seriously degenerated as both claimed to be legitimate leaders of the world communist movement, and for a time war along China's northern borders seemed imminent. In 1960, the split became open and acrimonious, and the USSR withdrew all aid to China. The Sino-Soviet split resulted in a decade of anti-Soviet and anti-US Chinese foreign policy (see Chapter 4 for a more detailed discussion). In 1972, both Beijing and Washington significantly changed their strategic outlook and embarked on negotiations about a bilateral alliance directed against Soviet hegemony. Following the 'ping-pong diplomacy' between the two architects of *rapprochement*, Henry Kissinger and Zhou Enlai, the US and China re-established diplomatic relations in 1978. After this, China rather profited from the deadlock between the two superpowers, which allowed it relative freedom from military threat to pursue its own modernization goals. From the US point of view, the Soviet Union was consistently perceived as the major threat until 1990, by which time China had in fact acquired a very secure status in Asia due to its successful economic development. In the early 1990s, US reaction to the new power of China appeared to be rather mixed, reflective of the transition from Cold War to the new global arena.

The post-Cold War era

When the era of bipolarity came to an end it was clear from an American perspective that any new world order would have to be built along the lines of US supremacy and thereby mirroring abroad American values and beliefs. However, the United States entered the immediate post-Cold War era as a weaker power than it used to be, especially in economic terms. The relative decline in US economic power had two reasons: the trade deficit and the budget deficit. The US trade deficit with Japan was in the region of US$50 billion, and with other Asian countries around US$25 billion in the early 1990s. At the same time, the US government was running a massive fiscal deficit, which necessitated a further reduction in spending on welfare programmes and the military. Although while within a few years, the US had balanced the budget and rode a wave of tremendous growth whereas Japan drifted deeper and deeper into crisis followed by the collapse of other East Asian economies during the 1997–98 meltdown, to many the scenario of the early 1990s pointed to a continued decline in US influence in the region (Okimoto *et al.* 1996). It is important to note that not all analysts subscribed to the 'declinist' argument, as most prominently put forward by Paul Kennedy (1988). Nye (1990) and Rapkin (1994) promoted the counter-hypothesis based on the assumption that global US primacy was unchallenged. However, the emergence of a strong neo-isolationalist impulse in some sections of the US political elite (Schlesinger 1995) further contributed to the perception of significant changes to America's global role. Among Washington's East Asian allies Japan and South Korea and other governments in the region, there was great concern that, 'with the ending of the Cold War and the US domestic reaction brought on by the trade deficit, the United States might "withdraw" from Asia' (Krauss 2000: 482). According to a widespread American view, the extremely successful economies of East Asia were now in a position to defend themselves without US assistance (Johnson and Keehn 1995: 104).

New strategies in the light of changed structures: the emergence of multilateralism

In the wake of structural chances and uncertainties, many key foreign policy actors in Washington perceived the need for new mechanisms to cope with the emerging challenges. In the early days of the first Clinton Administration, Assistant Secretary of State for East Asian and the Pacific Affairs, Winston Lord, wrote an incisive memo to Secretary of State Warren Christopher, warning that the United States was in deep trouble in Asia. Some Asian states had started to oppose American engagement in the region and perceived Washington an 'an international nanny if not bully', as one senior official within the administration put it (cited in Manning and Stern 1994: 86). The promotion of multilateralism was seen as a suitable strategy to keep the US involved in the region and to strengthen both credibility and legitimacy of Washington's position *vis-à-vis* other major regional actors. Unlike the Administration of George Bush, a majority of relevant actors of the first Clinton Administration welcomed multilateralism as a supplement (but never as an alternative) to existing bilateral arrangements. Hence, the United States supported approaches for strengthening existing multilateral dialogues (APEC) and creating new ventures, such as the ASEAN Regional Forum (ARF) (Baker 1998; McGrew 1998; Dosch 2000).

Contrary to transatlantic experiences and maybe for the first time in modern history, in the Asia-Pacific a multilateral system of inter-state relations has been initiated and significantly influenced by weak actors and not by the dominant regional powers. At the same time it is important to note that the role of the United States has been crucial to the emergence of multilateralism in the region, even though Washington did not initiate the process. Instead the ASEAN states take credit as the architects of the regional security dialogue. ASEAN saw the ARF concept as a way of keeping the United States engaged in the region and the rising powers such as China and Japan restrained. In the first half of 1993 the United States and Japan signalled their support for a multilateral security forum. Washington was interested in creating a vehicle to encourage dialogue between South Korea and Japan in the absence of any suitable bilateral forum. Japan was driven by the political will to search for supplementary ways to ensure its security without becoming too active, thus avoiding any reminders of the bitter days of Japanese hegemony. Hence, both Japan and the United States welcomed ASEAN's initiative to take the diplomatic lead in setting up a multilateral venture. When the *Washington Post* (26 July 1994) reported after the first ARF meeting in 1994 that the new institution had been built 'along lines advocated by President Clinton', it ignored the fact that the new forum was obviously more Asian-driven.

However, in a speech to the South Korean National Assembly in July 1993 Clinton endorsed security dialogues among Pacific countries. He proposed a number of overlapping security activities, from multilateral discussion on specific issues such as the Spratly Islands dispute to confidence-building measures such as discussion of defence doctrines, transparency in weapons acquisitions and conflict management. This proposal, which was part of Clinton's neo-Wilsonian 'engagement and enlargement strategy', marked a turn in US foreign policy towards the Asia-Pacific.

The first half of the 1990s were the heydays of the 'Pacific dream' when the terms future, prosperity and Asia-Pacific became almost synonymous. No actor, certainly not the United States, wanted to lose out on the 'coming Pacific century'. In his critical assessment of the Asia-Pacific vision, Rob Wilson writes:

> 'Asia-Pacific' is a utopic discourse of the liberal market, an emerging signifier of transnational aspirations for some higher, supra-national unity in which global/local will meet in some kind of 'win–win' situation and the open market will absorb culture and politics into its borderless affirmative flow.
>
> (Wilson 2000: 566)

In sum, the sheer volume of Asia-Pacific commerce animated US dreams of a Pacific Community. The figures were impressive indeed. While Asian economies counted for 4 per cent of global GDP in 1960, they had a share of 25 per cent in 1991 – roughly equal to the US portion at that time. Between 1972 and 1992, GDP in the Asia-Pacific grew by 141 per cent whereas West Europe and North America reached growth rates of only 55 per cent and 59 per cent respectively (Dibb 1995: 19). US Undersecretary of Commerce, Jeffrey E. Garten (1995), stated that East Asia could grow twice as fast as the United States in the next decade, and three times the rate of Europe. Consequently the US supported APEC as a cornerstone of the Clinton Administration's policy goal to sustain economic dynamism in the region. In a Congressional hearing on the future of US foreign policy in Asia and the Pacific, representatives of the Office of the United States Trade Representative (USTR), a major player in American foreign economic policy, talked of APEC as 'the regional centerpiece to our efforts to open markets and expand trade' (Barshefsky 1995). According to USTR estimates, any 1 per cent increase of the US market share as a result of co-operation within APEC was to create 300,000 new jobs in the United States (Barshefsky 1995). On Clinton's initiative, APEC began to take on a more significant role in 1993 when for the first time the member states' heads of government met in Seattle. Until then only ministers and senior government officials had been involved in APEC. The Seattle Summit gave trade liberalization initiatives a strong boost. A year later, APEC's 'Bogor Declaration' of 1994 called for the establishment of – *de facto* – an Asia-Pacific Free Trade Area by the year 2020. Since the mid-1990s, however, APEC in particular and regional multilateralism in general have gradually lost momentum, primarily as a result of the Asian crisis which has substantially changed the perception of the Asia-Pacific as the economic powerhouse of the twenty-first century. At the same time APEC, ARF and other multilateral forums are not irrelevant. In the absence of other suitable mechanisms they continue to provide a valuable framework for regular high-level meetings between states and their actors who otherwise would find it difficult to communicate. China and Taiwan, Japan and South Korea, the US and North Korea are cases in point. At the same time, multilateralism does not top the foreign policy agendas any more. As far as the United States is concerned, the outbreak of the Asian crisis in 1997 relieved all worries concerning the possible decline of US primacy. From the perspective of a once-again perceived American strength, multilateral co-operation lost its initial attraction and necessity as a means of promoting US interests. Proven uni- and bilateral strategies regained importance. The successful redefinition of the US–Japan alliance further influenced this change of perception. The renewed agreement significantly reduced the US uncertainties of the early 1990s about the Asia-Pacific's post-Cold War security architecture. The alliance was again seen as the strong backbone of security relations in the area, thus reducing the need for supplementary strategies.

The revival of the old pattern in US–East Asia relations: bilateralism prevails

The predominance of bilateral approaches to security in the Asia-Pacific is clearly reflected in the *Japan–US Joint Declaration on Security: Alliance for the 21st Century* of 16 April 1996. It describes in general terms the need for the two countries to 'work jointly and individually . . . to achieve a more peaceful and stable security environment in the Asia-Pacific region' (Ministry of Foreign Affairs of Japan 1996). The document stresses four major points:

- Co-operation with the People's Republic of China with the aim of encouraging China to 'play a positive and constructive role in the region'.
- Encouragement of co-operation with Russia's ongoing process of reform, and reaffirmation of full normalization of Japan–Russia relations as important to regional peace and stability.
- Continuation of efforts regarding stability on the Korean Peninsula in co-operation with South Korea.
- Development of multilateral regional security dialogues and co-operation mechanisms such as the ASEAN Regional Forum and eventually security dialogues regarding Northeast Asia.

A comparison of these points with the five 'foundation stones' of US–Asia policy named by then-Defence Secretary Caspar Weinberger in 1985 shows that Washington's priorities have not changed significantly:

- The key importance of the US–Japanese security relationship.
- The US commitment to stability on the Korean Peninsula.
- US efforts to build an enduring relationship with China.
- US support for ASEAN.
- The long-standing US partnership with Australia and New Zealand (cited in Grinter 1989: 22).

The Joint Declaration of 1996 and the new Guidelines for US–Japan Defence Co-operation released in New York on 23 September 1997, stimulated a lively academic debate on the meaning of the alliance for security relations in the Asia-Pacific. Generally it is acknowledged that the renewed American–Japanese alliance represents more than ever the backbone of the region's security architecture. It guarantees peace and security not only for Japan but for the entire Asia-Pacific area. Most regard the alliance as the second-best option in the absence of a multilateral security and defence structure as can be found in Europe. At the same time the fact that many in Asia (and perhaps in the United States as well) perceive the alliance as a counterweight against a potentially expansionist and aggressive China causes some concern.

After the short interlude of multilateralism neither the Clinton Administration nor the government of George W. Bush have principally questioned bilateralism on US terms as the key foreign policy approach towards the Asia-Pacific. If this structure was to change then a concert of power could emerge as a working alternative. One popular scenario that is discussed both by political actors and academics envisions the enlargement of the US–Japan alliance. South Korea (and maybe a future re-united Korea) and Australia are likely players in such a concert system that would give the US allies significantly more duties and responsibilities than today. However, the key question is whether China could qualify as a partner in the concert. If the answer was yes, then the Asia-Pacific could well resemble the increasingly inclusive transatlantic security structure centred on a broadening NATO.

The post-September 11 alternations to international relations further point in the direction of concerted efforts to establish a secure regional order in the Asia-Pacific. Despite unilateral tendencies in US foreign policy in the wake of the terrorist attacks on New York and Washington, the ongoing war on terrorism needs partners in order to achieve anything. The immediate implications for Southeast and Northeast Asia, however, have been limited so far. They are most visible in the Philippines.

Box 2.1 The war on terror in the Asia-Pacific: the Philippines as a second front?

Where? Basilan, a roughly 20-mile-by-30-mile island in the southern part of the Philippines, a province of the Mindanao region, is the stronghold of the Abu Sayyaf group. The terrorists or bandits – depending on one's personal view – are said to be linked with the Al-Qaeda terror network.

What did the US do? Originally labelled a training exercise, the joint mission with 3,800 Filipino troops is now referred to by the US side as 'Freedom Eagle – Philippines'.

What is the aim? The obvious aim is to destroy Abu Sayyaf. According to American think-tank sources the Philippines is a major planning hub for Al-Qaeda missions worldwide. These reports claim that the Abu Sayyaf group has well-established ties with Osama bin Laden's terror network. However, most observers and even the governments in Manila and Washington estimate that the real number of active Abu Sayyaf members is closer to 100. And many believe that the group is more interested in banditry than Islam extremism or international terror.

How did Abu Sayyaf catch international attention? In March 2000 Abu Sayyaf kidnapped 58 people from a Basilan school. Later that year the group abducted 21 hostages, including 10 foreign tourists, from a Malaysian diving resort. The hostages were freed when Libya paid over US$20 million in ransom. In May 2001 Abu Sayyaf kidnapped 20 hostages, 17 Filipinos and three Americans, from the Dos Palmas resort on the Philippine island of Palawan. The large-scale kidnappings have made many sceptical of Abu Sayyaf's self-proclaimed ideological foundations. The group's invocation to Islam seems to be designed to confer respectability to its criminal activities.

Is the US presence accepted? The deployment of American troops is controversial because the Visiting Forces Agreement of 1998, under which the US military presence is possible in the Philippines, prohibits American forces from engaging in combat while in the country or quelling insurgencies and criminal activities. The governments in Manila and Washington simply ignore this provision because the joint mission enjoys public opinion approval in both nations.

What is Washington's real interest? The US has been interested in closer military contacts with the Philippines ever since it lost its bases a decade ago. The joint operation has now opened the door for the restoration of a long-term US military presence in the country which is of geostrategic importance to Washington.

Will other Southeast Asian countries follow? Even though the Bush Administration is concerned that Southeast Asia could develop into a new breeding ground for terrorists, the joint operation in the Philippines is unlikely to be a model for the region. For the time being, US officials have concluded that it would be counterproductive to deploy troops in Indonesia, for example, given the anti-American sentiments in the world's most popular Muslim nation.

This historical overview has shown that despite major structural changes at historical junctions the United States has dominated the region since the dawn of the nineteenth century. The next section focuses on the factors that have significantly influenced or even determined the American approach towards the region.

A reflection on the US role in the Asia-Pacific: three variables

Any analysis of the United States in the Asia-Pacific has to take into account three core structural factors. The first is the American claim to international leadership or primacy; the second is the self-perception of the Pacific Ocean as a natural zone of American influence, as 'our lake'; and the third relates to the institutional dynamics of the US political system: i.e., the competition among a wide range of actors over the conduct of foreign policy.

Firstly, the US claim to global leadership or primacy which materializes in worldwide, sometimes aggressive promotion of democracy, human rights and market economy is typically justified on moral and special rights grounds. These perceived rights are embedded in the strong belief in exceptionalism and moralism or, according to Stanley Hoffmann's classical definition, 'the deep and lasting faith in the singular, unique, "unprecedented" and "unrepeatable" character of the United States . . .' (Hoffmann 1978: 6). The idea of exceptionalism dates back to the mystical concept of 'Manifest Destiny'.

Box 2.2 Manifest Destiny

In 1845, a democratic leader and influential editor by the name of John L. O'Sullivan gave the movement its name. In an attempt to explain America's thirst for expansion, and to present a defence for America's claim to new territories, he wrote:

'. . . *the right of our manifest destiny to over-spread and to possess the whole of the continent which Providence has given us for the development of the great experiment of liberty and federative development of self-government entrusted to us. It is right such as that of the tree to the space of air and the earth suitable for the full expansion of its principle and destiny of growth.*'

'Manifest Destiny became the rallying cry throughout America. The notion of Manifest Destiny was publicized in the papers and was advertised and argued by politicians throughout the nation. The idea of Manifest Destiny Doctrine became the torch that lit the way for American expansion.'
(Source: Rijksuniversiteit Groningen-Faculteit der Letteren: The American Revolution – an HTML project, http://odur.let.rug.nl/~usa/E/manifest/manif1.htm)

'No nation ever existed without some sense of national destiny or purpose. Manifest Destiny . . . revitalized a sense of "mission" or national destiny for Americans. The people of the United States felt it was their mission to extend the "boundaries of freedom" to others by imparting their idealism and belief in democratic institutions to those who were capable of self-government. It excluded those people who were perceived as being incapable of self-government, such as Native American people and those of non-European origin.'
(http://www.pbs.org/kera/usmexicanwar/dialogues/prelude/manifest/d2aeng.html)

The concept of manifest destiny, the missionary character of US foreign policy, is still very much alive. Not surprisingly this role concept clashes with Asian perceptions of the United States. Political elites in many East Asian states do not necessarily take for granted the missionary character of US foreign policy nor do they subscribe to the idea of US hegemony by default. Singapore's former ambassador to the United States, Tommy Koh, has summarized the discrepancy between the ego and the alter part of Washington's approach *vis-à-vis* East Asia:

> Many Asians do not understand America. America is not a normal country. From the time of its birth, Americans have believed that their country was founded with a divine mission – . . . Since this belief is an article of faith it is like America's secular religion. A believer on faith would not normally subject his beliefs to intellectual analysis or to the empirical test. Thus, Americans have never hesitated in their proselytizing mission abroad in spite of the vast discrepancies between American ideals and American realities at home.
>
> (Koh 1995: 91)

In some cases the notion of American exceptionalism is at odds with other nations' ideas of their own naturally given quasi-superiority. China is a case in point. The following quote stands for a common myth in US–China relations: 'China and the US will always confront each other. One country claims to be capitalist, while the other claims to be socialist, they should collide' (Shen Dingli, quoted in Agence France Presse 31 March 2002). A situation of competing economic systems may not provide an ideal framework for stable and peaceful bilateral relations but the impact and consequences of the capitalist–socialist/communist cleavage has been widely overestimated. At best, it is only part of a far more complex structure. The decisive element of this structure is rather the clash of self-perceptions and role concepts in international relations. In short, due to historical, geopolitical and ideological factors, both nations, the US and China, cling to their respective belief of being legitimately superior to any other actor in the Asia-Pacific, superior in terms of value systems and cultural features and as the result of a long-term hegemonic role in the area: the Chinese tribute system that lasted for many centuries versus American pre-eminence.

The second and closely related variable of any American role in the Asia-Pacific is the perception of the Pacific Ocean as a natural zone of American influence, as 'our lake'. This concept dates back to the late nineteenth century when the whole North Pacific Rim was in US hands at all important strategic points.

The annexation of Hawaii and the colonization of the Philippines on the eve of the twentieth century marked the key stages of American expansion into the Pacific. Historians have coined the terms 'Empire by invitation' or 'Sentimental Imperialists' to describe this initially more unplanned than strategically envisioned and always highly controversial process. The result of the American imperial involvement in the Asia-Pacific region is undisputed, however. For more than a century the Pacific Ocean has been perceived as a prime area for US opportunity: 'The Mediterranean is the ocean of the past, the Atlantic is the ocean of the present and the Pacific is the ocean of the future' (quoted in Wardhana 1994: 175). Secretary of State John Hay's early twentieth century account sounds strikingly similar to the prophecy of James Hodgson, then the US ambassador to Japan, about eighty years later: 'The now flourishing Pacific Region . . . constitutes nothing less than one of the great developments in human history – from now on the words "Pacific" and "future" will be synonymous' (quoted in Wardhana 1994: 175).

Thirdly, the lack of policy direction and the US political system. As Marvin Ott's epigraph to this chapter shows, the consistency of the United States' general foreign policy approach towards the Asia-Pacific is remarkable at first glance. However, many observers and analysts both within and outside the United States have complained about the lack of direction in Washington's Asia-Pacific policy, and called for a comprehensive and coherent long-term blueprint, strategy or even an Asia-Pacific Marshall Plan.

What is the reason for the alleged lack of direction in Washington's East Asia policy? The foreign policy-making process in general and strategies towards the Asia-Pacific in particular involve a wide range of actors representing different interests and pushing diverging agendas. The best example is Washington's China policy. The fact that US–China relations often appear to lack consistency and long-term vision is at least partly due to the high number of actors involved on Washington's side.

Whereas the making of foreign policy in most European democracies traditionally is the domain of governments, the US Constitution – to use the famous phrase of Edward Corwin (1984: 201) – creates 'an invitation to struggle for the privilege of directing American foreign policy'. As a result, in the US we can normally observe a gap between a more pro-China policy of the administration and more contra-China interests in Congress. During the Clinton presidency, for example, the administration favoured a strategy of engaging Peking and actively supporting the integration of the People's Republic into the international community of states, thereby making its foreign policy behaviour more predictable and reliable. However, from 1994 onwards the Republican-dominated Congress had increasingly challenged and undermined Clinton's co-operative approach. In 1999, the 'Cox Report', a Congressional study alleging that China had acquired sensitive technology through commercial satellite contracts, contributed to the perception of China being the United States' principal post-Cold War adversary. Not least, Congress's tough stand on Peking has been influenced by an anti-China coalition of (a) pro-human rights NGOs, condemning the PRC for its poor human rights record, (b) trades unions eager to prevent more relaxed US–China trade relations supposed to threaten American jobs, and (c) religious and environmental NGOs. At the same time any moves to constrain China's international position in general and its most favoured nation (MFN) status in particular were immediately countered by equally strong pro-China interests as articulated by trade lobbies and business groups such as the Business Coalition for US–China Trade. China's WTO membership has not reduced the potential for conflict. Quite to the contrary, trade disputes have become more intense in the wake of China's accession to the world trade body. In 2002 China's trade surplus with the United States hit a record US$103 billion and will exceed US$120 billion in 2003. Therefore, US officials have demanded that China move faster in meeting market-opening commitments, warning that failure to act could jeopardize Chinese access to American markets. The US administration has put pressure on China to revalue its currency which is pegged to the dollar; the US Department of Commerce – on the recommendation of the American textile lobby – imposed quotas on Chinese textiles with other products such as TV sets likely to follow. China has accused the United States of acting against the spirit of free trade and protecting its own industry.

In addition to the administration–Congress controversy and disputes between pro- and anti-China lobbies, a third cleavage refers to conflicting views on US–Taiwan relations. In 1995 influential pro-Taiwan activists among the political elite in Washington successfully pushed the administration to grant Lee Teng-hui, then president of Taiwan, a visa for a visit to his alma mater, Cornell University. The visit was heavily criticized by the government in Peking and interpreted as a step towards a diplomatic recognition of Taiwan. The matter eventually provoked serious tension in the Taiwan Strait in July of the same year. A few years on there is strong indication that 'the "one-China" principle that has been the mainstay of relations between the United States and China for 30 years is steadily fading' (Halloran 2003). Both houses of the US Congress have organized Taiwan caucuses and the House of Representatives unanimously adopted a pro-Taiwan resolution. Taiwan's President Chen Shui-bian was welcomed in New York in November 2003 on his way to Panama where he had a brief meeting with US Secretary of State Colin Powell. Shortly after, Taiwan and the US announced that they would hold comprehensive defence talks and take part in a computer-based war simulation exercise amid rising tensions between Taiwan and China (*The Australian*, 2 December 2003, p. 9). The Pentagon is particularly known for its anti-China and pro-Taiwan position and related reluctance to support any far-reaching engagement strategies towards China. On the eve of Hu Jintao's (then vice-president of the PRC; he became China's president in March 2003) visit to Washington in April 2002 Defence Department officials allegedly leaked intelligence details of Chinese missile deployments near Taiwan in an effort to embarrass Hu. At the same time, however, the Chinese vice-president became the most senior official of his country ever to visit the Pentagon.

It goes without saying that the whole picture of US–China relations is more complex.

None the less, this brief outline demonstrates that the variety of interests makes consistency, comprehensiveness and long-term planning in the foreign policy field hard to achieve for any US administration.

Having discussed the factors that determine the US foreign policy approach towards the Asia-Pacific, we now need to ask why the United States has been able to maintain primacy in the region. The answer relates to a combination of hard power based on military might and soft power based on America's cultural attractiveness and model character.

Hard power and soft power: the pillars of American primacy

Not only the notion of the Asia-Pacific as a focal point of Washington's foreign policy strategy has virtually remained unchanged. The key actors contributing to the lasting and profound Asia-Pacific engagement have been remarkably persistent too. Among them, the US Navy represents the most important.

Although the term 'hegemony' seems to be outdated in the globalized world of the post-bipolar era, most states in the Asia-Pacific, with the prominent exception of China, still consider and favour the United States as the prime stabilizer, broker and balancer within the area. Since the end of the Second World War US *hard power* in the region has been based on maritime superiority. Today this structural advantage could be even more important than in during the days of the Cold War, as Paul Dibb observes:

> From a defense planning perspective, it is important to understand that in the Asia-Pacific region potential military operations *will be essentially maritime* in nature. Apart from the Korean Peninsula, US military forces are not likely to be involved in large-scale ground-force operations. The dominant geopolitical change in the new security environment has been the virtual elimination for military planning purposes of allied continental commitments; the emerging struggle for power in Asia will focus on political fault lines that are maritime rather than continental in aspect. The development of China's military power and the response to it of India and Japan are likely to put pressure on the chain of America's friends and allies in the long littoral extending between South Korea and Taiwan in the north to the ASEAN countries and Australia in the south.
>
> (Dibb 2001: 1; original emphasis)

Potential adversaries of the US such as China might be able to build naval forces capable of partially restricting or even denying the American forces freedom of naval movement. But they lack the resources and means to establish naval power on a comparable scale. The actual dispute concerns the *degree* of American naval superiority rather than its *fact*.

The responsibility of the US Pacific Command (USARPAC) covers more than 50 per cent of the earth's surface, reaching from the west coast of the United States mainland to the east coast of Africa and from the Arctic to the Antarctic. Approximately 90,000 to 100,000 troops are currently forward-deployed in the Asia-Pacific, principally in Japan (especially on Okinawa where 60 per cent of the 47,000 US troops in Japan are stationed), South Korea, Guam and Diego Garcia. US naval power in this region is based on the presence and mission of the Seventh Fleet, which is part of the Pacific Fleet and one of the core forces within USARPAC. Established in 1943, the Seventh Fleet is the largest of the Navy's forward-deployed fleets, including 40 to 50 ships, 200 aircraft and about 20,000

Navy and Marine Corps personnel. Eighteen ships operate from the US facilities in Japan and Guam, representing the heart of the fleet. Other ships are deployed on a rotating basis from bases in Hawaii and the US west coast (US Pacific Command, http:// www.pacom.mil).

Unlike the Clinton Administration, which produced two security strategies for the Asia-Pacific region (1995 and 1998), the succeeding Bush Administration has not formulated a defence outlook for the region in spite of the area's growing strategic importance as a theatre for the war on terrorism. The 1998 report survived the change of governments and remains the authoritative blueprint – a further indication of rather persistent American interests and policies towards the Asia-Pacific. The tenor of the current US National Security Strategy confirms the principal policy approach based on a system of bilateral alliances which is partly supplemented by multilateral initiatives. The strategic goals and cornerstones are deliberately broadly formulated in order to allow for flexible responses.

Box 2.3 The US National Security Strategy (September 2002)

'The war against terrorism has proven that America's alliances in Asia not only underpin regional peace and stability, but are flexible and ready to deal with new challenges. To enhance our Asian alliances and friendships, we will:

- look to Japan to continue forging a leading role in regional and global affairs based on our common interests, our common values, and our close defence and diplomatic co-operation;
- work with South Korea to maintain vigilance towards the North while preparing our alliance to make contributions to the broader stability of the region over the longer term;
- build on 50 years of US–Australian alliance co-operation as we continue working together to resolve regional and global problems – as we have so many times from the Battle of the Coral Sea to Tora Bora;
- maintain forces in the region that reflect our commitments to our allies [military presence of 100,000 troops], our requirements, our technological advances, and the strategic environment; and
- build on stability provided by these alliances, as well as with institutions such as ASEAN and the Asia-Pacific Economic Co-operation forum, to develop a mix of regional and bilateral strategies to manage change in this dynamic region.

We are attentive to the possible renewal of old patterns of great power competition. Several potential great powers are now in the midst of internal transition – most importantly Russia, India, and China. In all three cases, recent developments have encouraged our hope that a truly global consensus about basic principles is slowly taking shape.'

(Source: *The National Security Strategy of the United States of America, September 2002,*
http://www.whitehouse.gov/nsc/nssall.html)

Table 2.1 US interests and policy approaches towards the Asia-Pacific under three administrations

	George Bush (1989–93)	Bill Clinton (1993–2000)	George W. Bush (since 2000)
General approach	'Preservation of American strategic access and influence'	'Engagement and enlargement'	'Global war on terror'
Global/regional governance	• Revival of neo-Wilsonian ideal of international co-operation • 'New world order' and US primacy (pre-eminence) • Flexible bilateralism as the main pattern of relations with AP	• Revival of neo-Wilsonian ideal of international co-operation • Bilateralism and multilateralism as parallel strategies towards AP • Promotion and enhancement of democracy and human rights	• Revival of unilateralism • Multilateralism as long as it clearly reflects the US national interest and is guided by Washington (NATO, IMF) • Key-country approach • Global coalition against terrorism
Security	• US–Japan alliance as cornerstone of security architecture (highest priority) • Strengthening of US–South Korea alliance • Strengthening the alliances with the Philippines (securing the military bases, Clark airbase and Subic naval base) and Thailand • Strengthening the partnership with Australia • Reduction of US troops in the AP to 100,000 personnel	*Bilateral* • 'Comprehensive, durable partnership' with Japan • Stability on the Korean Peninsula • Improvement of relations with China • Normalization of relations with Vietnam • Stability in Cambodia • No further reduction of US troops in AP *Multilateral* • Deepening of relations with ASEAN • Active support of regional security dialogues (ARF, CSCAP, NEACD) • Regional co-operation to enforce non-proliferation and to limit arms trade	*Unilateral* • Strengthening of US position in the Asia-Pacific based on national interest: TMD, US naval power (7th Fleet) *Bilateral* • Bilateral alliance system: US–Japan, US–South Korea *Multilateral* • 'Trilateral virtual alliance' (Ralf Cossa): US, Japan, South Korea with Australia as a salient co-opted partner • Ad hoc alliance/coalition-building: anti-terrorism • General interest in ASEAN and APEC as 'the principal engines of regional coherence' (Assistant Secretary James Kelly)

	George Bush (1989–93)	Bill Clinton (1993–2000)	George W. Bush (since 2000)
Economy	*Bilateral* • Reduction of trade deficit with Japan, China etc. • Liberalization of international trade relations • MFN status for China *Multilateral* • Reduction of trade deficit with Japan, China etc.	*Bilateral* • Reduction of trade deficit with Japan, China etc. • 'Promotion of free market democracy' • Liberalization of international trade relations • Fighting the Asian crisis *Multilateral* • Reduction of trade deficit with Japan, China etc. • Promoting free trade by means of active participation in regional forums (especially APEC) • Fighting the Asian crisis under IMF guidance and leadership	• China's accession into WTO • New round of trade talks • Free Trade Area of the Americas (FTTA)

The acceptance of a pre-eminent position of the United States in the Asia-Pacific has never been based on the sheer size of its military presence alone. The export of American culture and technology has played an equally important part. This is what Joseph Nye has called *soft power*:

> If [a state's] culture and ideology are attractive, others will more willingly follow. If it can establish international norms that are consistent with its society, it will less likely have to change. If it can help support institutions that make states wish to channel or limit their activities in ways the dominant state prefers, it may not need costly exercises of coercive or hard power in bargaining situations.
>
> (Nye 1990: 46)

While hard power materializes in military force or economic sanctions, soft power is based on values, ideology and cultural features. The sources of American soft power are liberalism and democracy and – maybe to an even greater extent – specific consumer patterns, pop culture and films. According to a popular cliché, McDonald's, Starbucks, MTV and Hollywood are the faces of globalization. This is, of course, a simplifying metaphor but a very powerful one and not very far from reality. Until very recently in Bangkok a cup of coffee would cost the equivalent of about 10 cents. Today it is fashionable to have the same black brew for ten times its former price. Today it is called *latte* and it is from one of the uncounted Starbucks outlets that spread over town. Last but not least American universities are an important source of soft power as they attract more than 500,000 foreign students each year who get in touch with – and not seldom absorb – American values and ideas before they return home. In his most recent book, Nye (2002) argues that while the US as a leading world actor needs to exert both hard and soft power, the information revolution and the phenomenon of globalization call for the exercise of soft more than hard power. He consequently criticizes the strong unilateral element in George Bush's foreign policy.

A concluding word on theory

IR theories in general and the main schools of thought, neo-realism, Idealism and liberal institutionalism in particular, do not solely explain observed reality. In addition to their purpose of providing a framework for academic analysis, very often they gain importance as foreign policy recipes. In this regard, IR theories are different from other social science hypotheses because academic analysis and foreign policy making are intertwined in a reciprocal relationship. Over the decades the ideas developed by Hans Morgenthau, the father of realism, and his many academic followers have had a significant impact on the conduct of foreign policy, especially in the United States. The realist concept of 'balance of power' even became a self-fulfilling prophecy during the Cold War. At the same time, the way policy makers perceive the international environment and react to challenges posed by it constantly refines IR theory. The most striking example is probably George Kennan's famous 'Long Telegram' of 1946 that best illustrated American anti-communism and general suspicion of Soviet aspirations and laid the foundation for Washington's containment strategy towards Moscow. The 'Long Telegram' was perhaps the most cited and most influential statement of the early years of the Cold War. At the time he authored the telegram Kennan was chief of mission at the American embassy in Moscow. In 1947 the essence of the document was published in *Foreign Affairs* under the title 'The Sources of Soviet Conduct' and signed by 'X', although everyone knew that Kennan was the author.

For Kennan, the Cold War gave the United States its historic opportunity to assume leadership of what would eventually be described as the 'free world'.

Although US foreign policy seems to follow realist patterns due to the strong influence of the realist/neo-realist school on policy making, Idealists (sometimes also called Wilsonists referring to President Woodrow Wilson, the architect of the League of Nations and model Idealist) and liberal institutionalists have equally put their mark on Washington's foreign policy interests and strategies. One of the best and recent examples is Harvard Professor Joseph Nye, who served in both the Carter and Clinton Administrations. As Clinton's Assistant Secretary of Defence for International Security Affairs he drafted the US Asia-Pacific Security Strategy of 1995 (even dubbed the 'Nye Report') which put the main emphasis on multilateral co-operation and significantly changed, for a short period, Washington's foreign policy and defence approach towards the Asia-Pacific. In the United States more than 1,000 private, non-profit think-tanks try to contribute their expertise to the governmental decision-making process. The influence of think-tanks and academics in the foreign policy process grows the more they are integrated in so-called epistemic communities or 'Track II' activities which bring them together with government officials who often attend these kind of meetings in their private capacity. In sum, the reciprocal relationship between theory as an analytical instrument and theory as a foreign policy recipe or even self-fulfilling prophecy is often ignored in the IR literature but should be kept in mind when we try to analyse international relations and the conduct of foreign policy.

References

Agence France Presse (2002) 'Year after spy plane crisis, China–US ties face new uncertainty', 31 March.

Baker, R. W. (1998) 'The United States and APEC regime building', in V. K. Aggarwal and R. Baker (eds) *Asia-Pacific Crossroads. Regime Creation and the Future of APEC*, New York: St Martin's Press, pp. 165–90.

Barshefsky, C. (1995) (2 February) Statement, in: The Future of US Foreign Policy in Asia and the Pacific. Hearings before the Subcommittees on International Economic Policy and Trade, Asia and the Pacific, and International Operations and Human Rights of the Committee on International Relations, House of Representatives, 104th Congress, First Session, 2 February, 9 February, 16 March and 27 June, pp. 5–10.

Corwin, E. S. (1984) *The President. Office and Powers, 1787–1984*, 5th edn New York: New York University Press.

Dibb, P. (1995) *Towards a New Balance of Power in Asia*, London: Adelphi Paper 295.

Dibb, P. (2001) 'Strategic trends – Asia at the crossroads', *Naval War College Review*, 54: 1 Online. Available HTTP:http://www.nwc.navy.mil/press/Review/2001/Winter/art 2-w01.htm (accessed 8 March 2004).

Dosch, J. (2000) 'Asia-Pacific multilateralism and the role of the United States', in J. Dosch and M. Mols (eds) *International Relations in the Asia-Pacific. New Patterns of Power, Interest and Co-operation*, New York: Palgrave, pp. 87–110.

Garten, J. E. (1995) 'Is America abandoning multilateral trade?' *Foreign Affairs*, 74: 50–62.

Grinter, L. E. (1989) *Security, Strategy, and Policy Responses in the Pacific Rim*, Boulder, CO: Lynne Rienner.

Halloran, R. (2003) 'Cross-strait tensions build as one-China principle fades', *Japan Times*, 1 December.

Hoffmann, S. (1978) *Primacy or World Order. American Foreign Policy since the Cold War*, New York: McGraw-Hill.

Johnson, C. and Keehn, E. B. (1995) 'The Pentagon's ossified strategy', *Foreign Affairs*, 74: 103–14.

Kennedy, P. (1988) *The Rise and Fall of the Great Powers: Economic Change and Military Conflict from 1500 to 2000*, London: Unwin Hyman.

Koh, T. T. B. (1995) *The United States and East Asia: Conflict or Co-operation*, Singapore: Times Academic Press.

Krauss, E. S. (2000) 'Japan, the US, and the emergence of multilateralism in Asia', *The Pacific Review*, 13: 473–94.

Manning, R. A. and Stern, P. (1994) 'The myth of the Pacific century', *Foreign Affairs*, 73: 79–93.

McGrew, A. (1998) 'Restructuring foreign and defence policy: the USA', in A. McGrew and C. Brook (eds) *Asia-Pacific in the New World Order*, London: Routledge, pp. 158–88.

Ministry of Foreign Affairs of Japan (1996) *Japan–US Joint Declaration on the Security–Alliance for the 21st Century*. Online. Available HTTP: <http://www.mofa.go.jp/region/n-america/us/security/security.html> (accessed 8 March 2004).

Nye, J. (1990) *Bound to Lead. The Changing Nature of American Power*, New York: Basic Books.

Nye, J. (2002) *The Paradox of American Power: Why the World's Only Superpower Can't Go It Alone*, New York: Oxford University Press.

Okimoto, D. I. *et al.* (1996) *A United States Policy for the Changing Realities of East Asia: Toward a New Consensus*, Standard, CA: Asia/Pacific Research Center, Stanford University.

Ott, M. (2001) 'East Asia: security and complexity', *Current History*, 645: 147–53.

Rapkin, D. P. (1994) 'Leadership and cooperative institutions in the Asia-Pacific', in A. Mack and J. Ravenhill (eds) *Pacific Co-operation*, St Leonards: Allen & Unwin Australia, pp. 98–129.

Schlesinger, A. Jr (1995) 'Back to the womb?', *Foreign Affairs*, 74: 2–8.

Umbach, F. (2000) 'The future of the US–Japanese security alliance', in J. Dosch and M. Mols (eds) *International Relations in the Asia-Pacific. New Patterns of Power, Interest, and Co-operation*, New York: Palgrave, pp. 111–54.

Wardhana, A. (1994) 'The Pacific Rim challenge', in H. Soesastro (ed.) *Indonesian Perspectives on APEC and Regional Co-operation in Asia-Pacific*, Jakarta: CSIS, pp. 173–81.

Wilson, R. (2000) 'Imagining "Asia-Pacific": forgetting politics and colonialism in the magical waters of the Pacific. An Americanist critique', *Cultural Studies*, 14: 562–92.

3 Japan in the Asia-Pacific

Michael K. Connors

When the football World Cup was hosted in Japan and Korea in 2002, an astute expatriate Japanese living in England observed how certain television channels recycled clichéd images of Japan in the opening sequences of football programmes. From 'a Kodo drummer, a couple of geisha, the rising sun' to the kitsch Japanese television-set design of 'cherry blossom pond and wood-and-paper shoji screens', it was clear that Westerners needed to conjure certain images in order to place Japan in its proper place: as something alien and exotic (Kawakami 2002: 6). The dozens of metropolises that make up Japan, the overwhelming high-tech advances, and the significant modernization and consumerization of Japanese society were conveniently glossed over in a display of conjured exoticism. This traditionalistic representation of Japan is not only symptomatic of international ignorance; indeed, the highlighting of Japanese difference and uniqueness is not conducted by outsiders alone. Japanese agencies themselves, as part of nation-building and the promotion of Japanese national identity, have attempted to project the image of a people fundamentally different to others, characterized primarily by groupist and hierarchical orientation (Mouer and Sugimoto 1986). These so-called cultural traits imply that Japan functions differently. Similar arguments are made for the uniqueness of Japanese business practices. At the same time, some suggest that there is a culturally derived form of diplomacy based on the pursuit of harmony and conflict avoidance (see Tamamoto 1993). In this vein, the former Japanese ambassador to the UK notes that:

> We prefer to work behind the scenes to promote agreements, just like the unseen feet of the water-fowl work to propel the bird gracefully along the water. This adaptation has been very profitable for Japan, though viewed by outsiders as 'reactive' and 'exceptional'. With the end of the Cold War we are to become 'normal', whatever that is.
>
> (Kazuo Chiba 1996: xix)

In many ways Japan has indeed gracefully glided across the water, rising from wartime devastation to becoming the world's second largest economy, after the United States. Kazuo's allusion to Japan becoming a 'normal nation' relates to the widespread observation of the anomaly between its economic prowess and its lack of influence in international politics. This 'paradox of unrealized power' is an avowedly realist notion, in that realist theory predicts an emerging power to utilize its power resources in order to augment its relative power in the international system. Japan, as yet, seems not to have taken this road (Drifte 1998: 5).

Perpetuating the mystery of Japan are the notoriously diffused foreign policy-making processes which work through the bureaucratic and executive system, lending little coherence to foreign policy. Some have gone so far to declare that Japan has 'no foreign policy, only entrepreneurial policies' (Scalapino 1977: 409). Such a claim reflects the centrality of the Ministry of Finance and the Ministry of International Trade and Industry, and the influence of the relevant *zoku* or party policy tribes within them, in Japan's international affairs for the promotion of Japan's economic position. The relatively small Ministry of Foreign Affairs was marginal during Japan's pursuit of economic growth, although in the post-Cold War world it is assuming greater importance (Drifte 1998: 18–20). As in any country, complex processes of contestation between ministries about appropriate policy belie the idea of a unitary rational state bent on a grand strategy. However, inasmuch as the focus is on Japan's external relations, the state does present a relatively unified stance enabling, at a basic level, an analysis of 'Japan's' foreign policy. It should be noted that this presumption is for analytical purposes; it allows complex material to be dealt with in an introductory manner. More in-depth foreign policy analysis would entail greater attention to domestic and international factors that shape the policy process. Within these limits, the aim here is to explore how Japan positioned itself during the Cold War, and how its elites are now groping for new strategies. Firstly, a brief history traces salient events and developments prior to the end of the Second World War. This historical perspective is important as past events continue to influence Japan's relations with its neighbouring countries. The discussion then moves towards examining Japan's position during and after the Cold War. At the end of the chapter the utility of these approaches for understanding Japan is addressed.

Opening Japan: black ships

The arrival of Commodore Perry's 'black ships' (so-called because of the black smoke of the coal engines) in 1853 marked the beginning of Japan's engagement with the Western state system. Arriving with a letter from the American president and with the useful prop of warships, Perry demanded that Japan open itself to trade. This event ended the Edo period (1600–1868), setting in motion the modernization of the Japanese state. From the 1870s to the 1940s Japan acted like similarly late industrializing states (Germany and Italy, for example) in that it adapted domestic conservative ideologies, such as the Samurai code of ethics and Emperor worship, to mobilize the population around industrialization, militaristic nationalism and imperial expansion (Pempel 1998: 4).

Through a conscious effort of 'catching up' with the great powers of Europe, Japan acquired a significant military and naval force, leading to its victory in the Sino-Japanese war (1894–95), and the Russo-Japanese war (1904–05). In the wake of these victories Japan moved to take control of Formosa (Taiwan) and Korea respectively. Its repression of independence movements in these countries was severe and uncompromising. Furthermore, it became increasingly belligerent regarding China, extending its position in Manchuria into formal rule, and displacing Russian prevalence more generally. Fearing the emerging nationalist movement in China, in 1932 the occupying Japanese force declared the puppet state of 'Manchukuo' and maintained tight control of the region. In 1936 an alliance of nationalist and communist forces emerged and the second Sino-Japanese war (1937–45) broke out for control of China's mainland. The Japanese captured the capital of the Chinese Republic, Nanjing, in 1937. Grotesque and brutal massacres of civilian populations were widely reported, with some 200,000 to 300,000 people slaughtered (see Yang 1999).

Throughout the Second World War, the Japanese controlled the eastern coastal areas of the Chinese mainland. The war in Europe provided a window of opportunity for the seizure of more territories. In 1940 Japan allied itself with Germany and Italy (Tripartite Pact), and entered a new period of expansionism. Following its bombing of Pearl Harbour, Japan moved to 'liberate' the western colonies of the Philippines, French Indo-China, Malaya, Indonesia and Burma (1941–42) (Beasley 1991).

The motives and ideology of Japanese imperialism

Understanding Japan's imperialist movements in the first wave of opening requires situating Japan in the international system of the times. The mid-nineteenth century was the heyday of free trade, but from the 1880s onwards, with the consolidation of states in Europe, Western powers began a scramble for empire in an effort to secure access to raw materials and guaranteed markets for their commodities. Many informal colonies became formalized, and imperialist states closed off access to rivals. Japan as a late-starter thus confronted an Asia dominated by Western powers and found its modernizing ambitions of 'rich nation, strong army' frustrated.

Responding to this situation, the Japanese elite began to propagate the idea of pan-Asianism – the idea that all Asian peoples had a common interest in defying the 'white man'. The flavour of this sentiment is found in the writings of Tokutomi Soho:

> The countries of the white men are already extending to the forefront of Japan. They have encroached on China, India and Persia. . . . We, Japanese, should take care of the yellow man. . . . We should proclaim that the mission of the Japanese Empire is to fully implement an Asian Monroe Doctrine.
>
> (Cited in Susumu 2001: 24)

The Japanese 'Asian Monroe Doctrine' found expression in Japan's declaration of the Greater East Asia Co-Prosperity Sphere in 1942. Occupied territories purportedly would be governed by the benign and civilizing Japanese elite who would assist in economic development. In constructing a Japanese-controlled region, Japan would form the industrial centre and the occupied territories from Korea to Southeast Asia would supply labour and raw materials. Of course, on its surrender in August 1945, Japan's control over the colonies was lost. The memory of Japan's actions remains potent today, and is a constant issue in Japanese bilateral ties with countries in the region. Japan has failed to present a clear historical record of these events through its education system, nor has it produced an apology acceptable to the region. Given this, there remains a lingering suspicion of Japanese intentions that dogs Japan's efforts to present as a regional leader.

From surrender to economic power

The dropping of atomic bombs on the cities of Hiroshima and Nagasaki by the United States in August 1945 brought forward Japan's already certain surrender. The use of the bomb conveniently signalled US superiority to advancing Soviet troops, moving through China (see Alperovitz 1996). The bombing was an initial redefining of world order, in which conflict between the emerging superpowers (the USA and the USSR) would be contained through the use of nuclear deterrence. For Japan, the consequences were two-fold. Firstly, in the years of Allied Occupation (1945–51), Japan, through a complex process of elite contestation, would emerge as a major ally of the United States and effectively became a client state that was subject to US hegemony. Secondly, having largely forfeited sovereignty on questions of foreign policy and, as a consequence, being marginalized in the construction of new international structures, Japan turned to economic means by which to pursue its interests.

The Allied Occupation of Japan from 1945–51 had as a principal objective the creation of a new Japan that would never again threaten Western interests and international order. In pursuit of these objectives Japan was to be democratized and demilitarized. Political prisoners were released, the ban on leftist parties was lifted and union rights were recognized. A purge against militaristic elements in the state was launched. During Yoshida Shigeru's first tenure as prime minister, Japan's new 'peace constitution' (1946), largely drafted by United States officials, established constitutional monarchy in Japan along the lines of a Westminster democracy (Stockwin 1999). Article 9 of the Constitution renounced war and pledged that Japan would never maintain 'land, sea and air forces, as well as other war potential.' . . . The right of belligerency of the state will not be recognized'. The Constitutional Preamble set a tone of liberal internationalism.

As the Cold War heated up, the United States' concerns shifted towards ensuring Japan's status as an ally. With this new focus, elements of the old militarist state re-emerged as did, in modified form, the business–state relationships that had fuelled Japanese imperialism. These were deemed tolerable developments as long as Japan was on the side of the 'free world', supporting US strategy. The Japan–US Security Treaty (1952, revised 1960) expressed the terms of the mutual alliance in which Japan, in return for guarantees of security, allowed the United States use of bases and port facilities for the occupation and forward deployment of its forces. The bases provided a crucial staging post for operations in the Korean and Vietnam wars. They remain central to US policy today (notwithstanding recent commentary on possible withdrawal) with close to 40,000 troops present, many on the island of Okinawa where a strong anti-bases movement exists. The Peace Constitution and the Treaty effectively paved the way for Japanese disengagement from military pursuits beyond self-defence. Constitutionally banned from waging war and maintaining offensive capacity, and dependent on the US for its security, Japan was to enter into a forty-year period of 'pacificism', never deploying troops, and playing a minimal role in world security affairs. In 1967 the government also adopted the three non-nuclear principles stating that it would never produce, possess or allow passage to nuclear weapons. The third principle has been routinely violated, with the Japanese government allowing passage to US aircraft and navy which operate under a 'neither confirm nor deny' policy regarding the carriage of nuclear materials.

Accepting US hegemony entailed benefits for the Japanese elite. Japan was identified as a Western-oriented industrial power. The US supported Japanese entry into GATT and the United Nations in the mid-1950s, and entry into the OECD in 1964. By the 1960s, a consensus had largely emerged within Japan around pursuing economic growth under the security umbrella afforded by its close relationship with the United States. This posture became known as the Yoshida Doctrine, and was essentially composed of three elements: to concentrate on economic rehabilitation through co-operation with the United States; maintain internal consensus on economic growth by not getting involved in international political and strategic affairs; and guaranteed security from the US in return for US right to bases on Japanese soil. However, it must be noted that the 'doctrine' and the peace constitution have always been open to interpretation, with successive debates about what Japan can do and what forces it can maintain. It has not only been internal pressures that have led to constant debate about the status of Japan's military capacity; external factors have played a major role. Although initially demanding Japan's disarmament, when the Cold War emerged as the new structuring principle of the international bipolar state system, the United States began to pressure Japan to take a greater share in its own defence, particularly after the outbreak of hostilities in Korea. As a consequence, the police force was re-organized in 1954, becoming Japan's Self-Defence Forces. Today these forces, numbering over 200,000, are among the best equipped in the world, equivalent to the United Kingdom's armed forces (Drifte 1998: 76).

The Security Treaty was deeply resented by both left-wing forces (seeking a more neutral pacifist stance) and conservative nationalists (seeking Japanese rearmament and independence), and became the focus of much protest and political struggle through the 1950s (Pyle 1996: 21–5). In the 1960s opposition to the Yoshida line was largely marginalized, as Japan embarked upon a massive programme of economic growth. In 1960, Prime Minister Hayato Ikeda, in the wake of mass demonstrations against the renegotiated Security Treaty, announced the Income Doubling Plan. This ideology of 'GNPism', as it became known, undercut radical politics and cohered the political and business establishment around a policy of economic nationalism. Japan was to once again 'catch up'. The aim of economic policy was to establish Japanese international competitiveness across a range of high value-added industries and protect domestic industries from foreign competition. Essentially a form of mercantilism, the state played a significant role in industrial policy, allocating credit and supporting Japan's technological advances. This project was driven by the emergence of a conservative regime that united business, bureaucrats, politicians and farmers, and locked out independently organized labour (Pempel 1998). The persistence of single-party rule under the Liberal Democratic Party from 1955 to 1993 demonstrates the strength of GNPism and the Yoshida Doctrine.

US concerns to nurture Japanese economic well-being, and thereby maintain its support in the Cold War, led the US State Department to promote geopolitical interests over specific US economic interests in the relations with Japan. In the 1960s, the US State Department issued a paper that recommended 'Firm Executive Branch resistance of American industry demands for the curtailment of Japanese imports' (Pyle 1996: 34). As Japan's economy grew to challenge the supremacy of the Western economies the close relationship between state and business was increasingly scrutinized, leading 'revisionist' commentators to argue that far from being on the road to Western-style liberalism, Japan's 'capitalist developmental state' devised mercantilist trade strategies that advanced national interest in relative terms, over and above the absolute interests that might be forthcoming by engaging in a liberalized and interdependent trading regime (Johnson 1982). In short, the argument was that while Japan had access to Western markets for its produce, it played the trading game unfairly; Japan's massive trade surpluses with the US in the 1980s and 1990s were seen as evidence of this. The trade surpluses were only one factor causing friction; sustained disputes between the two countries also broke out regarding market access, technology sharing and reciprocity (McDougall 1997: 66–71).

Tension also spilled over into the security sphere. With Japan rising economically and the US in seeming decline, there was a renewed call for Japan to play a greater burden-sharing role. With the United States wavering in its Asia commitment following defeat in the Vietnam War, and tightening Cold War conflict with the Soviet Union, the Japanese government announced in 1981 that it was ready to defend Japan's sea lanes to 1,000 nautical miles. However, public and political opposition led to backsliding. The staunch anti-communist Prime Minister Nakasone (1982–86) promised the US, in 1983, that in the event of a crisis Japan would close the three straits that pass it (effectively a blockade against the USSR), and that Japan would be made into an 'unsinkable aircraft carrier'. Nakasone also expressed interest in revising Article 9 of the Constitution, but found himself outplayed by interests still beholden to the Yoshida line. The US was also eager that the cost of its troops deployed in

Japan be paid by the host. Over time the amount Japan pays has increased, so that by 2001 Japan paid US$4.13 billion to maintain US military installations in Japan. NATO countries combined provide just over half of this. Currently, Japan pays the bulk of operating costs associated with the US presence in Japan (Iwamoto and Edirippulige 2002: 11).

During the Cold War, Japan's security concerns were effectively tied up with US interests and protection. It largely focused on economic matters in its relations with other countries. In this context, Japanese foreign policy circles in the late 1970s began to define what they saw as distinctive about Japanese foreign policy under the idea of 'Comprehensive Security'. Comprehensive Security was essentially an attempt to expand the basis of national security beyond a narrow military focus. In Japan the idea was understood as embracing resource security including energy and raw materials which come from overseas, and the provision of foreign aid as part of building economic growth and stability in the region, thus ensuring resource stability. The concept was effectively a translation of economic needs into a foreign policy idea. The idea of Comprehensive Security also allowed Japan to codify its regional and global role. By building up regional economic interdependencies, through investment, technology transfer and trade, Japan could claim to be a good international citizen, assisting in the growth of regional stability and thereby enhancing security. At the same time its budgetary commitments to the United Nations, second only to the United States, also signalled Japan's seeming commitment to peace and order. In this regard Japan has persistently pursued a permanent seat on the UN Security Council, but with little success given its inability to act as a full member in acts of collective security. Nevertheless, despite a reliance on the US security umbrella, Japan could paint a largely liberal picture of itself in world affairs. As one MITI official once candidly observed, 'Post-war Japan defined itself as cultural state holding the principles of liberalism, democracy and peace, but these were only superficial principles, the fundamental objective was the pouring of all our strength into economic growth' (cited in Pyle 1996: 36).

Japan, China and the region

The prioritization of economic diplomacy is seen very starkly in Japan's relations with China. Its avowed anti-communist stance was always directed principally at the USSR, not China. Yoshida, speaking in 1951, was clear on this: 'Red or white, China remains our next door neighbour. Geography and economic laws will . . . prevail in the long run over any ideological differences . . .' (cited in Mendl 1995: 78). Now, despite the existence of a strong pro-China lobby within business, the bureaucracy and among politicians, a condition of the Security Treaty was that Japan establish diplomatic relations with Taiwan and submit to US containment policy on China. However, by arguing a case for the separation of politics from economics (*seikei bunri*), Japan was able to maintain a level of trade with China. Although this was a troubled relationship with each side delivering political tirades against the other, separate interests in markets, raw materials and technology transfer brought them together (Edström 1999: 23). Japan only moved to formalize relations with China after it became apparent that the United States planned to do so. In September 1972 Japan signed a communiqué recognizing the People's Republic of China as the legitimate government of all China, and broke all diplomatic ties with Taiwan. Despite continuing friction over Japan's relationship with the US, minor territorial disputes and admissions of nuclear testing by China in 1995, economic matters have dominated the relationship. The economic relationship has grown in diversity, especially from the 1980s when China embraced a 'socialist market' economy. The closeness of the relationship was evident in Japan's response to the

Tiananmen Square massacre in 1989 when thousands of pro-democracy students were killed by government forces. China found itself internationally isolated and condemned, and facing economic and diplomatic sanctions. Japan was the first country to resume aid, and the first G-7 country to have its head of state visit China after the massacre. Japan's economic interests in China are immense, having poured tens of billions of dollars of FDI into the country (Mendl 1995: 85–7). Japan's economic interests in China are reflected in the fact that in the 1990s it was the greatest source of aid for China.

Japan also expanded its interests by developing ties with the economies of Southeast Asia in the 1960s and 1970s. These ties accelerated from the mid-1980s onwards. This was largely supported by the US, which as early as the 1950s well recognized the importance of Southeast Asia for Japan's economic reconstruction. As William Nester notes, 'Washington promoted a triangular economic division of trade between the United States, Japan and Southeast Asia in which America would provide high technology and capital goods, Japan intermediate and consumer goods and Southeast Asia raw materials and energy' (1992: 121). Such openness to Japanese interests lay in a security logic moulded by the Cold War. According to a joint chiefs of staff report in 1952:

> the United States must take into account Japan's dependence upon Southeast Asia for her economic wellbeing and . . . the loss of Southeast Asia to the Western world would almost inevitably force Japan into an eventual accommodation with the Communist controlled area in Asia.
>
> (Cited in Nester 1992: 121)

Several factors pushed Japan to seek a more active role in the region in the mid-1970s. Firstly, Japan's regional economic dominance, manifest in a flood of exports, created nationalist backlashes in a number of Southeast Asian countries in the early 1970s. Riots and boycotts against Japanese imports occurred in Thailand and Indonesia, for instance. Recognizing that economic diplomacy alone was not sufficient to maintain good relations with the region, Japan embarked on a new diplomacy with its Asian neighbours. Secondly, as the structure of power in the region began to unravel, with the US's defeat in Vietnam and communist victories in Indo-China, Japan was forced to rethink its position.

On assuming the prime ministership in 1977, Takeo Fukuda quickly moved to define Japan's foreign policy objectives and to restate Japanese pacifism in the face of the perceived US backout from Southeast Asia. Fukuda, in August 1977, articulated what became known as the Fukuda Doctrine. The doctrine, such as it was, committed Japan to peace and reaffirmed that Japan would not assume any military role in the region. It expressed a desire for co-operative relations with ASEAN and for 'heart to heart' understanding between Japan and Southeast Asia across politics, economics and culture. Finally, Fukuda pledged to pursue relationships with the communist Indo-Chinese countries based on mutual understanding. The doctrine effectively articulated a regionally specific policy of engagement that was to be underscored by the emerging economic interdependencies between Japan and the region (Edström 1988: 88–91). In subsequent years the rhetoric was to be backed by a massive flow of aid and FDI.

In the 1980s the idea of the flying-geese model, promoted by Japanese economic agencies, construed Japan as the 'lead goose', followed by the first-tier NICs and the second-tier NICs; China became a popular way of visualizing Japan's relationship with the region:

> As it flies forward, becoming more and more technologically advanced, Japan pulls the entire V formation along with it. It does so by successively shedding industries in which

it no longer holds comparative advantage. Through FDI, these industries ultimately find a new home among the less developed countries (the follower geese) of Asia. Over time, these developing countries master the new technology, upgrade their own industrial structure, and themselves begin shedding outdated industries.

(Hatch and Yamamura 1996: 27)

The NICs certainly underwent significant economic growth at faster rates than anywhere else in the world. They increasingly embraced new industries and constantly upgraded their technological capacities within the limits available to them. They did this most certainly through a mixture of domestic policy, Japanese guidance and foreign direct investment, and Japanese overseas development aid that was tied to Japanese goods and services. It has been argued that the best way to conceptualize these developments is to see Japan as the pre-dominant economic power in the Asia region integrating others into its global strategy of exports and growth. It has become a regional hegemon in economic terms, able to shape the regional economic environment, and by the force of its economic power, and ideology, able to win other states to its project of constructing a regional production alliance (Beeson 2001). By the processes of expanded foreign direct investment in selected countries, Japan taps into the region's international division of labour. It selectively locates factories, assembly plants and so on, and integrates these into a production process that is region-wide. As Hatch and Yamamura (1996) argue, Japan has used its regional production alliance as a platform to export to the US and Europe; this has the advantage of reducing Japan's controversial trade surplus. FDI in Asia enables Japan to enter new markets by jumping barriers to trade. Japan's strategy has led to some dramatic shifts in its trade profile. While the US remains a central market, diversification of export and import partners reduces Japan's strategic dependence on the United States.

Contemporary issues

With the end of the Cold War imminent in 1990, Prime Minister Kaifu Toshiki noted that:

> with dialogue and co-operation now replacing missiles and tanks as the tools for achiev-ing order, Japan has both the chance and the duty to apply its economic and techno-logical strength, along with its store of experience and its conceptual ability, to the creation of a new framework for international relations.

(Cited in Kelly 2002: 109)

However, as is frequently noted, optimism for a new world order based on the principles of liberal internationalism, economic interdependency and rational dialogue was rudely

Table 3.1 Shifting Japanese trade profile, 1965 and 1998 (per cent)

	1965			1998		
	Imports	*Exports*	*Total trade*	*Imports*	*Exports*	*Total trade*
EC/EU	4.8	5.7	5.3	13.9	18.4	16.5
US	23.9	30.5	27.7	29.0	29.3	29.3
East Asia	15.8	21.2	18.5	34.9	33.9	33.9

Adapted from Hook (2002). Figures for 1965 are for the much smaller EC.

disrupted by subsequent events; military power remains a key ingredient in deciding who gets what, when and how in the international system. Facing up to this reality, Japan has attempted to steer a course that adequately takes account of the realist security environment in which it perceives itself embroiled, while at the same time pushing forward elements of a liberal foreign policy based on multilateral institution building, trade and diplomatic activity through the UN. The *Japanese Diplomatic Bluebook* (2002) elaborates the three pillars of its contemporary policy: to maintain the US–Japan alliance, to moderately build up its defence capacity and to work towards peace and stability in the world (Ministry of Foreign Affairs of Japan 2002: 91). The *Bluebook* paints a picture of an unchanged Asia-Pacific security architecture built around US bilateralism, while recognizing the emergence of a new multilateral framework around the ASEAN Regional Forum and other bodies. What is significant here is that despite a decade having passed since the end of the Cold War, Japan's basic orientation to defence and security has changed little, nor have its threat perceptions. Its external policies reflect a perceived anarchical environment of competing powers. Fears of an emerging China, and concerns about the nuclear ambitions of the 'rogue state' North Korea, animate Japan's security dilemma and bolster the centrality of the US alliance to Japan. Exacerbating these developments is that they are occurring in a changed security environment. The basic structure of the Cold War capped local rivalries and disputes, as the balance of power maintained by the two superpowers disciplined regional actors into acceptance of the international order. With that order now gone, the question remains of whether US primacy will be sufficient to maintain order or whether order breakers will appear (this is how China is often seen). Japan's security environment then is marked by increased uncertainty. Regarding China, despite a basic orientation to engage economically in the hope of supporting graduated change, at another level Japan may be said to be facing the logic of an emerging rival power challenging its regional hegemony. Furthermore, China's designs on Taiwan and the extent to which these are increasingly achieved through belligerency may draw Japan, by virtue of its US alliance, into a regional conflagration.

Regarding North Korea, there would seem to be no greater immediate threat to Japan's security. Despite decade-long negotiations and diplomatic efforts to engage North Korea (with Japan playing a central role alongside China, the US and South Korea), it remains outside the US-led order, and repeatedly threatens its disruption. In 1998 North Korea fired test missiles over Japan, demonstrating an assault capability were it so inclined. More recently, North Korea's withdrawal from the Treaty on the Non-Proliferation of Nuclear Weapons in 2003, and its claim to have a nuclear weapons development programme, significantly intensifies the security dilemmas faced by Japan. Bluff or not, Japan's defence establishment is eager to meet any potential threat posed by North Korea, and this has manifested itself in support for the United States Theatre Missile Defence (TMD) programme. Such a programme, ostensibly targeted at North Korea, but arguably aimed at neutralizing China's nuclear arsenal, further plunges Japan into the downward spiral of a realist security environment, as the TMD can be expected to lead to an intense arms race. Given these developments, how has Japan responded?

Towards normalization?

Earlier it was noted that in the 1980s Japan began to expand its role in the US alliance. The 1990s were witness to a considerable expansion of its role, further accentuated by Japan's response to the events of September 11 2001. The augmentation has come in several stages: the United Nations Peace Keeping Operations Act of 1992 (revised 1998 and 2001), the

Table 3.2 Japan in action

Context	Action	Implications
1990–91: The Gulf War and Peace-Keeping: In August 1990 the US requests Japanese minesweepers in the Persian Gulf. Japan sends them in April 1991. Japan bankrolls Gulf War effort to the tune of US$13 billion dollars. The then US Secretary of State, James Baker criticizes Japan's 'checkbook diplomacy'. Japan is compelled to reassess its role in the post-Cold War environment.	October 1990: Japanese parliament debates the creation of non-SDF peace co-operation corps. The Bill lapses in the face of parliamentary opposition. In June 1992 parliament passes the 'Law Concerning Co-operation for United Nations Peace-keeping Operations and Other Operations' (known as the PKO law). This allows SDF participation in UN PKO and humanitarian operations according to five principles: an existent ceasefire; agreement by rival sides to UN and Japanese presence; impartiality; right to withdraw when the above not observed; use of weapons only in self-defence.	Japan breaks through a decades-long constitutional interpretation that disallowed dispatch of SDF forces. Japan is now in a position to play a greater international role. However, the five principles severely limit Japan's terms of engagement. Nevertheless, the PKO law is criticized by China, and others, as marking a departure from constitutional restraints on Japan's military role. Legislatively enabled, Japan engages in UN operations in Mozambique, Cambodia, Zaire and the Golan Heights. Later it participates in UN operations in Afghanistan and East Timor.
1996–99: Enhanced US–Japan Co-operation: In 1996 the US and Japan sign a Joint Declaration on Security that restates the primacy of the relationship in the post-Cold War context. In line with the US East Asia Strategy Review, from 1996–97 Japan and the US negotiate new guidelines for co-operation (unrevised since 1978). Cognizant of the new security environment, and the possibility of conflict breakout (China–Taiwan and the Koreas), the US and Japan negotiate new terms for the practical implementation of the US–Japan alliance. The revisions become law in 1999.	Basic provisions of Revised Guidelines Legislation: • Restatement of co-operation during peacetime, including sharing information, working together during UN operations, policy consultation. • Japan to be primarily responsible for defensive operations within Japanese territory, while the US provides support if Japan is attacked. • Japan to provide greater support to the US in 'situations in areas surrounding Japan that will have an important influence on Japan's peace and security'. This allows Japan to provide logistical support to the US, and to assist in search and rescue operations, evacuations and support for US activities in contingency crises in the region.	Japan's field of operations are extended outside of its own territory. The ambiguity of the term 'situations in areas surrounding Japan' is a thorn in the side of Sino-Japan relations as China interprets it as sanctioning Japanese involvement in any US-led operations related to the defence of Taiwan. While the role of the SDF remains couched in terms of self-defence, the sphere or operability has been significantly extended. The involvement in regional contingencies is open to interpretation, and provides justification for operations that take place well beyond those previously sanctioned (1,000 nautical miles). The guidelines are criticized by North Korea and China as a staging post for the re-emergence of a militarized Japan.

Context	Action	Implications
	• Japan to provide greater support to the US in 'situations in areas surrounding Japan that will have an important influence on Japan's peace and security'. This allows Japan to provide logistical support to the US, and to assist in search and rescue operations, evacuations and support for US activities in contingency crises in the region.	
1998 onwards: Missile Defence: After North Korea fires a test missile over Japan in August 1998, Japan and the US agree to initiate joint research and development of a theatre missile defence system that is capable of detecting and destroying incoming missiles.	Japan agrees to jointly fund research and development of the system, and by 2002 has contributed some US$50 million dollars. Despite enthusiasm among high-level defence personnel in Japan, the government delays making a decision until the feasibility of the technology is known. In 2002, the US withdraws from the Anti-Ballistic Missile Treaty of 1972, in order to proceed to the developmental stage of missile defence. In 2003 the Japanese government signals support for the development of a missile defence system in Japan.	The deployment of a TMD system in East Asia is likely to be seen as a measure directed not just at North Korea, but at degrading China's nuclear stockpile. China is against the system, seeing it as directly related to a growing US-Japan pact to dominate the region. Some are concerned that the deployment of a missile defence system in the region will embolden Taiwan to declare independence. Thus the system is seen as heightening, rather than attenuating, existent security dilemmas for states involved.
The 2001 Anti-Terrorism Law: In the wake of September 11 2001 terrorist attacks on the World Trade Center the US pressures its allies to come on side: President George Bush declares that, 'You're either with us or against us in the fight against terror'. The US pushes for Japanese involvement in Afghanistan and later in Iraq.	In October 2001 an Anti-Terrorism Special Measures law allows for the dispatch of the SDF to Afghanistan. The anti-terrorism law provides for: co-operation and support of US and allies in 'war against terrorism', participation in search and rescue missions for foreign forces and relief operations. Furthermore, the 1992 PKO law is revised in 2001, allowing the SDF the use of force in self-defence and to protect those 'under its care'.	The law sanctions, in unambiguous terms, the deployment of Japanese forces to foreign territory. Critics argue that the Terrorism Bill is being used to transform the SDF into a regular armed force. South Korea and China express concern at the development. The Anti-Terrorism Law, expiring in November 2003, was extended for a further two years.

Adapted from Mulgan (2000), Iwamoto and Edirippulige (2002), Singh (2002) and Katsumi Ishizuka (2002); also from various articles in *Japan Times* and *Asia Times* online.

Revised Guidelines negotiated in 1996 and legislated in 1999, joint research on Theatre Missile Defence with the US, and the new Act on Terrorism (see Table 3.2). These developments have been supplemented by new military hardware purchases enabling Japan to play a role well beyond its borders. For example, there is the deployment of forty-seven F-2 fighter bombers able to complete return missions of 850 kilometres, according to the Defence Development Programme of 2001–05, along with the acquisition of four air tankers able to refuel aircraft mid-flight (Kang and Kaseda 2001: 56). These developments stand in stark contrast to Japanese rejection of any role in security affairs prior to the 1990s, apart from its commitments under the US–Japan Security Treaty.

Taken together, the developments outlined in Table 3.2 suggest a significant shift from the Yoshida line, edging towards military engagement. In the latest development Japan passed a controversial special law in mid-2003 allowing dispatch of over 1,000 troops to non-combat zones in Iraq in support of the US and its allies. The law, in effect for four years, allows SDF to provide humanitarian, logistical and security assistance. As late as December 2003 the troops had not been deployed, reflecting uncertainty about how to define non-combat zones in countries where a strategy of guerilla warfare was being utilized. Despite the inconclusive nature of this debate Prime Minister Koizumi signalled a willingness to deploy troops. Raging debates about the dispatch of the SDF to Iraq reflects ongoing debates about the constitutionality of any overseas dispatch of the SDF. Currently Japan remains in the throes of a constitutional debate. While Article 9 has been interpreted as prohibiting anything other than self-defence, it is clear that understandings of self-defence are being broadened to encompass international commitments to maintain peace and order. While in the 1990s this entailed pushing for an expanded Japanese role in UN PKOs, since 2001 it has also entailed a strong identification with the US-led war on terror. There are significant forces in Japanese politics now seeking a revision of Article 9, so that Japan can cast off the constitutional restraints on its 'normalization'. For conservatives a constitutional change would be a better outcome than always having to pass special laws each time the SDF is dispatched.

The debate is often mired in constitutional metaphysics that are often incomprehensible even to the learned eye, but the intention is thoroughly clear. There is a strategic grouping of elites within political parties, the bureaucracies and the defence establishments who seek a definitive break from the Yoshida line. In 2001 the government established a Constitutional Review Committee to survey possible amendments to the Constitution. In early 2003 this committee tabled its report, surveying a range of possibilities. It is largely recognized that revision of Article 9 would most certainly lead to a regional crisis, with even US allies such as South Korea and a number of Southeast Asian nations interpreting such revision as the beginning of a new era of Japanese imperialism. Given this possibility, and the fact that constitutional revision requires a two-thirds majority of the parliament and subsequent support in a popular referendum, revision does seem unlikely in the near future. Also, the fact remains that significant sections of the elite continue to hold to the established line of pragmatic and incremental change, which thus far has allowed Japan to expand the range of operations without drawing retaliatory actions from neighbouring states. However, increasing instability in North Korea and souring relationships with China could lead to a dramatic sea change and the ascendancy of political forces seeking 'normalization'. Indeed, its current Prime Minister Junichiro Koizumi has used Japan's involvement in the 'war on terror' to once again argue the need for Japan to revise Article 9 (*Japan Times*, Online, 3 November 2003).

If the above suggests a strong focus on the US alliance and a deepening of Japanese commitment to that alliance through increased burden sharing, the 1990s were also marked by an increased interest in multilateral initiatives by Japan. It should also be noted that the expansion of Japan's role in UN PKOs reflects an increased contribution by Japan to that organization, on top of its massive financial support and the diplomatic initiatives it undertakes through the UN in support of non-proliferation, development and humanitarian assistance. Japan has also sought to improve its security environment through the support of regional security dialogue, especially through the ASEAN Regional Forum, the body established by ASEAN to establish dialogue on security matters between members ranging from China, the US, South Korea, Japan and ASEAN itself (see Chapter 5). The Japanese rationale for such engagement is given in typically liberal tones in official documents. There is a desire to build transparency, to share information, to build trust and confidence among states (Ministry of Foreign Affairs of Japan: 2002). Yet many conclude that in real terms, for all the rhetoric of multilateralism in Japan, the most significant feature of the post-Cold War era has been the hardening of Japan's reliance on the US, contrasted with its tentative dip into security multilateralism and liberal internationalism in the UN.

Making sense of Japan? Realism, liberalism and radicalism

Recently, eminent scholars on Japan issued a call for analytical eclecticism when it came to understanding Japan in the post-Cold War era (Katzenstein and Okawara 2001/02). For them, no single theoretical perspective can account for the often muddled, contradictory and wide ranging actions of the Japanese state across economic and security matters, nor can any theory capture the various levels at which states and other actors interact, nor determine the relative importance of structure and agency in outcomes. Be that as it may, it will be useful to discern in broad outline three interpretations of Japan.

At the most basic level a key question relating to the neo-realist perspective is whether, given the assumed condition of anarchy, the Japanese state may be expected to pursue substantially its own normalization, including nuclearlization. Just after the end of the Cold War neo-realist Kenneth Waltz wrote:

> For a country to choose not to become a great power is a structural anomaly. For that reason, the choice is a difficult one to sustain. Sooner or later, usually sooner, the international status of countries has risen in step with their material resources. Countries with great power economies have become great powers, whether reluctantly or not. How long can Japan and Germany live alongside other nuclear states while denying themselves similar capability?
>
> (Waltz 1993: 66)

From a realist perspective it is arguable that the developments outlined above represent a movement towards 'normality'. Japan may be moving to end the paradox of its unrealized power. For the neo-realist, Japan's behaviour is to be expected in the current uncertain security environment. Through its deepening alliance with the US, Japan is doing what all states do, balancing the power of potential rivals, and bandwagoning on US primacy. Furthermore, the incremental expansion of the SDF's role is seen as evidence of a classic self-help strategy in the specific circumstances of the constraints that Japan faces (Singh 2002: 85). Calls within Japan among right-wing nationalists for Japanese rearmament commensurate with its economic power adds force to the realist interpretation, although even when facing the North Korean crisis of 2003, the Japanese defence establishment made it clear that entering a nuclear arms race was not an option (Thompson 2003). A more cynical argument comes from those who see Japan as a neo-mercantilist state bent on economic supremacy and advantage. Japan's alliance with the US is seen as conveniently stripping Japan of military engagements that might hurt its economic interests. Japan, for example, is able to maintain good relations with Arab oil-producing countries, on whom it is heavily dependent, because it pursues active diplomacy promoting ties between Japan and the Middle East, and it does not have to bear the cost of the US's unpopular Middle East policy centred on defence of Israel. From this perspective Japan's incrementalism may be taken as shrewd 'dual hedging', in which it keeps up the alliance for the sake of its security in Asia, and yet downplays the importance of the alliance in the Middle East in order to maintain good relations with oil states (see Heginbotham and Samuels 2002).

For liberals, Japan's increased role in UN PKOs may be interpreted as a welcome sign of its engagement with emergent institutions of global security, under the leadership of what Ikenberry has termed US constructed liberal hegemony (Ikenberry 1999). Japan may indeed be moving, however cautiously, towards direct involvement in collective security, and this liberals can countenance. For liberals, Japan's constant engagement with the instruments of the UN reflects an abiding concern with internationalism and the development of international law. Japan's ratification of the Kyoto Protocol is similarly seen in these terms. Further, its multilateral pursuits may be interpreted in terms of liberal institutionalism. By supporting the ARF, Japan is seen as participating in an emergent regional security regime with the capacity to create new forms of order less dependent on power and self-help and more reliant on co-operation. In this light, Japan is an exemplar state, militarily defensive, a major contributor to global governance through its massive support of the UN budget, and its ODA programme. While recognizing the national interest that Japan pursues in all of these arenas, for liberals the logic of institution building ties Japan into a liberal internationalist perspective supportive of global trade and peace. The *Diplomatic Bluebook* of 2002 notes that 'The peace and prosperity of Japan are inevitably linked to the peace and prosperity of the Asia-Pacific region and of the world'. It then goes on to list Japan's efforts in ARF for CB methods, preventative diplomacy, in the UN for PKOs, and economic measures to ensure stability. This all points to the relevance of a liberal interpretation.

From a radical perspective Japan's failure to balance US power, and its continuing preference to augment US power in the region suggests that a structure of US-led hegemony is present. Japan sees its best chance of advancing its capitalist interests by working within the sphere of US hegemony. After all, Japan enjoys the twin benefits of economic growth and access to vital markets, as well as the security apparatus of the US machine (Van Ness 2001). In this perspective, Japan exists in a structured world system in which the rules of the game are set by US hegemony. Having accepted these rules, it is not driven to self-help strategies which would suggest nuclearization (an expectation of the neo-realists). Of course the neo-realist response to this line of analysis is that Japan is augmenting its economic power through opportunist mercantilist policies, and that nuclearization in Japan can occur relatively rapidly, in a matter of months, if the Japanese so choose.

It is abundantly clear that the three perspectives offer quite different answers to Japan's purpose. With reference to these approaches, it is appropriate that this chapter concludes with three questions. Is Japan intent on realizing its power (economic and military), and taking its seat at the table of great powers? Is Japan an exemplar trading state, pointing to the future where states are economically strong (through trade interdependencies with the world) and support international law and emerging norms of co-operation and peace? Or is Japan the still, but not forever, junior partner of the international capitalist enterprise led by the United States?

References

Alperovitz, G. (1996) *The Decision to Use the Atomic Bomb: And the Architecture of an American Myth*, London: Fontana.

Beasley, W. G. (1991) *Japanese Imperialism 1894–1945*, Oxford: Clarendon Press.

Beeson, M. (2001) 'Japan and Southeast Asia: the lineaments of quasi-hegemony', in G. Rodan, K. Hewison and R. Robison (eds) *The Political Economy of South-East Asia: An Introduction*, 2nd edn, Melbourne: Oxford University Press, pp. 283–306.

Drifte, R. (1998) *From Japan's Foreign Policy for the 21st Century: From Economic Superpower to What?*, Basingstoke: Macmillan.

Edström, B. (1988) *Japan's Quest for a Role in the World*, Stockholm: Institute of Oriental Languages, University of Stockholm.

Edström, B. (1999) *Japan's Evolving Foreign Policy Doctrine: From Yoshida to Miyazawa*, Basingstoke: Macmillan.

Hatch, W. and Yamamura, K. (1996) *Asia in Japan's Embrace: Building a Regional Production Alliance*, Melbourne: Cambridge University Press.

Heginbotham, E. and Samuels, R. J. (2002) 'Japan's dual hedge', *Foreign Affairs*, 81: 110–21.

Hook, G. D. (2002) 'Japan's role in the East Asian political economy: from crisis to bloc', *Asian Business and Management*, 1: 19–37.

Ikenberry, G. J. (1999) 'Hegemony and the future of American post-war order', in T. V. Paul and J. A. Hall (eds) *International Order and the Future of World Politics*, Cambridge: Cambridge University Press, pp. 123–45.

Iwamoto, Y. and Edirippulige, S. (2002) 'Japan's response to the war against terrorism', *New Zealand International Review*, 27: 9–12.

Johnson, C. (1982) *MITI and the Japanese Miracle: The Growth of Industrial Policy*, Stanford, CA: Stanford University Press.

Kang, S. E. and Kaseda, Y. (2001) 'Korea and the dynamics of Japan's post-Cold War security policy', *World Affairs*, 164: 51–9.

Katsumi Ishizuka (2002), 'The evolution of Japan's policy towards UN peace operations', paper presented at the 15th Annual Meeting for the Academic Council on the UN system, Cascais, Portugal, 21–23 June 2002.

Katzenstein, P. J. and Okawara, N. (2001/02) 'Japan, Asian-Pacific security, and the case for analytical eclecticism', *International Security*, 26: 153–85.

Kawakami, A. (2002) 'Japan? Not quite', *The Guardian*, 12 June, p. 6.

Kazuo, C. (1996) 'Japan: after the Cold War', in B. Edström (ed.) *Japan's Foreign and Security Policies in Transition*, Stockholm: The Swedish Institute.

Kelly, D. (2002) *Japan and the Reconstruction of East Asia*, Basingstoke: Palgrave.

McDougall, D. (1997) *The International Politics of the New Asia-Pacific*, Boulder, CO: Lynne Rienner.

Mendl, W. (1995) *Japan's Asia Policy*, London: Routledge.

Ministry of Foreign Affairs of Japan (2002) *The Diplomatic Bluebook*, Ministry of Foreign Affairs of Japan. Online. Available HTTP: <http://www.mofa.go.jp/policy/other/bluebook/2002/> (accessed 9 October 2003).

Mouer, R. and Sugimoto, Y. (1986) *Images of Japanese society: A Study in the Structure of Social Reality*, London: Kegan Paul International.

Mulgan, A. G. (2000) 'Beyond self-defence?', *The Pacific Review*, 12: 225–48.

Nester, R. W. (1992) *Japan and the Third World: Patterns, Power, Prospects*, Basingstoke: Macmillan.

Pempel, T. J. (1998) *Regime Shift: Comparative Dynamics of the Japanese Political Economy*, Ithaca, NY: Cornell University Press.

Pyle, K. (1996) *The Japanese Question: Power and Purpose in a New Era*, 2nd edn, Washington, DC: AEI Press.

Scalapino, R. A. (ed.) (1977) *The Foreign Policy of Modern Japan*, Berkeley, CA: University of California Press.

Singh, B. (2002) 'Japan's post-Cold War security: bringing back the normal state', *Contemporary Southeast Asia*, 24: 82–105.

Stockwin, J. A. A. (1999) *Governing Japan: Divided Politics in a Major Economy*, 3rd edn, Malden, MA: Blackwell.

Susumu, T. (2001) 'The global meaning of Japan: the state's persistently precarious position in the world order', in G. D. Hook and H. Harukiyo (eds) *The Political Economy of Japanese Globalization*, London: Routledge, pp. 19–39.

Tamamoto, M. (1993) 'The Japan that wants to be liked: society and international participation', in D. Unger and P. Blackburn (eds) *Japan's Emerging Global Role*, Boulder, CO: Lynne Rienner, pp. 37–54.

Thompson, J. (2003) 'Japanese nuclear arsenal looks unlikely', *Japan Times*, 10 August.

Van Ness, P. (2001) 'Hegemony, not anarchy: why China and Japan are not balancing US unipolarity', Australian National University, Department of International Relations, Working Paper 2001/4.

Waltz, K. (1993) 'The emerging structure of international politics', *International Security*, 18: 66.

Yang, D. (1999) 'Convergence or divergence? Recent historical writings on the rape of Nanjing', *American Historical Review*, 105: 1. Online. Available HTTP: <http://www.historycooperative.org/journals/ahr/104.3/ah000842.html> (accessed 17 June 2003).

4 China in the Asia-Pacific

Rémy Davison

A hundred years hence we will want it and fight for it. . . . And when I go to heaven to see God, I will tell him that for the present it is better to have Taiwan under the care of the United States.

(Mao Zedong to Richard Nixon, 1972)

Introduction

The emergence of China as a state of potentially global significance is the product of over fifty years of revolution, reform and renewal. By 2003, the People's Republic of China (PRC) was a state in transition, with the 'fourth generation' assuming leadership of the Chinese Communist Party (CCP). This chapter examines the main players in the Asia-Pacific region with which the PRC interacts: Taiwan, Hong Kong, North Korea, Japan and the US. The national security interests of these states are integrally linked, and the region has exhibited volatility in recent years, with tensions between the PRC and Taiwan, together with North Korea's resumption of nuclear weapons development. At the same time, the PRC has developed considerable economic linkages with its neighbours, which have profound implications for Chinese foreign policy in the region over the coming decades. In the concluding section, we examine how an emergent China is viewed through the prisms of realism, liberalism and neo-Marxism.

The emergence of the People's Republic of China

Mao Zedong's accession to power in 1949 represented a seminal moment in China's history, particularly as the formation of the People's Republic of China (PRC) came at a pivotal point of the Cold War. In 1948, the Soviet Union had effectively completed its takeover of most of Eastern Europe. Mao's revolution, and his alliance with the USSR, suggested that international communism was in the ascendant. The result was a freezing of relations between the PRC and the West for almost a quarter of a century. The Nationalist Kuomintang (KMT) regime, which retained control over Taiwan, was recognized as the *de jure* government of the Republic of China (ROC), and remained seated at the UN until 1971.

However, the relationship between the Soviet Union, the 'senior partner' in the relationship, quickly turned frosty, culminating in the Sino-Soviet split of 1957–61. Nevertheless, it took another decade before US policy makers appreciated the depth of the split, and the PRC remained a pariah state in international relations. Effectively, 1949 meant the separation of China into the 'four Chinas': British Hong Kong, Portuguese Macao, the PRC and the Republic of China (ROC), Taiwan. Within months of its formation, the PRC became embroiled in the Korean War, which is discussed in Chapter 8.

Box 4.1 Significant events in recent Chinese history

1925	Nationalist Government established under Kuomintang.
1931	Japan occupies Manchuria.
1937	The Manchurian 'incident' results in the massacre of over 100,000 people.
1949	Mao Zedong's Chinese Communist Party assumes power and establishes the People's Republic of China (PRC).
	Kuomintang Nationalist government occupies Taiwan and forms the Republic of China (ROC). ROC retains China's Permanent Membership of the United Nations Security Council (UNSC).
1950	Korean War commences. UNSC authorizes intervention, resulting in fighting between multinational forces, led by the US, and Communist-backed North Korean forces. 200,000 PRC 'volunteers' cross border to assist North Korean forces.
1953	Stalemate in Korea results in armistice and a demilitarized zone at the 38th parallel, dividing Korea into North and South.
1957–61	Sino-Soviet split.
1959	Soviets cease nuclear development assistance programme with PRC.
1964	France establishes diplomatic relations with the PRC.
	Soviet leader Khrushchev overthrown.
	PRC explodes first nuclear device.
1966	Commencement of the Cultural Revolution.
1971	Australian Labour leader Gough Whitlam visits Beijing during US Secretary of State Henry Kissinger's secret visit.
	US President Nixon announces that the US will support the PRC's entry into the UN.
	The UN General Assembly votes to admit the PRC to the UN and to expel the ROC. The ROC withdraws from the UN.
1972	US President Nixon visits Beijing.
	Japan recognizes PRC and establishes diplomatic relations. PRC renounces all war reparations claims against Japan.
	Australian government establishes diplomatic relations with PRC and recognizes PRC as government of China.
1973	PRC seated as a Permanent Member of the UNSC.
1976	Death of Mao. End of the Cultural Revolution. Ascendancy of Deng Xiaoping.
1977	Deng establishes 'open door' trade and investment policy and Special Economic Zones.
1979	US formalizes relations with PRC.
	Deng initiates economic reforms integrating 'socialism with Chinese characteristics'.
1989	Deng orders suppression of Tiananmen Square uprising.

1994	Jiang Zemin assumes effective control of government.
1996	PRC recommences nuclear tests.
	PRC conducts a series of weapons tests off the coast of Taiwan.
1997	Death of Deng. Formal succession of Ziang Zemin.
	PRC reassumes sovereignty over Hong Kong.
2000	US President Clinton signs China Trade Relations Act.
2001	PRC and Taiwan enter the World Trade Organization.
2002	US government grants permanent normal trade status to PRC.
2003	Retirement of Ziang Zemin. Hu Jintao assumes presidency, with Wen Ziabao as prime minister.

Rapprochement: China turns West

The dilemma in the US of how to contain their communist adversaries was a classic case of the policy divisions between conservatives and realists. For realists, such as Hans Morgenthau, a state was a state was a state; it made no difference whether it was communist or capitalist; totalitarian or democratic. All states, Morgenthau asserted, had similar interests: security and survival (Morgenthau 1948). Conversely, conservatives, such as Kennan (1947), argued that communism was a new and inherently aggressive type of ideological force which needed to be contained at all costs. However, conservatives failed to acknowledge that the Chinese response to the Korean War was a realist response to the threat on its border, not a consequence of its alliance with the USSR.

The conservative ascendancy in US foreign policy led to no significant policy shifts towards China until 1969, when Richard Nixon assumed the presidency. Both Nixon and his National Security Adviser (later Secretary of State), Henry Kissinger, adopted realist responses to the 'China question'. Conservatives had not treated the 1957–61 Sino-Soviet split with sufficient seriousness. Conversely, realists argued that Chinese and Soviet interests were *national* interests, driven by security, while conservatives tended to tar all communist states – the USSR, China, North Vietnam, North Korea and Cuba – with the same brush. All were notionally satellites of Moscow, rather than independent national entities with distinctly different interests. Neoliberals, conversely, argued that if the US was acting in its national interests, it would have allied itself with China in order to balance Soviet power. According to Hemmer and Katzenstein (2002: 584), 'Although conceivable in terms of material balance of power, for ideological reasons, communist China was not a plausible alliance partner for the United States after 1949'.

The turning point in Western relations with the PRC came in 1971–72, with the visit of Australian Labor leader (later prime minister) Gough Whitlam to Beijing in 1971. At the same time, US National Security Adviser Kissinger had taken a secret flight to Beijing, resulting, days later, in the announcement that US President Richard Nixon would visit the PRC in 1972. For both China and the US, this represented a critical turning-point in China's relations with the world; for the US, it was a significant diplomatic victory over the Soviets. Mao famously told Nixon, 'We will criticize you, but not much; and you can criticize us, but not much. But this is for domestic consumption'. Some commentators credited the US's diplomatic triumph with a thaw in Soviet–US relations, resulting in the 1972–79 period of *détente* between the superpowers.

Sino-American *rapprochement* resulted in the ROC's removal not only from permanent membership of the UN Security Council (UNSC), but also from the General Assembly. In effect, as a sovereign state, the ROC ceased to exist in 1971. In December 1972, the Australian government recognized the PRC, establishing diplomatic relations for the first time since 1949. In 1972, the PRC was also seated as one of the five permanent members of the UNSC. Nevertheless, the question of Taiwanese independence persisted. In response, the US developed the 'one China' policy which meant that the US recognized the *de facto* and *de jure* sovereignty of the PRC. However, in practice, it did not mean an end to US support for Taiwanese political and economic independence from the mainland, which resulted in an increasingly complex relationship between Beijing, Taipei and Washington by the end of the twentieth century.

The 'one China' issue

Nixon's remarkable *volte-face* on US–China relations led to the 1972 joint communiqué which set out the principles of the US's 'one China' policy. Although it satisfied Mao's government, it was deliberately couched in ambiguous terms: 'The United States recognizes that all Chinese on either side of the Taiwan Strait maintain there is only one China and Taiwan is a part of China'. By couching the 'one China' policy in deliberate ambiguity, the clear intent of the Nixon Administration was to avoid offending Taipei, while simultaneously recognizing there were not two *de jure* governments of China. Concrete US confirmation of its recognition of the PRC's primacy came in 1971 with the removal of the ROC from its permanent seat on the UNSC and the seating of the PRC in its place.

Having stabilized relations with China following Nixon's 1972 visit, the US deprioritized the PRC, content with issuing three communiqués (1973, 1978, 1982) which dealt with US recognition of China, the 'one China' policy, and reductions in arms sales to Taiwan, respectively. Despite warmer relations, the US did not recognize the PRC until 1979, by which time Cold War hostilities with the USSR had recommenced. Simultaneously, the US passed the US–Taiwan Relations Act, which committed the US to 'oppos[ing] any effort to determine the future of Taiwan by other than peaceful means'. In 1994, Premier Ziang Zemin sought a fourth US–China communiqué which would eradicate any possibility that the US would either initiate high-level official visits to or from Taiwan, or countenance the establishment of diplomatic relations between Washington and Taipei. The Clinton Administration refused overtures to develop a fourth communiqué and declined to host an official visit from Ziang, arguing that only democratic countries or states which shared the US's ideals were permitted state visits. Ultimately, a compromise was reached, with a Clinton–Jiang meeting at the fiftieth anniversary of the United Nations in New York in 1995 (van Kamenade 1997: 48–9). But the episode revealed that cracks were emerging in the US–China relationship following a long period throughout the Carter–Reagan–Bush Administrations where China was relegated to the second-order agenda during the US's 'second Cold War' with the USSR (1979–86) and, subsequently, *rapprochement* with the Soviet Union (1986–91).

Following the abortive conflict in the Taiwan Strait in 1996, the US launched several initiatives aimed at defusing tensions between Washington and Beijing. Firstly, the Clinton Administration opted to follow a 'national interest' approach to its China policy, abandoning half-hearted attempts at containment during the early 1990s. US Secretary of State Warren Christopher argued that, 'We reject the counsel of those who seek to contain or isolate China. . . . That course would harm our national interests, not protect them. Demonizing China is as dangerously misleading as romanticizing it would be' (van Kamenade 1997: 51).

Nevertheless, events such as the 1999 American bombing of the Chinese embassy in Belgrade, and the US and Chinese aircraft collision in 2001, demonstrated that US–China relations were easily ruptured.

During the 2000 US presidential election, Clinton and Vice President Gore argued that China was a partner of the United States. Conversely, Republican candidate George W. Bush asserted that China was a competitor, not a partner. However, despite some diplomatic hostilities in 2001 following the crash of a US spy plane, China's relationship with the US since Bush's election has been relatively cordial. Two significant events suggested US policy towards China was demonstrably conciliatory. Firstly, the US welcomed China's and Taiwan's entry into the WTO in 2001. Secondly, the US granted China 'permanent normal trade status' in 2002 (Embassy of the PRC 2001a; 2001b; 2001c). However, China's WTO entry also meant that it would be subject to tighter monitoring by both the WTO and the US. For example, in May 2003, the US employed a WTO clause to safeguard its market against increases in Chinese textile exports to the US (*People's Daily* 2003).

Considerable diplomatic differences remain in key areas of Sino-US relations. Although the Chinese government declared its public support for the US's 'war on terror' (Embassy of the PRC 2002b), the two states were at significant variance over policy on Iraq, with the US favouring military intervention, and China arguing that US action without UNSC authorization was a gross breach of international law. Furthermore, the Chinese government protested strongly over the US's 2002 Defense Authorization Act, which it argued contained 'anti-China' clauses. Beijing remains particularly concerned about the sale of high-tech US naval destroyers and Maverick missiles to Taiwan. At the same time, US intelligence has pointed to mounting evidence of the PRC's covert support for North Korea and its nuclear programme (*Washington Times* 2002c).

However, China demonstrated some solidarity with the US following the September 11 2001 terrorist attacks. The PRC has its own problems with terrorist groups, with Islamic separatists active in Xinjiang, and attacks in both Xinjiang and Beijing, by persons believed to have been trained by Al-Qaeda in Afghanistan. However, as Christensen argues, Beijing has also used September 11 as a cover for summary arrests and executions of a number of disparate groups and activists, including Falun Gong (Christensen 2001). Nevertheless, China's opposition to the US-led war on Iraq in 2003 demonstrates that it is moving closer to the Russian and French multilateralist position in an attempt at containing the American 'hyperpower'. In recent years, France has abandoned its criticism of China in the UN Human Rights Commission, in marked contrast to the US Premier Li Peng's 1998 visit to Paris, whose lavish reception provoked criticism of France's China policy in the National Assembly, led the French foreign minister to respond that the US's 'realist approach' to China had not produced 'concrete results' (Védrine 2001: 147).

China's integration into the global economy

China has become heavily dependent upon FDI flows. The PRC was the destination of 10 per cent of total global investment in 2002 (US$53 billion) and 70 per cent of all inward Asian FDI in 2001 (Mahani 2002: 1269). Even prior to the PRC's accession to the WTO, 51 per cent of total trade was conducted by foreign firms, and trade as a proportion of GDP was 44 per cent in 2001. By contrast, developed economies, such as Germany, export only 23–25 per cent of their GDP. China also depends heavily upon the US market as an export destination; the US took 20.4 per cent of mainland Chinese exports in 2001

(US$54.3 billion). As mainland re-exports from Hong Kong are categorized separately, and a substantial proportion of the PRC's trade with the US is exported from Hong Kong, Chinese exports to the US are even more significant than the 'direct' trade figures suggest.

Japan has emerged as China's most important source of imports, with 17.6 per cent of imports originating from Japan (US$42.8 billion) in 2001. Taiwan and the US were the second- and third-largest sources of imports, with 11.2 per cent and 10.8 per cent, respectively. Fourth and fifth were South Korea and Germany, both with approximately 8 per cent of the Chinese market. Following two decades of significant economic reform, China entered the WTO, together with Taiwan, in November 2001. Although WTO membership is likely to lead to a tremendous increase in FDI and trade with China, accession to the WTO also requires China to follow stringent regulations. These include not only sweeping anti-piracy measures in accordance with WTO agreements on trade in intellectual property services (TRIPS), but also structural reforms to asset ownership and financial services deregulation. These include areas such as domestic currency lending by foreign banks; market access for foreign international financial institutions, including insurance companies; domestic currency deposits; and geographical distinctions governing market entry. Under WTO regulations, all international financial institutions are now subject to 'national treatment' (i.e., the Chinese government cannot discriminate between domestic and foreign service providers). Of even more significance has been the partial lifting of the restriction upon foreign ownership of Chinese financial sector assets. 50 per cent is now the maximum permissible level of ownership, although this means there will be no wholly owned foreign subsidiaries in mainland China. Moreover, even under the WTO regime, China's regulation of pension funds and securities remains tight; foreign firms are restricted to 33 per cent ownership in this sector, rising to 49 per cent by the end of 2004 (Lardy 2001a). In Hong Kong, yuan trading is restricted to state-controlled banks, locking up 10 billion yuan that is unavailable for investment in Hong Kong (*Tax News Hong Kong* 2003).

Nevertheless, due to potential financial sector collapses, the PRC may be forced to remove these restrictions at a faster rate than the WTO requires. Lardy argues that poor accounting and budgetary practices, non-performing loans and profligate lending by the Bank of China, one of the country's four biggest banks, could lead to a 'full-blown fiscal crisis', with bad loans comprising 39 per cent of the Bank's portfolio in 1999. In 2000, the four largest banks jointly held somewhere between US$240 and 600 billion in non-performing loans, equivalent to 40–75 per cent of China's GDP. Chinese non-adherence to Western accounting practices also suggests that government reporting of fiscal deficits and debt is grossly understated and misleading (Lardy 2001b). With a loan : GDP ratio of 117 per cent (Bonin and Huang 2002: 1077), there are considerable risks that China will find itself increasingly exposed to shocks during periods of international financial turbulence. This is the result of China's accession to the WTO, and its growing level of integration with world markets means that its interests and national policy preferences are now increasingly affected and constrained by the global political economy.

China and the Asia-Pacific region

China and North Korea

The 1953 armistice left the Korean Peninsula question unresolved. As South Korea developed into a tiger economy in the 1980s, North Korea remained a relic of the Cold War; a diplomatically isolated communist state with high levels of poverty. China has remained North Korea's largest trade partner and it supplies an estimated 70 per cent of Pyongyang's oil (*China Reform Monitor* 2003a). By 2003, the North Korean regime of Kim Jong-il had expelled UN weapons inspectors and announced the recommencement of the country's nuclear weapons programme. More ominously, Pyongyang's two ballistic missile tests over Japan and the Sea of Japan provoked alarm in Tokyo.

The Bush Administration labelled North Korea as part of the 'axis of evil', which included Iraq and Iran. However, Beijing proved conspicuously silent in the midst of North Korea's new-found assertiveness. The *Asian Wall Street Journal* (2003) editorialized,

> China is the one country most reluctant to dislodge Kim Jong-il. For all the giveaways in Seoul's 'sunshine policy', the amount of aid that flows from South Korea is still only a fraction of the support Beijing provides in propping up its faltering communist neighbour.

The CIA, in a report presented to Congress in January 2003, alleged that North Korea had secured raw materials for its ballistic missile programme via North Korean firms based in China. US intelligence also asserted that Pyongyang had also purchased chemicals designed to extract material from spent nuclear fuels to aid its plutonium programme from China (*Washington Times* 2002a; 2002b; 2002c). Beijing responded by tightening up its previously lax control of Chinese industries exporting 'dual use' materials (Christensen 2002).

China's intercession as mediator between the US and North Korea is largely designed to portray the PRC as an 'honest broker' in regional affairs. Beijing hosted trilateral talks between the US, North Korea and China in April 2003. However, it was clear that Beijing sought a *quid pro quo* on US–Taiwan relations as a result of its mediation efforts with North Korea. President Bush reportedly told Jiang Zemin in late 2002 that the US 'opposes' Taiwan's independence (Christensen 2002). However, Beijing has frustrated Washington by its refusal to take a harder line on North Korea. Although it is not in the PRC's interest to see Pyongyang develop a nuclear weapons capability, should this occur, it will at least in part be due to Beijing's lax non-proliferation policies, which have previously resulted in Chinese assistance for Pakistan's nuclear weapons programmes. Although it is highly unlikely that Beijing would support North Korean military action against South Korea in the event of a pre-emptive attack, China's support for UNSC-sanctioned resolutions against Pyongyang is an even more remote possibility. However, there are strong incentives for Beijing to moderate North Korea's behaviour. As Christensen argues, 'Taiwan is not the most likely flashpoint for US–China relations in the near term . . . North Korea is' (Christensen 2003).

China and Taiwan

Tensions in the China–Taiwan relationship had their origins in the 1949 establishment of rival regimes in Taipei and Beijing. The ROC remained a Permanent Member of the UNSC until 1971, when it left the UN, rather than face a vote of expulsion. The PRC assumed Taiwan's UNSC seat in 1972. However, although Taiwan has moderated its claims regarding its legal jurisdiction over mainland China, it has largely conformed with the US-mandated doctrine of a 'one-China' policy.

The 1950–53 Korean War saw an escalation in the PRC–ROC conflict as Beijing saw US intervention in Korea as a possible prelude to an invasion of the Chinese mainland in support of the Nationalist government. However, the stalemate in Korea, together with US policy-makers' conviction that the Moscow–Beijing–Pyongyang triangle formed a holistic communist bloc, froze relations between the US and China for almost twenty years, and American administrations continued to support the Taipei government. US–Chinese *rapprochement* from 1971 politically and diplomatically isolated the ROC. In international law, Taipei was no longer the *de jure* government of China. Taipei had supported a 'Dual Representation Complex' proposal, which involved keeping both Taipei and Beijing within the UN, while Beijing took over Taipei's seat on the UN Security Council (*Taipei Times* 2001: 3).

The security of Taiwan became – and remains – a linchpin of American policy in the region. The Taipei–Beijing relationship reached a flashpoint in 1996 during the Taiwanese elections, which threatened the introduction of a democratic Taipei government on China's doorstep. In March, Beijing provocatively announced surface-to-surface missile tests in close proximity to two Taiwanese ports; airforce and naval exercises employing live ammunition in the Taiwan Strait; and a third set of air and sea-based exercises late in March. The US response was to send two aircraft carriers to the Strait, purportedly in order to monitor both the PRC military exercises, as well to ensure regional stability during the Taiwanese elections. Although no confrontation took place, the crisis prompted a rethink of policy on both sides, which resulted in serious attempts at *rapprochement* during the second Clinton Administration. In 2001, China's ambassador to the US said that, 'The question of Taiwan has always been the most important and most sensitive issue at the heart of China–U.S. relations' (Jiechi 2001).

In 1995, Taiwan's president, Lee Teng-hui, made a strong speech calling for international recognition of Taiwan's legal independence of the PRC. The ROC has always rejected Beijing's 'One Country, Two Systems' doctrine, which implies that Taiwan lacks sovereignty. However, Lee's provocative stance did not go as far as rejecting official US or PRC policy concerning the 'one China' issue. In 1999, Lee clarified Taipei's position, stating that Taipei's position on the PRC was 'unchanged' and that peaceful unification with a democratic mainland China remained the objective. He consistently referred to Taiwan as a 'sovereign nation' and argued that the PRC should recognize Taiwan as a state (CNN 1999). However, US liberals argue that the very ambiguity of America's 'one China' policy is a strength, and encouraging Taiwanese independence merely gives the impression that the US is a threat to Chinese interests in the region (Bush 2002a). As Ross argues, 'rather than needlessly challenge Chinese security, the United States should use its strategic advantage to expand co-operation with China and maintain the security of Taiwan' (Ross 2002: 85). However, there are indications that the Bush Administration is beginning to move away from the long-held US policy of 'strategic ambiguity' over Taiwan, although the longer-term implications of this shift are not yet clear. Despite the considerable volume of US arms transfers to Taipei, President Bush explicitly ruled out support for Taiwanese independence. President Chen Shui-bian moderated his independence rhetoric in 2003, with the Taipei administration cautiously moving towards acceptance of a 'Hong Kong' model, albeit a strict Taiwanese interpretation, as a last-resort basis for negotiations with the mainland, should direct economic links between Taiwan and the mainland fail to be established (Christensen 2003). Nevertheless, Chen reasserted his 'two countries' doctrine in late 2003 as he sought re-election, with the rival KMT also supporting independence (*The Australian* 2003).

The ROC's renewed independence movement inflamed Beijing. However, the Taiwanese population has not been supportive of declarations of independence, despite widespread popular rejection of the PRC's 'One Country, Two Systems' policy, demonstrated by the solitary seat held by the New Party, the only party to advocate reunification, in the December 2001 elections. Taipei has also attempted to regain membership of the World Health Organization (WHO) as a pre-accession attempt at applying for membership of the UN. The World Health Assembly (WHA) rejected five attempts by Taipei between 1997 and 2001 to join the WHO. Membership is open only to sovereign states, and the PRC has effectively blocked Taipei's moves, despite support for Taiwan from the US House of Representatives. During the 2003 SARS epidemic, the PRC offered Taiwan assistance, which was rejected. Without Beijing's permission, WHO representatives could not enter the island.

The PRC continues to protest strongly against states which exchange high-level representatives with Taipei. Arms sales to Taiwan are another potential flashpoint. In the 1982 US–PRC joint communiqué, the US pledged to gradually reduce arms sales to Taiwan. However, the US continues to supply sophisticated weapons to Taipei, while the Pentagon co-operates with Taiwan on anti-ballistic missile research. The visit of Taiwan's defence chief, Tang Yiau-ming, to the US in March 2002, increased friction between Beijing and Washington. China had opposed the visit, and the Chinese ambassador to the US argued that, 'The move has severely violated the "One China" principle and runs counter to the three Sino-US joint communiqués' (Embassy of the PRC 2002a). US neo-conservatives, while supportive of the 'one China' doctrine, have done little to defuse Beijing's suspicions that America may ultimately support an independent Taiwan. Equally, however, Congress is suspicious enough of the PRC's Taiwan strategy to order annual studies of China's military modernization. The 2003 Pentagon report alleges that China is not only acquiring short-range missiles capable of striking across the Taiwan Strait much faster than previously thought, but the PRC, according to intelligence, may also be pointing missiles at US targets in an effort to prevent any attempt by US forces to block a possible future invasion (*International Herald Tribune* 2003).

Conversely, although liberals differ over support for the 'one China' policy, they are united in their opposition to a stance on Taiwan which would commit the US to an armed conflict (Berry 2000). Richard Bush argues that, 'Beijing is willing to tolerate much about the United States' ties with Taiwan, but it cannot accept a public US rejection of its claims on this issue' (Bush 2002b). Liberals argue that the US should reiterate its commitment to the 1979 Taiwan Relations Act, which would compel the US to intervene only if China-Taiwan integration is not achieved by peaceful means. Rather than damaging trade relations, deploying BMD or supplying military assistance to Taiwan to 'reassure Taiwan and deter China, it will not suffice for Washington merely to transfer a few high-technology weapon systems, like Aegis-class cruisers for missile defence, to Taiwan', Cohen (2000) argues. He posits that although the US should continue supplies of military material to Taiwan, it should not use trade leverage as a means of deterring China from an assault on Taiwan. Further integration of China into the global economy might be more likely to achieve a peaceful resolution of the PRC–ROC issue.

China and ASEAN

China and ASEAN have only developed strong links since the early 1990s, with Chinese representatives attending the 24th ASEAN Ministerial at Kuala Lumpur in 1991. ASEAN's accordance of full dialogue status to China in Jakarta in 1996 recognized the significance of

China to the region. Significant initiatives included the formation of the ASEAN–China Joint Co-operation Committee and the ASEAN–China Co-operation Fund. A key area of mutual interest has been establishing a code of conduct in the South China Sea, as well as studies conducted by the ASEAN–China Joint Co-operation Committee examining the implications of a free trade agreement between China and ASEAN.

However, both the FTA and South China Sea issues have involved difficult diplomatic negotiations. Both sides have agreed to demonstrate 'restraint' in the South China Sea. A China–ASEAN FTA is much more complex, given the gross disparities in market power which exist between the two parties. Consequently, China has agreed to an extensive liberalization of its market in order to offset the negative impact of investment divergence away from ASEAN caused by China's accession to the WTO (Breckon 2003). However, following the November 2002 ASEAN–China meeting at Phnom Penh, Taiwan reportedly proposed an ASEAN–Taiwan FTA, although it is unlikely ASEAN would consider such an overture seriously. A China–ASEAN FTA would constitute the world's largest single market, comprising 1.7 billion consumers, a GDP of US$2 trillion and two-way trade totalling over US$1.2 trillion. However, ASEAN studies of the benefits of a China–ASEAN FTA have shown few gains from such an agreement, estimating the benefits at only 0.9 per cent of ASEAN GDP (US$5.4 billion) and 0.3 per cent of China's GDP (US$2.2 billion). Nevertheless, the study envisages a 48 per cent increase in ASEAN exports to China and a 55 per cent rise in Chinese exports to ASEAN. A major incentive for a China–ASEAN FTA is more likely to be a growth in Japanese, US and EU investment in the bloc (ASEAN Secretariat 2001: 30–1). However, as Chapter 9 notes, the ASEAN itself may face considerable difficulties meeting the AFTA schedules for the liberalization of ASEAN markets which, in turn, suggests that an FTA with China would not be accomplished easily. Nevertheless, China potentially offers ASEAN a great deal more than Japan, which could only deliver a vague commitment to a possible FTA within ten years at the Phnom Penh summit. As ASEAN becomes a less competitive climate for investment compared to China, this is likely to consolidate calls for closer ASEAN–China economic relations, and the APT is a potential vehicle for this form of co-operation.

China–ASEAN and APT relations have consolidated the PRC's bilateral links with ASEAN member countries. Under the Chiang Mai APT agreement, China agreed to a US$1.5 billion currency swap with Malaysia in 2002. The PRC has also developed closer relations with Vietnam and Indonesia in the area of military exchanges and co-operation and, although China–Vietnam border issues remain sensitive, they are not potential flashpoints. Dialogue between the two states continues on maritime issues. China has also committed to financing some Philippines infrastructure projects, which has prompted Manila to take a softer line on incidents such as illegal Chinese fishing in the Philippines' exclusive economic zone (EEZ). China has also expanded its economic links further south of the region, signing a liquefied natural gas (LNG) deal in 2002 with an Australian firm, valued at more than US$25 billion, and a similar arrangement with Indonesia's West Papua province to supply Fujian province with LNG worth US$8.5 billion (*China Reform Monitor* 2002).

China has been a particularly enthusiastic advocate of the ASEM process as it views the forum as a means of strengthening the multilateral process, characterized by the IMF, WTO and World Bank. Realists argue that China's objective is to use ASEM as a multilateral forum in order to avert continued US dominance of international institutions. Chinese governments view multilateralism as a means of furthering China's national interests by counter-balancing US financial and military power, which has remained relatively unchecked since the collapse of the USSR. In many respects, the structure of the international system since 1991 has been unipolar (Bin 2003). China's aim is to achieve strategic bipolarity in the longer term, with a multipolar framework as an interim objective. ASEM, to some extent, represents one pillar in China's attempt to build support for its initiatives in an inter-regional, multilateral forum.

China and Japan

Since the 1931 Japanese invasion of Manchuria, Sino-Japanese relations have been characterized by a mutuality of suspicion, which were exacerbated by Mao's accession to power in 1949 and the PRC's support for North Korea. The Japanese surrender in 1945 had resulted in the return of Taiwan and Penghu Islands to the Republic of China, and the Japanese government formally recognized the Nationalist government of Chiang Kai-shek. Japan's geostrategic location, together with its membership of the US-dominated Western alliance, meant it was much more vulnerable to potential attack from the communist triangle of the PRC, North Korea and the USSR.

Throughout most of the Mao era, Japan adopted a position of 'uncertainty' on jurisdiction over Taiwan. However, Sino-US *rapprochement* from 1971 forced Japan to assume a more conciliatory position towards China. In 1972, Japan recognized the PRC and established diplomatic relations, adopting the US's 'one China' policy at the same time. Article 3 of the Sino-Japanese Joint Statement on 29 September 1972 noted that:

> The government of the People's Republic of China reiterates that Taiwan is an inalienable part of the territory of the People's Republic of China. The government of Japan fully understands and respects this position of the government of the People's Republic of China, and shall firmly abide by the principles under Article 8 in the Potsdam Proclamation.

As a *quid pro quo*, the PRC renounced all war reparations claims against Japan. However, a number of issues remain outstanding. China continues to dispute the legality of the peace treaty signed between Japan and the ROC government at the conclusion of the Second World War. Moreover, China consistently raises objections to official contacts between Japanese governments and the Taipei regime.

The steady marketization of the Chinese economy from 1979 – which coincided with Japanese financial power reaching its zenith – saw Sino-Japanese trade and investment achieve impressive growth. As the engine of Asian financial and industrial growth, it was clear that modernization and industrialization in China would require strong links with Japan. By 1999, Japanese loans to China totalled 2.9 trillion yen (US$27 billion). In 2001, two-way trade reached a record US$89.1 billion.

Nevertheless, irrespective of closer Sino-Japanese economic relations, the two states remain major economic and strategic competitors within the region. Despite the economic stagnation of Japan after 1990, China is dwarfed by Japanese economic power and investment by Japanese firms in mainland China is increasing rapidly. As early as 1994, more Japanese FDI projects were directed to mainland China than to any other country (Hatch and Yamamura 1996: 10–11). Firms such as Sony, Toyota, Matsushita and Canon have expanded their manufacturing and production facilities in China. It is becoming increasingly evident that Japanese business is consolidating its presence in the PRC, particularly as it seeks to offset its structural trade surplus with the US by exporting finished goods from China. By contrast, Chinese ownership of Japanese productive assets is nominal, suggesting that Japan's economic ascendancy will remain a dominant factor in the relationship.

However, difficulties in the Sino-Japanese relationship have remained, as China continues to be one of the key strategic actors in the region. Renewed attempts to remove or amend Article 9 of the Japanese constitution also causes alarm among Beijing elites, who view constitutional strictures as the key to maintaining Japan's largely defensive posture within the region. Moreover, a Japan capable of greater military assertiveness would be likely to increase its military co-operation with the US, 'encircling' China, a strategic outcome Beijing wishes to avert at all costs. Three major issues have emerged as dominant issues on the contemporary Sino-Japanese security and diplomatic agenda. These are (i) the threat of a nuclear-capable North Korea; (ii) the US–Japanese military relationship; and (iii) Japan's relationship with Taiwan.

The North Korea issue

The test launch of two ballistic missiles by North Korea in 1998 created alarm in Japan as one missile landed in the Sea of Japan, while the other flew over Japan. In May 2003, Japanese Prime Minister Koizumi sought Chinese President Hu Jintao's intercession over the North Korean issue to defuse tensions between the US and North Korea. Three days of talks took place between Chinese, North Korean and US officials, although China refused to include Japan, Russia or South Korea in the trilateral dialogue. Despite Beijing's claim that it is a mediator in the dispute, few doubt China's need to stress its great power status and its unrivalled influence over North Korean policy. Not only was Japan excluded, but China has kept the UN at arm's length, in marked contrast to its policy on Iraq. If US conservatives and intelligence are correct, then China will continue to supply the North Korean regime with raw materials, foodstuffs – and possibly weapons-related technologies and supplies – in order to play the 'Korea card' when dealing with Japan or the US on sensitive issues of national policy, such as Taiwan or trade-related matters.

The US–Japan military relationship

The US–Japan agreement in December 1998 to conduct joint R&D on upper-tier missile defences provoked alarm among Beijing elites; it confirmed their suspicions that the US was embarking upon a programme of 'hostile encirclement' of China. However, Japan has con-solidated its strategic relationship with the US recently. North Korea's admission that it was continuing weapons of mass destruction (WMD) development drew a forceful response from Japan in the form of a renewed emphasis upon its defence relationship with the US. In 2003, Japan announced it would aim to deploy a new US-designed missile defence system within three years. Japan will deploy the Patriot Advanced Capability–3 missile system, which will also involve upgrades of its Aegis-class naval destroyers. This will give Japan considerable navy-wide theatre defence capabilities. Theatre-based missile defence has been touted within the US military since at least 1983, and the development of Aegis-based technology gives the US and its allies in the Asia-Pacific region significant defensive capabilities.

Neo-conservative commentators argue that China's ultimate objective is the complete removal of US forces from the Asia-Pacific region, including South Korea and Japan. This, it is conjectured, will force Seoul and Tokyo to come to non-confrontational accom-modations with Beijing (*China Reform Monitor* 2003a). However, US withdrawals of land-based forces from Subic Bay (the Philippines) and Okinawa (Japan) are likely to be replaced by sophisticated and flexible naval-based BMD systems, such as Aegis, which will give the US arguably stronger defensive capabilities in the region. US withdrawals should not be interpreted as part of a systematic 'disengagement' from the region either, a perspective which gained wide currency during the Clinton era. In 2003, the US had troops in 136 countries, including several states bordering or neighbouring China, such as Japan, South Korea and Tajikistan, which suggests that the US is unlikely to disengage from the region.

China, Japan and the Taiwan issue

The rapid growth of Taiwan as a key centre of manufacturing and investment has encouraged Japanese business to contract out many of its consumer electronics manufacturing projects to Taiwanese firms, including Sony, NEC, Matsushita, Sharp and Toshiba. This has led to increased levels of contact between Japanese business and the Taipei government.

However, China has been clear on the legal ambiguity of Japan's post-war settlement with the ROC, which led Japan to adopt the 'theory of uncertainty of the jurisdiction over Taiwan' after 1949. The agreement between the Mao and Tanaka governments in 1972 ensured that Japan accepted the 'one China' policy. However, democratization movements in Taiwan in recent years have led to reassertions of Taiwanese independence. During his 1998 Tokyo visit, Jiang Zemin reiterated that Japan was expected to refrain from engaging in official contacts with Taiwan, or encourage independence movements (Consulate of the PRC 2003).

China and Japan have also experienced recent trade friction, caused partly by Japan's growing trade deficit with the PRC, which reached US$24.88 billion in 2001, on a total two-way trade volume of US$85.73 billion. Although Japanese FDI is a key source of investment in China, with around US$4 billion flowing to the PRC in 2001 alone, Japanese firms view China chiefly as a low-cost, offshore manufacturing base, not as a potential export competitor. In 2001, under pressure from its farm lobby, Japan imposed tariffs on a number of Chinese foodstuffs; China retaliated with tariffs on Japanese cars, mobile phones and air conditioners. However, Japanese firms have been the main exporters from China back to Japan, particularly in key sectors such as consumer electronics and cars (*Business Week* 2001). The trade disputes illustrate a growing rift between the policy objectives of Japanese government and business; firms need open trade with China, but Japanese administrations are wary of large-scale – potentially structural – trade deficits with their giant competitor.

China's 'New Security Concept'

Since 1998, China has developed what some commentators have identified as a new security doctrine. This 'New Security Concept' (NSC) is based upon a number of key premises, summarized in Box 4.2. Tow and Hay (2001: 40), argue that it 'poses a direct and serious challenge to US regional security diplomacy'. They further assert that the NSC, 'proposes an alternative security blueprint to the US bilateral alliance systems that have dominated Asian security politics for half a century by envisaging a new multilateral regional security framework devoid of any alliance structures' (Tow and Hay 2001: 40). Liberals, conservatives and realists agree that China poses a potential challenge to traditional US hegemony in the region, although they differ considerably over how to counter or accommodate China's emergence as a regional power. Liberals argue the 'engagement' thesis – that China is becoming enmeshed in the global economy and socialized into economic norms, such as free trade. Conversely, realists assert that China, as a rising power, will not be satisfied with the status quo; that is, an Asia-Pacific region dominated by US security interests, and a global economy under US hegemony (Johnston 2003: 5–6).

Thayer (2000: 69) credits Hu Jintao, former vice president and now president of China, with the development of the NSC. Beijing has attempted to develop the new concept through forums such as the ARF, ASEAN Plus Three and the ASEAN Post-Ministerial conference. China has sought to reduce tensions over the South China Sea by supporting a Code of Conduct, although Thayer notes the PRC would not discuss the issue at the 7th ARF meeting.

Tow and Hay (2001) argue that China has developed its NSC as a means of balancing US hegemony. They assert that the post-Cold War structure has pushed Beijing and Moscow closer together, with considerable increases in advanced military hardware exports from Russia. Military equipment is now Russia's biggest export to China, while Russian oil is of increasing importance to China. Beijing and Moscow, together with Paris and Berlin, were strident opponents of the Anglo-American invasion of Iraq, and Li notes that Russian President Putin describes China as a 'strategic partner', with Russian Foreign Minister Ivanov declaring that 'Russia and China will work to deepen relations of strategic partnership. Lately, the coordination of the two sides' efforts in the international arena has markedly increased' (Bin 2003). Analysts also point to the 'Shanghai Five' process which has resulted in confidence-building measures (CBMs) between China, Russia, Tajikistan, Kyrgyz and Kazakhstan since 1996, including reductions in military forces along common borders (Embassy of the PRC (Germany) 2002; Swaine 2003).

Box 4.2 Key elements of Chinese foreign policy

The Five Principles of Peaceful Co-existence:

1   Mutual respect for sovereignty and territorial integrity.
2   Mutual non-aggression.
3   Non-interference in each other's internal affairs.
4   Equality and mutual benefit.
5   Peaceful coexistence in developing diplomatic relations and economic and cultural exchanges with other countries (*People's Daily* 1999).

China's 'New Security Concept' (*People's Daily* 2002):

- That the Asia-Pacific region and the world are moving inexorably towards multipolarity and that regional dialogue and co-operation are the best way to ensure peace and security.
- Smoothing relations with its immediate neighbours through border agreements and related confidence-building measures.
- Collaborating with Russia to counterbalance US international security postures related to arms control and peace enforcement.
- Implementing a regional diplomacy of 'anti-hegemony' designed to shape a regional security environment where US alliance systems will no longer be relevant or necessary (Tow and Hay 2001).

Moreover, China did not threaten to exercise its UNSC veto on the Iraq question, in marked contrast with France and Russia, which demonstrated distinct caution on the part of the 'fourth-generation' leadership in its handling of the bilateral relationship with the US (Davison 2004). Finkelstein and McDevitt (1999) argue that China's NSC, outlined in Beijing's 1998 Defence White Paper, places 'strategic partnerships' – such as the Sino-Russian partnership – at the centre of Beijing's shift from alliance politics to 'strategic' partnerships. This means that China will attempt to develop partnerships with states and organizations, such as the EU and ASEAN, which can play a significant part in the PRC's economic and military strategies. As the progenitor of this type of coalition, the Sino-Russian partnership is likely to be an exemplar of the NSC. As Finkelstein and McDevitt (1999) argue, 'The concept is also an attempt to present a more benign and less threatening face in East Asia. Beijing wants to debunk the China threat theory and be perceived as a responsible actor in Asia'. However, Finkelstein (2001) also argues that 'Frankly, nothing in the concept is very new or extraordinary . . . [it] is merely a repackaging of China's time-honoured "Five Principles Of Peaceful Coexistence" '.

Nevertheless, US neo-conservatives and realists remain suspicious of claims that China is a benign power in the region, exemplified by the US's release of its 1998 paper, *Security Strategy for East Asia*, which represents continuity in the US's traditional alliance diplomacy throughout the region. For realists, China's resort to an NSC, comprising multilateralism, strategic partnerships and peaceful coexistence, represents weakness, not strength. It seeks to balance US hegemony by forging relations with other, similarly weak, second-order powers such as Russia and France. Neo-conservatives argue that China's multilateralist thrust is merely a cover for its covert programme of deploying advanced BMD, air and naval technologies within the present decade (*China Reform Monitor* 2003b).

In reply, China cites its record on disarmament, pointing to the 1 million reduction in personnel in the People's Liberation Army (PLA) between 1985 and 1997. China has moved to downsize its forces' personnel by a further 500,000 since 1997. However, conservative US think-tanks, such as the American Foreign Policy Council, are more sceptical about China's military designs, pointing to Beijing's drive to become a high-technology weapons producer of global significance. The Chinese armed forces modernization programme includes the development of a copy of the Eurofighter 2000 aircraft, strategic bombers, cruise missiles, the development of sea-based nuclear forces, and a dramatic increase in the numbers of nuclear and diesel-electric submarines. China is also reportedly developing a theatre missile defence (TMD) system in response to the US's National Missile Defence (NMD) and TMD. China possesses some twenty missiles with multiple independently-targeted re-entry vehicle (MIRV) warheads, which can strike up to ten targets simultaneously. Although China lags far behind the US in MIRVs, there are claims that China plans to increase its MIRV warheads to more than 100. Long-range ICBMs by 2005 are also claimed to be part of China's armaments programme (*China Reform Monitor* 2003b). In 2002, Foreign Minister Zhu Rongji asked France to cease arms sales to Taiwan, and sought a lifting of the EU embargo on arms sales to China. Zhu said that China had earmarked US$260 billion in foreign exchange for arms purchases (Agence France Presse 2002). US intelligence also confirmed that in 2002 China sold dual-use chemicals to an Iraqi firm manufacturing solid missile fuels (*China Reform Monitor* 2003c). Realists argue that this suggests China's NSC is no more than window dressing as the PRC steadily develops its nuclear arsenal.

If the NSC is to be interpreted as a significant policy shift, the diplomatic posture Beijing adopts in the medium term will determine the extent of its importance. There is little evidence that the NSC is, in fact, a radical departure from past Chinese foreign policy practice. In 1954, Premier Zhou Enlai outlined the 'Five Principles of Peaceful Coexistence' (Finkelstein 2001: note 1) and this found exceedingly limited, if genuine, expression in 1964 with China's establishment of diplomatic relations with another multilateralist power, France. Sino-Russian co-operation is not a recent development either; diplomatic relations improved considerably under Gorbachev (1985–91), and the volume of Russian military and non-military exports to China increased significantly from 1991 (Bazhanov 1995). Consequently, the significance of the NSC will be evidenced by China's actions and initiatives, both regionally and globally, rather than in the rhetoric of its leadership.

Emergent China: contending perspectives

How do realists, liberals and neo-Marxists approach the question of emerging Chinese power in the Asia-Pacific region? Should China be contained, balanced and encircled? Or should it be integrated into the political economy of the Asia-Pacific? Does China represent a new pole of politico-economic power, having outlasted the USSR and eclipsed Russia, while developing as a major competitor of Japan, both economically and strategically?

Realists argue that a state's ultimate aim is to ensure its security and survival in a conflictual and hostile international system. As a result, the state's resources are directed towards the maximization of its military capabilities. Concomitant with this is the development of a relatively self-sufficient economy which itself drives the process of modernization, techno-logical advancement and military sufficiency. 'Hard' military power has downstream benefits in terms of 'soft' power, which can give a state considerable diplomatic leverage. In China's case, its military power always meant it was a significant actor in regional affairs. However, its increasing economic strength also means that China's emergence as an economic actor has *global* significance. As a destination for FDI and a global manufacturing hub, China's centrality to the international economy is not restricted to the Asia-Pacific region. In addition, as a permanent member of the UNSC, and as a participant in the ARF, APEC and APT, realists assert that China has – or will – become a serious challenger to US hegemony because its strategic interests – chiefly, those concerning North Korea, Taiwan and Japan – in the region invariably draw it into conflict with those of the US.

US policy makers tend to believe the international system works best with a single leader; conversely, China, together with Russia and France, has sought to balance US power through sponsoring multilateral initiatives. However, to this point, they have singularly failed to balance American unilateralism. Realists argue that China's resort to multilateralism is merely an indication of weakness, not strength, and only by building bilateral and multi-lateral alliances throughout the region – such as with ASEAN – can it hope to galvanize sufficient support to oppose, modify or block the US's dominant politico-economic role in the Asia-Pacific.

By contrast, liberal approaches stress co-operation, rather than conflict, and integration, rather than division, when dealing with China's emergence as a great power. The liberal position was exemplified by the Clinton Administration, which sought to draw the PRC into the US-led multilateral system of trade, finance and security. Economic liberals recognized the centrality of China to the US investment and manufacturing sectors, and encouraged Washington to see the PRC as a partner, rather than a rival in the global economy. Clinton encouraged the inclusion of both the PRC and Taiwan as members of the WTO, as this would benefit both China and the US. WTO membership would also compel China to liberalize its markets and adhere to a rules-based international trading regime. China, liberals argued, would then become more heavily dependent upon, and integrated with, the

Western economies. Despite the threat of confrontation across the Taiwan Strait in 1996, liberal perspectives remained dominant in the Clinton Administration's dealings with China. Nevertheless, Clinton's 'liberalism' should not be overstated; it was upon Assistant Secretary of Defence Nye's initiative that the concept of an expanded defence role for Japan was explored and implemented from 1997. In addition, it was Clinton who approved and signed NMD into existence, a defence system which has been widely viewed by the Chinese leadership as not only directed at containing China, but also as a means of encircling China.

From a neo-Marxist perspective, China's ability to transform itself from a first-tier NIC to a core state in the world system is critical to its emergence as a power of truly global significance. In this respect, China will need to avoid the pitfalls of dependency which have befallen other significant actors, such as India and South Korea. China arguably remains on the semi-periphery of the world economy (Wallerstein 1998); despite its rapid development, it is still a country with a large rural sector and high levels of poverty outside the major cities. Nevertheless, neo-Marxist perspectives frequently view China's emergence as a counter-hegemonic, countervailing force in the region as a direct response to US–Japanese military and economic dominance of the Asia-Pacific. However, Wallerstein (1997) argues that it is difficult to predict whether China will be able to displace Japan as the dominant Asian power in the region. For dependency theorists, the main question regarding China is whether it can successfully pursue a model of capitalist economic development, similar to that of Japan, or whether it remains on the fringes of the world economy, dependent largely upon FDI and foreign technology. The post-war Northeast Asian development experience suggests that China is more likely to join the core than remain on the semi-periphery.

Conclusions

China is commonly viewed as a less of a threat both regionally and globally because it is a civilizational 'soft' power, which cannot be seen as serving its own interests only. As Dellios and Field (2002) argue, 'China views itself as a great power, but projects itself as strategically different from other major powers, emphasizing peaceful coexistence'. This is in marked contrast to what is widely viewed as US global 'imperialism'. Regardless of Chinese foreign policy-makers' avowed profession of China's 'difference', PRC foreign policy has been realist in its articulation and implementation. However, realists, neo-conservatives and liberals differ markedly over how to deal with China's growing military and economic importance. Realists stress alliance diplomacy and balancing Chinese power, while neo-conservatives argue that China needs to be contained, exemplified by the Bush Administration's attempts to develop reconfigured security alliances in the region with Japan and Australia. Conversely, liberal approaches, articulated by the Clinton Administration, seek to integrate China into the globalization project, arguing that an economically interdependent PRC is less likely to threaten others by placing its own national interests in jeopardy. However, as China's influence in the region grows, it may pose a serious counter-hegemonic challenge to the US's traditional dominance in the region, and this in itself suggests that the first-order issues between China and the US will remain politico-military, rather than economic, in nature.

The future of the CCP itself is not assured. Like the former Soviet Union, the CCP is a melting pot of hardliners and reformers, who face a myriad of business and military interests. Most of the last vestiges of the CCP gerontocracy have disappeared, and the emergence of a new generation of leaders, represented by Wen Jibao and Hu Jintao, may signal a reduced emphasis upon the CCP's leading and guiding role in Chinese politics. However, former leaders, such as Jiang Zemin, may retain control of much of the policy process, albeit from the background. Li (2001) posits that the 'fourth-generation' Chinese leaders are 'techno-nationalists', who view their task as economic and technological modernization, as well as political reform. However, one of the major problems the new leadership must confront is the growing independence movement in Taiwan, which Li argues, 'place[s the] fourth generation leaders in a very difficult situation. Any major policy mistake from either side of the Taiwan Strait may profoundly jeopardize the course of China's modernization' (cited in Bush 2002a). However, Gill argues that China's relative weakness itself poses a danger both domestically and regionally. Gill asserts that the weakness of the regime led to the Tiananmen Square massacre, and that the fourth-generation leaders will want to avoid 'looking weak' in the face of an independence movement across the Taiwan Strait, particularly as the US remains committed to Taiwan's security. This was exemplified by Wen Jibao's warning that China would 'pay any price' to block Taiwanese independence (*The Australian* 2003). The new security dilemma China faces as a consequence of the US's forceful BMD agenda is likely to compel the CCP leadership to disguise its weakness with occasional declarations of false belligerence and increased defence spending (Gill 2001a). However, the fourth generation is only too aware that China's nuclear capabilities comprise a barely adequate deterrent and an ineffective – possibly non-existent – second strike capability (Gill 2001b). Liberals, such as Gill, argue that China and the US have a mutual interest in keeping the Chinese nuclear arsenal small, and that Washington neo-conservatives need to give Beijing an incentive to remain a second-tier nuclear power. Given this context, critics of Washington conservatives warn that aggressive policies aimed at containing China may, in fact, achieve the obverse.

References

Agence France Presse (2002) 'Zhu asks European Union for weapons sales', 27 September.

ASEAN Secretariat (2001) *Forging Closer Asean–China Economic Relations in the Twenty-First Century*, report submitted by the ASEAN–China Expert Group on Economic Co-operation, October, pp. 30–1.

Asian Wall Street Journal (2003) 'China props up an evil regime', 16 January.

Australian, The (2003) 'China warns US on Taiwan stand', 24 November.

Bazhanov, E. (1995) 'Russian policy toward China', in P. Shearman (ed.) *Russian Foreign Policy since 1990*, Boulder, CO: Westview, pp. 159–80.

Berry, N. (2000) 'Maintaining the one-China policy makes good sense: a commentary', Center for Defense Information, 24 August. Online. Available HTTP: <http://www.cdi.org/asia/fa082400.html> (accessed 18 March 2003).

Bin, Y. (2003) 'China–Russia relations: at the dawn of a unipolar world', *Comparative Connections*, 1st Quarter (January–March). Online. Available HTTP: <http://www.csis.org/pacfor/cc/0301 Qchina- rus.html> (accessed 23 June 2003).

Bonin, J. P. and Huang, Y. (2002) 'Foreign entry into Chinese banking: does WTO membership threaten domestic banks?', *The World Economy*, 27: 1077–93.

Breckon, L. (2003) 'China caps off a year of gains', CNA Center for Strategic Studies Paper.

Bush, R. C. (2002a) 'China's leadership transition: implications for cross-Strait and US–China relations', Brookings Institution, Center for Northeast Asian Policy Studies, 16 November.

Bush, R. C. (2002b) 'American ambiguity on Taiwan's sovereignty increases the island's safety', *Insight*, 4 December.

BusinessWeek (2001) 'China vs. Japan: a phony trade war', 9 July.

China Reform Monitor (2002), 469, 2 October.

China Reform Monitor (2003a) 'Beijing's Korea goal: remove U.S. military and political influence from Asia', 483, 6 February.

China Reform Monitor (2003b) 'China's drive to become a world-class weapons producer: the integration of military and civilian hi-tech production', 484, 11 February.

China Reform Monitor (2003c) 'China sold Iraq chemical for missile fuel', *China Reform Monitor*, 489, 17 March.

Christensen, T. J. (2001) 'Terrorism, Taiwan elections, and tattered treaties: PRC security politics from September 11 through year's end', *China Leadership Monitor*, December.

Christensen, T. J. (2002) 'The party transition: will it bring a new maturity in Chinese security policy?', *China Leadership Monitor*, 5 June.

Christensen, T. J. (2003) 'Optimistic trends and near-term challenges: Sino-American security relations in early 2003', *China Leadership Monitor*, June.

CNN (1999) ' "One-China" policy remains unchanged, Taiwan says', broadcast 14 July.

Cohen, E. A. (2000) ' "One China" policy is obsolete', *Wall Street Journal*, 21 March.

Consulate of the PRC (Australia) (2003) 'The question of Taiwan in China–Japan relations', press release, February.

Davison, R. (2004) 'French security after September 11: Franco-American discord', in P. Shearman and M. Sussex (eds) *European Security After 9/11*, Aldershot: Ashgate.

Dellios, R. and Field, H. (2002) 'China and the European Union: potential beneficiaries of Bush's global coalition', *Australian Journal of International Affairs*, 56: 83–98.

Embassy of the PRC (Germany) (2002) 'China's position paper on the New Security Concept', press release, 6 August.

Embassy of the PRC (US) (2001a) 'US seriously violates international law', press release, 15 April.

Embassy of the PRC (US) (2001b) 'Bush hails China's entry into WTO', press release, 11 November.

Embassy of the PRC (US) (2001c) 'US president grants permanent normal trade status to China', press release, 28 December.

Embassy of the PRC (US) (2002a) 'China protests US official contacts with Taiwan', press release, 14 March.

Embassy of the PRC (US) (2002b) 'China welcomes US stance on anti-terrorism', press release, 26 August.

Finkelstein, D. (2001) 'China's "New Concept of Security" – retrospective and prospects', paper presented at the National Defense University Conference on the Evolving Role of the People's Liberation Army in Chinese Politics, Fort Lesley J. McNair, Washington, DC, 30–31 October.

Finkelstein, D. and McDevitt, M. (1999) 'Competition and consensus: China's "New Concept of Security" and the United States security strategy for the East Asia-Pacific Region', *PacNet Newsletter*, 8 January.

Gill, B. (2001a) 'China's weakness is what makes it so dangerous', *Los Angeles Times*, 6 April.

Gill, B. (2001b) 'China's nuclear agenda', *The New York Times*, 7 September.

Hatch, W. and Yamamura, K. (1996) *Asia in Japan's Embrace: Building a Regional Production Alliance*, Cambridge: Cambridge University Press.

Hemmer, C. and Katzenstein, P. J. (2002) 'Why is there no NATO in Asia? Collective identity, regionalism, and the origins of multilateralism', *International Organization*, 56: 575–607.

International Herald Tribune (2003) 'Strategy menaces Taiwan, report says', 31 July.

Jiechi, Y. (2001) 'Cold War mentality vs. warm hopes for the new century', speech to the US–China Policy Foundation, 23 April.

Johnston, A. I. (2003) 'Is China a status quo power?', *International Security*, 27: 5–56.

Kennan, G. F. (1947) 'The sources of Soviet conduct', *Foreign Affairs*, 25: 566–82.

Lardy, N. (2001a) 'Open doors: foreign participation in financial systems in developing countries', paper presented at the Brookings/World Bank/International Monetary Fund Conference, April.

Lardy, N. (2001b) 'China's worsening debts', *The Financial Times*, 22 June.

Li, C. (2001) *China's Leaders: The New Generation*, Lanham, MD: Rowman & Littlefield.

Mahani, Z.-A. (2002) 'ASEAN integration: at risk of going in different directions', *The World Economy*, 27: 1263–77.

Morgenthau, H. J. (1948) *Politics Among Nations*, New York: Knopf.

People's Daily (1999) 'China's foreign policy', 14 September.

People's Daily (2002) 'China offers new security concept at ASEAN meetings', 1 August.

People's Daily (2003) 'China "deeply regrets" US possible import restrictions', 27 May.

Ross, R. S. (2002) 'Navigating the Taiwan Strait: deterrence, escalation, dominance, and U.S.–China relations', *International Security*, 27: 48–85.

Swaine, M. (2003) 'China's perspective on Northeast Asian security', paper presented at Carnegie Endowment for International Peace, Washington, DC, 12 February.

Taipei Times (2001) 'Taiwan and the United Nations – withdrawal in 1971 was an historic turning point', 12 September.

Tax News Hong Kong (2003) 'Hong Kong lenders urge Beijing to lift restrictions on yuan', 22 May.

Thayer, C. A. (2000) 'China's "New Security Concept" and ASEAN', *Comparative Connections*, 2, 3. Online. Available HTTP: <http://www.csis.org/pacfor/cc/003Q.pdf> (accessed 23 June 2003).

Tow, W. and Hay, L. (2001) 'Australia, the United States and a "China growing strong": managing conflict avoidance', *Australian Journal of International Affairs*, 55: 37–54.

van Kamenade, W. (1997) *China, Hong Kong, Taiwan Inc.: The Dynamics of a New Empire*, New York: Knopf.

Védrine, H. (2001) *Les Cartes de la France à l'heure de la mondialization*, trans. P. H. Gordon, *France in an Age of Globalization*, Washington, DC: Brookings Institution Press.

Wallerstein, I. (1997) 'The rise of East Asia, or the world-system in the twenty-first century', keynote address at Institute of International Studies Symposium on Perspective of the Capitalist World-System in the Beginning of the Twenty-First Century, Meiji Gakuin University, 23–24 January.

Wallerstein, I. (1998) 'The so-called Asian crisis: geopolitics in the Longue Durée', paper presented at the International Studies Association Meeting, Minneapolis, 17–21 March.

Washington Times, The (2002a) 'North Korea seeks aid from China on nukes', 9 December.

Washington Times, The (2002b) 'China ships North Korea ingredient for nuclear arms', 17 December.

Washington Times, The (2002c) 'Panel to probe China's nuclear-related sales to N. Korea', 20 December.

5 Southeast Asia and the Asia-Pacific: ASEAN

Jörn Dosch

Introduction: what is ASEAN?

Following a recent assessment, it is interesting to note that pre-1990s writings on the international politics of Southeast Asia rarely strayed outside the realist camp, and that on the whole Southeast Asia provoked little theoretical debate. However, 'In the 1990s, Southeast Asia generated more theoretical interest as the realist orthodoxy was confronted with a twofold challenge: liberal institutionalism and institutional constructivism' (Rüland 2000: 421–2).

It is easy to see why Southeast Asia attracted renewed interest in the 1990s. The Association of Southeast Asian Nations (ASEAN), which was expected to face a major identity crisis after the end of the Cold War virtually reinvented itself, firstly as a grouping with regional economic ambitions, and secondly as an embryonic security dialogue body, the first of its kind in the region. If in the 1970s ASEAN might have been portrayed as a club of dictators, in the contemporary period significant political change in Southeast Asia – democratization and market reform in nominally socialist economies – means that ASEAN demands attention as an organization with the potential to significantly impact on region formation and shape the major powers' intervention in the region. However, as we will see, this capacity has been uneven, especially as ASEAN proved to be a weak organization in terms of the impact of the Asian economic crisis.

What is the Association of Southeast Asian Nations (ASEAN)? An international organization? A forum for co-operation and policy co-ordination among governments in Southeast Asia? A free trade area? Something like the European Union? Integration in Southeast Asia has many facets but is strikingly different from the European experience.

ASEAN came into existence in 1967 as a child of the Cold War which had just reached a new peak as the result of the Vietnam War. Although never officially stated, we know today that ASEAN's 'founding fathers saw intensified regional co-operation as a means of strengthening Southeast Asia's position in the Asia-Pacific area and thereby reducing the risk of becoming a victim of great power rivalry'. Over the following three decades the association successfully institutionalized a network of regular meetings among the member states that enabled the governments of Southeast Asia to liaise on problems or challenges the region faced. ASEAN has gained a reputation for having orchestrated Vietnam's withdrawal from Cambodia and the subsequent Paris Peace Agreements of 1991 that ended the Indo-China conflict. One of the most remarkable successes of ASEAN has been the ability of its member states to (seemingly) harmonize their foreign policies and often speak with one voice in international affairs. This in turn allowed ASEAN to establish formal relations with the leading regional and global powers such as the United States, the European Union,

China and Japan within the framework of annual conference series and forums like the ASEAN Post-Ministerial Conferences (PMCs) and the ASEAN Regional Forum (ARF). After the outbreak of the Asian crisis in 1997, however, some observers became rather sceptical and even suggested that ASEAN might dissolve. The organization has been criticized for holding on to what seem to be decades-old, outdated concepts, such as the strict adherence to the principle of non-interference and the necessity of reaching consensus on every single issue, no matter how marginal it may be. According to these views, ASEAN has not found any effective way of dealing with today's pressing challenges such as globalization or Islamic militancy and terrorism. Then again, few deny that ASEAN has prominently contributed to the management of regional order: after all, war among member states has been absent for more than three decades. Moreover, after many unsuccessful and half-hearted attempts at regional trade liberalization, ASEAN finally committed itself to economic integration, with the first stage of the ASEAN Free Trade Area (AFTA) coming into effect in 2002.

Any attempt to evaluate ASEAN's achievements and shortcomings needs first to address the issue of regionalism and regionalization in general terms. The idea of the *regionalization* of international relations refers to the underlying, often undirected, processes bringing adjoining states, societies and economies into intensified interaction such that a particular cluster of states may be said to have a distinctive orientation to each other and may be said to constitute a region. The term *regionalism* is more complex. According to Joseph Nye, 'in the descriptive sense [it means] . . . the formation of interstate associations or groupings on the basis of regions; and in the doctrinal sense, the advocacy of such formations' (Nye 1968: vii). Or as a prominent voice from Southeast Asia, Hasnan Habib, puts it:

> Regionalism is the expression of regional consciousness that develops from a sense of identity among states situated in geographical proximity which motivates them to mutually cooperate in one or another mode to attain common goals, satisfy common needs, or to solve political, military, economic, and other practical problems . . .
>
> (Habib 1995: 305)

Thus while regionalization is what happens, regionalism can be understood as a conscious orientation by actors to bring about specific forms of regionalization. Taking the debate on regionalism as a starting point, there can be little doubt that a sense of regional consciousness has emerged in Southeast Asia and that the region's states have actively promoted the idea of mutual co-operation.

This chapter will, firstly, shed some light on the structural framework for community building in Southeast Asia; secondly, describe the development of ASEAN over the past thirty-five years; thirdly, discuss the organization's achievements; fourthly, take a closer look at the typical features of Southeast Asian regionalism, the so-called 'ASEAN way' of co-operation; before turning to a concluding critical evaluation of co-operation in the region. A discussion of the comparative strengths and weaknesses of neo-realism, liberalism and social constructivism in the analysis of Southeast Asian regionalism will form the red thread of this chapter.

Box 5.1 ASEAN at a glance

Founded in August 1967 in Bangkok by Indonesia, Malaysia, the Philippines, Singapore and Thailand.

Later joined by Brunei (1984), Vietnam (1995), Laos and Myanmar (1997) and Cambodia (1999).

Organizational structure
- Meetings of the heads of government (formally every three years supplemented by 'informal meetings').
- Annual Ministerial Meeting (AMM) of the Foreign Ministers (annually): *de facto* the most important ASEAN meeting.
- Frequent meetings of other ministers, senior officials etc. (400+ meetings per year).
- ASEAN Secretariat in Jakarta (founded 1976): can advise the ASEAN governments but does not have any decision-making power.

Foreign relations
Annual meetings:
- ASEAN Post-Ministerial Meetings (PMCs), gradually developed since the early 1970s → ASEAN + Australia, Canada, China, EU, India, Japan, New Zealand, Russia, South Korea, United States.
- ASEAN Regional Forum (ARF), founded 1993 (first official meeting 1994) → ASEAN + Dialogue Partners + Mongolia, North Korea.
- ASEAN Plus Three, founded 1999 → ASEAN + China, Japan, South Korea.
- Frequent inter-regional meetings with EU and Latin American states etc.

Milestones of co-operation and important agreements

1907	Bangkok Declaration → Founding Document, stresses the need for economic, political and cultural co-operation and exchange.
1976	Treaty of Amity and Co-operation (TAC) → guidelines for the management of intra-regional relations, including mechanism of confict resolution; in reality more symbolic than binding.
Late 1980s/early 1990s	ASEAN successfully and significantly contributed to the resolving of the Cambodia conflict.
1992	Agreement on the establishment of an ASEAN Free Trade Area (AFTA) to be implemented by 2010 → first stage came into effect on 1 January 2002.
2001	Hanoi Declaration on narrowing development gap for closer ASEAN integration.
	ASEAN Declaration on Joint Action to Counter Terrorism.

2002	ASEAN–China agreement on the Spratly Islands.
	Agreement on establishing an ASEAN–China Free Trade Area by 2010.
	ASEAN–US Joint Declaration for Co-operation to Combat International Terrorism.
2003	Accord on the establishment of an ASEAN Economic Community (AEC), *de facto* a Southeast Asian Common Market modelled on the European Union, by the year 2020 (Declaration of ASEAN Accord II).

The structural setting

When the foreign ministers of Indonesia, Malaysia, the Philippines, Singapore and Thailand established the Association of Southeast Asian Nations (ASEAN) in August 1967, they presented very different descriptions of what they had launched. 'A structure for peace and progress', was how the then Philippines Foreign Minister Narciso Ramos called it. Thailand's Thanat Khoman described it as 'a new society'. Singapore's Sinnathamby Rajaratnam declared 'that we have now erected the skeleton and must give flesh and blood to it', and the next moment he referred to it as 'a child sired up by five fathers' (cited in *Philippine Herald*, 15 August 1967). However, there is reason to believe that their different sobriquets reflected a difference in form, not substance. For, to be precise, they were all agreed on the idea of establishing a new operational regional organization, one initiated and run by Asians themselves.

Looking back, today's analyst can even go one step further: Although the *Bangkok Declaration*, ASEAN's founding document, stressed the importance of regional economic co-operation and cultural exchange among the young nations of Southeast Asia, the main objective was clearly security. ASEAN was born at a time when the region's political leaders had strong reasons to believe that their countries could get prominently involved in the global game of East–West confrontation in general and the Vietnam War in particular. The United States had just revived President Eisenhower's *Domino Theory* of 1954 (see Chapter 2 on the United States), making Southeast Asia leaders aware of world communism's aggressive expansionism. The states, which had achieved independence from colonialism for only a short while, wanted to avoid a situation of new dependence at all costs. They did not want to see the emergence of repeated great power rivalry on their doorstep.

ASEAN leaders have generally shared the view that their national development required a regional international order in which the balance of power would operate, and alternations in the distribution of power would occur peacefully and within an international context of negotiated neutrality. In real terms there can be no doubt that the governments demonstrated a favourable disposition towards an American predominance of power in the region and a suspicion on Soviet motives and activities. Although the ASEAN members never made any comments of anti-communism in their official declarations and documents, nevertheless it was anti-communism which served as an effective common bond. Between official neutrality and sub-official commitment, ASEAN as an organization had managed to stay formally neutral during the Cold War, despite the virulent anti-communism of its members and their engagement in US-assisted counter-insurgency operations. By remaining neutral,

ASEAN was able to negotiate its position in respect of possible hegemony, even though Southeast Asia was one of the 'hottest' regions in geopolitical and geostrategic terms. In other words, ASEAN has successfully played the big powers off against each other. This point is best summarized by former Malaysian Foreign Minister Ghazali Shafie: 'The past [decades] had shown the resilience of ASEAN in manoeuvring the turbulences of Cold War and intense East–West rivalries, despite the varied affiliations or non-alignment of its members' (cited in *Jakarta Post*, 17 October 1992).

In general, the clear structure of bipolarity and East–West confrontation served ASEAN well. It kept the United States engaged in the region as a guaranteed power for a secure geopolitical environment. At the same time the Cold War contained the power projection interests of all three major actors, i.e. the US, the Soviet Union and China. Not surprisingly, uncertainties concerning the new regional political-security architecture arose in the wake of the Cold War, including:

- shifting power relativities between the major states;
- the gradual rise of a multi-polar security environment with the major Asian powers playing a larger role;
- significant increases in military capabilities and local defence industries;
- the possibility of ethnic and national tensions, economic rivalry, disappointing aspirations for prosperity, and religious or racial conflict.

The profound changes at the system level of international relations in the early 1990s, the alternations to the overall distribution of power and capabilities after the Cold War, first seemed to result in a power vacuum in the Asia-Pacific. Unlike Europe there was no 'iron curtain' in the Asia-Pacific that separated the American and Soviet zones of hegemonic influence and no 'wall' that came down to symbolize the beginning of a new international era. The end of the Cold War left the Asia-Pacific with many question marks. Would the US stay as a regional balancer? Would China try to seize the opportunity and aggressively pursue an alleged national interest of becoming the region's next pre-eminent power? And would Japan change the pacifist nature of its foreign and defence policies? ASEAN actively participated in the emerging debate on multilateral institution-building as an alternative to the hegemonic settings of the Cold War days. Among other initiatives, in 1993 ASEAN initiated a regional dialogue scheme on security matters called the ASEAN Regional Forum. Among the members are the United States, the European Union, China and Japan.

At first glance ASEAN seems to prove neo-realist thinking in international relations. According to the realist view, the founding of the organization in 1967 and its evolution during the Cold War can be explained as the product of balance-of-power considerations. ASEAN's strong anti-communist posture and the fact that the organization was set up by states that already had strong linkages with the US (the Philippines and Thailand) or Indonesia, Malaysia, Singapore, could be interpreted as a typical power-balancing behaviour of small and medium states, namely to jump on the bandwagon of a super power (the US in this case) in order not to be absorbed by the other (the Soviet Union). It is not surprising that for realists 'Southeast Asia's turbulent post-war history was proof that under the conditions of anarchy survival constitutes the overriding interests of states in the region. Foreign policy was thus described in terms of self-help and military power' (Rüland 2000: 422). Now if that was the case during the Cold War, it remains relevant in the post-Cold War era, as Sorpong Peou notes (2002: 121):

> Realism continues to be a key conceptual approach in Southeast Asian Studies. . . .
> There is no 'peace divided' in Southeast Asia after the Soviet collapse; [and some
> scholars] see the region as one rife with growing bilateral tensions after the Cold
> War . . .

Indeed, neo-realists argue that ASEAN still exists today because its member states face
similar external threats, despite the obvious ideological differences that would normally
divide them, and perceive the need to balance these threats. It is particularly the China
threat, so the argument goes, that unites states with political systems ranging from military
authoritarianism (Myanmar) and communist one-party rule (Vietnam, Laos) to liberal-
democracies in the making (Thailand, the Philippines and perhaps Indonesia). As long as
China remains a possible threat, the neo-realist approach seems to explain the rationale for
ASEAN's existence. Furthermore, economic realities seem to underpin the neo-realist view
of regional order and stability as a function of great power strategic dominance. As Amitav
Acharya summarizes:

> the Asian economic crisis has amply underscored the economic and strategic depend-
> ence of . . . Southeast Asia on the great powers. In the economic sphere, the region's
> ability to ride out the crisis has depended on China's pledge not to devalue its currency,
> the ability of Japan in getting its own economy back on track as well as its willingness to
> provide substantial aid to the crisis-stricken economies, and the rescue missions under-
> taken by the International Monetary Fund (IMF), an institution widely seen as a tool of
> the West, especially the United States . . .
>
> (Acharya 1999: 6)

There is some truth in the neo-realist perspective on ASEAN. However, it fails to address the
impact of institution-building in Southeast Asia on regional peace and stability. Liberal
institutionalists challenge the neo-realist standpoint by arguing that co-operation among the
states of Southeast Asia has generated a set of agreed norms, principles and rules, in short
International Regimes, which have increased transparency and trust and reduced uncertainties and hostilities in intra-regional relations. According to this perspective it has been primarily a process of institution-building, not US-bandwagoning, that facilitated security and
welfare in Southeast Asia. Looking at the following achievements of ASEAN-driven
regionalism, liberal institutionalism does indeed seem to offer the more powerful argument.

Achievements of Southeast Asian regionalism

The analysis of ASEAN's general achievements can be based on six broad arguments:

ASEAN is a successful collective actor on the international stage

The strong links that ASEAN members have forged amongst themselves enable them to
negotiate and bargain with third countries with greater confidence and success. Like no
other group of non-Western countries, ASEAN as a collective actor has managed to gain the
industrial nations' attention through its well-established dialogue mechanisms, which belong
to the most recognized international forums in the world. Given this, ASEAN has been
described as 'politico-diplomatic coalition vis-à-vis the outside world' (Sopiee 1991: 320).
Since 1972 when ASEAN took the initiative to conduct an institutionalized dialogue with

the European Community, ASEAN has developed a network of regional and global meetings that today involve more than a dozen global players such as the United States, the European Union, Japan and China. At the core of these activities are annual conferences on economic and political issues that affect the region. By setting up the ASEAN Regional Forum (ARF) in 1993, a framework for the discussion of developments related to regional security, the association prominently contributed to shaping a new security order in the Asia-Pacific. ASEAN has also played a central role in the establishment of APEC. ASEAN's successful strategy of 'networking the region' is remarkable because the existing dialogue forums enable the Southeast Asian heads of state, ministers (especially foreign ministers) and senior officials to regularly meet with their counterparts from Washington, Beijing, Tokyo, Brussels and so on. Taking advantage of these extensive dialogue networks, even small powers like Cambodia or Laos are in the position to have an, at least, annual exchange with the US Secretary of State, for instance. No other groups of nations outside Europe have ever created for themselves such a favourable position within the international system. The latest international achievement in this respect is the institutionalization of co-operation within the broader East Asian region. ASEAN's initiative to foster relations with China, Japan and South Korea started with an informal gathering in 1997, which was soon formalized and named the 'ASEAN Plus Three Meeting (APT)'. The APT takes place annually involving the member states' heads of government, with frequent meetings of ministers and senior officials in between summits, and addresses economic and security issues of regional importance, such as closer trade and investment relations, transnational crime and terrorism. The feasibility of a gradual formation of an East Asia Free Trade Area is currently being studied. Some believe that ASEAN Plus Three is a step closer towards a loose East Asian alliance.

ASEAN as a regional conflict mediator

ASEAN has demonstrated its will to find regional solutions for regional problems. Most importantly, in the late 1980s ASEAN contributed to the political solution of the Cambodian conflict as one, if not as the most important major player in the peace negotiation process. Furthermore, in 1992, ASEAN adopted the 'Declaration on the South China Sea', which was regarded as a first step towards a peaceful settlement of the Spratly Islands dispute. The Spratlys are a collection of mostly barren coral reefs, atolls and sand bars – many of which disappear at high tide – which covers an area of some 70,000 square miles. This area is claimed, in whole or in part, by China, Taiwan, Vietnam, Malaysia, Brunei and the Philippines. With the exception of Brunei, all of the disputants maintain a military presence on some of the islands. Throughout the 1990s there were intermittent incidents involving the various claimants, ranging from complaints about construction of buildings on islands to the arrest or detention of fishermen. Friction most recently erupted in August 2002 when Vietnamese troops based on one islet fired warning shots at Filipino military planes.

At an ASEAN–China Summit in 2002, heads of government of the ASEAN members and Chinese premier Zhu Rongji signed a so-called declaration of conduct, agreeing not to attempt to occupy the Spratlys. Sometimes referred to as the 'Spratly Islands Pact', the agreement aims at avoiding conflict by means of 'confidence-building activities between ASEAN and China' (ASEAN 2002: para. 28). Although the agreement is not binding and depends on the goodwill of the signatory states, senior officials from ASEAN and China believe the 'pact' will help ensure regional security. To this end, in 1995 the ASEAN states also signed a treaty which – on paper – bans the development, acquisition, use, testing and stationing of nuclear arms in Southeast Asia. However, since the ASEAN states do not possess nuclear weapons themselves and the nuclear powers, particularly the US and China, have so far objected to an accession to the Southeast Asia Nuclear Weapons-Free Zone (SEANWFZ), the agreement is more of a symbolic value.

ASEAN as a security community

ASEAN is not a military alliance but a security community in the sense that probably no ASEAN member would seriously consider the use of military force as a means of problem solving in inter-member relations. ASEAN has successfully managed to keep the residual conflicts between the members – especially territorial disputes – on a low-key level. Armed confrontation or any other kind of seriously threatening behaviour in the ASEAN region had been avoided since the end of *Konfrontasi* (the war-like conflict between Indonesia and Malaysia/Singapore, 1963–65) despite the existence of more than a dozen territorial conflicts among the ASEAN members, regular rows over migration issues (especially between Malaysia and Indonesia) and heated discussion on the distribution of resources (between Singapore and Malaysia about water, for example). Furthermore, in 2002 ASEAN adopted a Declaration on Terrorism which aims to prevent, counter and suppress terrorist activities in the region.

ASEAN as an inter-personal network

High-ranking bureaucrats, government officials, scholars and the representatives of the private initiative within the ASEAN framework have forged a close network of personal links. In this way border-crossing communications and activities have increased and interactions have become much easier. If one takes into consideration that only about forty years ago the different national elites in Southeast Asia were practically not talking to each other, this network building within ASEAN (with its 400-plus annual meetings) is one major achievement of Southeast regionalism. It has resulted in transparency and confidence building.

ASEAN as a framework for economic development

Taking these four aspects together, ASEAN has created for itself a peaceful and stable regional situation. This situation in turn has contributed to a conductive climate for ASEAN countries to pursue their national economic development. The Asian crisis had briefly interrupted the development process and the perception of Southeast Asia as a stable region and prime destination for FDI. Although Indonesia has yet to fully recover from the crisis, most countries in the region are described by many commentators as back on track, having already reached or exceeded their macroeconomic pre-crisis levels.

ASEAN as a free trade area

Perhaps the most tangible achievement of recent years is the agreement on establishing an ASEAN Free Trade Area (AFTA), signed in 1992. Nattapong Thongpakde (2001) gives a good summary of AFTA's origins and main purposes:

During the early 1990s, there was considerable progress in regional co-operation. The United States and Canada had reached a bilateral agreement in 1989, and the enlargement to the North American Free Trade Agreement (NAFTA) to include Mexico, was discussed and became effective in 1994. . . . In addition, the economic integration of the European Union with the aim of integrating into a single market, gave the best example of regional co-operation. . . . With regional co-operation and trade negotiations intensifying in the Uruguay Round, the ASEAN members had to review its concrete economic co-operation measures. In the Fourth Summit in Singapore (1992), the ASEAN Free Trade Area (AFTA) was formed under the Common Effective Preferential Tariff (CEPT) scheme. The primary objective of AFTA is to enhance ASEAN's competitiveness in the world market. The aims are also to expand intra-ASEAN trade and to gain economies of scale and specialization to further deepen economic co-operation. Finally, it is anticipated that greater foreign direct investment will flow into the region as a result of ASEAN economic integration.

Despite these clear economic incentives, it took the member states ten years to implement even the first stage of AFTA because – given their different levels of economic development – they could not agree on definite schedules for and scope of tariff reductions. Many ASEAN governments seemed to have spent more time working on exclusion lists naming the products they refused to include under the AFTA scheme than trying to implement the agreement as quickly as possible. According to the current schedule (see below) import duties among the six old ASEAN members will only be fully eliminated by 2010; and there is still a big question mark behind the integration of the four new ASEAN members into AFTA. The general problem is still the diversity of the ASEAN members and the different stages of economic development within the region, ranging from Singapore as one of the five wealthiest nations in the world to Laos as one of the poorest. In addition, the benefits of a Southeast Asian Free Trade Area are limited because, unlike in the case of Europe for example, intra-regional trade as a proportion of the countries' total trade is less than 20 per cent, which is a rather small figure. In other words, the most important trading partners for the individual ASEAN members are the United States, Japan and the European Union but not the neighbouring economies.

However, even before the full implementation of AFTA has been achieved, ASEAN and China agreed in principle on the establishment of an ASEAN–China Free Trade Area by the year 2010 for the old ASEAN members and 2015 for the new ones, a potential market of 1.7 billion people with annual output of US$2 trillion. While it seems to be a painful process for both sides to agree on the concrete terms of how to achieve this ambitious goal, as senior officials involved in the negotiations between ASEAN and China admit, the political value of the project is obvious. Following China's admission into the WTO the proposed FTA has further enhanced Beijing's position as a regional power – to the expense of Japan as many observers have suggested. Tokyo reacted with alarm to the plan and subsequently entered into talks on a Japan–ASEAN FTA. ASEAN has certainly benefited from the regional 'FTA fever' as it puts the organization on the map and, coming back to the first argument presented here, shows its resilience as a successful collective actor on the international stage.

Box 5.2 The schedule for the implementation of AFTA

- On 1 January 2002 the first six signatories to the AFTA agreement (Brunei, Indonesia, Malaysia, the Philippines, Singapore and Thailand) dropped tariffs to 0–5 per cent on most of the products traded among them, in accordance with the tariff-cutting schedules to which they had previously committed themselves (the *Common Effective Preferential Trade* or CEPT Agreement). The average tariff on intra-ASEAN trade is now down to 3.2 per cent.
- The lowering of tariffs was accompanied by an expansion of intra-regional trade – from US$44.2 billion in 1993 to US$97.8 billion in 2000.
- In 1999, ASEAN's leaders agreed to eliminate all import duties among the first six members by 2010 and by 2015 for the newer members (Vietnam, Cambodia, Myanmar and Laos). However, the 'ASEAN Integration System of Preferences' allows these four member states to gain tariff-free access to the more developed ASEAN markets by 2003, seven years ahead of the agreed target of 2010.
- In 2003, at the 9th ASEAN Summit in Bali, the Southeast Asian Heads of Government expressed the vision of working towards the establishment of an ASEAN Economic Community as 'the realization of the end-goal of economic integration . . ., to create a stable, prosperous and highly competitive ASEAN economic region in which there is a free flow of goods, services, investment and a freer flow of capital, equitable economic development and reduced poverty and socio-economic disparities in year 2020' (ASEAN 2003).

From a theoretical point of view, the recent ASEAN–China *rapprochement*, materializing in the ASEAN–China agreement on the Spratly Islands and the proposed FTA, challenges the neo-realist assumption that ASEAN's *raison d'être* is a commonly perceived 'China Threat'. Quite to the contrary, ASEAN seems to prosper as a result of the gradual elimination of this threat perception and emerging co-operation between the two actors. At the same time, while most agree that the achievements listed here are notable, they do not necessarily prove the liberal institutionalist assumption either. For example, while ASEAN has been good at conflict avoidance, the association has never successfully practised conflict resolution. Again the recent 'Spratly Islands Pact' and also ASEAN's 'Declaration on Terrorism' (which is discussed in more detail in the next section) are cases in point. Both documents address and discuss vital security issues, which is an important achievement in itself, but do not resolve the underlying conflicts and disputes. There is no hard empirical evidence that, for example, relations between Singapore and Malaysia have remained peaceful because of both governments' integration within ASEAN, or rather, as a neo-realist would argue, as the result of a balance of power in their military capabilities. The institutions (norms, principles, rules, decision making procedures) that do exist within ASEAN are 'soft institutions' which are not legally binding because they are based on convention and informal agreement rather than formal treaties. The pillar of ASEAN is voluntarism not legalism. This 'soft approach' to co-operation has been labelled the 'ASEAN way'.

The case of soft institutionalization: the 'ASEAN way'

Box 5.3 The 'ASEAN way'

At the core of the so-called 'ASEAN way' of diplomacy in Southeast Asia stand six norms:

- sovereign equality;
- the non-recourse to use of force and the peaceful settlement of conflict;
- non-interference and non-intervention;
- the non-involvement of ASEAN to address unresolved bilateral conflict between members;
- quiet diplomacy;
- mutual respect and tolerance.

Source: Haacke (2003: 1)

These six norms form the basis for four broad principles (see Acharya 1997 for details):

- *Open regionalism:* a set of features including, in the first place, promotion of transparency, avoidance of discrimination among intra-regional and between intra- and extra-regional actors, mutual reassurance, and non-exclusive order maintenance and conflict regulation.
- *Cooperative security:* inclusiveness as far as possible or a commitment that the dialogue must be open to all relevant actors and a concept of building security with others rather than against them; in short, the opposite of a military bloc which implies exclusive membership and a clear-cut perception of friends and enemies. The concept ideally also includes norms like non-interference, respect for national identity and territorial integrity.
- *Soft rules:* a non-legalistic approach to co-operation on the basis of voluntary membership (which means that every actor keeps an exit option), non-binding decision making, conventions and informal networks (rather than formal contracts or treaties), a loose organizational structure and the absence of any supra-national agents
- *Consensus building:* a commitment to finding a 'way of moving forward by establishing what seems to have broad support' (*Straits Times*, 13 November 1994, p. 17). Thus, consensus should not be confused with unanimity and consequently does not require total agreement by all parties.

A good example of ASEAN's adherence to soft institutionalization is the organization's response to the threat of terrorism in general and radical Islamic groups in particular (see Collins 2003: 200–11, for a more detailed discussion). The *2001 ASEAN Declaration on Joint Action to Counter Terrorism* commits the member states 'to counter, prevent and suppress all forms of terrorist acts in accordance with the Charter of the United Nations and other international law, especially taking into account the importance of all relevant UN resolutions' without prescribing a specific institutionalized pattern of dealing with the problem. Although ASEAN has established a regional framework for fighting transnational crime and adopted a Plan of Action outlining a regional strategy to prevent, control and neutralize transnational crime, the organization's overall response to the threat and realities of terror-ism clearly mirrors its traditional policy for not committing its members to any specific responsibilities. The Plan of Action is based on the principle of voluntary contribution. The cautious approach of some ASEAN states to anti-terror co-operation is also prominently reflected by the *US–ASEAN Joint Declaration for Co-operation to Combat International Terrorism*. The document includes a paragraph the US side was initially unwilling to accept: 'Recognizing the principles of sovereign equality, territorial integrity and non-intervention in the domestic affairs of other states'. The paragraph was added in the declaration at the request of Indonesia and Vietnam, which feared such an anti-terror accord with the US could lead to the basing of US troops in Southeast Asia. In sum, both documents reflect the lowest common denominator and do not create any binding obligations for ASEAN mem-bers because of a missing consensus on an exact definition of terrorism and, equally import-ant, because the issue touches upon the sensitive field of national sovereignty. As we will show in the concluding section, ASEAN members are not yet prepared to allow any substan-tial outside interference with national policies or even to partly surrender their national sovereignty.

A critical evaluation of Southeast Asian regionalism

Why does ASEAN cling to soft co-operation and not attempt deeper integration? Estrella D. Solidum (1974) of the Philippines, a pioneer of the Southeast Asian debate on regionalism, observed that co-operation among ASEAN nations was more realistic and successful the more it dealt with 'safe' or non-sensitive issues. Matters of high politics, such as the creation of defence alliances or common markets, were not susceptible to the early stages of co-operation among heterogeneous polities. Malaysian political scientist Pushpa Thambipillai (1980) primarily employed Karl W. Deutsch's hypotheses on community building. She con-cluded that ASEAN differed from the process of community building described by Deutsch. Contrary to his assumption that adjoining states and societies strove for political community building ('amalgamation' in Deutsch's terminology), within Southeast Asia the idea not to unite politically but to preserve autonomy had prevailed. Accordingly, although inter-dependence (as conceptualized by Joseph Nye and Robert Keohane) among ASEAN mem-bers had been growing, the states of Southeast Asia were still concerned to maintain and entrench their respective national identities by subscribing to the principle of non-interference in neighbouring countries' affairs.

An important strand of the academic debate has focused on the historical burdens of Southeast Asian regionalism and the relating obstacle to integration. Chung-si Ahn, for instance, observed that the growth of regionalism in Asia was slow due to the bitter memor-ies of colonialism and the Second World War. In his view, both contributed to tensions, disputes and distrust among the regions' nations. Therefore, Chung-si Ahn (1980) described regionalism as coexistent with strong tendencies of nationalism in Asia. The nations' polit-ical leaders were reluctant to accept any proposal for regional co-operation that may infringe upon the national sovereignty and independence.

Although the studies mentioned here were published many years ago, most of their findings remain resilient. Today ASEAN's institutional structure is not much different from what it used to be two or even three decades ago. More than thirty-five years of regional co-operation have not generated any kind of supranationality. The ASEAN secretariat, which was established in 1981, mainly contributes to the co-ordination of the organization's day-to-day business and, to a degree, works as the organization's internal think-tank but does not have authority to make decisions for or on behalf of the member states. Any centralized decision making is difficult to achieve and rejected by most actors, because some member states (particularly Indonesia) are still preoccupied with the process of nation building; any transfer of national sovereignty to a supranational level is thus out of the question.

Table 5.1 shows that while motivations and aims of EU and ASEAN member states have been strikingly similar, the ways of reaching these goals differ significantly. As suggested above, at the end of the day the most crucial difference comes down to the nature of institutions, 'hard' or legally binding institutional arrangements in the case of the European Union, 'soft' or voluntary and informal institutional setting in Southeast Asia. Until the outbreak of the Asian crisis most academics (both within and outside Southeast Asia) and regional politicians alike had argued that the moral power of informal, soft procedures could determine relations between actors as effectively as legally binding hard rules. However, ASEAN's handling of the regional financial crisis has been seen as ineffective inside and outside the region. On this point Bantarto Bandoro wrote:

> ASEAN will definitely become less cohesive and more distracted, and long-standing rivalries within the grouping may resurface. This will make the association a whole lot more susceptible to penetration by external powers or actors. . . . ASEAN is not only at the crossroad, but it is also on the brink of depression and disintegration . . .
>
> (Bandoro 1998: 298–9)

Not all agree though. Some have argued that ASEAN did not fail in the wake of the Asian crisis but that it was rather an expectation–reality gap that triggered the association's downgrading. According to Shaun Narine (2002):

> The expectation that ASEAN could have effectively addressed the economic crisis is entirely unreasonable. ASEAN lacks the economic resources and the institutional architecture to deal with financial crises. Nonetheless, before the crisis, ASEAN had strongly expressed the desire to be an important regional economic institution. It proceeded from the assumption that it could meet this goal through mechanisms like AFTA. AFTA was designed to attract foreign investment to ASEAN by facilitating regional free trade. It lacked any capacity to address the regional upheaval and was certainly not designed to deal with such events. ASEAN could not claim to be a meaningful economic institution yet lack any ability to confront the worst economic downturn in the region's modern history. ASEAN created the impression in the international community that it was an effective economic organization, but it could not meet these expectations at a crucial time.

A third view argues that the 1997 watershed did not have any specific long-term positive or negative impact on ASEAN but changed the scope of regionalism in the Asia-Pacific. As Derek McDougall (2002) explains, whereas before the Asian crisis regionalism had developed at both an Asia-Pacific-wide (APEC, ASEAN Regional Forum) and sub-regional level (ASEAN, South Pacific Forum), the post-1997 period has seen a stronger East Asian focus in terms of regionalism generally, most clearly in the case of the new ASEAN Plus Three forum.

In fact, in the late 1990s many actors within ASEAN came to believe that it was time for a change. High ranking politicians such as the then Thailand's Foreign Minister Surin Pitsuwan were no longer satisfied with the traditional 'Asian way' of dealing with problems and

Table 5.1 Regionalism in Europe and East Asia compared

	European Community / European Union	ASEAN
Motivation and Aims *What goals should be reached or supported?*	• West Integration (during the Cold War as a contribution towards building a bulwark *vis-à-vis* the Soviet bloc) • Co-operation among former adversaries (Germany and France, for example) and thereby contributing to the creation of a stable and peaceful regional order • Prosperity through means of economic integration	• Neutrality (during Cold War) • Co-operation among former adversaries (Indonesia and Malaysia, for example) as a means of establishing regional stability and prosperity • Conflict management through regular meetings • Economic prosperity
Actors *What characterizes the member states?*	• Industrialized nations • Democracies • Despite obvious national differences, member states are homogeneous in many respects (similar political systems, common cultural traditions, shared historic experiences)	• Medium and small powers • Mostly NICs but also developing nations • Mostly young nation states in different stages of nation building • Overall very heterogeneous actor spectrum (different stages of economic development; different political systems; ethnic and religious differences)
Integration *How far has institutional evolution gone?*	• All-embracing economic and political integration • 'Supranationality' in most areas except foreign and defence policies	• Gradual implementation of a Free Trade Area and, although very vaguely so far, an Economic Community modelled on the EU Common Market • No political integration, no supranationality • Sovereignty rests with the member states
External Federator *Which outside forces / actors have had a uniting effect?*	• Communism (during the Cold War) • United States	• Communism (during the Cold War)
Decision Making	• Various procedures, consensus and majority vote	• Strict consensus • Non-interference in member states' internal affairs (although this approach seems to be gradually changing)

challenges and thereby sounded the bell for a new phase of regionalism. In 1998 Thailand, supported by the Philippines, proposed that ASEAN's non-interference policy should be replaced by 'flexible engagement'. Even though the concept was not well received by the majority of ASEAN's foreign ministers and was finally re-named 'enhanced interaction', it shook up the status quo of foreign relations in Southeast Asia. Surin believed the time was right for reforms within ASEAN:

> In 31 years, diversity has become a problem for ASEAN [. . .]. Diversity which used to be a source of strength has become a source of weakness [. . .]. We have no freedom and flexibility of expressing our views concerning some members. We have to be silent because we are members of the family. This is not fair, not just.
>
> (Pitsuwan 1998)

Back then Surin's challenging of the sacrosanct 'ASEAN way' seemed to be premature. But the foreign minister had won a growing number of colleagues over to his idea. In 2000 the foreign ministers formally approved Thailand's concept of an 'ASEAN troika'. The new mechanism enables the sitting chair to activate a three-member task force to tackle specific problems that have regional implications. While the arrangement has to be considered as one of ASEAN's most important attempts at the institutionalized management of regional order, its effectiveness remains questionable. Partly modelled on the 'EU troika', it seems hard to believe that, analogous to the European Union, ASEAN's present chairman, his immediate predecessor and designated successor would have a formal mandate to act on behalf of the other members. If Thailand, Singapore and Vietnam (a hypothetical troika) had authority to deal with border disputes between ASEAN members, or even terrorism and ethnic-religious violence in Indonesia, ASEAN would have reached the stage of a supra-national organization or indeed something like the European Union. This is not even a distant possibility at present. There is no indication yet that ASEAN is willing or capable of making use of new institutional mechanisms. It would not be realistic and maybe not even desirable for ASEAN, especially not for the new members such as Vietnam who have opposed any attempts to leave the traditional path of consensus building and non-interference, to commit itself to such a high degree of integration. At the same time, it is quite obvious that strict adherence to the 'ASEAN way' and particularly the norm of non interference is a normative and guiding principle more than a practical reality. Most member states have long started to follow their own concept of 'flexible engagement' in inter-member relations, which often means open criticism of the neighbours' policies. For example, in 1998 politicians from Indonesia and the Philippines openly criticized the treat-ment of Anwar Ibrahim in Malaysia (who was jailed for charges of sodomy and corruption); many believe, however, that the real reason for the sentence was to prevent the prominent leader of the Malaysian reform movement from challenging the power of Prime Minister Mahathir Mohammad). And in February 2002 Singapore's elder statesman Lee Kuan Yew warned that the people of Southeast Asia were exposed to a continuing security risk because the ringleaders of extremist cells roamed freely in Indonesia.

To many, the real test case for 'flexible engagement' came in 2003 when ASEAN came under international pressure to deal with the situation in Myanmar and repeatedly called for the release of Aung San Suu Kyi, the leader of the oppositional National League for Democracy. When the regime in Rangoon turned a deaf ear, ASEAN looked for a way to use the troika as a conduit to exert influence inside Myanmar. Mahathir even warned that Myanmar's continued detention of Suu Kyi might ultimately lead to the country's expulsion from ASEAN. Although currently the organization neither seems to be ready for such drastic steps nor – in more general terms – to seriously consider the option of humanitarian intervention, the fact that ASEAN actors have started to revise their formerly strict and unconditional adherence to the principle of non-interference might indicate a gradual change of the group's approach to the management of regional security. If non-interference in the ASEAN context is understood 'in terms of a state's freedom from unsolicited, usually verbal, involvement by foreign state-linked authorities in what are considered its home affairs' (Haacke 2003: 168), the Myanmar case can already be called 'a rather drastic change in ASEAN's position', as Sunai Phasuk, spokesman for the regional human rights organization Forum Asia, put it (cited in *Far Eastern Economic Review*, 14 August 2003, p. 19).

Where do we go from here as far as IR theory is concerned? While both neo-realism and liberal institutionalism contribute to our understanding of ASEAN as they provide complementary rather than mutually exclusive approaches to the study of Southeast Asian regionalism, even in combination they cannot solve the central puzzle: how has ASEAN been able to successfully manage intra-regional relations and become an important and respected collective actor on the international stage? To answer this core question, 'more and more scholars have now turned to social constructivism for insights in explaining ASEAN regionalism' (Sorpong Peou 2002: 122). Jürgen Rüland explains the essence of the approach which, as many believe, offers more powerful explanations than the traditional strands in the IR debate:

> While realism and institutionalism are committed to rationalism, constructivists share a reflexive concept of science. Their key concern is the relationship between ideas, identities and material interests, which change through interaction of agents (states) and structure. Identities and interests are thus not exogenously given – through anarchy or self-help as suggested by realism – but rather socially and politically constructed. Institutional constructivists seek to explain cooperation by the formulation of collective identities. They search for shared principles, values and traditions with the power of shaping the region's common interests. With liberal institutionalism they share a process-oriented concept of integration, a normative outlook, voluntarism and a firm belief in the learning effects of cooperation. In other words: cooperation breeds more cooperation . . .
>
> (Rüland 2000: 423)

According to the social constructivist perspective on international relations regional identities play a crucial part in the process of community building. In two influential books, the main proponent of the constructivist approach, Amitav Acharya (2000; 2001) argues that over the past thirty-plus years, the Southeast Asian states have forged a strong collective identity among themselves as the result of political, strategic and functional interactions and interdependencies. Drawing on Benedict Anderson's classic concept of the nation state, Acharya describes ASEAN as an 'imagined community' (Acharya 2001: 2; for a discussion see Sorpong Peou 2002). To John Ravenhill even negative experiences can have a major impact on identity formation:

> Few would question the role that the financial crisis played in fostering a sense of common identity [for ASEAN], the image of a region in adversity besieged by outsiders 'ganging up' in their attempts to exploit the difficulties that East Asian governments faced . . .
>
> (Ravenhill 2002: 175)

In sum, we may argue that ASEAN, or the process of integration in Southeast Asia in general, has advanced as a combination of three factors: coalition building *vis-à-vis* common threat perception and extra-regional powers, soft institution building, and an emerging regional identity.

References

Acharya, A. (1997) 'Ideas, identity, and institution-building: from "ASEAN way" to the "Asia-Pacific way"?' *The Pacific Review*, 10: 319–46.

Acharya, A. (1999) 'Realism, institutionalism, and the Asian economic crisis', *Contemporary Southeast Asia*, 21: 1–29.

Acharya, A. (2000) *The Quest for Identity: International Relations of Southeast Asia*, Oxford: Oxford University Press.

Acharya, A. (2001) *Constructing a Security Community in Southeast Asia: ASEAN and the Problem of Regional Order*, London: Routledge.

ASEAN (2002) *Press Statement by the Chairman of the 8th ASEAN Summit, the 6th ASEAN + 3 Summit and the ASEAN–China Summit*, Phnom Penh, Cambodia, 4 November. Online. Available HTTP: <http://www.aseansec.org/13188.htm> (accessed 4 December 2002).

ASEAN (2003) *Declaration of ASEAN Concord II (Bali Concord II)*. Online. Available HTTP: <http://www.aseansec.org/15159.htm> (accessed 27 October 2003).

Bandoro, B. (1998) 'The implication of economic turbulence: ASEAN on the brink of depression and disintegration', *Indonesian Quarterly*, 26: 298–300.

Chung-si Ahn (1980) 'Forces of nationalism and economics in Asian regional co-operation', *Asia Pacific Community*, 7: 106–18.

Collins, A. (2003) *Security and Southeast Asia. Domestic, Regional, and Global Issues*, Boulder, CO: Lynne Rienner.

Haacke, J. (2003) *ASEAN's Diplomatic and Security Culture. Origins, Development and Prospects*, London: RoutledgeCurzon.

Habib, H. A. (1995) 'Defining the "Asia-Pacific region" ', *Indonesian Quarterly*, 23: 302–12.

McDougall, D. (2002) 'Asia-Pacific security regionalism: the impact of post-1997 developments', *Contemporary Security Policy*, 23: 113–34.

Narine, S. (2002) 'ASEAN in the aftermath: the consequences of the East Asian economic crisis', *Global Governance*, 8: 179–94.

Nattapong, Thoagpakde (2001) 'ASEAN Free Trade Area: progress and challenges', in C. L. Gates and M. Than (eds) *ASEAN Enlargement: Impacts and Implications*, Singapore: Institute of Southeast Asian Studies, pp. 45–79.

Nye, J. S. (ed.) (1968) *International Regionalism: Readings*, Boston, MA: Little, Brown.

Pitsuwan, S. (1998) Speech at the Foreign Correspondence Club, Bangkok, 11 August; transcript by Jörn Dosch.

Ravenhill, J. (2002) 'A three bloc world? The new East Asian regionalism', *International Relations of the Asia-Pacific*, 2: 167–95.

Rüland, J. (2000) 'ASEAN and the Asian crisis: theoretical implications and practical consequences for Southeast Asian regionalism', *The Pacific Review*, 13: 421–51.

Solidum, E. D. (1974) *Towards a Southeast Asia Community*, Quezon City: University of the Philippines Press.

Sopiee, N. (1991) 'ASEAN and Indo-China after a Cambodian settlement', in D. Alves (ed.) *Change, Interdependence and Security in the Pacific Basin. The 19th Pacific Symposium*, Washington, DC: National Defense University Press, pp. 315–36.

Sorpong Peou (2002) 'Realism and constructivism in Southeast Asian security studies today: a review essay', *The Pacific Review*, 15: 119–38.

Thambipillai, P. (1980) 'Regional cooperation and development: the case of ASEAN and its external relations', unpublished thesis, University of Hawaii.

6 Australia in the Asia-Pacific

Michael K. Connors

Australia, for the most part, is invisible in international politics and rarely rates a mention in the international media; little is known about its politics by those who do not live there. When, for example, Australia responded to a wave of refugees by turning them away and having them land elsewhere, the *Los Angeles Times* ran a story entitled 'G'way mate' (a playful twist on the Australian greeting 'G'day mate') and mistakenly referred to Prime Minister John Howard as John Hunt. As recently as the beginning of 2003, after more than six years in office, the BBC placed a picture of John Howard in a story on Vermont Governor Howard Dean. While Australian prime ministers are far from assuming the status of US governors, they are known to routinely invoke the special nature of the US–Australia relationship. Indeed, so close is the relationship that one commentator suggests that Australia petition for union with the United States so that the US would 'get a State instead of a colony' and Australians would no longer 'have to go on pretending our soul's our own' (Watson 2001: 54–5). While the suggestion should be read as a satirical one, Australia's involvement in the US-led war on Iraq in 2003 highlights Australia's constant attempt to implicate itself in US global and regional strategy. This enduring feature of Australian foreign policy, dating from the 1950s, will serve as the plot line for this chapter. Despite pendulum swings in the relationship, official rhetoric about special relations with other nations and public announcements of international good citizenship, the strategic importance of the US in elite calculations of national interest has barely wavered. Indeed, understanding Australia's role in the Asia-Pacific largely involves understanding its relationship to the US.

Not surprisingly, the closeness of the relationship has caused disquiet, domestically and internationally. In 2000, for example, when the Australian government indicated support for National and Theatre Missile Defence systems proposed by the US, the Chinese official organ *Renmin Ribao* offered the following advice: 'The Australian government should take a lesson from the past and not act as a cat's paw anymore' (cited in Malik 2001: 124). The attack nicely echoes much of the domestic criticism within Australia against successive governments' apparent willingness to be tied to US strategy. Dissent of this nature is expressed from the left and the right of the political spectrum (Fraser 2001; Stott-Despoja and Bartlett 2001), pointing to the fact that there is opposition to the way Australian elites have developed particular constructions of the 'national interest' and concepts of security. A key issue in public discussion on Australian foreign policy for many years has been the extent to which Australia's alliance with the US comes at the expense of its national interest in improving relations with its Asia-Pacific regional environment. This will be the second plot line of this chapter.

This chapter is divided into four sections. The first provides a historical overview of Australia's foreign policy until the end of the Cold War. It then moves into the contemporary era, looking at an attempt to recast Australian foreign policy in an internationalist mould in the wake of the end of the Cold War. More recent developments in relation to 'national interest' diplomacy are explored in the third section. The final section explores the implications of Australia's alliance diplomacy in the light of recent events.

From one great and powerful friend to another

Reflecting its origins as a British colony, for the first forty years of the twentieth century Australia's foreign policy was essentially devised in London and its interests represented by British diplomatic missions. If one considers the formation of Australia's strategic culture at this time (the manner in which its history, values and perceptions of the localized security environment combine to produce an Australian approach to international relations) it is obvious that fear of its Asian neighbours was very prominent. As one author explains,

> Australia has always been a 'frightened country'. The constant fear of attack or conquest by external and predominantly Asian 'others', coupled with the belief that Australia cannot defend itself . . . has led Australia's policy makers to look to 'great and powerful friends' for reassurance and protection.
>
> (Cheeseman 1999: 273)

Securing great power support in the region has been a staple foreign policy objective. Historically, this has its origins in the founding of a state through the seizure of a massive continent with vulnerable borders. While the nineteenth and first half of the twentieth century were characterized by heavy dependence on the British, although the US was welcomed in the region, the onset of the Second World War led the Australian government to turn emphatically towards a new and powerful friend. With the impending advance of Japanese troops throughout Southeast Asia, in late 1941 John Curtin, Australia's prime minister, announced, 'I make it quite clear that Australia looks to America, free of any pangs as to our traditional links or kinship with the United Kingdom' (cited in Evans and Grant 1995: 22). The shift, uneven at first, marked the beginnings of Australia's entry into international relations without the obligatory British stamp of approval. Australian policy makers have, ever since, struggled to define the country's role as a small-to-medium power with a modestly sized population of European origin in a region that was and is perceived as hostile and unpredictable.

In the early years after the Second World War, the Australian government sought to promote an active security and ordering role for the United Nations, believing that small and middle powers such as Australia were vulnerable to the consequences that would flow from great power conflicts. At the same time, the government saw itself as a regional leader, seeking the establishment of a regional grouping for security co-operation with the involvement of the United States and the United Kingdom. However, overtures on security regionalism were rejected by the United States, and instead the US brought into being a series of bilateral relationships, or the so-called hub-and-spoke system (see Chapter 2), of which Australia would be but one ally. The two countries also differed on the terms of a peace settlement with Japan, Australia being adamant that the occupying powers of defeated Japan impose demilitarization. The Truman Administration began to take a softer line in the context of the Cold War, seeing Japan as a central ally in the region. Truman made it clear that the US would commit itself to Japan's defence, and support a defensively armed Japan. Australia succumbed to the loose bilateralism offered by the US, and when the Korean War broke out and fears turned towards Chinese communism, Australia consented to the 'soft' peace treaty with Japan. Partly in response, in 1951 Australia was rewarded with the Security Treaty between Australia, New Zealand and the United States (ANZUS), which promised consultation in times of need (Dalby 1996: 114). ANZUS was less than a security guarantee, as Article 4 spelled out:

> Each Party recognizes that an armed attack in the Pacific Area on any of the Parties would be dangerous to its own peace and safety and declares that it would act to meet the common danger in accordance with its constitutional processes.

Throughout the 1950s, the conservative administration of Robert Menzies made it clear that Australia was tied to both the United States and the United Kingdom. Australian links with the Commonwealth led to military action with the British in Malaya against communist insurgency in the 1950s. In the mid-1960s Australia also joined British and Malaysian troops against Indonesian border incursions in the regions of Sabah and Sarawak in northern Borneo. Such involvement indicates the resolute connection Australian elites felt towards the old British empire. This historical connection lives on today in the form of the Five-Power Defence Arrangements (FPDA) which involves Australia, New Zealand, Malaysia, Singapore and the United Kingdom in limited co-operation. As Russell Ward noted, until the mid-1960s white Australians largely saw themselves as having a dual identity and '[f]or most . . . national and imperial patriotism were complementary, not contradictory' (cited in Bell 1997: 195). Concomitant to this was the maintenance of the White Australia Policy, which since the early 1900s had systematically blocked Asian migration into Australia. As the United Kingdom, Canada, the United States and the United Nations moved against racial discrimination, Australia held firm to its race line, only beginning to dismantle it in 1966 when Asian trade more forcefully entered calculations (Meaney 1995: 178–9).

While the white British connection served to maintain a sense of separateness from the region, in the 1960s the anchors of Australian identity were becoming increasingly uncertain. Inevitably, the UK's strategic impotency and drift from Commonwealth commitments, marked respectively by the Suez Canal débâcle and moves to enter the European Community, moved Australia closer to the United States. Australia's increasing entanglement with US global strategic objectives is evidenced by its involvement in the Korean and Vietnam wars, and its membership of SEATO (1954–77). Along with the increasing significance of the alliance, Australia's earlier 'race' fears of Asia were conflated with fear of communism. Throughout the 1950s, the Menzies government endorsed the notion of forward defence, claiming that Australia was better defended 'as far from our own soil as possible' (Gurry 1995: 22). The alliance took concrete form in the stationing of three important US bases on Australian soil from the 1960s onwards, used for intelligence and communications purposes. These bases are deemed by some commentators as the most important contribution Australia offered to the US alliance, and Desmond Ball (2001) has described them as 'the real ties that bind' the United States to protection of Australia.

To summarize this section, from the 1950s, Cold War calculations determined Australian foreign policy. Faced with a seemingly adventurist China and communist insurgencies in Southeast Asia, the Australian government committed itself to the US alliance, and accepted the terms of that alliance as requiring followership of US strategy. This, however, did not mean the complete eclipse of its historical relationship with the British Commonwealth.

Towards Asia

Even as Australia integrated itself into the Cold War perspective of its great and powerful friend, it also moved to advance its economic interests in the regional neighbourhood. The shift in Australia's trade patterns was dramatic over the decades. Even on the eve of troop commitments to Vietnam in 1964, the external affairs minister expressed what would become a habitual incantation: 'Friendship with Asia, reciprocal trade, closer cultural relations and a clearer understanding of Asia and its people are in the forefront of Australian policy' (cited in Bell 1997: 198). Modestly paced at first, Australia's attempt to relate to the economic dynamism of the region gathered steam. The dominant focus in this shift was Japan, which emerged as a mighty economic power to which Australia increasingly gravitated. The economic relationship was codified in the 1957 Commerce Treaty. This was followed by the more wide-ranging Basic Treaty of Friendship and Co-operation and Protocol (1976), which set the tone for future relations as partners in the region sharing similar goals of economic integration and complementarity – a relationship that remains constant into the contemporary period (see Mackerras 1996; Tereda 2000).

Another factor pushing Australia closer to the region was the gradual withdrawal of US troops from Vietnam in the light of the Nixon Doctrine of 1969. The Nixon Doctrine compelled US allies in the region to move their national security strategies towards self-reliance, and also raised the question of greater co-operation among states in the region. Beginning in the 1970s, the Australian government began to pursue lines of diplomacy clearly at a remove from the United States, but within the framework provided by ANZUS. Most significant in this regard was the tentative move to Asian engagement which would become an obsession in later years. Australia established diplomatic relations with China in 1972, and entered intensive dialogue with ASEAN countries. These developments gathered pace in the 1980s as Australian political economy underwent profound change. In the 1980s the government responded to economic troubles and declining returns in trade by floating the Australian dollar and opening the country to greater foreign direct investment and capital flows. The aim was to move Australia beyond its historical dependence on primary commodity exports and to graduate to the export school of elaborately transformed manufactures. Tapping into the Asian economic miracle was a principal objective of this economic strategy, and increasingly defined the prime objectives of foreign policy.

Australia's 'post-Cold War' era

It has been remarked that for Australia the end of the Cold War came well before the collapse of the Soviet Union in 1991. In the mid-1980s it was all too clear that communist China was intent on economic modernization that entailed partial integration with the rules of global capitalism. Its domestic focus made it clear that it no longer constituted a genuine threat to Australian security interests. Secondly, Soviet influence in the Pacific was decidedly on the decline, removing fears of Soviet expansionism. It was in this context that the idea of 'middle power diplomacy' increasingly informed Australian foreign policy. The growing use of the term in Australia from around the late 1980s was associated with Gareth Evans, Australia's 'liberally oriented' foreign minister from 1988–96. Evans argued that middle power diplomacy entailed a recognition that countries have 'a self interested preference for the peaceful resolution of conflict, acceptance of international law, protection of the weak against the strong, and the free exchange of ideas, people and goods' (Evans and Grant 1995: 344).

There is no consensus on what constitutes a middle power in International Relations theory. However, most writers who engage in using the term are likely to agree that a middle power is a state less powerful than great states and more powerful than weak or marginal states. Such a banal definition reflects a lack of agreement on more precise grounds. Furthermore, there is general agreement that 'the use of the term assumes a state-centric conception of the international community in which "powers" are defined as geographically delineated' (Chapnick 1999: 73). In Australian understandings of the term, the idea of middle power has been deployed to delineate a particular form of state behaviour by 'middle-sized' states. Cooper *et al.* define middle powers as those states that behave in a particular way: 'their tendency to pursue multilateral solutions to international problems, their tendency to embrace compromise positions in international disputes, and their tendency to embrace notions of "good international citizenship" to guide their diplomacy' (1993: 19). What this suggests is a state that attempts to build international order through co-operative institution building as a counterbalance to the security dilemmas and self-help strategies that crowd the system of international anarchy. In this respect the idea of a country being a middle power is clearly associated with neoliberal institutionalist approaches to international relations.

At a policy level a middle power orientation implied a shift from alliance diplomacy and the centrality of the US in Australian foreign policy towards a more independent stance. Indeed in the mid-1980s the then Labor government raised the possibility of linking the presence of the US bases to a future reform of America's export enhancement programme which was seen as hurting Australian farmers' economic interests (Ravenhill 2001). Furthermore, when New Zealand moved towards prohibiting the entry of US nuclear-powered vessels capable of bearing nuclear weapons, Australia dallied with the idea. If the US alliance was central to the Australian government's overall sense of strategic purpose, it is telling that at times the government had to be prodded on the issue. In 1986 the government issued a paper on Australian defence capabilities. The paper was deemed too 'Australian focused' by the US, which pushed for Australian conceptions of 'self-reliance' to be hitched more firmly and explicitly to the alliance. Henceforth the idea of self-reliance was understood as being 'set firmly within the framework of our alliances and regional associations' (Dibb 1997: 63). At the same time, the *Defence White Paper* of 1987 clearly articulated Australia's position in the balance of power in the Cold War divide.

Yet, as indicated earlier, realist security logic was increasingly overshadowed by new, arguably liberal diplomatic initiatives relating to trade and the Asia-Pacific. In the 1990s Gareth Evans began to promote the idea of co-operative security. He proposed no less than a transformation of ways of seeing the security environment: 'consultation rather than confrontation, reassurance rather than deterrence, transparency rather than secrecy, interdependence rather than unilateralism' (Evans 1994: 7). In line with this new thinking, Australia began to voice ideas of building 'a sense of regional community' (Department of Defence 1993).

It is notable that in 1990 Evans proposed, at an ASEAN post-ministerial conference, the establishment in Asia of something like the European Conference on Security and Co-operation. The objective was:

> to develop a security dialogue between states in the region aimed at developing shared perceptions of the strategic landscape; giving and receiving assurances about the role of military forces; strengthening links with existing friends and reaching out to former adversaries; and building a co-operative capacity to tackle jointly regional issues . . .
>
> (Evans and Grant 1995: 116–17)

The US rejected the idea in an attempt to maintain the status quo security arrangement. It feared that co-operative security arrangements would bring into question its own strategies and deployments. Nevertheless, as ASEAN began to come to terms with the post-Cold War environment it looked to Australia's earlier proposals in the design of the ASEAN Regional Forum.

However, balancing this incipient liberal institutionalism was the rather more realist take on the region by the Department of Defence. The 1994 *Defending Australia White Paper* (Department of Defence 1994) pessimistically evaluated that the security environment was fraught with insecurities. Reporting on the volatility of the China–Taiwan issue, the Spratly Islands dispute and the Korean Peninsula stand-off, the paper argued that the US should remain as a stabilizing force in a region subject to fluid structures of power and military modernization of Asian countries. But in a genuflection to the idea of self-reliance it was noted that the US 'neither seek nor accept the primary responsibility for maintaining peace and stability in the region' (Department of Defence 1994: 8).

Australian attempts to engage with Asia, despite the inhospitable security environment, led to a bold refashioning of Australian identity. By the end of the 1980s Australia was a much transformed country. The final dismantlement of the White Australia Policy had occurred in 1973 and Australia's ethnic composition was rapidly changing. As Australia turned its focus towards Asia, commentators spoke of the 'Asianization' of Australia. Underlying this shift was the same broad shift from geopolitics to geo-economics that was taking place elsewhere in the world. However, the government chose to see it as a matter of redefining Australia's sense of place in the world:

> for most of the two hundred years since European settlement, Australia has fought against the reality of its own geography. We thought of ourselves, and were thought of by just about everyone else, as an Anglophonic and Anglophilic outpost – tied by history, language, culture, economics and emotion to Europe and North America.
>
> (Evans and Grant 1995: 348)

Thus, a significant consequence of middle power diplomacy towards the Asia-Pacific was the reorientation of Australia to its region by making the population 'Asia' literate through the promotion of Asian studies and languages in universities and schools. This was not about making Australia 'Asian', but rather a recognition of Australia's interests being tied to its immediate environment and the need to move towards enmeshment with it in a multidimensional way (Evans and Grant 1995: 350–1). There was a powerful reason compelling Australia to engage – the phenomenal growth Asia had experienced in the preceding decades. Rather than see this as a threat, Australians were urged to see it as an opportunity. Indeed, the famous and influential report *Australia and the Northeast Asian Ascendancy* written by Ross Garnaut (1989) called for Australia to open itself to more investment from Asia and to learn from Asia's economic success.

Middle power diplomacy found expression in a number of areas. Australia was, with Japan, a frontrunner in the establishment of the Asia-Pacific Economic Co-operation grouping, that eventually tied over twenty countries into a multilateral organization promoting open regionalism in accord with GATT prescriptions of non-discrimination (McDougall 2001). Australia also intimated that it would like to create links with the emerging ASEAN Free Trade Area. It supported the formation of the ASEAN Regional Forum, seeing this as an important initiative in regionalizing security issues. Yet significant bilateral diplomacy was also embraced in this period. Australia signed the Agreement on Maintaining Security with

Indonesia in 1995. Australia had long courted Indonesia for two basic reasons: Indonesia was a major regional power, and good relations with it were seen as necessary to advance Australia's own regional interests and engagements. Moreover, this country of over 200 million people is by far the most likely place through which any hostile power would advance towards Australia. The significance of the relationship is evident in that successive Australian governments recognized Indonesia's annexation of the former Portuguese colony of East Timor in 1975, despite obvious and ongoing human rights atrocities and questionable claims to sovereignty. The successful conclusion of the bilateral security agreement between Australia and Indonesia in 1995 was seen as a culmination of the fundamental shift towards Asia.

Even if the US alliance remained central to Australian security perceptions in this period of Asian engagement, it is not hard to conclude that in the early 1990s Australian policy elites were laying the basis for a move beyond alliance diplomacy. By laying the foundations of multilateralism and by reconceptualizing the region as a place of enmeshment, the underlying rationale for the alliance (security) was indirectly challenged. While the government believed that the US was central to the security architecture of the Asia-Pacific, middle power diplomacy pushed at the limits of a regional alliance arrangement that could not countenance the transformation of regional security along genuinely multilateral lines. Australia at this point in its foreign policy was clearly seeking to direct the terms of the alliance in the direction of regionalization, to envelop or surround the hub-and-spoke arrangement with emergent structures of security multilateralism. The difficulty of achieving this end was clearly evident to all concerned, hence the continuing centrality of the alliance, even if a different future was being glimpsed.

Australia in a new world

In 1996 a new conservative government assumed office and remains in office at the time of writing. The government immediately set to work on revitalizing the ANZUS alliance, based on a belief that it, above all else, was central to Australian security, especially in the uncertain environment of the post-Cold War period. The merit of the alliance in the post-Cold War environment was spelled out by Australia's new defence minister in 1996:

> America's security commitment to the region is essential to ensure strategic stability into the long-term. Continued US involvement in regional security is critical for the region to realize its full economic potential. While Australia's interests will not always be identical with those of the United States, there is much common ground. Australia's long-term interests in the Asia-Pacific largely converge with those of the United States. Our alliance with the US is a unique asset, enabling us to influence US policies in this part of the world.
>
> (*The Australian*, 26 July 1996, p. 34)

In 1996, the US and Australian governments issued a Joint Security Declaration announcing greater security co-operation, new joint exercises and extension of the lease on the Pine Gap intelligence base. Prime Minister Howard declared that, 'The ANZUS Pact between Australia and the United States has done more to deliver security of the Australian nation in the years that have gone by since the WWII than any other international agreement' (Howard 2001).

Effectively, Howard was claiming that Australia's security has been best served by the US alliance and not by the UN and the international order it regulates, nor by its own regional and bilateral efforts in the Asian region. Howard's 2001 statement reflected the fact that between assuming office and making the statement, Australia's engagement with Asia and the varied attempts at economic and security multilateralism had been found wanting. Renewed alliance diplomacy with the US reflected realist pessimism on the nature of the security environment. The language of 'regional community' and 'co-operative security' that had characterized the earlier response to the post-Cold War environment was displaced by concerns relating to emergent security dilemmas in the region. The government's foreign affairs White Paper, *In the National Interest* (1997) firmly described Australia's national interests as tied up with doing what it could to mitigate strategic competition between regional powers, to thwart the emergence of a regionally dominant hostile power, to work towards a benign security environment in Southeast Asia and to move against the proliferation of weapons of mass destruction (Department of Foreign Affairs and Trade 1997: 8). Such objectives easily twinned with those of the US in the region, particularly the US's desire to thwart the emergence of a regional hegemon.

The government also rejected the implicit idealism of the previous administration, and opted for a firm statement of naked national interest:

> Preparing for the future is not a matter of grand constructs. It is about the hard-headed pursuit of the interests which lie at the core of foreign and trade policy: the security of the Australian nation and the jobs and standard of living of the Australian people. In all that it does in the field of foreign and trade policy, the Government will apply this basic test of national interest.
>
> (Department of Foreign Affairs and Trade 1997: 2)

In keeping with this definition of national interest, the government outlined what it saw as the strength of bilateral approaches to international politics and diplomacy, given its perception that multilateral institutions were too sluggish to develop relevant and sustained approaches to various problems. Of course this did not entail withdrawal from international or regional organizations, but it did mean a greater resource commitment, at the expense of multilateralism, to pursuing bilateral relations in order to advance the national interest. This is most evident in the government's enthusiastic pursuit of bilateral trade agreements which critics argue undermine multilateral negotiations in the World Trade Organization and elsewhere. The new approach also entailed criticism of the instruments of internationalism, such as the United Nations, seeing these in realist terms as beholden to the states that compose them rather than encompassing an emerging liberal logic that transcends state sovereignty:

> Australia must be realistic about what multilateral institutions such as the United Nations system can deliver. International organisations can only accomplish what their member states enable them to accomplish. If the reach of the UN system is not to exceed its grasp, it must focus on practical outcomes which match its aspirations with its capability.
>
> (Department of Foreign Affairs and Trade 1997: Overview 6)

More recently, after the war on Iraq (2003) Australia's foreign minister, Alexander Downer, spoke about the increasing impotence of the UN and the need for Australia to participate in security actions with other 'coalitions of the willing' (Downer 2003). In its own 'Pacific backyard', the government has moved towards 'humanitarian interventions' in the Solomon Islands without a prior United Nations mandate.

At a regional level the conservative government consciously moved away from the previous administration's rhetorical hug and kiss relationship with the region. In practice, Australian national interest diplomacy openly pursued relations for the sake of pure national interest, and dispensed with the rhetoric of Special Relations with Asian countries. This development is seen in Australia's relationship with China. The new government earned the disfavour of Beijing for its support of US naval deployments into the Taiwan Strait in 1996. Fearing the consequences of displeasing Beijing, the government quickly distanced itself from Sino-US tensions by highlighting economic aspects of the relationship with China. In a visit to China in 1997 the government proposed to develop further economic linkages with China and to channel discussion on human rights into a private bilateral dialogue between the two states. The then Chinese Premier Li Peng asked John Howard that Australia withdraw from an annual UN human rights resolution criticizing China. Australia complied (*Weekend Australian*, 5 April 1997, p. 21). A veteran Australian journalist aptly captured the thrust of national interest diplomacy in relation to China:

> How does Howard define the national interest with China? First, economic results – trade, investment, jobs. Second, a personal relationship with China's leadership. Third, a political relationship that minimises the disruption caused by different values. Fourth, formal but somewhat ritualistic support for China's engagement . . .
>
> (Kelly 1997: 21)

The government saw itself as advancing Australian national interests through practical, bilateral relationships based on acquirable objectives, eschewing the 'big picture' approach of the previous administration. More generally, various events during the tenure of the present government have further intensified this commitment to national interest diplomacy and the centrality of the US alliance. Three significant events – the Asian economic crisis, the East Timor crisis and September 11 – have contributed to a discernible shift in the way Australia defines its place in the region.

The Asian economic crisis of 1997 brought into question the extent to which Australia's economic future lay with the region. The crisis also undermined the prevailing sense of Asia as a role model for economic development. Such factors fuelled the government's new orientation towards centre-staging links with the US and more practical and goal-based engagement with Asia. After all, hitching the country's future to an Asia that appeared to be in decline hardly seemed prudent. Nonetheless, Australia contributed to the 1997 IMF rescue packages, and was also reputedly responsible for mitigating some of the harsher demands of the IMF in relation to Indonesia. This was seen as earning credit in the region (*Australian Financial Review*, 22 September 1998, p. 4). However, by the same token, the economic crisis was used by the government to extol the virtues of Western-style capitalism. Within the affected countries there was a feeling that strict loan conditionality and economic restructuring were nothing less than an attempt to break Asia from its own historic forms of capitalism. In response, there was a growing resentment of the IMF and the 'globalization project' of deregulation, privatization and good governance (Higgott 1999; So 2001), with which Australia publicly identified (Downer 1999). Indeed, when Indonesia fell into political disarray as a result of the economic crisis in 1997, Australia was able to turn its support of the globalization project into practical policy by actively supporting the democratization and liberalization of that state.

However, it was mostly Australia's response to the emerging crisis in East Timor that coloured Australia's relations with the rest of the region. The bare facts are as follows. In

1999, as a result of a UN-brokered agreement between Portugal and Indonesia, East Timorese were given an opportunity to vote on autonomy within Indonesia. A negative vote would lead to independence. Close to 80 per cent rejected autonomy in August 1999, setting the scene for gradual independence. Facing loss, forces close to the occupying Indonesian military went on a brutal rampage leading to the destruction of the country's infrastructure, and the loss of hundreds of lives. As the crisis unfolded on Australian television the government faced massive pressure from concerned citizens to intervene. In this context, and with permission from a reluctant and internationally pressured Indonesia, Australia led a UN-mandated peacekeeping force. Although 'invited' by Indonesia, that country's displeasure was evident when it abrogated the 1995 security agreement with Australia. Howard made it clear that as far as he was concerned this was a cost Australia could bear: 'It has been left to a Coalition government to reverse 25 years of over-accommodation to Indonesia' (*Weekend Australian*, 11 December 1999, p. 25).

While Australia's intervention was widely praised, the image management of its role led to criticism of it as an overbearing and aggressive country. For example, the intervention was publicly discussed in the Australian media as an opportunity for Australia to extend its leadership in the region. Moreover, Howard invested the intervention with a presumed moral superiority: 'We were defending the values we hold as Australians. We were willing to be in dispute with our nearest neighbour, to defend those values' (Brenchley 1999: 22). In words reminiscent of the 'civilizing mission' of an earlier time he explained that Australia had a duty 'above and beyond' to the region:

> We have been seen by countries, not only in the region but around the world, as being able to do something that probably no other country could do, because of the special characteristics we have; because we occupy that special place – we are a European, Western civilisation with strong links with North America, but here we are in Asia.
>
> (Brenchley 1999: 23)

Compounding this, in a much publicized interview Howard did not shirk from suggestions that Australia was acting as the regional deputy sheriff of the United States (Leaver 2001). It took over a week for the government to formally reject the idea, by which time predictably severe criticisms had been aired. Malaysian Prime Minister Mahathir Mohammad put it like this 'Australia is talking about becoming the deputy to the United States in policing Asia. This is unmitigated arrogance' (*Sydney Morning Herald*, 26 October 1999, p. 13).

The notion of the region being policed by two Western powers went stridently against the region's own sense of an emerging security community. A Thai foreign affairs official noted that, 'ASEAN must play the primary role in Southeast Asia. ... The role of the US is important, but over the long-term we'd like to see a regional order based on multilateral security co-operation' (*International Herald Tribune*, 27 September 1999). It is argued by some commentators that Australian posturing throughout the crisis has further alienated Australia from the region. A test of this is the fact that Australian attempts to push forward a trade linkage with ASEAN have failed to develop legs, and Australia has virtually given up its attempt to join the ASEM process.

Finally, it should be noted that the impact of the terrorist attacks on the US in 2001, and then the bombings in Bali in October 2002, have further strained relations with the region and further intensified Australian strategic proximity to the US. Australia formally invoked the ANZUS alliance in the wake of the attack on the World Trade Center, despite the misfit in terms of that treaty's objectives. Australia has also been an avid supporter of the US 'war on terrorism', supporting the wars in Afghanistan and Iraq while neighbouring countries with large Muslim populations such as Indonesia and Malaysia were highly critical. Furthermore, Australian defence policy, which is closely watched in Asia, has progressively moved away from notions of continental defence towards greater integration with US operations, and strategic deployments abroad (Monk 2003). All of the above developments are seen as driving Australia further away from integration with the region and into a newly intensified relationship with the world's sole superpower. As the new century opened it looked as if Australia had returned to rest on the shoulders of its great and powerful friend.

Australia and the United States: a cat's paw?

The foregoing narrative of Australia's international relations in the Asia-Pacific raises questions of whether Australia was merely a dependent mimic, echoing every twist and turn of US policy, and whether it has sacrificed independence in its foreign policy approach in order to serve the United States. These are questions that have long exercised observers of Australian foreign policy and below we explore a number of possible responses.

In popular Australian nationalist discourse, Australia's close relationship with the United States is seen as embroiling it in distant adventurist campaigns linked to US objectives (see, for example, Broinowski 2003). In contradistinction, it may be argued that Australia's involvement in military campaigns reflected a strategy to ensure United States presence in the region, it was not mere lapdog behaviour. Far from being dependent it may be argued that successive Australian governments have pursued, via the alliance, their own positions and interests, and have pursued their own strategic independence. Historically, during the early years of the Cold War, a key component of strategic independence was the deliberate amplification of the communist threat in Southeast Asia as a means of ensuring continuing US engagement. After 1954 when President Eisenhower first enunciated the domino theory – the idea that if Vietnam went 'communist', others would follow suit like 'falling dominos' – the Australian government regularly invoked the threat of communism in the region. Indeed, well before Eisenhower, in 1950 Australia's minister of external affairs noted that:

> Should the forces of Communism prevail and Vietnam come under the heel of Communist China, Malaya is in danger of being outflanked and it, together with Thailand, Burma and Indonesia, will become the next direct object of further Communist activities . . .
>
> (Cited in Millar 1978: 239)

Now, despite this early articulation of the 'domino theory', Australia's rhetoric was hardly matched with physical force and resource commitment throughout its various troop deployments. As one war historian notes:

> Less than one-tenth of the total Australian forces (86,000 personnel) were in Vietnam at the period of maximum commitment. During the war the Australian armed forces constituted about 0.7 per cent of the Australian population, and Australian defence expenditure averaged between 4 and 4.5 per cent of Gross National Product. By way of comparison, the American armed forces constituted 1.6 per cent of the total population and American defence expenditure averaged 9 per cent of Gross National Product during the same period.
>
> (Ekins 2003)

The same kind of misproportionality, between stated threat and actual troop commitment, may be observed in minimal Australian deployments in Afghanistan and Iraq in recent times. Explaining this apparent paradox takes us to the question of Australia's independence in the alliance relationship. While there are many commentators who argue that Australia effectively surrendered its capacity for making independent foreign policy by coat-tailing the US, others argued that Australia managed the alliance to suit its needs. Spender, Australia's external affairs minister at the outbreak of the Korean War, in very telling terms that remain relevant today, hints at Australia's strategic interests in following the US:

> from Australia's long-term point of view any additional aid we can give to the United States, now, small though it may be, will repay us in the future one hundred fold. . . . Time in Korea is rapidly running out and if we refrain from giving any further aid we may lose an opportunity of cementing friendship with the United States which may not easily present itself again . . .
>
> (Cited in Firth 1999: 15)

Regarding Australia's commitment in Vietnam, commentators note Australia was hardly a puppet of American foreign policy in Vietnam, although this is a popular perception. Australia's support for the war in Vietnam was largely related to its perception of the war as Chinese-communist inspired and its generalized fear of China (see Camilleri 1979: 23–4, 49–57). Fearing the long-term dominance of that country in its immediate Southeast Asian neighbourhood, the Australian government actively campaigned for strengthening the American commitment in Vietnam. As one commentator observes of the escalation of conflict in Vietnam in 1965:

> . . . beyond doubt the real initiative did not come from the Americans, but from the Australians. . . . What a study of the available documents from that period reveals is that the relevant parts of the Australian government desired an increased American involvement in the Vietnam conflict at every level . . .
>
> (Sexton 1981: 1)

What we have here is a picture of a regional power in the context of the Cold War seeking to engage a global power in its immediate neighbourhood. Its leverage is to share in the same threat perception of communism, and to highlight the existence of this threat in the region surrounding Australia. As T. B. Millar (1978: 216) explains:

> The main purpose was to show the United States that Australia was a willing ally, one that stood up to be counted and thus deserved to be stood up *for* if necessary, as well as to encourage the United States to remain committed to the defence of Australia's South East Asian neighbourhood against militant communist action . . .

Even during the 1980s when there was a discernible divergence of threat perception between the two states, Australia clung firmly to the US alliance despite a number of reservations about trade, nuclear weapons and the half-hearted US approach to multilateralism in the Asia-Pacific. With the return of a conservative government in 1996 Australia moved once again towards viewing the world in a manner congruent with US strategy and more stridently embraced the alliance.

Richard Leaver has discerned a particular pattern in Australia's relationship with the

United States, traced from the 1950s to the present day, which he describes as 'counter-cyclical'. The latter term indicates a constant pattern of divergence between the US and Australia on policy and perception (within the terms of the alliance). As agents of Australia's role in the international system, policy makers have attempted to steer a course that avoids both entrapment, or complete subsumption into US policy, and abandonment, or a condition of irrelevance to US strategic thinking (Leaver 1997: 89). In pursuit of this objective Australia has found itself at odds with the United States on a number of issues; it has not always merely toed the line. Australia had differences regarding the prosecution of the Korean War. It was opposed to the Indonesian takeover of Irian Jaya, which the United States endorsed, and it has been more supportive in a long-term perspective of multilateral institutions. The thrust of Leaver's critique is to argue against the dominant theme of dependency that is often read into Australian foreign policy. Why, Leaver (1997: 89) asks, is there a stronger narrative of dependence in discussions of Australian foreign policy when a different interpretation might paint Australia's role as that of loyal opposition? Furthermore, Leaver's approach illuminates the very real space in which Australian governments can manoeuvre within the alliance. Thinking in terms of 'counter-cyclical' aspects of the relationship allows Australian foreign policy practice to be interpreted as an attempt to define an independent position while avoiding the dangers of entrapment or abandonment in relation to its major and far more powerful ally. The approach also allows observers to situate Australia as an active and self-aggrandizing participant in a foreign policy. By extension, it may be argued that Australia has actively benefited from its relationship with the US because it shares the same global and regional interests.

From a Marxist perspective, that Australia shares a fundamental strategic interest with the United States, as a Western capitalist state, dependent on the maintenance of international order, is not surprising. In a point that could be taken in a Marxist direction, writing of the 1960s Pemberton argues that 'Australia's strategic and economic interests demanded that Western hegemony be maintained in that region [Southeast Asia]' (Pemberton 1987: 333). In a realist manner, Coral Bell makes the point that Australia's relationship to the US was structured by its own interests in the maintenance of existing international order through the system of alliances (Bell 1988).

More recently, the post-Cold War era has seen Australia align itself with the globalization project, most associated with the American state and its aligned multilateral institutions such as the World Bank and the IMF. Australia has also associated itself with both US regional strategy in the Asia-Pacific and its more global strategy of hegemonic dominance. These developments are differently explained by realist, liberal and Marxist understandings of politics.

In a realist and Marxist frame, Australia as a significant regional ally of the US can be seen as hitching itself to the fortunes of the major world economy and the institutions which serve those purposes in order to advance its own perceived national interests. In both perspectives Australia is seen as a supporter of the maintenance of international order by a hegemonic power. The most recent foreign affairs White Paper from the government, *Advancing the National Interest* (2003), would seem to corroborate this point:

> The depth of security, economic and political ties that we have with the United States makes this a vital relationship. No other country can match the United States' global reach in international affairs. . . . Further strengthening Australia's ability to influence and work with the United States is essential for advancing our national interests.
>
> (Department of Foreign Affairs and Trade 2003)

The difference between the two frames, realist and Marxist, is of course that one supports the alliance, while the other critiques it. From a broadly neoliberal frame it could be argued that Australian foreign policy has largely sought to advance the cause of interdependence through its support for the globalization project, but that it realistically recognizes this project is far from easily pursued via multilateral institutions. It thus chooses to pursue its interests via bilateralism as well as supporting multilateral institutions. Furthermore, until security dilemmas in the region are diminished it necessarily orients itself decisively in the direction of the US.

Conclusion

In conclusion, the experience of Australia offers instructive insights for students of the Asia-Pacific. A predominantly European-identifying country (at least in terms of elite decision makers), Australia aspires towards a global and regional order that can further secure its perceived national interests in terms of the expansion of global capitalism, buffeted by security arrangements that keep in check potential security dilemmas. Historically Australia has not so much been a pawn of its great and powerful friends, but rather an active participant in the various economic and security mechanisms through which it pursues its national interests. Its attempt at regional integration, and its subsequent retreat, tells us much about the volatile nature of international relations in the region. In some senses the country is caught in a pincer movement set in motion by potentially countervailing forces. On the one hand, it is pressured into regional economic integration by virtue of its own economic interests. Yet, from the other side, it feels the pressure of its security needs, which thus far have driven it away from the region and closer to the United States. How these twin pressures exert themselves in the future will not only reveal Australia's fortunes, but that of the Asia-Pacific in general. Whatever pressures it does face, it is likely that foreign policy makers will continue to pursue, within the terms of the US alliance, objectives they perceive to serve Australia's national interests.

References

Ball, D. (2001) 'The strategic essence', *Australian Journal of International Affairs*, 55: 235–48.

Bell, C. (1988) *Dependent Ally: A Study of Australian Foreign Policy*, 2nd edn, Oxford: Oxford University Press.

Bell, R. (1997) 'Anticipating the Pacific century? Australian responses to RE-alignments in the Asia-Pacific', in M. T. Berger and D. A. Borer (eds) *The Rise of East Asia*, London: Routledge, pp. 193–218.

Brenchley, F. (1999) 'The Howard defence doctrine', *The Bulletin*, 28 September, pp. 22–4.

Broinowski, A. (2003) *Howard's War*, Carlton North, Victoria: Scribe Publications.

Camilleri, J. A. (1979) *An Introduction to Australian Foreign Policy*, South Melbourne: Jacaranda Press.

Chapnick, A. (1999) 'The middle power', *Canadian Foreign Policy*, 7: 73–82.

Cheeseman, G. (1999) 'Australia: white experience of fear and dependence', in K. Booth and R. Trood (eds) *Strategic Cultures in the Asia-Pacific Region*, Basingstoke: Macmillan, pp. 273–98.

Cooper, A., Higgott, R. and Nossal, K. (1993) *Relocating Middle Powers: Australia and Canada in a Changing World Order*, Vancouver: University of British Columbia Press.

Dalby, S. (1996) 'Security discourse, the ANZUS alliance and Australian identity', in G. Cheeseman and R. Bruce (eds) *Discourses of Danger and Dread Frontiers: Australian Defence and Security Thinking After the Cold War*, St Leonards: Allen & Unwin, pp. 108–33.

Department of Defence (1987) *The Defence of Australia*, Canberra: Commonwealth Government of Australia.

Department of Defence (1993) *Strategic Review*, Canberra: Commonwealth Government of Australia.

Department of Defence (1994) *Defending Australia*, Canberra: Commonwealth Government of Australia.

Department of Foreign Affairs and Trade (1997) *In the National Interest: Australia's Foreign and Trade Policy: White Paper*, Canberra: Commonwealth Government of Australia. Online. Available HTTP: <http://www.dfat.gov.au/ini/overview.html> (accessed 10 September 2003).

Department of Foreign Affairs and Trade (2003) *Advancing the National Interest: Australia's Foreign and Trade Policy White Paper*, Canberra: Commonwealth Government of Australia.

Dibb, P. (1997) 'Australia's defence policies in the post-Cold War era', in J. Cotton and J. Ravenhill (eds) *Seeking Asian Engagement: Australia in World Affairs, 1991–1995*, Oxford: Oxford University Press, pp. 61–77.

Downer, A. (1999) 'Australia and Asia – traders and partners', speech given at Perth, 19 August. Online. Available HTTP: <http://www.dfat.gov.au/media/speeches/foreign/1999/990819_asia_society.html> (accessed 12 September 2003).

Downer, A. (2003) 'Security in an unstable world', speech given at the National Press Club, 26 June. Online. Available HTTP:<http://www.foreignminister.gov.au/speeches/2003/030626_unstableworld.html> (accessed 12 September 2003)

Ekins, A. (2003) 'Impressions: Australians in Vietnam', Official History Unit, Australian War Memorial Online. Online. Available HTTP: <http://www.awm.gov.au/events/travelling/impressions/overview.htm> (accessed 19 June 2003).

Evans, G. (1994) 'Cooperative security and intrastate conflict', *Foreign Policy*, 96: 3–20.

Evans, G. and Grant, B. (1995) *Australia's Foreign Relations in the World of the 1990s*, 2nd edn, Carlton: Melbourne University Press.

Firth, S. (1999) *Australia in International Politics: An Introduction to Australian Foreign Policy*, St Leonards: Allen & Unwin.

Fraser, M. (2001) 'An Australian critique', *Australian Journal of International Affairs*, 55: 225–34.

Garnaut, R. (1989) *Australia and the Northeast Asian Ascendancy*, Canberra: Australian Government Publishing Service.

Gurry, M. (1995) 'Identifying Australia's "region": from Evatt to Evans', *Australian Journal of International Affairs*, 49: 17–31.

Higgott, R. (1999) 'The international relations of the Asian economic crisis: a study in the politics of resentment', in R. Robison, M. Beeson, K. Jayasuriya and H.-R. Sim (eds) *Politics and Markets in the Wake of the Asian Crisis*, London: Routledge, pp. 261–82.

Howard, J. (2001) 'Transcript of the Prime Minister the Hon MP address at Federation Frontline Centrepiece Event, Darwin', 19 February. Online. Available HTTP: <http://www.pm.gov.au/news/speeches/2001/speech760.htm> (accessed 8 May 2003).

Kelly, P. (1997) 'Marriage of convenience', *Weekend Australian*, 5 April, p. 21.

Leaver, R. (1997) 'Patterns of dependence in post-war Australian foreign policy', in R. Leaver and D. Cox (eds) *Middling, Meddling, Muddling: Issues in Australian Foreign Policy*, St Leonards: Allen & Unwin, pp. 69–90.

Leaver, R. (2001) 'The meanings, origins and implications of "the Howard Doctrine" ', *The Pacific Review*, 14: 15–34.

Mackerras, C. (ed.) (1996) *Australia and China: Partners in Asia*, South Melbourne: Macmillan Education Australia.

Malik, M. (2001) 'Australia and China: divergence or convergence of interests?', in J. Cotton and J. Ravenhill (eds) *The National Interest in a Global Era: Australia in World Affairs, 1996–2000*, Melbourne: Oxford University Press, pp. 109–29.

McDougall, D. (2001) 'Australia and Asia-Pacific security regionalism: from Hawke and Keating to Howard', *Contemporary Southeast Asia*, 23: 84.

Meaney, N. (1995) 'The end of "White Australia" and Australia's changing perceptions of Asia, 1945–1990', *Australian Journal of International Affairs*, 49: 171–89.

Millar, T. B. (1978) *Australia in Peace and War: External Relations, 1788–1977*, Canberra: Australian National University Press.

Monk, P. A. (2003) 'Strategic changing of the guard', *Australian Financial Review*, 6 June, p. 6.

Pemberton, G. (1987) *All the Way: Australia's Road to Vietnam*, Sydney: Allen & Unwin.

Ravenhill. J. (2001) 'Allies but not friends: the economic relationship', *Australian Journal of International Affairs*, 55: 249–59.

Sexton, M. (1981) *War for the Asking: Australia's Vietnam Secrets*, Ringwood: Penguin Books.

So, A. Y. (2001) 'The "globalization project" and East Asia: an opportunity or a trap?', in J. C. Hsiung (ed.) *Twenty First Century World Order and the Asia-Pacific*, New York: Palgrave, pp. 135–56.

Stott-Despoja, N. and Bartlett, A. (2001) 'ANZUS? ANZ who?', *Australian Journal of International Affairs*, 55: 287–300.

Tereda, T. (2000) 'The Australia–Japan partnership in the Asia-Pacific', *Contemporary Southeast Asia*, 22: 175–98.

Watson, D. (2001) 'Rabbit syndrome: Australia and America', *Quarterly Essay*, 4: 1–59.

7 Europe and the Asia-Pacific

Jörn Dosch

Introduction

As elsewhere in the world after the fall of the Berlin Wall and the end of the Cold War, academic and public discussion in Europe focused on whether the so-called new world order would be dominated by the United States or would develop into a multipolar system with the United States, East Asia and the European Union as its principal centres. In 1992 when ASEAN announced the gradual implementation of a Southeast Asian Free Trade Area (AFTA) and in 1993 when the APEC countries' heads of state met for the first time in Seattle, European newspapers published scenarios presenting AFTA and APEC as emerging trading blocs and direct competitors of the European Common Market. Although it soon became clear that economic co-operation in the Asia-Pacific will not lead in the foreseeable future to a level of integration comparable to Europe's, many in Bonn, Paris, Rome and other capitals worried that a 'Pacific Century' could leave Europe as the odd man out in the new international order. Special attention was given to the role of the United States. It was believed that Washington would shift its main foreign policy focus from transatlantic to transpacific relations (although the United States was a Pacific power long before it became an Atlantic one). Concern was caused by trade figures showing that in 1995, for example, 66 per cent of total US trade was carried out within the Asia-Pacific area (including Canada). At the same time, of the ten biggest US trading partners five were Asian economies (Japan, China, Taiwan, South Korea and Singapore, in this order) but only three were European (Germany, the UK and France).

As a result of this perception, both the EU and individual member states have strengthened their relations with East Asian states on both the Track I and the Track II levels. Among the most important achievements are the Asia–Europe Meeting (ASEM) launched in 1996 which, according to Tommy Koh, Singapore's ambassador-at-large, 'is as important as APEC and the ASEAN Regional Forum' (*Asiaweek*, 4 February 1997). ASEM is supported by the Asia–Europe Foundation (ASEF), a Singapore-based think-tank that aims to boost intellectual and cultural interaction between the two regions. Collaboration between ASEM as the Track I forum and ASEF on the Track II level is paralleled by the ARF/CSCAP structure. Due in part to these activities, the international order of the post-Cold War era approaches a model in which relations between (a) the United States and the European Union, (b) the United States and Asia, and (c) Asia and the European Union form the three major strands.

For most of the past decade the vaguely formulated 1994 document 'Towards a New Asia Strategy' had formed the authoritative basis for the EU's strategic perception of East Asia. The paper reflected Europe's fear of becoming marginalized in a prosperous Asia-Pacific which was supposed to be the world's prime economic powerhouse by the year 2000 (EU 1994). However, the economic and political face of the region has significantly changed since the mid-1990s and so have European perceptions, strategies and policies. Despite the lack of grand visions, new developments in Europe's relations with East Asia are obvious. The fourth Asia–Europe Meeting (ASEM IV), which took place in Copenhagen in September 2002, clearly stressed the importance of inter-continental co-operation on security matters in addition to the trade agenda. The Chairman's statement is very explicit in this respect:

> Leaders underlined their resolve to fight international terrorism, while taking into account the multiple reasons leading to the emergence of terrorism. They pledged to work closely together to combat this threat to global peace and security, sustainable economic development and political stability. ... Leaders adopted the ASEM Copenhagen Co-operation Programme on Fighting International Terrorism. ... Leaders also endorsed the initiative to hold an ASEM Seminar on Anti-terrorism ...
>
> (ASEM 2002)

Although ASEM's current security agenda is largely driven by September 11 and subsequent events on the world stage, security is not a new issue in Europe–Asia relations, as this chapter tries to explain.

Here, the concept of security refers to both *hard security* (aspects of military defence) and *soft security* (the broad area of comprehensive security, including for instance diplomacy and confidence building, political and economic stability, human security etc.). Firstly, we will outline the state of institutionalization in Europe's relations with Southeast and Northeast Asia. We will then turn to the main actors on the European side and their strategic security interests *vis-à-vis* the Asia-Pacific. This will include a brief analysis of patterns in foreign policy making and a comparison with the role and position of the United States in the region. We will argue that interest cleavages between various actors, such as governments, parliaments and societal groups, constantly tend to hinder the formulation of coherent and comprehensive long-term East Asia strategies on the European sides. At the same time we will show that, contrary to popular belief, European actors have a long tradition of constructive post-colonial involvement in East Asian security, with a strong focus on soft security, however.

This chapter is written from a European perspective, or the European Union angle to be precise. Although it takes into account Asian perceptions, it cannot give a comprehensive analysis of Asian views on security in Europe–Asia relations due to the natural limitations to the space of a book chapter. In addition, the following will address the wider context of Europe–Asia security rather than focus exclusively on EU–ASEAN relations. Overall the chapter will primarily apply a liberal view as institutionalism seems to provide a better framework than neo-realism to explain the dynamics of co-operation between the two regions.

The institutionalization of relations between the European Union and the Asia-Pacific

EU–ASEAN

When the foreign ministers of Indonesia, Malaysia, the Philippines, Singapore and Thailand gave birth to ASEAN in August 1967 (see Chapter 5 on ASEAN), one main objective was 'to

Table 7.1 Europe and East Asia: a short historical overview

16th to 18th centuries	Missionaries and growing economic interests
	→ Age of trading companies
19th to mid-20th centuries	Age of colonialism and imperialism
	→ All Southeast Asian states (except Thailand) become colonies; China becomes a semi-colony
	→ Transfer and adaptation of European ideas, ideologies and political, social concepts:
	• Nationalism
	• Communism
	• Political order
	• Economic systems
Post-Second World War	All colonies become independent
	→ Fading European impact
	1950s: attempts to strengthen formal links (in the sense of creating military pacts) with East Asia fail (FPDA, etc.)
Early 1990s	Fears of being the 'odd man out' in the Asia-Pacific
Mid-1990s	Intensified inter-regional institution building (ASEM etc.)
Today	Growing economic links
	Strengthening of multilateral dialogues
	Occasional conflicts within the EU and between the EU and ASEAN on how to deal with China and Myanmar

maintain close and beneficial co-operation with existing international and regional organizations with similar aims and purposes', as stated in the Bangkok Declaration, the organization's founding document. Five years later, in April 1972, ASEAN launched a Special Co-ordination Committee (SCANN) to conduct an institutionalized dialogue with the European Community. This way, the EC became ASEAN's first 'Dialogue Partner'. A few months later, this initiative led to the establishment of the ASEAN–Brussels Committee (ABC), comprising ASEAN ambassadors accredited to the EC to act as its outpost in Europe. The ABC – which was the first ASEAN Committee in a third country – stands for the beginning of formalized ASEAN–EC/EU relations. In 1974 a Joint ASEAN–EC Study Group was established as an alternative to the commercial co-operation agreements that had been negotiated bilaterally between the EC and the Commonwealth countries. And in November 1979 the first ASEAN–EC Ministerial Meeting (AEMM) took place.

The signing of the ASEAN–EC Co-operation Agreement in Kuala Lumpur in 1980 marked an important step in the co-operation process between the two organizations. Of particular importance was the statement in the agreement that 'such co-operation will be between equal partners', without disclaiming that it will 'take into account the level of development of the member countries of ASEAN and the emergence of ASEAN as a viable and cohesive grouping, which has contributed to the stability and peace in Southeast Asia'. This new effort was particularly motivated by the urgency of working jointly at the international level to deal with major economic issues. Since the early 1990s both sides have been trying to reach a new co-operation treaty. So far, however, different opinions concerning questions of if, in what form and to what extent aspects of human rights and sustainable development should be stressed in the new treaty as well as divergent views on Myanmar and East Timor (at least until the referendum in 1999) have hindered the successful formulation of a draft acceptable to both sides.

Apart from these exclusive ASEAN–EU forums and dialogue mechanisms but closely connected with them is the Asia–Europe Meeting (ASEM) which stands for the most ambitious initiative to foster co-operation between the European Union and the Asia-Pacific. ASEM groups all EU and ASEAN member states (except Myanmar) as well as China, South Korea and Japan. ASEM has been the joint European–East Asian answer to the ongoing process of transpacific co-operation as materialized in APEC and other organizations. ASEM is meant to close or at least to narrow the institutional gap between Europe and Asia by providing the long missing 'third link' of the post-Cold War triangular world order. Although the endeavour – as the name states – involves more than just EU and ASEAN members, the process is so far dominated by these two organizations. Singapore was its main initiator (strongly supported by France), and Thailand the first host. The first meeting was held in Bangkok in March 1996, followed by summits in London (1998), Seoul (2000) and Copenhagen (2002).

Additionally, non-governmental actors within the EU and ASEAN have strengthened their relations amongst each other on the so-called 'Track II' level. Among the most recent achievements are the Council for Asia–Europe Co-operation (CAEC), the Asia–Europe Foundation (ASEF) and other institutionalized mechanisms. The CAEC links seven think-tanks in Europe (Berlin, Leiden, London, Paris, Stockholm, Trier and Warwick) with seven in Asia and Australia (Beijing, Canberra, Jakarta, Manila, Seoul, Singapore and Tokyo). ASEF is a Singapore-inspired think-tank that aims to boost intellectual, cultural and economic interaction between the two regions.

EU–Northeast Asia

Although the pattern of European–Northeast Asian relations differs from EU–Southeast Asia interactions due to the absence of an institutionalized group-to-group dialogue, strong economic incentives for co-operation are equally obvious. In recent years the EU's relationship with Japan has moved beyond narrow trade disputes to embrace broader economic and political co-operation. South Korea is an increasingly important trading partner for Europe as is China. By 1997 the People's Republic had become the EU's fourth most important trading partner. Formalized dialogue mechanisms between the EU and the states of Northeast Asia are significantly younger than EU–ASEAN links and bilateral in direction.

The relationship with *Japan* is certainly the most developed bilateral link. Official EC–Japan trade negotiations began in 1970. In 1991 the two sides signed the landmark EC–Japan Declaration in Brussels, which provided for an annual meeting between the presidents of the European Council and the Commission and the Japanese prime minister as well as other officials to discuss a variety of issues including not only the trade agenda but also 'international security' issues. The Declaration was partly modelled on the previous year's EC–US transatlantic equivalent, which had been designed to renew the relationship in the wake of massive structural changes as posed by the end of the Cold War and the transformation of Eastern Europe. Recently, Japan has established itself as a leading player within the framework of ASEM. As a result of the political dialogue, EU–Japan relations have moved beyond the narrow trade disputes that characterized the early stage. However, the EU continues to press for further opening up of Japan's markets.

EU trade with ASEM countries, 1980–2002 (in billion ECU/euro)

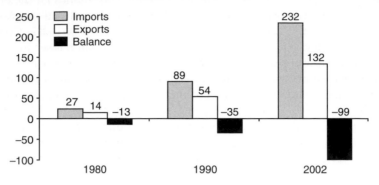

EU trade with ASEM countries, 1980–2002 (in % of total EU trade)

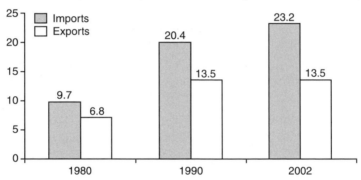

Main products in EU–ASEM trade, 2002 (ASEM share of total EU trade by product in %)

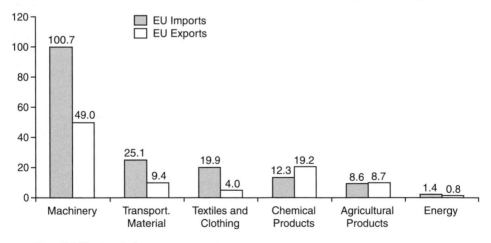

Figure 7.1 Trade relations
Data source for all charts: European Commission, http://www.europa.eu.int/comm/trade/issues/bilateral/data.htm; for the still most comprehensive analysis of economic relations between Europe and East Asia see Dent (1999).

Political relations between EU and *South Korea* are based on the 'Joint Declaration on Political Dialogue Links with South Korea'. The EU is also a member of the Korean Peninsular Energy Development Organization (KEDO) and contributes financially to the organization together with Japan, the US and South Korea. KEDO's main objective is to channel *North Korea's* nuclear ambitions by building two light-water reactors and thereby preventing Pyongyang from developing nuclear weapons. The EU contributed some US$65 million to KEDO from 1997 to 2000 and holds one of KEDO's directorships (Maull 2001a: 67). Contrary to the EU, the Clinton Administration had never been able to play an active role in KEDO due to the Congressional strategy of blocking Washington's agreed financial contributions as a means of opposing the president's engagement approach on more than one occasion and of pushing for a tougher US approach towards North Korea. In addition to KEDO-related activities, the first ever exclusive dialogue between EU and North Korean officials took place in December 1988, allowing the Commission to address the issue of human rights and non-proliferation. The EU was also one of the largest donors to humanitarian aid to North Korea in 1997 and 1998.

As Hanns Maull explains:

> the most dramatic sign of Europe's active involvement in the Korean Peninsula came with the visit of the EU troika on May 2–3, 2001 to Pyongyang and Seoul, at a time when the official inter-Korean dialogue had come to a halt and the new administration in Washington was still reviewing its policy toward North Korea. In this situation, the visit by the troika was widely seen as an attempt to inject momentum into both the inter-Korean détente process and America's policy review. The effort failed to produce immediate results, clearly demonstrating the limits of European influence on the Peninsula, but may still have been useful in providing an indirect communications link between the two Koreas at a critical moment. It also may have helped Washington to make up its mind . . .
>
> (Maull 2001b: 130)

Although the ongoing crisis on the Korean Peninsula (see Chapter 8 on regional security) has questioned the overall effectiveness of multilateralism in Northeast Asia, KEDO and other activities on the Peninsula have provided a good opportunity for European actors to promote 'European-style' co-operative approaches to security based on multilateral institution building. Similarly, EU actors had initially hoped to develop the ASEAN Regional Forum (ARF), founded in 1993, into a CSCE (Conference on Security Co-operation in Europe)-like institution suitable to handle security-related problems and challenges in a comparable way.

Of all Northeast Asian states *China* poses the greatest economic potential. The EU has therefore tended to adopt a 'pragmatic approach' to China. Senior EU trade officials have often claimed that the EU's soft approach in dealing with Asia's economic powers, and China in particular, has proved to be more effective in boosting business for its companies than, what some have called, the 'megaphone diplomacy' applied by the United States. The EU established diplomatic relations with Beijing in 1975 and signed an economic trade and co-operation agreement three years later. The EC–China Trade Agreement of 1978 was the first that the EC had concluded with a non-market economy. This agreement was renewed and extended in 1985. China was granted a modified MFN status as it was not a member of GATT then. Relations temporarily flagged after the 4 June 1989 Tiananmen Square massacre but rapidly improved in the second half of the 1990s. The EU–China human rights dialogue resumed in 1997 and, since then, the EU has actively engaged in a political dialogue with Beijing aiming at the full integration of China into the international community.

Given the EU's official 'one China' policy, dialogue with *Taiwan* is limited and consists of low-intensive annual consultation. In February and March 1996, however, the European Parliament, the EU's legislative but largely powerless arm, passed two resolutions urging China to halt any preparations for military action against Taiwan. In a similar vein, foreign ministers of the fifteen member states issued a joint statement condemning Beijing for conducting missile tests on Taiwan's doorstep. Whereas Taiwan naturally appreciated the position as a moral support, China strongly condemned it as a 'wanton interference in China's internal affairs and a reckless violation of the principles enshrined in the United Nations Charter' (BBC 1996).

In sum, compared with two decades or even ten years ago, today European–Asian relations are fairly institutionalized. The 'third link' of the international order is not comparable to highly formalized transatlantic relations but has come close to match transpacific links. What are the consequences for Europe's involvement in East Asian security?

Actors and strategic interests

It seems to be impossible to discuss Europe's security role in Asia without mentioning the United States:

> The United States is the only superpower in history to exercise its power in East Asia by invitation. Japan, South Korea, Thailand, and the Philippines by choice sought the security umbrella that comes with alliance membership with the United States. Other regional states such as Singapore provide host facilities for the United States military. The United States provides the military power that bolsters the security of these states . . .
>
> (Dickens 2000: 77)

Even though not any given government in the Asia-Pacific would subscribe to this view, it correctly points to the striking difference between Europe's and America's involvement in the Asia-Pacific security order. Americans *are*, Europeans *used to be* major actors in the arena of East Asian security. Whereas transpacific military relations are highly institutionalized, Europe–East Asia links lack any attempt to strengthen hard security co-operation except for occasional joint manoeuvres organized by Great Britain and France as part of their arms-selling activities. While Europe has legitimate reasons to become involved in Asia-Pacific security, the structural setting of EU security interests and strategies towards the region differ significantly from those of the United States, for five reasons.

Firstly, and most important, contrary to the role of the US as the pre-eminent military power, balancer and broker in the Asia-Pacific, Europeans have never returned as significant military actors to the region since the end of the colonial empires in the long aftermath of the Second World War and the British decision to withdraw its troops east of Suez (1968). Attempts to establish military relations with East Asian states, such as the Five-Power Defence Arrangements (FPDA) of 1971, grouping Great Britain, Malaysia, Singapore, Australia and New Zealand, have failed as military pacts. However, FPDA continues to provide a framework for joint exercises and consultations on security matters. Additionally, neither the EU as a collective actor nor most respective member states (with the partial exception of Great Britain and France) have direct hard security interests in the region other than the general aim to contribute to stability and a peaceful regional order.

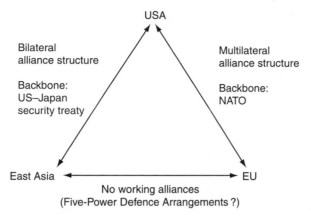

Figure 7.2 The global defence triangle

Secondly, unlike in the field of economic policies, EU members have neither *de jure* nor *de facto* yet surrendered their sovereignty in the area of foreign relations. Although the EU troika and the Commission act on behalf of the whole Union on the international stage, the respective member states still cling to their autonomy in foreign affairs. Every EU standpoint communicated to the external world reflects a compromise reached in a constant, never-ending process of interest harmonization among fifteen ministries of foreign affairs, often including other departments and the offices of prime ministers and presidents too. In some instances common positions were out of reach, as in the case of how to deal with China. Formally, Article J.13 of the Maastricht Treaty

> speaks of qualified majority in adopting joint actions, common positions or taking any other decision on the basis of a common position. So, the journey towards commonness in CFSP [Common Foreign and Security Policy] has begun. However, this Article provides for a Member State to abstain constructively in adopting common positions and joint actions pointing to considerations of national interest . . .
>
> (Lim 1999: 1)

Thirdly, and closely related, given the diversity of national interests within the EU and historical patterns of relations between the respective member states and East Asia, European governments tend to follow their own agenda first before adopting or sponsoring joint policies. Traditionally, the former colonial powers Great Britain, France, the Netherlands and to some extent Portugal (on the East Timor issue for many years) have been more active in outlining and shaping Europe–Asia relations but were joined by a pro-active German government in the 1990s. Denmark and – to a lesser extent – Sweden have successfully tried to put their mark on specific topics such as the controversial human rights question.

Fourthly, and as a result of the factors explained in the previous points, although hard security issues are also being tackled (as in the case of KEDO, for example) the EU is more likely to concentrate its efforts in the area of soft security, focusing on the democratization of East Asia's political systems, the rule of law and the reduction of informal institutions (such as corruption), human and civil rights, environmental and, not least, economic stability or more specifically crisis solving and prevention.

Fifthly, compared with the United States, public opinion and societal interests have a significantly lesser impact on both the EU's and its member states' relations with East Asia.

This is not only because of smaller and less well organized ethnic Asian communities but also due to the limited role of the legislature in the foreign policy arena. Historically and different to Anglo-American political thought, in most European nations the primacy of the executive in foreign policy making is taken for granted. In general, neither do constitutions provide for an active part of the legislature nor have many parliaments taken the initiative to exert substantial influence over the shaping of foreign relations. The case of the European Parliament is slightly different though. Although usually more active than national legislative bodies, as frequent resolutions on Europe's political and economic relations with the region demonstrate, the European Parliament lacks the formal power to play an important role within the framework of the Common Foreign and Security Policy (CFSP).

Similarly to the US, *relations with China* demonstrate best the nature of cleavages and diverging views among actors involved in the process of foreign policy making. There is a striking structural difference though. In the American case the lines of conflict are within the political system or more specifically between the executive and legislature on a horizontal level and among the spectrum of non-governmental actors vertically and informally linked especially with Congress. Intra-EU cleavages are purely horizontal in direction referring to disputes between the respective national governments. Neither parliaments nor societal groups are prominently involved. Tensions exist, for example, about how to balance economic interests and the promotion of human and civil rights in the case of EU–China relations. In 1995 and the following year the EU sponsored a resolution in the United Nations Human Rights Commission (UNHRC) criticizing China for human rights violations in Tibet and elsewhere. In 1996 however,

> some cracks in the European unity were beginning to appear as some EU member countries argued for doing a deal with China in which, in return for dropping the resolution, China would ratify one important international covenant on civil and political liberties. The deal was not struck in the end, but the French in particular were becoming increasingly impatient to adopt a different approach to the human rights issue. . . . Germany, Italy, Greece and Spain came round to the French line of thinking

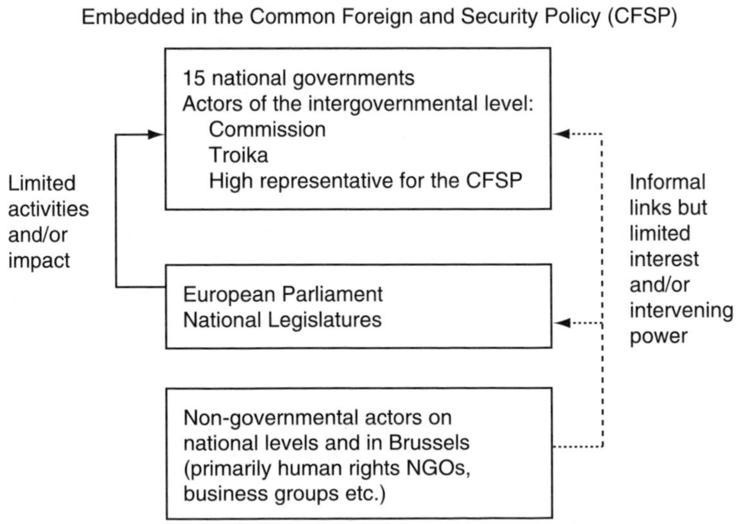

Figure 7.3 Actors in EU foreign policy making

and blocked a joint EU sponsorship for the April 1997 resolution. In the end, Denmark, a consistent supporter of human rights, with strong support from the Netherlands and the UK, took on the task of sponsoring the resolution. . . . But with China mobilizing developing country support around its position, the resolution failed even to be debated . . .

(Bridges 1999: 107–8)

The disunity was also obvious when no other EU member country joined the British government in its boycott of Hong Kong's handover ceremony.

Why are most European actors more flexible to weigh up business and *human rights interests* compared with the United States which seems to be under constant pressure to push for human rights in Asia? One answer suggests that US foreign policy is more moralistic in direction than European strategies of dealing with the outside world. The different national roles of the United States and European countries in international relations based on historic experiences, foreign policy traditions, socio-economic and power-related positions etc. certainly contribute to this attitude. But this is only part of the explanation. As already hinted, different patterns of the political systems and political cultures must be considered, too. The European approach towards China is a case in point. In the absence of strong European public interest towards China and given the lack of significantly organized ethnic interests, European policy makers do not have to be extremely moralistic in their China approach. Human rights issues and especially the situation of Tibet are never left out in bilateral meetings but in general EU governments can primarily concentrate on trade relations and thereby preparing the ground for investment opportunities.

In view of all these structural framework conditions and patterns of actor behaviour, what are the *specific implications for Europe's security interests and strategies in East Asia*? Obviously, due to the weak institutionalization of the CFSP and the variety of different, partly conflicting national interests, the EU has not yet produced any explicit East Asia security strategy like the Pentagon's East Asia strategies of 1995 and 1998. And more than defining its strategic interests *in the region*, the EU tends to outline potential and promising areas for co-operation *with the region*, which is again a significant difference in comparison with the US.

Apart from highlighting the general importance of intensified political dialogues, the 1994 EU document *Towards a New Asia Strategy* primarily stressed:

- (regarding the area of hard security) the importance of working towards arms control and the non-proliferation of weapons of mass destruction (nuclear, chemical, biological, ballistic missiles);
- (considering the field of soft security) the necessity for 'the development and consolidation of democracy and the rule of law and respect for human rights and fundamental freedoms' and the need to take joint measures against drug trafficking, drug production and drug consumption, since they would present 'a problem to Asian regions and [have] significant repercussions on the European economies and EU security and stability' (EU 1994).

The Asia–Europe Co-operation Framework (AECF) of 2000 further specifies these strategic interests. European and East Asian actors should, among other measures,

- strengthen efforts in the global and regional context towards arms control, disarmament and non-proliferation of weapons of mass destruction;

- combat illicit trafficking in and accumulation of small arms and light weapons;
- tackle the global environmental issues and striving for sustainable development;
- managing migratory flows in a globalized world;
- combat transnational crime, including money laundering, the smuggling and exploitation of migrants, the trafficking of persons in particular women and children, international terrorism and piracy, and fighting against illegal drugs (EU 2000: Article 14).

The strategy paper *Europe and Asia: A Strategic Framework for Enhanced Partnership* (EU 2001), adopted by the EU in September 2001, further adds to the security agenda by, among other issues, focusing on

- strengthening EU engagement with Asia in the political and security fields;
- building global partnerships with key Asian partners (in areas like UN reform, WTO, environment or other challenges such as international crime, terrorism and the spread of HIV/Aids).

Although it seems inconspicuous at first glance, probably the most important recent achievement towards a harmonization of European and East Asian perceptions and interests related to soft security is the acknowledgement of the universality of human rights. The Chairman's Statement of the Third Asia–Europe Meeting, which took place in Seoul in October 2000, stresses: 'Leaders committed themselves to promote and protect all human rights, including the right to development, and fundamental freedoms, bearing in mind their universal, indivisible and independent character as expressed at the World Conference on Human Rights in Vienna' (ASEM 2000: para. 8). Conflicting views of the concept of human and civil rights have been the most serious intervening variable in Europe–East Asia relations since 1991 when the EC had decided to make human rights clauses compulsory elements of its international treaties.

The inclusion of formally tabooed core soft security issues such as human rights, rule of law and good governance on the Asia–Europe agenda does represent a new quality in intra-regional relations. According to Michael Reiterer,

> the new commitments made in the AECF 2000 in the fields of good governance, human rights and the rule of law are significant and this document will steer the ASEM process during the next decade, so it would be difficult to back away from these commitments now they are agreed . . .
>
> (Reiterer 2001: 17)

This is, however, only part of the story. While the vast majority of actors, both on the European and the Asian side, today do subscribe to the idea that any serious inter-regional dialogue needs to focus on principal aspects of soft security, the views on the translation of the debate into a working agenda significantly differ. The question, if and to what extent the Asia–Europe co-operation process in general should be conditional to the adherence of human rights remains particularly controversial. On the eve of ASEM IV, for instance, some European members, especially Sweden, expressed a strong interest in explicitly linking anti-terrorism activities with human rights. The tenor on the European side was to make it clear that the fight against terrorism must not be carried out at the expense of human rights. However, neither the *ASEM Copenhagen Declaration on Co-operation against International Terrorism* nor the *Copenhagen Programme on Fighting International*

Terrorism nor the *Concept Paper on ASEM Seminar on Anti-Terrorism* establishes such an explicit link. Instead, the *Declaration* states in a rather indirect fashion, that 'the fight against terrorism must be based on the principles of the UN Charter and basic norms of international law' (para. 2) and 'we reject any attempt to associate terrorism with any religion, race or nationality' (para. 3).

The predominance of soft security issues in Europe–Asia relations does not imply the complete absence of hard strategic thinking on the EU side. The fact that Asian states possess nuclear weapons or have capabilities to build them (China, North Korea, India, Pakistan) does cause concern not only in the US but in Europe too, to put it mildly. The EU, like many actors in the Asia-Pacific, has articulated and demonstrated a strong strategic interest in dealing with the problems and challenges of nuclear (and conventional) armament and proliferation in a preventive way. The EU's active role in the Korean Energy Development Organization (KEDO) is a case in point. At the same time, specific hard security interests in the Asia-Pacific do not rank high on the respective national foreign policy and security agendas, with the notable exception of Great Britain and France. Responsibilities as permanent members of the UN Security Council in both cases, Britain's continued political commitment to the Five-Power Defence Agreements (FPDA) and the French military presence in the Indian Ocean and the South Pacific (totalling some 16,000 troops) provide both the motivations and the means to maintain at least a minimal hard security presence in East Asia (see Bridges 1999: 212). In addition, France and the UK are the main European suppliers of arms and arms technology to East Asian countries. During the 1990s the European market share of the military supply sector in the region rose from about 10 per cent to more than 20 per cent (Maull 1999: 61).

Table 7.2 Types of EU promoted security co-operation in the Asia-Pacific

	Hard security	*Soft security*
Bilateral	Activities between individual EU members and East Asian States: • British Gurkha infantry and some helicopters stationed in Brunei • Joint naval exercises (Great Britain and France respectively) partly to boost arms sales • Security dialogues with Japan involving defence ministries among other actors (Great Britain, France, Germany respectively) • Military dialogues with the Chinese armed forces (Great Britain, France, Germany respectively)	(a) EU dialogues with key countries broadly addressing issues of international security, for example: • EC–Japan Declaration • Joint Declaration on Political Dialogue links with South Korea • Dialogue between EU and North Korean government officials (b) Wide range of diplomatic activities in the field of confidence-building measures and support of economic and political reforms, which are supposed to help prevent further crises, lead to democracy and a more stable regional order
Multilateral	Activities involving a group of states either on the European *or* East Asian side or on both sides: • European and Asian contribution to the UN Transitional Administration in East Timor (UNTAET)*	Participation in Asian-Pacific non-military security forums and dialogues on both the Track I Track II levels: • ASEAN Regional Forum (ARF) • Council for Security Co-operation in the Asia-Pacific (CSCAP)

- Five-Power Defence Arrangements (FPDA, Great Britain, Australia, New Zealand, Malaysia, Singapore) officially continue to exist (joint exercises but no military pact)
- Central EU role in the Korean Peninsular Energy Development Organization (KEDO)
- Joint activities in the area of arms-control co-operation

Security-related issues (transnational crime, money laundering, drug trafficking etc.) also being addressed within the framework of exclusive Europe–Asia dialogues:
- Multilevel EU–ASEAN dialogue
- Asia–Europe Meeting (ASEM)

Twilight zone hard/soft security Anti-terrorism co-operation in the wake of September 11 2001 (ASEM Copenhagen Co-operation Programme on Fighting International Terrorism etc.)

---

* The following European, Southeast Asian and Northeast Asian states have contributed civilian and/or military personnel to UNTAET: Portugal, Austria, Denmark, France, Spain, Sweden, Great Britain, Thailand, Singapore, Philippines, Malaysia, Japan and South Korea.

Source: Dosch (2003: 14).

Conclusion and outlook

The EU and its member states entered the post-Cold War era being confronted with the problem of becoming largely marginalized as actors in East Asia. The fear of being the odd person out in the Asia-Pacific resulted in the search for the so-called missing link in international relations, a popular reference to 'under-institutionalized' Europe–East Asia relations. Some pundits even suggested counterbalancing American military influence and superiority in the region, thus mostly reflecting the old British and French dream of returning as decisive security players to East Asia. As in the case of the United States, for Europeans the Asian crisis of 1997–98 painted a new picture of global power relations, putting East Asia's position in perspective and postponing the 'Pacific Century'. Above all, post-crisis relations between the EU and East Asia are significantly less influenced by ideology or value debates. This has contributed to a favourable atmosphere for a less heated debate on the importance of soft security (democratization, human rights, economic stability etc.) for a stable regional order. EU–ASEAN relations are not necessarily a never-ending success story though. Since the end of the Cold War relations have also suffered from setbacks. In the 1990s, the bilateral conflict between Indonesia and Portugal over East Timor and disputes resulting from different perceptions of human rights and good governance had blocked any institutional evolution and the drafting of a new co-operation treaty. But it has been especially Myanmar's accession to ASEAN in 1997 that contributed to the worsening of relations. Several official meetings were cancelled due to the inability to find a compromise concerning the legitimacy and extent of Myanmar's participation in the dialogue. Although neither the EU nor ASEAN represented united opinion blocks, both organizations managed to officially speak with one voice. Whereas ASEAN insisted on the inclusion of its member, the EU rejected any participation of the Myanmar military junta.

In view of these and other differences in group-to-group relations between the EU and ASEAN, the broader ASEM structure may offer the greater potential for fruitful long-term interaction between the two regions. Despite its explicit character as an informal dialogue programme the quickly growing topical agenda and the absence of US actors and American interests has opened the door for the development of alternative views on security in East

Asia, for example. ASEM has gradually gained importance to the extent that today and as far as institution-building is concerned, Europe–Asia relations are primarily centred upon ASEM and no longer on the EU–ASEAN dialogue. When talking in private, senior officials involved in the management of the EU–ASEAN co-operation scheme tend to confess that it had been difficult to keep the group-to-group dialogue alive given its downgraded importance on the foreign policy agendas of most member states and the subsequent absence of new initiatives. Whereas various EU–ASEAN meetings have recently produced only one new security-related initiative, a conference on piracy, ASEM has generated more than half a dozen schemes ranging from the anti-terrorism agenda and support for the process of inter-Korean reconciliation and co-operation to soft security issues such as transnational crime, anti-money laundering and trafficking in women and children. But ASEM's potential in this area seems to be limited.

Even though some actors within ASEM perceive the need to balance US influence and counter increasing US unilateralism, the stark reality is that neither the EU nor the Asian ASEM members are able to act in concert: 'The EU is still sorting out a common foreign and security policy, and the Asians are still hesitant about institutionalizing their inter-state co-operation' (Yeo Lay Hwee 2000: 122). ASEM's current anti-terrorism agenda provides a good example. China, which has more and more established itself as an informal leader among the Asian participants in the absence of other actors' (especially Japan's) interest to play such a role, was keen on organizing a meeting on terrorism before the ASEM Copenhagen Summit to balance Washington's global opinion-leadership on the issue of anti-terrorism. Although the European side rejected the idea of a special meeting and put the discussion off until the summit, the case shows that 'Asians, for their part, have sought to balance what they perceived as an increasingly dominant role of the US in Pacific Asia' (Rüland 2000: 62). However, while any kind of balancing is hard enough to achieve in the economic field, it is next to impossible in the security arena. One has to keep in mind that ASEM's organizational structure consists of an economic, political and cultural/intellectual pillar but has not yet established a security pillar. The maximum that ASEM can achieve for the time being is to pursue a strategy of complementing the American role by emphasizing the importance of soft security for regional order and stability guided by the assumption that political and social processes in the Asia-Pacific are closely related to regional peace and stability.

References

ASEM (2000) 'Chairman's Statement of the Third Asia–Europe Meeting', Seoul, 20–21 October. Online. Available HTTP: <http://europa.eu.int/comm/external_relations/asem/asem_summits/asem3_stat.htm> (accessed 10 July 2002).

ASEM (2002) 'Chairman's Statement. Fourth Asia–Europe Meeting (ASEM 4)', Copenhagen, 23 September. (This and all other ASEM documents as well as a wide range of other useful sources can be found on the recently launched 'ASEM Research Platform' website: http://www.iias.nl/asem.)

BBC (1996) 'Foreign ministry appreciate EU parliament support', *Worldwide Monitoring*, 15 March.

Bridges, B. (1999) *Europe and the Challenge of the Asia-Pacific. Change, Continuity and Crisis*, Cheltenham: Edward Elgar.

Dent, C. M. (1999) *The European Union and East Asia: An Economic Relationship*, London: Routledge.

Dickens, D. (2000) 'The United States military presence in East Asia', *Panorama*, 4: 77–95.

Dosch, J. (2003) 'Changing security cultures in Europe and Southeast Asia: implications for inter-regionalism', *Asia Europe Journal*, 1: 1–19.

EU (1994) 'COM(94) 314 final', Brussels, 13 July. Online. Available HTTP: <http://www.europa.eu.int/comm/external_relations/asem/asem_process/com94.htm> (accessed 10 August 2002).

EU (2000) 'Europe and Asia: a strategic framework for enhanced partnership'. Online. Available HTTP: <http://europa.eu.int/comm/external_relations/asem/asem_process/aecf_2000.htm> (accessed 10 July 2002).

EU (2001) 'COM(2001) 469 final'. Online. Available HTTP: <http://europa.eu.int/comm/external_relations/asia/doc/com01_469_en.pdf> (accessed 10 July 2002).

Lim, P. (1999) *The EU's Common Foreign and Security Policy and Asia – A Statement, Asia Update Executive Summary for the Conference 'Asia and the European Union's Common Foreign and Security Policy'*, 24 November, European Parliament, Brussels.

Maull, H. (1999) 'European Union', in C. E. Morrison (ed.) *Asia-Pacific Security Outlook 1999*, Tokyo: Japan Centre for International Exchange, pp. 55–64.

Maull, H. (2001a) 'European Union', in C. A. McNally and C. E. Morrison (eds) *Asia-Pacific Security Outlook 2001*, Tokyo: Japan Centre for International Exchange, pp. 60–7.

Maull, H. (2001b) 'Europe–East Asia relations: building an Asia-Pacific connection', *Comparative Connections*, 3: 128–35. Online. Available HTTP: <http://www.iias.nl/asem/publications/Maull_ europeandeastasiaCC.pdf > (accessed 10 July 2002).

Reiterer, M. (2001) 'ASEM – the Third Summit in Seoul 2000: a roadmap to consolidate the partnership between Asia and Europe', *European Foreign Affairs Review*, 6: 1–30.

Rüland, J. (2000) 'Transnational forum at the crossroads', in W. Stokhof and P. van der Velde (eds) *Asian–Europe Perspectives. Developing the ASEM Process*, Richmond, Surrey: Curzon Press, pp. 60–76.

Yeo Lay Hwee (2000) 'ASEM: looking back, looking forward', *Contemporary Southeast Asia*, 22: 113–44.

8 Regional security in the Asia-Pacific

Sources of conflict and prospects for co-operation

Jörn Dosch

Introduction

What exactly is security and how does it come about? Security is not the product of any predictable rules, depends on individual threat perceptions, differs greatly according to an actor's status and position within the international system and, most importantly, is subject to interpretation. Historically, security was understood in terms of threats to state sovereignty and territory. This traditional concept is called hard or military security. During the Cold War, it was generally thought, firstly, serious armed conflict in the Asia-Pacific would only take place between the superpowers, or their clients; and, secondly, that it would be in one of four areas: the Sea of Okhotsk; the Korean Peninsula; Taiwan Strait; or the Sino-Soviet border. This security threat to the region changed dramatically in the late 1980s. Soviet nuclear submarines no longer use the Sea of Okhotsk as a strategic haven in preparation for a strike at the US. The dispute about islands there is a relatively minor affair. Furthermore, the Sino-Soviet border tension is much reduced following better relations between China and Russia. There has been an all-round amelioration of relations at a bilateral level, and some movement towards a more constructive regional dialogue on security issues. At the same time, globalization has produced a simultaneous emergence of localization with more emphasis on local issues, revival of traditional local (intra-national) conflicts, which had been suppressed by ideological divide of the Cold War and nuclear deterrence, and not least the terrorist movements. Such tensions inevitably impact on regional stability.

In sum, the structural changes of the post-Cold War era have resulted in new views on the definition and nature of security. Security is now widely interpreted as meaning more than the avoidance of war and military violence. Insecurity is no longer seen as a phenomenon primarily associated with military threat nor does it exclusively concern the state. According to the new understanding, security covers societal and even individual dimensions, economic, environmental, criminal, humanitarian and human rights issues, as well as those of the illegitimate use of violence. This broader idea of security is generally referred to as non-traditional or soft security. The terrorist attacks of September 11 2001 and the subsequent war on terror have, probably been the most visible manifestation of the post-Cold War security agenda, and have had significant implications for many states and governments in the Asia-Pacific and in some cases have compounded pre-existing problems: 'The new circumstances are particularly hard on weak states with large Muslim populations and new and/or weak leadership, such as Indonesia and Pakistan' (McNally and Morrison 2002). Drug trafficking, piracy, environmental degradation, growing competition for economic resources and poverty are other decisive issues which are related to regional security and stability. None the less, despite the emergence of non-traditional security, the basic security perspectives and problems in the region remain essentially unchanged. Hard security challenges such as the Korean Peninsula, the Taiwan Strait and unresolved territorial disputes between numerous states in the region remain as potential flashpoints for serious conflicts and continue to dominate the agenda.

This chapter aims to outline the various sources of conflict and looks in more detail at some of the potential flashpoints, namely Taiwan, Korea, the Spratly Islands issue and local tensions. It then presents some of the arguments for, and against, the potential for conflict in the region and concludes by presenting two scenarios for regional order-building from the neo-realist and liberal institutionalist perspectives.

Nature and areas of potential conflict

In the early 1990s economic development and military security became intertwined in a way never seen before. At the same time, the post-Cold War period in International Relations has been characterized by the recognition of highly uneven patterns of change in different components of development, and the technological and political changes often labelled globalization. One consequence has been the emergence of the concept of human security. As fostered by the United Nations Development Programme (UNDP), this term usually means 'freedom from fear and want' (King and Murray 2002: 585). The UNDP *Human Development Report* (1994) stressed:

> The concept of security has for too long been interpreted narrowly: as security of territory from external aggression, or as protection of national interests in foreign policy or as global security from the threat of nuclear holocaust. It has been related to nation-states more than people. . . . Forgotten were the legitimate concerns of ordinary people who sought security in their daily lives. For many of them, security symbolized protection from the threat of disease, hunger, unemployment, crime, social conflict, political repression and environmental hazards . . .
>
> (UNDP 1994: 22–3)

Human security has not emerged as the only alternative security concept. As Table 8.1 shows, security can be understood as a wide array of inter-related issues. Many elements of this multidimensional concept of security are present in the Asia-Pacific, thus contributing to the perception that the potential for conflict in the region is generally quite high. Among the crucial factors are:

- the prevalence of weak states;
- an uneven distribution of economic development and prosperity within regions;
- a wide range of territorial and resource disputes;
- an arms race fuelled by economic growth and inter-state tensions;
- unresolved conflicts of the Cold War era (e.g. North/South Korea; Taiwan);
- major environmental problems, migration and other non-traditional security issues (see Tan and Boutin 2001 for a comprehensive analysis);
- the absence of a broad regional security order.

Table 8.1 Alternative security concepts

Tradition and origin	Form of security	Focus	Specific emphases: what is at risk?	Threats to security
Traditional, realist-based	National	State	Sovereignty, territorial integrity	Other states (and non-state actors in post-Cold War period)
Traditional and non-traditional, realist- and liberal-based	'Social'	Notional, societal groups, class and economic focus, political action committees/interest groups	National unity, quality of life, wealth distribution	States themselves, nations, migrants, alien culture
Non-traditional, liberal-based	Human	Individuals, humankind, human rights, rule of law	Survival, human development, identity and governance	State itself, globalization, natural catastrophe and change
Non-traditional, potentially extreme	Environmental	Ecosystem	Global sustainability	Humankind: through resource depletion, scarcity, war, and ecological destruction

Source: Liotta (2002: 475, Table 1).

Table 8.2 summarizes possible areas of conflict.

Table 8.2 Conflicts in the Asia-Pacific

	Territorial and sovereignty issues	Bilateral security issues	Intra-national issues, resistance, secessionist
Northeast Asia	• Russia/Japan: competing claims to the southern Kurile Islands • Japan/Korea: Competing claims in the southern Sea of Japan • China/Taiwan: dispute regarding the legitimacy of the government of Taiwan • China/Japan: competing claims over islands in the East China Sea • China/Russia: border disputes	• Japan/North Korea: North Korea's nuclear and weapons programme • Japan/China: perceive each other as threats	• Korea unification (non-peaceful scenario) • China internal secessionist movements
Southeast Asia	• China/Vietnam: competing claims to the Paracel Islands and border disputes • China/Vietnam, Brunei, Malaysia, Philippines, Taiwan: competing claims to the Spratly Islands in the South China Sea • Indonesia/Vietnam: boundary disputes		• Philippines: Muslim and Communist insurgencies • Malaysia: Sabah separatism • Papua New Guinea: Bougainville secessionist • Indonesia/Irian Jaya: resistance

Southeast Asia	• Malaysia/Vietnam: boundary dispute on their demarcation line for the continental shelf in the South China Sea • Cambodia/Vietnam: border disputes • Philippines/Malaysia: dispute over Sabah • Malaysia/Singapore: competing claims to Pedra Branca (Pulau Batu Putih) Island • Malaysia/Indonesia: competing claims to the Celebes sea islands – resolved in December 2002* • Malaysia/Thailand: border disputes • Malaysia/Vietnam: boundary disputes on their offshore demarcation line • Thailand/Myanmar: border disputes	• Aceh: independence movement • Moluccas: violence between Muslims and Christians • Myanmar: pro-democracy, communist insurgency, secessionism
South Asia	• Myanmar/Bangladesh: border disputes • China/India: border disputes • India/Pakistan: competing claims over the legitimate government of Kashmir; border disputes • Bangladesh/India: border disputes	

* The International Court of Justice (ICJ) based in The Hague, the Netherlands, ruled in December 2002 that Malaysia has the full sovereignty over two tiny islands, Sipadan and Ligitan, thus shutting down the protracted territorial disputes between Indonesia and Malaysia.

Sources: Ball and Kerr (1995: 42, Table 4.1) (the original list is also available at http://www.lib.adfa.edu.au/military/info_guides/territoral_ea.htm); Flamm (1997: 21); Umbach (2002: 36–45).

Regional flashpoints in Northeast Asia: Taiwan and Korea

Possibly the two most volatile hotspots in the Asia-Pacific are the Taiwan Strait and the Korean Peninsula, areas where problems date back to the late 1940s.

China and Taiwan

> *Box 8.1* China and the security of the Asia-Pacific: key issues
>
> *The impact of September 11*
>
> • For all the goodwill created by China's co-operation against terrorism, distrust survives on both sides, Washington and Beijing, and could again result in rather problematic if not hostile relations. According to James B. Steinberg, director of the Brookings Institution's Foreign Policy Program, 'there has been some highlighting between the United States and China of the co-operation on terrorism,

but that has been more symbolic than substantive. And we are beginning to see traditional issues come back on the agenda' (quoted in *White House Weekly*, 9 April 2002: 'China policy reverts to pre-Sept 11').

- Richard Bush, the unofficial US ambassador to Taipei, defined the limits of co-operation in a 28 January 2002 speech in which he ruled out concessions over Taiwan in return for Beijing's support for the war on terrorism: 'And some of you may be worried that Beijing may try to play upon American gratitude in order to extract political concessions for Taiwan', he said. 'Let me assure you as categorically as I can: It could not happen' (*Far Eastern Economic Review*, 14 February 2002, p. 27).
- Likewise Chinese officials have reminded their American counterparts that 'Anti-Terrorism is not our top priority. Taiwan is our top priority' (quoted in *Far Eastern Economic Review*, 14 February 2002, p. 28).
- In March 2002, the Bush Administration faulted China (and other US allies in its war on terror) in its first worldwide human rights report. The report accuses China of using September 11 as a pretext for further crackdowns on Muslim Ulighurs. The document, which is supposed to serve as a guide for policy decisions, has been described as part of an overall US commitment to human rights that requires fighting governmental abuses as well as terrorist attackers.

The issue of non-proliferation
- China and the US argue over a bilateral non-proliferation agreement signed during the last days of the Clinton Administration in November 2000. At issue is whether the agreement binds China to cancel contracts made before that date, whether Chinese entities have made shipments of missile-related items since then and when China will unveil a missile-export control regime, which it committed to in the agreement.
- China has allegedly shipped missile components and equipment that could be used to produce chemical weapons to Iran, Pakistan and – before 1990 – to Iraq.
- Over the past ten years or so, Beijing is said to have sold at least US$1 billion worth of arms to the Myanmar regime.

The development of China's military power
- 'The development of China's military power and the response to it of India and Japan are likely to put pressure on the chain of America's friends and allies in the long littoral extending between South Korea and Taiwan in the north to the ASEAN countries and Australia in the south' (Dibb 2001).
- China might be able to built naval forces capable of partially restricting or even denying the American forces' freedom of naval movement.
- China's White Paper *The One-China Principle and the Taiwan Issue* of February 2000 has contributed to intense speculation about China's military aims. The document harshly criticizes Taiwan's political leadership and changes the terms under which Beijing will use military force against Taiwan.

Since 1949, the governments of Taiwan or the Republic of China (ROC) and the People's Republic of China (PRC) have both claimed to be the only legitimate governments of the whole of China. Until 1972, the ROC's claim was fully endorsed by the US, and the ROC was a key factor in the whole anti-communist containment strategy. The serious nature of the US commitment became evident in 1954–55. In July 1954 the Chinese media began to proclaim the intention to 'liberate' Taiwan, and kept up heavy artillery bombardment of Taiwanese offshore islands through the winter, while the US dispatched a naval task force to the area. In 1955, the US threatened explicitly to use tactical nuclear weapons in the event of a Chinese assault on Taiwan, after which the PRC government defused the situation. Chinese bombardment was resumed in 1958, and again was met by a very determined US response. This crisis is thought to have been one of the catalysts for the Sino-Soviet split: the Chinese leadership were deeply angered that Khrushchev would not risk confrontation with the US in support of Beijing's claim to Taiwan.

However, after the Nixon–Mao agreements of the early 1970s, the US recognized the government in Beijing, which led to a rapid deterioration in Taiwan's international position as it was removed from the UN, and lost diplomatic recognition by almost all foreign governments. Its isolation was intensified because both Taiwan and Beijing refused to have diplomatic relations with any state that recognized its rival. Many nations followed the Americans in handling this problem: from 1972 to 1979, they maintained formal diplomatic ties with Taiwan, and quasi-diplomatic ones with Beijing; from 1979 until now, the formal ties are with Beijing, and relations with Taiwan are conducted through a number of semi-official offices, institutes, councils, delegations etc., which in effect conduct diplomatic business.

In the 1980s, relations between the two states appeared to be improving. Neither government relented on its basic policy, but economic contacts increased dramatically, mainly through indirect trade and investment from Taiwan into south China, filtered through Hong Kong. During the relatively calm period of the 1980s and early 1990s, Taiwan also sought to improve its international position. Its principal resource was its enormously successful economy, which to some extent could compensate for its political weakness. It began to upgrade its commercial, quasi-governmental offices in many countries, especially the US. Another tactic was to join international organizations, from which the PRC had previously excluded it at all costs (for example, the Asian Development Bank, Asia-Pacific Economic Co-operation or APEC). It is a very high priority for Taiwan to continue its search for at least some form of diplomatic recognition and international protection. It is extremely keen to develop its role in organizations like APEC, and would like to enhance relations with ASEAN. A major step towards the goal of a more prominent international role was Taiwan's admission into the WTO (under the name of Chinese Taipei) which came into effect on 1 January 2002 following China's accession a few weeks earlier. Overall Taipei's foreign policy has been based on a strong national defence against invasion by the PRC, and on flexible, informal and difficult attempts to upgrade its diplomatic status.

The US and other Western countries have continued to sell military equipment to Taiwan, whose booming economy allowed it to become one of the most powerful states in East Asia; despite improving relations with the PRC, and an apparently peaceful international environment, Taipei insisted on maintaining a very high level of military preparedness. This proved to be a wise precaution, because since the mid-1990s, Beijing has increasingly become vocal and aggressive towards the ROC, in contrast to its conciliatory behaviour of the late 1980s. There may be several reasons for this. Partly, the old generation of CCP leaders was retiring from politics, and they felt deeply frustrated at their lack of success over Taiwan, which in many respects had outdone China itself. They felt that the much higher standard of living on Taiwan, coupled with a reasonably democratic polity, reflected poorly on the achievements of the PRC. But most important, they were alarmed by the growth of a strong independence movement on Taiwan, which asserted itself in various ways: increasing assertion of Taiwanese relations around the world and demands for complete secession from China and the formation of a new nation state.

Consequently in March 1996, Beijing authorized highly provocative and aggressive military exercises just outside Taiwanese waters, with warnings that any further moves towards independence would be met with an invasion. Since then the warning has been repeated on various occasions. Most people viewed this threat relatively seriously, even believing that China would destroy its own economic development to prevent Taiwanese independence. The PRC's increasingly aggressive rhetoric continues to threaten Taiwan's future. The main worry for Taiwan is whether the US will remain as committed to its security in the twenty-first century as it was in the previous one. For this reason, one can anticipate that Taiwan will for the medium term continue to support one of the largest, most modern, and best equipped armed forces in Asia. As well as its overseas purchases, it has developed a major national defence industry, capable of building missiles and guided missile frigates that are at least a generation ahead of the PRCs.

Reducing tension with the PRC: long-term merger

There is a more optimistic scenario in the long term: that Taipei and Beijing could produce some kind of agreement along the 'one country, two systems' model, that was in fact developed by Beijing with reference to Taiwan before being applied to Hong Kong. The Taipei government at various times responded with counter-suggestions, such as 'one country, two governments' or 'one country, two areas', and with the suggestion that the state of civil war should be formally ended. The Chinese government and many neutral observers are optimistic that the ever-increasing economic co-operation between China and Taiwan would inevitably lead to a political reconciliation, presumably one that would allow both sides to retain face and dignity and postponing the most difficult decisions until a very distant future. The PRC is Taiwan's most important trade partner, top destination for FDI and the most important source of Taiwan's trade surplus.

From the PRC's perspective the current situation looks as follows:

> Beijing's long-standing threat to use military force if the island declares independence is still there, but mainland officials are at pains to downplay it: 'We will do anything and everything we could to pursue peaceful reunification,' [a Chinese government] official said, adding that any effort to force China to use military means to attain reunification 'is not so easy.' He said China was committed to stable cross-strait relations both for their own sake and for the sake of good relations with Washington, which Beijing sees as the key to its dreams of reunification and continued modernization.
>
> (*Far Eastern Economic Review*, 6 February 2003, p. 6)

However, Taiwan is wary of greater engagement with the PRC and remains sceptical of Beijing's intentions. As Chien-min Caho, a Taiwanese scholar, puts it,

> Concerns were raised when Chen Shui-bian of the Democratic Progressive Party (DPP) was elected President of Taiwan in March 2000, because of his pro-independence stand. On the eve of the election, Chinese Premier Zhu Rongji warned Taiwan voters

to think twice before casting their ballots for the 'candidate of independence' lest they regret it afterwards. [Since then] relations across the Taiwan Strait have seemingly been stabilized. . . . Yet the relatively calm facade can hardly conceal the tensions beneath. While commenting on the results of the election, a spokesman from Beijing's Office of Taiwan Affairs reiterated the old policy that Chen and his administration would have to return to the 'one China' principle before contacts could be resumed between the two.

(2003: 125)

The Korean Peninsula

By the seventh century, Korea had evolved into a unified state that persisted until the end of the Second World War. Because of this history and ethnic unity, the division of Korea along the 38th parallel in 1945 represents a traumatic separation. There is no historical justification for the division of Korea and it is not based on language, culture, ethnicity or natural geography. And the decision to divide the country along the 38th parallel was arbitrary, if not absurd. Following Japan's surrender on 15 August 1945, John J. McCloy of the State-War-Navy Coordinating Committee (SWNCC) directed two young colonels, Dean Rusk and Charles H. Bonesteel, to withdraw to an adjoining room and find a place to divide Korea in thirty minutes. Despite the fact that two distinct states have emerged (Republic of Korea/ROK in the south and the Democratic People's Republic/DPRK in the north) and the death of 4 million Koreans during the civil war (1950–53) Koreans on either side of the demilitarized zone still identify the country as one 'nation'. Roland Bleiker, however, takes a more critical view:

> In contrast to this mythical homogeneity we find the reality of half a century of political division, during which the two Koreas have developed identities that are not only distinct, but also articulated in direct and stark opposition against each other. Over the years these antagonistic forms of identity have become so deeply entrenched in societal consciousness that the current politics of insecurity appears virtually inevitable. It is the tension between these two contradictory aspects of Korea politics – the strong myth of homogeneity and the actual reality of oppositional identity practices – that contains the key to understanding both the sources of the existing conflict and the potential for a more peaceful peninsula.

(2001: 121)

Like Taiwan, the ROK has to take account of an ever-present military threat, invasion from the North. Following the Korean War, the US signed an ROK–US Mutual Defense Treaty, according to which US troops would be stationed in the ROK (in the 1980s and early 1990s there were typically around 50,000), for which the ROK would make a substantial payment. While many Koreans accept the need for this, it has also been unpopular. A US commander is, in effect, in charge of ROK forces, and the ROK courts have only limited jurisdiction over the US military. Many Koreans would prefer to see the US forces downgraded if not withdrawn. Also, many Koreans resent support given to unpopular dictators by the US. In the early 1990s, US forces were in fact slightly reduced.

Among the most decisive problems in North–South relations are the bankruptcy and unpredictable state of the North Korean regime. Reports suggest that the economy is so weak that there are serious food shortages, and that it may be almost impossible to continue as a viable unit for much longer. Although in July 2002 the DPRK introduced a number of important economic changes, including first steps towards the decentralization of economic planning, scope and impact of the reform programme are as difficult to determine as the overall policy goals and intentions of the ruling elite. One scenario put forward is that in desperation the DPRK may launch an attack on South Korea, something that has been threatened for many years. Another issue that may provoke international conflict is North Korean failure to adhere to international norms, and pressure, concerning the production of nuclear weapons: a nuclear stand-off brought the Peninsula to the brink of war in 1994. However, the crisis was resolved following a series of meetings between the US and DPRK which resulted in the Geneva Agreed Framework (1994). Under this non-proliferation agreement North Korea promised to freeze its nuclear programme. In return the US agreed to develop North Korea's civilian nuclear power capabilities by providing two 1,000-megawatt light-water reactors. Furthermore, Washington gave formal assurances against the use of the threat of nuclear weapons against North Korea and agreed to take steps to lift economic sanctions and to improve political relations. The Korean Peninsular Energy Development Organization (KEDO) was founded to co-ordinate and implement the provisions of the Agreed Framework. KEDO is an international organization comprising thirteen member states with South Korea, Japan, the US and the European Union at the core (see also Chapter 7 on relations between the European Union and the Asia-Pacific). However, a new crisis began in October 2002 when North Korea acknowledged its secret nuclear weapons programme and re-started its nuclear reactor in February 2003. The five-megawatt reactor at the Yongbyon nuclear complex could produce enough plutonium for three warheads every two years, according to US sources. Pyongyang is believed already to have one or two nuclear bombs, and may have extracted plutonium from 8,000 spent nuclear fuel rods to build more. In addition North Korea has threatened to test a bomb. The nuclear stand-off between Pyongyang, Washington and Seoul has not shown any signs of a quick resolution. The US administration has made it clear that it did not want to engage in any bilateral negotiations with the DPRK and favoured a multilateral approach instead. One aspect of the Korean situation is that it gives some leverage to China as Beijing appears to be the only state with some influence in Pyongyang, which is otherwise almost completely isolated diplomatically. China's role has been instrumental in organizing 'Six-Party Talks' that took place in Beijing in August 2003 with the participation of North and South Korea, the US, China, Japan and Russia. Although no agreement was reached, the Six-Party Talks are likely to continue and are widely seen as the most promising route to a peaceful solution to the nuclear stand-off.

Long-term goal of reunification

To this day the Korean Peninsula represents the Cold War's final frontier with a total of 2 million troops on either side of the demilitarized zone. In his inaugural speech in February 1998, then President Kim Dae-jung called for a new approach towards the North. The new strategy, initially termed the 'sunshine policy', centred on the idea of moving from 'a deeply entrenched politics of containment towards a more active engagement that promotes "reconciliation and co-operation between the South and the North" ' (Bleiker 2001: 130). The president's initiative resulted in the historic summit between the two heads of state, Kim Dae-jung and Kim Jong-il in June 2000, which 'signalled the beginning of the end of the 50-year-long cold war on the Korean Peninsula' (Yong-Chool Ha 2000: 30). After years of refusing to deal over nuclear and other North–South matters with anyone but the US, on the ground that South Korea's leaders were just America's 'puppets', the summit signalled North Korea's acceptance of South Korea as a legitimate – and equal – partner. Equally important was the change of rhetoric that has accompanied the new summit diplomacy. No longer was Kim Jong-il described in negative terms as a 'brutal, insane, licentious and impetuous drunk and playboy'. Instead, shortly before the summit Kim Dae-jung referred to the North Korean head of state as 'a pragmatic leader with good judgement and knowledge', a move that initially created a major political storm (Bleiker 2001: 126).

In September of the same year Kim won the Nobel Peace Prize for his continuous efforts of bringing the North and the South closer together. Kim's revolutionary approach also motivated the Clinton Administration to modify US policies towards the Korean Peninsula. *The Perry Report* (1999), the central document in this respect, called for a 'fundamental review of US policy towards Pyongyang' (North Korea Policy Review Team 1999). After a series of bilateral high-level meetings in 2000 and 2001, however, the process of *rapprochement* has slowed down. Although the new South Korean President Roh Moo-hyun is committed to the sunshine policy, the approach has come to a halt due to the nuclear crisis.

Flashpoints in Southeast Asia

Unlike Northeast Asia where the security agenda is still dominated by traditional threat perceptions, the situation in Southeast Asia is increasingly characterized by intertwined hard and soft security issues. As Collins summarizes:

> the financial crisis of 1997–1998 had not only an economic impact on the region, but also political ramifications, most spectacular in Indonesia where it brought to an end the thirty-year rule of Suharto's New Order regime. Since 1997, other security issues have come to [the] fore. In the environment sector, the forest fires in Indonesia have created security problems, in terms of both health and lost tourist revenues, and led to diplomatic squabbles between states. The region is home to a host of other nontraditional security problems, such as drug trafficking, human trafficking (slavery), and organized crime . . .
>
> (2003: 1)

Not all of these security challenges can be discussed in detail in this part which will primarily focus on local tensions and the South China Sea dispute as the potentially most explosive international conflict in the region.

Local tensions

Local tensions and conflicts within countries are likely to be highly damaging to the participants, and possibly to neighbours who may suffer from spillover.

Insurgency movements where politically inspired groups seek to overthrow national governments by armed struggle: examples in the past decade have been the communist movement in the Philippines, and, perhaps the most destructive, the Khmer Rouge in Cambodia until about 1997. China perceives its national security to lie with the 'Balkanization' of Indo-China, i.e. it would probably prefer to see Indo-China weakened and split into numerous warring factions, rather than allow Vietnam to be a clear regional hegemon. It is not impossible that China would back more insurgencies in Indo-China to curtail Vietnamese power. At the same time Vietnam–China relations have significantly improved since the two states re-established diplomatic ties in 1991.

Box 8.2 Communist insurgencies in the Philippines

When the Communist Party of the Philippines (CPP) entered a period of steep decline in the late 1980s and subsequently factionalized due to internal power struggles, the communist insurgency movement no longer seemed to pose a critical threat to the government in Manila. By the mid-1990s the CPP and its armed wing, the New People's Army (NPA), were in disarray because of a lack of funds and successful counter-operations by the Philippine government. However, in 2002 the US designated the CPP/NPA as a Foreign Terrorist Organization. What is the history of the guerrilla movement and how can its re-emergence be explained?

The communist insurgency movement in the Philippines is one of the most resilient in the world. Various Marxist organizations emerged in the countryside soon after the Philippines had achieved independence in July 1946. The *Huk* rebellion of 1950 posed the most critical challenge to the young Philippine government when the *Hukbong Mapagpalaya ng Bayan* (People's Liberation Army) threatened to enter Manila. The *Huks* were eventually defeated but communism was not. In 1968 José María Sisón, a student leader at the University of the Philippines, formed a new Philippine Communist Party along Maoist lines. In March of the following year a military arm of the party, the NPA, was established with the aim of overthrowing the government through protracted guerrilla warfare. The movement quickly became the largest in the ASEAN region. By the time President Ferdinand Marcos was ousted in 1986, the communists controlled some 20 per cent of the villages and urban neighbourhoods in the Philippines. The success of the CPP/NPA was mainly the result of economic decay, increasing mass poverty, and the repressive, corrupt and exclusionary politics of the Marcos regime. The fight for radical political change has been extremely violent. Over the past three decades more than 40,000 people were killed due to the communist insurgency. Post-1986 events saw the CPP and its wings rapidly losing popular support partly due to internal conflicts and subsequent splits within the party. However, the movement regained strength a few years ago. According to estimates, the CPP/NPA have nearly 12,000 members, twice as many as in the mid-1990s. Part of the problem is the government's inability to contain the communist threat at the negotiation table. Peace talks between the government and the NPA, which started in 1992, have suffered from regular setbacks and failed to produce a peace accord.

Even more than in the case of Abu Sayyaf (see Chapter 2 on the US), however, it is increasingly difficult to determine whether acts of terror committed by communist groups do really follow any ideological pattern or are rather money-generating activities. The US State Department admitted in a 1999 report, 'distinguishing between political and criminal motivation for many of the terrorist-related activities in the Philippines was difficult'. As in other countries – Latin America certainly comes to mind – decades of insurgency movements have produced 'full-time' guerrillas who survive on robbery, extortion of so-called revolution taxes and kidnapping. Even if the government and the NPA succeeded in reaching a peace accord one day – as unlikely as it seems today – it would not solve the problem of bandit groups generated by the disintegration of the NPA. Movements such as the *Alex Boncayo Brigade* or the *Merlito Glor Command* would not follow any order 'to give up the so-called armed struggle . . . and will continue to terrorize the countryside', suggests a *Manila Times* editorial.

Ethnic and religious disturbances are a constant worry in countries where populations are so mixed. Among potential victims are the overseas Chinese communities in Malaysia and Indonesia which suffered enormously during race riots and even massacres during the 1960s, and again in the 1990s. Another factor is Islamic fundamentalism, and more recently terrorism, which used to be relatively low-key in the region but which has now increasingly come to the forefront in Indonesia, Southern Thailand and the Southern Philippines.

Box 8.3 The issue of Islamic fundamentalism in Indonesia

On 12 October 2002 the radical Islamic group Jemaah Islamiah ('Islamic Community') committed a bomb attack on a nightclub on the Indonesian island of Bali killing about 200 people. The United States and some Asian countries had long been concerned about Indonesia's vulnerability to Muslim militarism. For example, Singapore's elder statesman Lee Kuan Yew warned that the people of Southeast Asia were exposed to a continuing security risk because the ringleaders of extremist cells roamed freely in Indonesia. Indonesia has a long history of conflicts involving religious groups dating back to the days of Dutch colonialism. One of the hot spots of communal violence has been Aceh, the northern-most province of Sumatra. After a long history of confronting the colonial masters, the Acehnese first enthusiastically supported Indonesian nationalism and independence. However, when it became apparent that Aceh would not be granted a certain degree of autonomy within the Republic of Indonesia, political and social unrest soon took hold. Aceh became the seat of a Muslim-inspired rebellion known as Darul Islam ('House of Islam'). It rapidly extended its activities into Java and profoundly challenged the secular, unitary state. Although the rebellious movement was finally defeated in 1962, Darul Islam's legacy has lived on.

During the New Order regime of President Suharto (1966–98) hard-line Islamic groups were perceived as a threat to political stability and the fragile process of nation-building, and became a major target of state surveillance and repression. While the pluralistic environment of post-Suharto Indonesia has opened a window of opportunity for the emergence of Islam as a prominent political force, the democratic elections of 1999 and 2004 did not give any indication of a far-reaching Islamization or even radicalization of Indonesian politics. Despite the existence of radical groups such as *Laskar Jihad* ('Holy War Warriors'), *Pembela Islam* ('Islamic Defender Front') or the Indonesian Mujahedin Council Indonesia is unlikely to see the radicalization of moderate Islamic organizations or to go the same way as Algeria or Egypt, for several reasons:

- Unlike in the Arabic world, there is generally little tendency towards religious fanaticism among the Javanese who form the majority of the Indonesian population. Javanese are traditionally open in their personal approach to religion, even polytheistic according to some, rather than adhering to a conservative or fundamentalist Islam.

- Although some new urban Muslim leaders seem to be orientated towards Saudi Arabia and Pakistan in their concept of Islam, most influential Islamic leaders and scholars are more inclined to Western culture, partly because of their US-based education, and believe in a dynamic and progressive Islam. Among them are former President Abdurrahman Wahid, chairman of *Nahdlatul Ulama* (NU) from 1984 to 1999; Amien Rais, a leading Muhammadiyah figure and currently speaker of the People's Consultative Assembly (MPR); intellectual Deliar Noer; or scholar Syafei Maarif. They and many others have had a decisive impact on Indonesia's return to democracy. While elsewhere in the Islamic world – Egypt is a case in point – liberal thinkers and moderate institutions are often isolated, Indonesia's moderate Islamic groups and their leaders are the very visible and highly respected key voices in any debate on religion.

- Any attempts to change the secular nature of the Indonesian nation have failed. For example, the Indonesian parliament rejected a proposal to pass a constitutional amendment that would have allowed the full imposition of the Sharia on Indonesian Muslims.

- As a result of secularism, Indonesia is more sensitive to gender rights than most other countries with Muslim majorities. There is a strong opposition towards any moves that could jeopardize the modern status of women in society.

Some radical groups might have found it useful to ride the global jihad bandwagon and it is not impossible that they have received financial support from Al-Qaeda. On balance, however, their agendas tend to be local rather than international.

The South China Sea disputes

In the previous sections, mention was made of the predominance of ethnic and religious tensions. While this tends to remain a serious issue within the countries concerned, and can spill over into neighbouring areas, a more likely cause of armed conflict *between states* is control over shipping lanes, or territories that impinge upon them, such as the Taiwan Strait, the Straits of Malacca and so on. It is of particular concern to Japan and the US to keep all these lanes open and free from conflict, to allow their massive import/export shipments. Almost all Pacific nations are therefore increasing the strength of their navies, and are alert to any incursions from foreign powers.

This concern about shipping lanes is greatly exacerbated in the South China Sea (SCS) by an additional factor – the reserves of oil close to the Spratly Islands, which are thought to provide a serious risk of armed conflict. The Spratlys are a collection of mostly barren coral reefs, atolls and sand bars – many of which disappear at high tide – which cover an area of some 70,000 square miles. This area is claimed, in whole or in part, by China, Taiwan, Vietnam, Malaysia, Brunei and the Philippines. The other major area of dispute in the

South China Sea concerns the Paracels, which are claimed by China and Vietnam. With the exception of Brunei, all of the disputants maintain a military presence on some of the islands. Although a resolution of the disputes is not in sight, a first step towards a peaceful settlement could be the 'ASEAN Declaration on the South China Sea' of 1992, which was also signed by China in 2002 (see Chapter 5 on ASEAN). Furthermore, Vietnam signed a land border treaty with China in 1999, and another treaty on the demarcation of the Gulf of Tonkin in 2000. Although the latter has not yet been completely implemented, these treaties have narrowed down the scope of territorial disputes at least between these two countries relating to the Paracel and Spratly archipelagos.

Cases for conflict and conflict avoidance

Arguments for conflict

The period since the late 1990s has seen some potential conflicts developing into actual conflict – East Timor, Aceh, Ambon in Indonesia; tension in Malaysia; North Korean missiles over Japan, to mention just a few. Arguments for further escalation of conflict in the near future tend to be based on the following considerations:

- *Lack of strong unitary regional security network*; low level of institutionalization and binding legal agreements.
- *Prevalence of weak states* (marked by domestic instability, itself caused by economic disparities, political problems, ethnic tensions can spill over and become a source of regional tension).
- *Lack of mature democracies* (apart from Japan, the region is made up mainly of new democracies or else authoritarian regimes): studies have shown that while democracies tend not to go to war with each other, fragile democracies may be more likely to go to war.
- *Asymmetrical development*, i.e. North–South issues: poor states versus rich states (promotes intra-regional tension); economic interdependence might promote more, not less, friction; less transparency than in the West; potential for trade friction due to the competition for the same markets etc., labour migration is a potential source of tension.
- *Unresolved pre-Cold War conflicts*: traditional ethnic/religious rivalries that can spill over into neighbouring states to involve members of same ethnic/religious background.
- *Rapid increase in military expenditure* in contrast to reverse trends in the West.

Annual defence expenditures in Asia have increased significantly since the end of the Cold War. It should be noted that they had been doing so in the 1970s and 1980s too, but the trend became more marked (and more alarming to Western observers) in the 1990s given Asia's growing economic development and, perhaps more importantly, the fact that in the West the trend was towards arms reduction and a preference for negotiation and prevention. Defence budgets were being concentrated not only on the development of conventional arms but also on indigenous weapons and systems, the purchase of weapons of mass destruction (chemical/nuclear), the development of power projection capabilities (China and Singapore) and of high-tech weaponry (Japan, Taiwan harnessing technology already being developed in other domestic industries). The build-up of arms was fuelled not only by the success of the Asian economies but also by increasing competition and sales pressure among Western arms manufacturers. China's armaments programme was pushed forward by generals who were desperately worried by the US success in the Gulf in 1991. They persuaded Chinese leaders that China urgently needed a new generation of weaponry, which was partly purchased from the West, partly home-produced and partly purchased cheaply from Russia.

Various reasons can be cited to explain the arms build-up:

- regional instabilities still exist in the post-Cold War order, and there is a greater need for self-reliance;
- need to ensure maritime routes safe;
- need to access oil/gas/fisheries;
- uncertainty about the long-term role of the US.

In 2002, among the ten states with the largest defence budgets worldwide, three were from the Asia-Pacific region: Japan (2nd), China (5th), and South Korea (10th). Overall, however, mainly as a result of the Asian crisis and its long-term implications, defence spending in the Asia-Pacific has slowed over the past five years – with the notable exception of the US and China.

Arguments for peace / conflict avoidance

While there is potential for conflict, there is also cause for optimism. For example, there has been some partial resolution or at least preliminary discussion on some of the potential sources of concern in the region. China has begun to discuss the Spratly Islands issue in multilateral forums and some bilateral tensions have been eased (e.g., China–Russia border disputes, Celebes Island disputes between Malaysia and Indonesia). One could argue that:

1   Increased economic integration constrains conflict (the liberal view). For example, 'countries that trade with each other are less likely to go to war'; armed conflict would be too costly.

2   The political leaderships' primary security concern is to maintain domestic stability and economic prosperity (and thereby their own power/influence) and conflict would be detrimental to these interests.

3   Universal (inevitable?) trend towards democratization and pluralism, therefore greater prospects for peace.

4   Although arms build-up has taken place, it is wrong to conceive it as a *'competitive arms race'*. Arms build-up need not lead to conflict and should be understood in terms of 'catching up'; the need to acquire technology to defend 200-mile EEZs (exclusive economic zones); the need to hedge against uncertainty, to enhance national prestige; acquire arms technology for civilian applications etc.

5   There has been an increase in dialogue and co-operation, or an increase in official and informal multilateral dialogues.

6   The US maintains its presence and alliances with Japan and ROK and acts as a balancer in regional security, prevents escalation of tension (see the chapters on the US and Japan).

7   There have been improvements in bilateral relationships (especially in Northeast Asia) but also across former ideological divides China and Russia, Vietnam, India, North Korea, Indonesia and Singapore; Moscow and South Korea, US and North Korea.

Table 8.3 Defence expenditures in the Asia-Pacific, 1998–2002 (in billion US$, at constant 2000 prices and exchange rates, and percentage of GDP)

Rank	Country	1998		1999		2000		2001		2002	
		(bn) US$	% of GDP	(bn) US$	% of GDP	(bn) US$	% of GDP	(bn) US$	% of GDP	(bn) US$	% of GDP
1	USA	289	3.1	290	3.0	302	3.1	304	3.1	336	3.1
2	Japan	45.4	1.0	45.5	1.0	45.8	1.0	46.3	1.0	46.7	1.0
3	China*	17.8	1.7	20.7	1.9	23.0	2.1	26.3	2.1	31.1	2.3
4	South Korea	12.4	3.1	12.1	2.8	12.8	2.8	13.1	2.8	13.5	2.8
5	Taiwan	9.7	3.3	8.6	2.8	7.8	2.5	7.8	2.6	7.3	2.6
6	Australia	7.0	2.0	6.8	1.8	6.6	1.7	6.7	1.7	6.8	1.7
7	Myanmar	6.7	2.3	6.7	2.0	9.0	2.3	..	0.8	..	0.8
8	Singapore	4.4	5.4	4.5	5.4	4.3	4.7	4.4	5.0	4.7	5.0
9	Thailand	2.4	2.1	2.1	2.1	1.8	1.5	1.8	1.4	1.8	1.5
10	Indonesia	1.5	1.1	1.3	0.9	1.7	1.1	1.8	1.1	..	1.0
11	Malaysia	1.3	1.6	1.7	2.1	1.7	2.1	1.9	2.2	1.9	2.2
12	North Korea	1.3	..	1.3	..	1.4	..	1.4	..	1.5	25 (est.)
13	Philippines	0.8	1.2	0.8	1.1	0.8	1.1	0.8	1.0	0.9	1.5
14	New Zealand	0.6	1.3	0.7	1.3	0.7	1.3	0.6	1.3	0.6	0.9
15	Brunei	0.5	8.7	0.4	6.8	0.3	6.1	0.3	7.4	0.5	4.8
16	Cambodia	0.1	4.5	0.1	3.9	0.1	3.5	0.1	3.0	0.1	..
17	Laos	0.02	1.6	0.04	2.2	0.04	2.0	0.04	2.0	..	2.1

est. = estimated. No data available for Vietnam.
* SIPRI estimates; China's official defence budget is currently about US$20 billion.

Data sources: International Peace Research Institute (SIPRI); SIPRI Military Expenditure Database: <http://projects.sipri.se/milex/mex_data_index.html> (accessed 8 March 2004); Commonwealth of Australia (2003).

Outlook: two scenarios for regional order

The neo-realist scenario: alliances, strategic triangles and a concert of power

From a neo-realist perspective the most likely scenario for the regional order is a continuation of the bilateral alliance system centred on US primacy in the region (see Chapter 2 on the US). The US–Japan military alliance is based on agreements reached in the 1950s and 1960s, whereby the the US essentially is responsible for security in Northeast Asia, and has large numbers of troops based there (approximately 100,000 troops, 330 warplanes and 60 warships). For the time being, this gives the alliance a clear superiority in the region. There is a growing tension between the two states, however, centred on Japan's huge trade surplus with the US. There are ever-increasing voices in Washington arguing that Japan should share the defence burden by increasing its military expenditure, something that did happen in 1995. A neo-realist ideal would be a multilateral Asian defence alliance along the lines of NATO, but this has so far proved elusive.

In the long term there will probably be four leading powers in East Asia: the US, Russia, China and Japan. For the time being, however, it seems likely that Russia will be very weak because of its political chaos and feeble economy. In the medium term, then, security in the region is likely to be dominated by a 'strategic triangle' comprising the US, China and Japan.

Of these, it seems likely that the US–Japan will attempt to maintain the status quo, while China will attempt to maximize its benefits from the situation to become even more powerful, until such a time as it may become a challenger, or at least able to carve out a satisfactory sphere of influence for itself. For the time being at least, China should, logically, maintain good relations with both Japan and the US. Indeed, it may be able to benefit from any tensions between them. China is still relatively under-developed, and its leadership knows it must continue its modernization programme for several decades more, during which time it will need technology, capital investment and access to markets in the West. It should therefore also be reluctant to escalate any conflict. The dynamics of this new strategic triangle are being closely observed by academics and policy makers alike, since the way the three powers interact with each other and react to regional stimuli will to a large extent determine the stability of the region as a whole. In particular, their handling of the Taiwan issue and the 'North Korea problem' will be crucial to the peace of Northeast Asia.

If this structure was to change then a concert of power could emerge as a working alternative. One popular scenario which is discussed both by political actors and academics envisions the enlargement of the US–Japan alliance. South Korea (and maybe a future reunited Korea) and Australia are likely players in such a concert system that would give the US allies significantly more duties and responsibilities than today. However, the key question is whether China could qualify as a partner in the concert. If the answer was yes, then the Asia-Pacific could well resemble the increasingly inclusive transatlantic security structure centred on NATO.

Box 8.4 The concert of power in international relations

The origins of the concept. In 1815, at the close of the Napoleonic Wars, the Congress of Vienna laid the foundation for a European collective security order based on a system of alliances and networks, formal and especially informal negotiations, and consensus building among the foreign policy elites of the continent's leading powers: Great Britain, France, Prussia, Austria and Russia. The participants agreed to work together to monitor political-security developments and to resist aggression as well as to orchestrate collective initiatives whenever necessary. This concert of powers guaranteed a stable regional security order for almost half a century. The nineteenth century was not free of war but compared to the troubled times Europe experienced before and afterwards it was a relatively peaceful one, characterized – due to the efforts of the 'concert' – by a predictable scheme of international relations for many decades.

What is the scenario for the Asia-Pacific? Despite its eventual failure, the European concert of powers has attracted attention and been discussed as a potential model for regional and global order building. Not surprisingly, the concept was revived after the Cold War's bipolar global order came to an end. Some suggested that the time was right for a new European (or, correctly, Atlantic) 'concert' built by the United States, Russia, Britain, France and Germany. Others favoured a global concert, including the United States, Russia, the European Union, Japan and China. The discussion among academics and policy makers has also focused on whether and how an Asian-Pacific 'concert' consisting of the United States, Japan, China, Russia (and maybe a reunified Korea) could work. The long-time emergence of a concert comprising the United States, Japan, South Korea (or a reunified Korea) and possibly Australia, however, has been perceived as the most likely scenario if American pre-eminence was ever to decrease as either the result of structural changes or a more self-restrained US foreign policy.

The international relations perspective. If one considers a balance-of-power mechanism as the worst-case scenario or the baseline against which anything else is measured, then a concert-of-power instrument is worth a deeper look. Both are classical concepts of realistic thinking in international relations. Unlike the balance-of-power mechanism which is most likely to prevail ad hoc in the absence of other regulating forces, as experienced in the Asia-Pacific for centuries, a concert of powers emerges by design. In other words, while the balance-of-power model may guarantee order and security because a certain number of powers are containing each other, the 'concert' is a co-operative approach to security (not in a neoliberal sense, however, since states, usually the large ones, are the only actors involved in the 'concert').

The liberal institutionalist scenario: the emergence of multilateralism

Scenarios for multilateral institution building in the Asia-Pacific often draw on European experiences. Centuries-lasting painful experiences with unilateralism, often in combination with nationalism and fascism, have shaped a structure that *de facto* prescribes multilateralism as the only possible answer to the challenge of managing regional order in Europe. The fact that some of the institutionally most advanced multilateral organizations have flourished in Western Europe and in transatlantic relations is primarily due to a large set of shared norms and values which, in turn, have provided a solid basis for generating binding rules and procedures that effectively constrain actor behaviour. In sum, multilateral institution-building in Europe was driven by the need for West-integration *vis-à-vis* the Soviet Union during the Cold War and, equally important, the perception that co-operation among former adversaries (Germany–France, for example) was an essential contribution to peace and stability. However, we should not blind ourselves to the fact that European multilateralism in security affairs is the result of a long process which is still far from being completed. Despite a large set of shared norms and values and mostly compatible foreign policy interests it took the Western European states almost four decades from the foundation of the European Economic Community in 1957 to the first steps towards the institutionalization of a European security policy. The EU's Common Foreign and Security Policy (CFSP) came only into existence as the result of the Maastricht Treaty in 1993 while the more elaborated European Security and Defence Policy (ESDP) was born in 1999.

Given the difficulties of security co-operation in the relatively homogeneous cultural and political environment of Europe, it remains questionable whether European organizations could serve as a model for the highly heterogeneous Asia-Pacific region which is still suffering from a high degree of mistrust and lack of transparency in international relations. Among the European international organizations which have been discussed as potential models for the management of security and order in the Asia-Pacific is the Conference/Organization of Security and Co-operation in Europe (CSCE/OSCE). The ASEAN Regional Forum (ARF) which goes back to Australian, Canadian and Japanese ideas of having an Asia-Pacific Conference on Security and Co-operation was at least partially modelled after the European CSCE. In July 1993 the then six ASEAN states plus Australia, China, the EU, Japan, Laos, New Zealand, Papua New Guinea, Russia, South Korea, the United States and Vietnam launched the ARF. The forum was later joined by Cambodia, India, Myanmar, Mongolia and North Korea. The ARF's first regular working session took place in July 1994 in Bangkok. Since then the forum has met annually.

The primary objective of the ARF is to have nations of the Asia-Pacific, including potential rivals, engaged in constructive dialogue on regional security, and to build mutual trust through confidence-building measures (CBMs) etc. It is essentially an initiative 'attempting to build a level of East Asian regional identity through consultation and preventive diplomacy' (Brook 1998: 235). The significance of the ARF is that it was the first post-Cold War regional security grouping and it broke with former reliance on bilateralism, enhancing the debate about the role and impact of multilateral institutions on security in the post-Cold War era.

Box 8.5 ARF: aims and process

- Based very much on the 'ASEAN model' of regional co-operation, with the emphasis on building trust and confidence through regular and informal contacts.
- Aims – to encourage high-level consultation and dialogue to prevent misunderstandings from arising and to allay mutual fears and suspicions – preventive diplomacy.
- Method is a step-by-step process and gradual discussion of more and more sensitive issues, but moving forward at a pace which is comfortable for all members.
- Three-step process – first confidence building, then development of preventive diplomacy and finally conflict resolution.

The ARF's aim of emphasizing a gradualist, consensual approach over a legalistic, functional approach demanding legally binding treaties and agreements gains the support of most East Asian governments and means that more countries are at least willing to engage in dialogue than would otherwise be the case. China, in particular, experiencing its first official foray into a multilateral security organization (except the UN), placed particular emphasis on consensus.

Another example of multilateralism in the Asia-Pacific is KEDO. Even in view of the current crisis North Korea's periodic integration into a multilateral co-operation structure has been one of the most successful attempts to multilateral crisis solving at an advanced level in the region. The Geneva Agreed Framework of 1994, which provided North Korea a set of benefits in return for a freeze and eventually dismantlement of its nuclear weapons programme and the subsequent formation of KEDO as the organizational structure to implement the Agreed Framework, had clearly shown elements of efficient multilateral security management from 1994 until 2002. Most political actors involved in the negotiations and academic analysts alike agree that the Agreed Framework and KEDO effectively channelled and institutionalized North Korea's behaviour in the mid- and late 1990s. Had the Agreement not come into existence and North Korea continued its weapons programme in 1994, 'by now it could have produced enough separated plutonium for 60–80 nuclear weapons' (Maull and Harnisch 2002: 40). According to other sources, North Korea would have even produced by now at least 100 nuclear weapons and would likely have the capacity to produce at least thirty additional weapons each year (CSIS 2003: 5).

However, multilateralism in the Asia-Pacific has its drawbacks since neither ARF nor the Agreed Framework/KEDO nor any other multilateral forums are based on legally binding rules and treaties. Instead, existing agreements rely essentially on the goodwill of member states who are under no legally binding obligation to, for example, produce defence papers or make their processes more transparent. Furthermore, unresolved territorial disputes, deep historical suspicions, long-standing rivalries, and nationalistic tendencies all undermine the process of socialization on which the ARF is based. Perhaps one of the major achievements of the group is to engage China in a multilateral structure, and gain its agreement to discuss contentious issues (such as the Spratly Islands) with all ASEAN members, rather than at a strictly bilateral level. The ARF meetings also provide a useful venue and good opportunity to defuse tension between two governments. The key test of the ARF is whether it can deal effectively with say territorial disputes in Southeast Asia, or eventually, some of the more serious problems in Northeast Asia (China–Taiwan, North Korea). Stumbling blocks are the difficulties of co-ordinating and gaining agreement of a large, disparate group with various bilateral tensions and rivalries. Furthermore, while North Korea was admitted to the forum in 2000, Taiwan is not a member as this would be unacceptable for China.

In sum and from the perspective of IR theory, liberal institutionalists and social constructivists are optimistic that multilateral co-operation in the Asia-Pacific will contribute to the gradual emergence of a stable security order in the region: 'They believe that strong feelings of trust and community can be generated over time, thereby allowing states to avoid conflicts of interest or settle them without resorting to violence' (Garofano 2002: 503). Neo-realists, however, are less optimistic. In their view, most multilateral organizations such as the ARF or KEDO do not possess the hard power capabilities to deal with order-building in the Asia-Pacific and are largely irrelevant. According to the neo-realist perception, the management of regional order is determined by zero-sum games and the states' overriding concerns for their own security.

Acknowledgements

The author wishes to thank Caroline Rose, University of Leeds, for her valuable contributions to this chapter.

References

Ball, D. and Kerr, P. (1995) *Presumptive Engagement: Australia's Asia-Pacific Security Policy in the 1990s*, Sydney: Allen & Unwin.

Bleiker, R. (2001) 'Identity and security in Korea', *The Pacific Review*, 14: 121–48.

Brook, C. (1998) 'Regionalism and globalism', in A. McGrew and C. Brook (eds) *Asia-Pacific in the New World Order*, London: Routledge, pp. 230–45.

Chien-Min Caho (2003) 'One step forward, one step backward: Chen Shui-bian's mainland policy', *Journal of Contemporary China*, 12: 125–43.

Collins, A. (2003) *Security and Southeast Asia. Domestic, Regional, and Global Issues*, Boulder, CO: Lynne Rienner.

Commonwealth of Australia (2003) *Defence Economic Trends in the Asia-Pacific 2002*, Canberra: Department of Communications, Information Technology and the Arts.

CSIS (Center for Strategic and International Studies) (2003) *Nuclear Confrontation with North Korea: Lessons of the 1994 Crisis for Today*, Seoul, March. Online. Available HTTP: <http://www.csis.org/isp/crisis_peninsula/seoulRTtranscript.pdf> (accessed 11 November 2003).

Dibb, P. (2001) 'Strategic trends: Asia at the crossroads', *Naval War College Review*, 56: 1. Online. Available HTTP: <http://www.nwc.navy.mil/press/Review/2001/Winter/art2-w01.htm> (accessed 10 January 2003).

Flamm, D. (1997) 'Impact of China's military modernisation in the Pacific region', *Asian Defence Journal*, 2: 16–21.

Garofano, J. (2002) 'A security community for Asia? Power, institutions and the ASEAN Regional Forum', *Asian Survey*, 42: 502–21.

King, G. and Murray, C. L. (2002) 'Rethinking human security', *Political Science Quarterly*, 116: 585–610.

Liotta, P. H. (2002) 'Boomerang effect: the convergence of national and human security', *Security Dialogue*, 33: 474–88.

Maull, H. W. and Harnisch, S. (2002) 'Embedding Korea's unification multilaterally', *The Pacific Review*, 15: 29–61.

McNally, C. and Morrison, C. E. (eds) (2002) *Asia-Pacific Security Outlook 2002*, Regional overview. Online. Available HTTP: <http://www.jcie.or.jp/thinknet/outlook2002.html> (accessed 15 June 2003).

North Korea Policy Review Team (1999) *Review of United States Policy Toward North Korea: Findings and Recommendations (The Perry Report)*, Washington, DC: US State Department. Online. Available HTTP: <http://www.state.gov/www/regions/eap/991012_northkorea_rpt.html> (accessed 8 March 2004.

Tan, A. and Boutin, K. (eds) (2001) *Non-Traditional Security Issues in Southeast Asia*, Singapore: Select Books.

Umbach, F. (2002) *Konflikt oder Kooperation in Asien-Pazifik? Chinas Einbindung in regionale Sicherheitsstrukturen und die Auswirkungen auf Europa*, München: Oldenburg.

UNDP (1994) *UN Human Development Report*, New York: Oxford University Press.

Yong-Chool Ha (2000) 'South Korea in 2000', *Asian Survey*, 41: 30–9.

9 Globalization and regionalism in the Asia-Pacific

Rémy Davison

Anyone who believes that globalization can be stopped has to tell us how he would envisage stopping economic and technological progress.

(Renato Ruggiero, WTO Director-General)

Introduction

This chapter examines the impact of globalization and regionalism on the global economic and political order, as well as the role that regionalism now plays in the strategies of individual states to maintain or strengthen their positions in the global political economy. Part one examines how East Asian states have responded to the challenge of globalization, and examines the growth and development of a number of regional initiatives. Part two considers the links between economic globalization and the growth of regionalism, particularly regional organizations. Both trends may reinforce each other: the spread of globalization can inhibit the ability of the state to implement national policy preferences and, as a result, globalization may encourage the state into closer regional co-operation. In summary, the thrust of this chapter is that globalization and regionalism are integrally interdependent and mutually reinforcing.

Globalization is a relatively new term, popularized by the mass media during the 1990s. In this chapter, we focus on the political economy of globalization, and discuss how states have reacted to, and attempted to accommodate, globalization. To accomplish this, we examine the realist, liberal and neo-Marxist perspectives and also evaluate some of the more sceptical views of globalization. An important theme in this chapter is the centrality of the state: how important is the state as a political and economic actor in an era of globalization? Proponents of globalization argue that global linkages have developed to such an extent that it is no longer sufficient to speak of merely 'China' or 'Indonesia' in territorial terms. Consequently, radical commentators argue that one can no longer equate territoriality with the traditional Westphalian view of state authority; globalization has become so intensive and extensive that the state cannot reassert itself as a central actor (Ohmae 1995: xiv).

The rise of globalization

The study of globalization has become the major focus of international relations and political science research in recent years. The development of globalization presents international relations with complex and difficult issues that have an impact on a range of theoretical and conceptual concerns. One of the most fundamental of these is the shift from internationalization to globalization, what drives it and how it affects the nation state. A key concern is conceptualizing globalization as both a political and economic development, and how states respond to, and manage, the demands created by the forces of globalization. These are crucial issues in the study of international relations.

Firstly, it is important to distinguish between *global, international* and *transnational* processes. *International* transactions take place *between nations*, such as international relations, international economics and international trade. Conversely, *transnational* relations take place *across* nations. The international and the transnational appear to be almost-interchangeable terms, and often they are used in this way; many commentators use the transnational corporation (TNC) or multinational corporation (MNC) to mean one and the same thing: a corporation operating in two or more states. However, the transnational and international have at least one thing in common: they contain the word *nation*, which suggests that transactions take place at the level of the state, or *between* or *across* nations. Generally speaking, most authors understand the international to refer to interactions between states. On the other hand, transnational processes may take place at the *sub-national* level, between non-governmental organizations (NGOs), such as business networks, or human rights groups. Conversely, the *global* refers to actors (states, firms, networks, organizations) conceiving of the world in spatially and geographically planetary proportions.

Globalization is difficult to define; when we speak of 'globalization', what do we mean? Are we referring to the globalization of international finance, of production, of trade? Do we mean technology, communications and transport? Or perhaps we can speak of the globalization of culture and language? Arguably, the international environmental agenda, such as air and ocean pollution, as well as access to critical resources like water and fishing grounds, has also become not merely regional, but global in its implications. According to Keohane and Nye (2001: 2), 'For a network of relationships to be considered "global," it must include multi-continental distances, not simply regional networks'.

The problems inherent in the concept of globalization are compounded by the enormous range of definitions available (Scholte 1997). Globalization has been referred to as universalization, internationalization, Westernization, Americanization or liberalization. More radical perspectives argue that globalization represents the development of a 'borderless' world (Ohmae 1990; 1996). Irrespective of definitional difficulties, globalization represents a challenge to the traditional notion of sovereignty and its notion of exclusive jurisdiction within a state's territorial borders. However, due to a combination of forces (international capital, non-state actors, global communications, technology), the state has arguably become more porous, less autonomous and susceptible to infiltration by non-state actors. As a result, the state has been forced to accommodate the forces of globalization, to the detriment of its own policy-making autonomy. In some instances, the state has beaten a 'strategic retreat' to the relative safety of regionalism, which we discuss in the second part of this chapter. In many respects, regionalism represents a halfway house, which states employ in an attempt to control, or at least ameliorate, some of the negative effects of globalization.

Globalization: realist perspectives

Perspectives on globalization differ markedly. In previous chapters, we have discussed three key theoretical perspectives, which may be classed broadly as Realist, Liberal and neo-Marxist. These three main paradigms not only contest the significance of globalization, but whether it is accurate to describe the breakdown of traditional national borders as globalization at all. Realists assert that liberal claims of the increased levels of interconnectedness and interaction wrought by globalization is exaggerated, and that most international transactions still involve the state. Realists also argue that the management of global finance, trade and debt by intergovernmental organizations (such as the G-7, WTO and IMF) remain inherently statist institutions, dominated by the powerful states in the system.

Realists generally argue that what we are witnessing is not globalization, but the 'Americanization' of national economies and culture. For realists, this has occurred because of the US's clear military dominance since 1945 which, in turn, has fuelled the expansion of American finance, firms and culture. Realist perspectives, emphasizing US dominance, are reflected by policy makers, such as US Trade Representative (USTR), Robert Zoellick (2002):

> We will promote free trade globally, regionally and bilaterally. . . . By moving forward on multiple fronts, the United States can exert its leverage for openness, create a new competition in liberalization, target the needs of developing countries, and create a fresh political dynamic by putting free trade on to the offensive. America's trade policies are connected to our broader economic, political, and security aims.

In many respects, the realist view appears to overlap with Kindleberger's hegemonic stability theory, which argues that a hegemonic state is required to provide international public goods. These include an international monetary system, an open trading regime and military security. The US provided these goods in the form of the gold: dollar standard and the GATT regime, while also delivering military security to its allies throughout the Cold War. As a result, the US exported its financial and, to a lesser extent, its ideological system to critical areas of conflict, such as East Asia. While China, North Korea and Vietnam experienced virtual isolation from international capitalism and experimented seriously with centrally planned economies, South Korea, Japan, Taiwan, Hong Kong and the ASEAN countries were the recipients of American technology and, with the exception of Japan, significant US direct investment and loans from the American-dominated IMF and World Bank. The difference here is that hegemonic stability theorists adopt a hybrid realist–liberal position, which argues that hegemony combines military power with liberal internationalism. Conversely, realists assert that the projection of financial and ideological power flows from a state's military capabilities. With the Soviet Union's collapse in 1991, the restrictions upon US influence were far fewer and, as a result, American military and economic power expanded to global proportions during the 1990s. According to some commentators, the 1990s were characterized not by globalization, but by the emergence of the US as a *hyperpower* (Gordon 2002). The post-Cold War emergence of the US as the sole superpower gave rise to a number of influential perspectives arising out of America's global preponderance. These included Fukuyama's (1992) liberal 'end of history' thesis, and Huntington's (1996) neo-conservative prediction of a 'clash of civilizations'. In many respects, these two concepts reflected different sides of the globalization coin.

Globalization: liberal perspectives

Economic globalization largely reflects the dominant neoliberal paradigm. Generally, liberal theorists view political and economic liberalism as interlocking, complementary forces which have expanded beyond the Western world, served to democratize societies and raised living standards in a number of regions. However, liberals differ markedly in their interpretations of globalization. Keohane and Nye (2001) view the development of globalization as an opportunity to determine how the new world order will be governed. The current institutional framework, they argue, is dominated excessively by the G-7, leading to heavy-handedness, such as IMF conditionality imposed upon East Asian states in the wake of the currency crisis. Keohane and Nye (1977) refer to this as 'vulnerability interdependence' (states possess few policy tools to deal with exogenous shocks). Arguably, the extent of East Asian states' vulnerability in 1997 was exacerbated under conditions of economic globalization. The difference here is stark; whereas *economic interdependence* generally denotes mutual dependence between states, *economic globalization* reduces governments' influence to the extent that they are unlikely to be able to assert control over capital flows.

One may distinguish here between the co-operative, consensus-building liberalism of Keohane and Nye with the *economic liberals*, who, broadly speaking, dominate national government departments and international institutions, such as the World Bank, IMF and OECD. Economic liberals, such as Zoellick, advocate zero tariffs and deep cuts to agricultural subsidies to promote free trade which, economic liberals argue, results in significant welfare gains for all countries engaging in free trade. This sits uneasily with the disposition of East Asian governments to protect key industry sectors, to subsidize development, and to engage in political cronyism to the detriment of economic welfare. Michel Camdessus, the IMF chairman during the 1997 currency crisis, said that the collapse was in reality a 'blessing in disguise', as it would force closed markets open and ensure both governments and the private sector developed more prudential lending practices. East Asian states, as a result of the crisis, were compelled to accept the liberal prescriptions of the IMF. Economic liberals argue that this represents the homogenizing power of globalization, in that it sweeps away state intervention and regulation, resulting in a more 'level playing field'. Conversely, governments in the East Asian NICs saw the IMF's intervention as promoting a culture of economic dependency upon the major powers. Krugman refers to post-crisis 'fire-sale FDI', pointing to the FDI boom in affected East Asian economies, which itself was sparked by the relaxation of foreign ownership controls demanded by the IMF. Consequently, US, European and Japanese firms acquired significant assets at nominal prices, such as GM's acquisition of Daewoo, Ford's stake in Kia, and the sell-offs of Seoul Bank and Korea First Bank (Krugman 1998).

Neo-Marxist perspectives

The expanding reach of international capital, in combination with the 1997 East Asian economic crisis, has prompted some authors to rearticulate theories of dependency to accommodate the phenomenon of globalization. Wallerstein's (1979) world-systems theory predicted the development of globalization in many respects, when he argued that there was a single world economy, a single world system: the capitalist world economy. The uneven distribution of benefits of globalization has also reignited the North/South debate. Yoshihara (1988) argues that the type of growth experienced in Southeast Asia is 'technologyless growth'; that is, growth *without development*. Yoshihara points to trends in investment and technology flows which suggest that the bulk of these move primarily from North to South, while high value-added trade remains largely between developed market economies. Yoshihara argues that the consequence is globalization embeds inequalities in the world system, and global wealth may be rearranged to some extent, but not redistributed.

Cox (1996) and Gill (1990) adopt alternative neo-Marxist perspectives, arguing that international capitalism encourages the formation of a transnational capitalist class. Global elites identify similar interests (liberal–capitalist ideology; the importance of co-optition as well as competition in international business) and achieve domination through consensual bargaining (effective use of military power to ensure international stability). For Cox, this results in the development of an 'historic bloc', a coalition of like interests which govern international public and private policy, via a network of state, intergovernmental and corporate actors. Gill argues that organizations, such as the Trilateral Commission (US–Japan–EU), have successfully exported liberal capitalism, building a historic bloc and, therefore, maintaining US global hegemony.

Globalization moves beyond both the international and the transnational to describe a range of interactions which are truly global in nature. For example, international trade may only take place between a select number of states; this was the case after the Second World War, when membership of the GATT comprised predominantly the advanced industrial states, such as the US, Japan and Western European countries. However, in 1994, the GATT evolved into the WTO, which reflected its increasingly global membership. Irrespective of whether we are referring to the globalization of trade or culture, globalization suggests, implicitly, a 'borderless' world, where there is a relatively unfettered flow of goods, services, capital, labour, ideas, culture and language. Whereas international transactions may affect only a few states, the impact of globalization affects *all* states to some extent or another. In summary, then, globalization refers to the intensification of interconnectedness between a vast array of human activities; no longer are states and citizens affected only by what governments may do.

Globalization: critical perspectives

Hirst and Thompson (1996: 2) provide one of the most forceful critiques of globalization, arguing that its effects have been uneven, rather than diffuse. They critique globalization on three grounds: firstly, that the 'new' global economy differs little from the 'previous' model; secondly, that the internationalization of production does not automatically suggest that global market forces have gained some form of autonomy; and, thirdly, that globalization itself represents a break in a historical continuum, a unique development which will persist well into the future. Hirst and Thompson contend that globalization's impact has been restricted largely to the industrial 'North', with only some aspects penetrating East Asia and South America, and that it has not infiltrated Central Asia and Africa to any significant extent. Hirst and Thompson also assert that it has been firms predominantly from the industrialized North, such as the US, Japan and Western Europe, which have dominated the internationalization of finance and production. Although some South Korean *chaebols* emerged as some of the world's top 200 firms during the 1990s, this trend proved short-lived, and Northern firms have reasserted their dominance, particularly since the 1997 East Asian crisis.

Hirst and Thompson assert that the state has not surrendered key areas of sovereignty to the forces of globalization; rather, they argue that the state can still assert its power in areas such as preventing or restricting population flows. While states have encouraged some trends, such as increased flows of foreign investment and trade, they also preserve their ability to impose restrictions on these flows. For example, during the 1997 crisis, the Malaysian government placed restrictions on short-term speculative investments which had wrought severe damage upon the economy. In addition, the Malaysian government also switched off a critical communications satellite's transmissions; as a result, pictures of clashes between rioters and police could not be transmitted to foreign television networks. In this context, Hirst and Thompson argue that the internationalization of capital and communications opens up a new type of space which exists *alongside*, but does not *displace* the sovereign state.

Even some liberal commentators are sceptical about some of the more radical claims made about globalization, such as homogenization, universality, equality or global integration. As Keohane and Nye (2001: 2) argue, '[Globalization] does not imply either homogenization or equity . . . an integrated world market would mean free flows of goods, people and capital, and convergence in interest rates. That is far from the facts'. Keohane and Nye even eschew the term 'globalization', arguing that 'globalization' and 'deglobalization' merely represent an increase or decline in 'globalism'.

A number of theorists also argue that the negative impact of globalization has been restricted largely to the global South (Evans 1987; Haggard and Cheng 1987). Critics of globalization contend that liberalizing reforms associated with globalization benefit the already powerful, widening disparities between North and South. Although Northern economies have experienced some negative effects, such as manufacturing unemployment as industrial production has shifted to the South, this has been offset to a large degree by the development of tertiary industries in the North which have created new areas of employment.

The diffuse impact of globalization

A key characteristic of globalization is its centrifugal force that appears to draw states inexorably into a web of economic and financial interconnectedness. Major powers are not immune; while they may have the option of remaining outside a system, their capacity to do so indefinitely may be limited, and the transaction costs may be high. An example of this was China's quest to obtain permanent MFN status in the WTO. To some extent, this represents the centrifugal force of the global trading system; it was too costly for China to remain outside the WTO, as it sought to deploy an export-oriented industrialization strategy to ensure high rates of growth, as well as economic development. This demonstrates, realists argue, American dominance of the global trading regime, as well as the ability of US Congress to accord or deny China MFN status. Although realists claim this gives US administrations a strategic advantage over China, liberals would reply that China's importance to global manufacturing and trade is such that the US has been locked into China's economic success; American firms have developed a significant dependence on unrestricted access to the huge variety of cheap consumer goods and manufacturing components exported from China. As a result, the US has been drawn into the web of globalization as well, and the costs it would incur by withdrawing would be considerable, if not insurmountable. This does not mean that globalization has resulted in a 'borderless world'; it does mean that restrictions upon states' domestic and foreign policy autonomy are heavily influenced by exogenous events beyond their capacity to predict or control. Woods (2001) argues this means that, 'The loss of autonomy associated with globalization falls unevenly with powerful states better able to insulate themselves. . . . Those states that are able to resist "internationalization" will emerge far more powerful than those that fail to do so'.

Over US$1 trillion in foreign exchange is traded daily, which exceeds the total paid-up capital of all IMF members. Bank computers now operate 24/7, monitoring market trends and buying and selling currencies, shares and bonds, even while traders are absent. As Mahathir (2001) noted,

> [Speculators] do not work in concert of course. Nor do they enter a conspiracy. But they do behave like herds. Thus when one of the more important members swing in one direction, the others will follow. The effect is not unlike acting in concert . . .

Programmed to follow market trends, bank computers respond to panic selling in the market, which can lead to an electronic frenzy of activity across the globe. Automated trading is merely one recent technological advance, which was certainly not available to financial institutions prior to the 1980s. As a result, the revolution in information technology of the 1980s and 1990s made an overwhelming contribution to the globalization of the world's communications infrastructure.

Debate also surrounds the impact of economic globalization on inequality, although the general consensus is that its effects vary considerably according to the level of national development. In 2002, the *Financial Times* argued that, 'Evidence suggests the 1980s and 1990s were decades of declining global inequality and reductions in the proportion of the world's population in extreme poverty' (Wolf 2002). However, the difficulty is *how* to measure the negative and/or positive aspects of globalization. A number of economists have used the level of openness of economies to determine the extent to which larger trade and investment flows have raised living standards and increased purchasing power. Lutz (2001) argues that the outcomes are complex, and that the empirical evidence, based on factors such as firm productivity or national economic growth, is ambiguous. Nevertheless, Asia as a whole (including central Asian states, such as India) continues to display considerable regional variations in terms of the impact of economic globalization. Nor is globalization and the economic growth it tends to encourage necessarily a panacea to income inequality. For example, although China has made significant gains in terms of growth and income since 1978, its GDP per capita position *relative* to the US, Japan and Germany has not changed a great deal. Lutz argues in his analysis of globalization and open markets that, 'We are thus left with the conclusion that the potential benefits of greater openness and, by implication, increased globalization for developing countries have been significantly overstated. There simply is [not] the empirical evidence to substantiate the claims'.

The World Bank itself has produced entirely different sets of numbers in two of its reports, one claiming that the number of persons living in poverty decreased by 200 million between 1980 and 1998; the other estimates that global poverty *increased* by 20 million during 1987–98. In summary, considerable confusion prevails regarding the diffusion of gains arising from the spread of economic globalization, and an exceptionally wide range of variables need to be assessed within individual countries in order to reach any firm conclusion regarding the extent to which its impact is positive or negative upon all, or parts of, national populations. Similarly, one must be cautious about declaring globalization the harbinger of greater poverty, inequality and insecurity, as there are clear gains for some regions of the world. Therefore, it does not appear unreasonable to argue that economic globalization is highly diffuse in its effects or, as Rodrik (1998: 156) puts it, 'it is not *whether* you globalize that matters, it is *how* you globalize'.

Inequalities in the capacity of states means that their responses to encroaching globalization demonstrates how diffuse the impact of globalization can be. For example, the Asian economic crisis – itself a product of the globalization of investment and trade flows – meant that the policy options of Thailand, Indonesia, Malaysia and South Korea were strictly limited by the extent of the currency collapse. What alternatives other than the IMF prescriptions did these states have? Clearly, their respective governments decided 'none'. The Indonesian government had determined that some IMF demands were simply unacceptable and the government would not withdraw funding from certain industries, such as aircraft manufacture. However, in order to secure the IMF's support, President Suharto agreed to all of the IMF's conditions. His successor, Habibie, achieved a high implementation rate of the IMF's programme. President Wahid also agreed to stringent IMF conditions, despite the fact that the Indonesian state's capacity to implement them had declined markedly (Boediono 2002). However, as Woods (2001) argues, 'since the East Asian financial crisis, the G-7 countries have determined that developing countries must meet certain codes and standards of economic behaviour if global economic stability is to be preserved'.

Globalization has forced most East Asian states into trade and economic alliances, primarily due to individual weakness, and the state remains a key actor in this regionalization process. However, globalization has also compelled East Asian states to retreat from their role in the market, particularly since the 1997 crisis. States are unwilling to surrender large portions of their economic sovereignty to the forces of globalization or regional institutions, but they are nevertheless obliged to cede an increasing number of policy areas, which were previously the preserve of the state, to transnational actors.

Conclusions

Globalization in multifarious forms poses a number of challenges to the state. The traditional concept of territoriality and the ability of the state to implement its national policy preferences have become increasingly constrained due to the impact of factors such as increased flows of capital and the coexistent pressures to further liberalize markets. Added to these are environmental issues, which are of increasingly global significance. Global civil society movements, such as opposition to the WTO's Seattle meeting, Nike's use of child labour, or the international reaction China's repression of the Tiananmen protests provoked, point to a world which is becoming more interconnected on a number of levels. Military security has also developed global dimensions as a result of technological advances, as well as the likelihood of conflicts escalating well beyond the initial war theatre. More recently, terrorism has arguably developed truly global proportions, as disparate groups are interconnected by common objectives. The globalization of terrorism is perhaps one of the most dangerous outcomes of globalization, as targets may be found in any state, and traditional territorial borders are no longer a guarantee of security, even for great powers. In summary, globalization is a process which is far from complete; indeed, we may be witnessing only its embryosis; and, in that context, it is probably far too early to assess or predict what its ultimate outcomes might be. However, one clear consequence of globalization is the emergence of regionalism, which we examine in the next section.

The development of regionalism in East Asia

In this section, we examine various forms of regionalism found in East Asia. We also discuss the various East Asian regional forums which have emerged over the last four decades, such as the AFTA, APEC and APT. According to Nye, regions consist of 'a limited number of states linked by a geographical relationship and by a degree of mutual interdependence' and can be differentiated according to the level and scope of exchange, formal organizations and political interdependence (cited in Butler 1997: 410). The founder of integration theory, Ernst Haas (1989: 135), argues that, despite historically weak regional economic relations, the Asia-Pacific has staged 'a remarkable shift from heavy external economic ties and dependence to an increasing amount of interregional and regional economic relations'. Even prior to the formation of APEC, Lampert (1989: 472) could write that, 'Asian neighbours already export more to Japan than the US does. Japan's total trade with Asian countries, even excluding China, now exceeds that of America'.

The growth of regionalism

Regionalism and globalization are integrally connected; arguably, regionalism is in many ways a *response* to globalization, in that the state is experiencing a significant decline in its capability to control, regulate and develop its own territorial space. While military security has had a regional dimension for some decades (for example, NATO, SEATO, ASEAN and the Warsaw Pact), it was only during the 1980s that saw a marked intensification of economic regionalism, with forty-one GATT notifications of regional trade agreements (RTAs) in 1990–94 alone. More than 100 regional FTAs are registered with the WTO.

The rise of regionalism is at least partly attributable to the economic insecurity of the 1970s and 1980s, as both states and firms faced significant global shocks (oil crises, financial and monetary instability), as well as intense competition for world market shares. The decreasing capacity of states to compete individually in a world of proliferative non-trade barriers (NTBs) and other trade barriers, led even the strongest economies such as Japan (APEC), the US (NAFTA) and Germany (EU) to develop closer regional links with their trade partners.

During the 1970s, the global economy experienced severe instability, caused by a number of international shocks, the effects of which extended well into the 1980s. The 1971 collapse of Bretton Woods, and the 1973 and 1979 oil crises, exposed states to the ravages of intense competition for world market shares in a recessionary global economy. Increasingly, individual states were unable to deal with the demands of inflation, debt, current account deficits and state-led investment. This was demonstrated by the IMF rescue packages of the ASEAN economies of the 1970s and early 1980s.

The first significant regional response to economic uncertainty was the EU's establishment of its Single European Market (SEM) programme in 1986. Effectively, this amounted to a single internal market comprising twelve (later fifteen) West European states. The SEM would have a market of 300 million people and it would also be the largest internal market in the world. The importance of the EU's regional integration project was that it prompted similar responses in North America and East Asia. In 1989, the US responded with the Canada–US Free Trade Association (CUSTA), which became NAFTA in 1994 with the inclusion of Mexico. Although East Asian responses to the challenge of trade blocs emerged quickly, the inequality of the players in the region, and their disparate interests, meant there was a lack of coherence and co-ordination in the various initiatives.

Prior to the 1980s, East Asian regional agreements had been largely restricted to security arrangements, such as the Five-Power Defence Arrangements (1971) and ASEAN (1967). While closer economic co-operation had been suggested for some time, it was not until the SEM and CUSTA initiatives that East Asian states began to take the threat of 'closed' or discriminatory regionalism seriously. Although EU and North American diplomats argued that the 'new regionalism' did not mean closure of these key markets to third countries, states outside trade blocs feared both discriminatory or 'closed' regionalism, allied with substantial trade and investment diversion within the new regional blocs.

East Asian regionalism

By the mid–1990s, East Asian economies had grown so rapidly that they collectively produced the largest proportion of global GDP. In 1995, East Asia produced 31 per cent of the world's output, compared with the EU (30 per cent) and NAFTA (24 per cent). Admittedly, the largest proportion of East Asian GDP was produced by Japan, the world's second-largest economic power, but this was not to deny the phenomenal growth and output figures of China and the first-tier NICs. Even the Philippines, the 'laggard' economy of the second-tier NICs, produced average growth rates of 7 per cent between 1985 and 1995. The tremendous spurt of growth experienced by East Asia from the mid–1980s until 1997 demonstrated the region's importance as the engine of growth for the world economy. This performance was all the more impressive, due to the collapse of the Japanese economic bubble from 1990.

Although analysts frequently distinguish between political and economic development, Northeast and Southeast Asia, one can identify four main groupings within the region. These are the first-tier NICs (South Korea, Taiwan, Hong Kong and Singapore); the second-tier NICs (Thailand, Indonesia, the Philippines and Malaysia); the socialist/post-socialist states (China, Vietnam and North Korea); and Japan. Within the region, Japan is a unique actor which is not only a dominant regional player, but also a global economic power.

The new regionalism

Analyses generally draw a sharp distinction between the 'old' regionalism of the 1950s to 1960s, and the emergence of the 'new regionalism' in the 1980s. 'Old' regionalism was represented by the minimalist customs union models, exemplified by the EC and the Caribbean Common Market, which emphasized formal agreements and institution building. Conversely, the 'new regionalism' is largely market-led, an outgrowth of complex economic interdependence driving firms, markets and states closer together, which Hurrell (1995) characterizes as 'regionalization' (Box 9.1). Regional economic linkages spill over into regional agreements, which have served to deepen the process of integration. Examples of market-led regional integration include Hong Kong and Taiwan's outgrowth into extensive production and labour networks within mainland China, a development which received little or no state assistance. What is distinctive about the new regionalism is that politics tends to *follow* markets; AFTA and NAFTA, for example, placed institutional and legal frameworks upon regional markets which were already a *fait accompli*. However, regional agreements, such as APEC, have a tendency to steer states and markets in directions they do not necessarily wish to go, as evidenced by APEC's debate on tariff elimination and the development of 'open' versus 'closed' regionalism.

Competing regionalisms: open versus closed

Open regionalism

The concept of 'open regionalism' first found expression in APEC's Bogor Declaration of 1993. Wei and Frankel (1998: 441) define open regionalism as 'external liberalization by trade blocs'. Concrete proposals for open regionalism were delivered by APEC's Eminent Persons' Group (EPG) in their 1994 report, which argued for the adoption of a quadripartite approach:

- the highest possible levels of unilateral liberalization;
- unilateral extension liberalization by individual APEC members to non-members on a conditional or non-conditional basis;
- the extension of regional liberalization to third countries on a reciprocal basis;
- member commitments to reduce internal barriers within APEC, while also reducing barriers to non-member countries (APEC 1995).

On the basis of these proposals, issues arise concerning the costs and benefits of membership under conditions of open regionalism. Why pay the transaction costs arising out of membership (e.g., tariff reductions) when non-members accrue the same benefits? Clearly, the temptation would be for third countries to 'free ride', enjoying the benefits of open regionalism, while paying none of the costs. The answer is two-fold. Firstly, blocs adopting open regionalism will tend to have high tariff barriers to begin with, which is certainly the case in much of East Asia. Secondly, the concept of reciprocity is critical; if, for example, APEC countries were to reduce market entry barriers to the EU, this would be conditional upon the EU granting similar tariff concessions to either individual APEC countries, or to APEC members as a whole.

Box 9.1 Regionalism: five different forms

Hurrell (1995) identifies five core explanatory variables of regionalism which are summarized briefly below. These are regionalization; regional awareness and identity; inter-state regional co-operation; state-prompted regional integration; and regional cohesion.

- *Regionalization*: flows of goods, services, capital and technology across state boundaries, driven largely by networks of private-sector actors (MNCs, markets, business groups). Firm-led M&A, FDIs and the internationalization of production are the key elements of the regionalization process, although there are inter-societal interactions which develop without the necessity of state intervention.
- *Regional awareness and identity*: the extent to which regional social networks have developed, and the level of social and cultural cohesion within a region.
- *Inter-state regional co-operation*: the building of institutions, frameworks, treaties, agreements and forums for the development and implementation of intra-regional agendas. The state is a key actor in this context, as regional co-operation may be bilateral or multilateral, and takes place at the levels of both high and low politics.
- *State-prompted regional integration*: regional integration refers to specific government policy decisions designed to increase levels of economic integration in order to reduce barriers upon the flow of goods, services, labour and capital.
- *Regional cohesion*: the extent to which the regional links alluded to in the first four categories have deepened to the point where the regional becomes the organizational base for multilevel (regional, national, local) policy development. Regional cohesion also refers to the role the region may perform in determining relations between member states.

In forming regional trade blocs, states reduce their internal barriers (technical, physical and financial barriers to trade) to promote market growth. This may take the form of a customs union or preferential trade agreement, where members of the bloc receive benefits unavailable to outsiders. For example, the EU has removed tariff barriers between its fifteen members, but retains a Common External Tariff on imports from third countries. Nevertheless, since 1958, the EU has effectively abrogated Article XXIV of the GATT, which dealt with regional associations. The GATT attempted to ensure that regional groupings would be open, rather than closed, by stating that

> Duties and other regulations of commerce imposed at the institution of any such union . . . shall not on the whole be higher or more restrictive than the general incidence of duties . . . prior to the formation of such union.
>
> (GATT Secretariat 1947: Art. XXIV (5))

The EU never received a waiver of this condition, and the GATT never ruled on the legality of the EU's interpretation of Article XXIV. As a result, discriminatory regionalism persisted in Europe, while the GATT pursued a free trade agenda. The number of RTAs grew to the extent that GATT could identify at least sixty-nine by 1994. Of these, only six were found to comply with GATT rules, although none was found to be in breach of GATT regulations; GATT compliance by most RTAs surveyed was found to be inconclusive.

Closed regionalism

Closed regionalism extends preferential trade only to members of a bloc. While internal liberalization takes place, third countries face external tariffs and, possibly, quantitative restrictions. Examples include the EU and NAFTA, although AFTA falls into this category to some extent. Closed regionalism means producers and consumers enjoy the benefits of liberalization, lower prices and reduced market entry costs. Conversely, non-members face restrictions and more barriers to market access.

Proponents of closed regionalism argue that international competitiveness does not automatically arise from liberalization and deregulation. Instead, states must act to protect strategic industry sectors until they become sufficiently competitive. By participating in closed regionalism, firms gain access to larger markets, without being forced to pay the full costs of competition. As recently as 1991, the EU negotiated a ten-year Voluntary Export Restraint (VER) with Japan, limiting Japanese auto firms to 15 per cent of the EU market, until EU auto-makers could become competitive.

Closed regionalism versus open regionalism closely approximates older debates between developmental and *laissez-faire* capitalism. A key feature of East Asian development has been the capitalist developmental state, exemplified by MITI and the MoF's roles in Japan's industrial restructuring, as well as South Korea under the Park regime. While market deregulation and liberalization increased markedly in East Asia from the 1980s, the history of economic development in the region is such that it is likely to prove difficult to extricate the state from the economy. The 1997 crisis, as well as the stalled APEC and AFTA processes, suggest that the state in East Asia is not quite through as an economic unit.

Expansionist regionalism

Certain regions have also engaged in overt expansionism in recent years, while others have widened their membership considerably. The EU's absorption of a number of Eastern European countries is one example of an expansionist regional strategy. Conversely, APEC has attempted to integrate various Asia-Pacific groupings and states into a single trading zone, with its members drawn from four continents. Recently, talks on a Free Trade Area of the Americas (FTAA) could link North and South America together in a single trade bloc.

Blocism

A number of analysts in the 1980s and early 1990s conjectured that the international trading system would fragment into three major trade blocs: NAFTA, the EU and an East Asian 'yen bloc' dominated by Japan. Blocism was seen as both a response to globalization, as well as the fear of discriminatory or 'closed' regionalism in other parts of the world. However, Nye predicted correctly that states in the post-Cold War order would be increasingly preoccupied with internal affairs, as the security threat was removed (Nye *et al.* 1991). However, the 'three-bloc' thesis, which gained some currency during the early 1990s, was undermined by the fact that the US remained heavily involved in European and Asia-Pacific security.

Box 9.2 Multilateral trade, open regionalism and closed regionalism compared

Model	Characteristics	Examples
Multilateral trade	• Free trade based on national treatment • Application of most-favoured nation (MFN) principle	• GATT • WTO
Closed regionalism	• Preferential trade area or customs union • Elimination or substantial reduction of internal barriers to free movement of goods, services, capital within the bloc • Restrictions on free movement of labour may or may not be included in regional agreement • Significant external barriers to non-members • Discrimination against countries via tariff barriers, quantitative restrictions or non-tariff technical barriers	• EU • NAFTA • CERTA • EFTA • CARICOM • MERCOSUR • Free Trade Area of the Americas (FTAA) [2005] • SAARC (South Asian Council for Regional Co-operation)
Open regionalism	• Preferential trade area • Elimination or substantial reduction of internal barriers to free movement of goods, services, capital within the bloc • Restrictions on free movement of labour may or may not be included in regional agreement • Few restrictions upon third-country trade and investment • Principle of non-discrimination based on MFN principle applied	• APEC • AFTA

Nevertheless, the threat of blocism remains in the forefront of the mind of many policy makers in East Asia, and can prompt states to undertake regional or bilateral initiatives in order to counter possible market access discrimination or trade diversionary measures taken in NAFTA or the EU. Following the Japan–South Korea agreement to boost co-operation in the IT and investment sectors, a MITI official was quoted as saying, 'With economic blocism expanding in Europe and in the United States, Korea and Japan must take the initiative in setting up a cooperative economic entity in these parts of Asia' (*Korea Times* 2000). Although North American and European officials argue that their regional blocs do not discriminate against outsiders, the perception remains that NAFTA and the EU are relatively closed to non-members which, in turn, affects and conditions the international public policy responses of East Asian states.

Regional trade, financial and dialogue forums

The Asian Development Bank (ADB) (1966)

Predating even ASEAN, the ADB has grown from thirty-one members at its inception to sixty-one in 2003. Membership is open to all members of the UN Economic and Social Committee. Thus, the ADB draws its membership from not only Asia, but also Europe, North America and the Pacific. Based in Manila, the ADB employs over 2,000 staff in over fifty countries. The ADB resembles in many ways a smaller version of the World Bank. Like the World Bank, the ADB relies upon both the contributions of its members, as well as international bond markets to raise capital to finance its loans. ADB loans are primarily made in areas such as agriculture and rural programmes, although health, education and water supplies have become the focus of increasing attention in recent years. The ADB also makes technical assistance loans available, although at around US$150 million, these comprise a small part of the bank's lending activities.

The dominant actor in the ADB is Japan, and the chairman of the ADB is always Japanese. The ADB (2003: 2) explains that, 'By tradition, the President is Japanese. The charter states that the President must be from a regional member country'. The IMF operates in a similar fashion: from 1944 until 1999, the chairman of the IMF was always a Frenchman. There are key historical and strategic factors behind the Japanese ascendancy in the ADB. Firstly, Japan was clearly the rising economic power of Asia in the 1960s; secondly, Japan was and remains Asia's largest aid donor, a position it has employed effectively to cement its investment and export position within the region. Japanese aid is mostly 'tied', meaning agricultural funding is often granted with the condition that Japanese farming equipment is purchased with the loan capital. Thirdly, from a realist perspective, the ADB provides Japan with some considerable strategic economic influence within the Asian region, as states such as Indonesia, China, Pakistan and India are the largest debtors to the ADB. Bank loans have also served to build a great deal of local infrastructure in the Asian region, which have largely benefited Japanese firms as they have relocated production throughout East Asia.

Nevertheless, while it is an important vehicle for Japanese economic strategies, the ADB is dwarfed by the financial depth of the IMF and World Bank. ADB lending in recent years averaged only US$5 billion per annum. Consequently, it would be incorrect to think of the ADB as a fledgling Asian central bank, built to provide liquidity and loans at times of crisis. However, in the wake of the 1997 currency crisis, Japan proposed an Asian Monetary Fund (AMF), which received some support within ASEAN, due to the disenchantment in the region with the IMF's post-crisis prescriptions.

However, there have been concrete proposals for a Northeast Asian Development Bank (NEADB), covering Northeast China, Mongolia, the Korean Peninsula, the Russian Far East and Japan. An Ad Hoc Committee for an NEADB, under the chairmanship of a former vice president of the ADB, established a forum in South Korea in 1993. NEADB proposals include loans to cover transportation, energy, communications and finance, and the Committee has expanded on these proposals in a forum held in China in 2000. The NEADB proposals include the utilization of Japan's 'chronic' trade surplus to fund development in the Northeast Asian region The forum recommended initial capitalization of US$50 billion for the NEADB, which would provide 'a new financial mechanism capable of intermediating long-term capital from international capital markets to Northeast Asia for infrastructure investments' (Cho and Katz, 2001: 4). The NEADB has not moved beyond the level of a forum, however, and it is unlikely that the US would support a 'mini-IMF' in the region. Equally, Japanese governments are increasingly reluctant to support investment in regional financial mechanisms while their domestic financial system remains fragile and debt-burdened.

ASEAN (1967)

As we noted in Chapter 5, ASEAN has developed into the linchpin of Southeast Asian co-operation, encompassing a wide range of security, trade, investment and banking agreements, including the ARF, AFTA, ASEM (see Chapter 7) and the APT. The growth in the importance of the Southeast Asian region has been such that ASEAN has developed into one of the main drivers of regional co-operation in the East Asian region as a whole. Most recently, ASEAN has launched a number of 'framework' agreements designed to encourage trade and investment within the region. These include the Framework Agreement on the ASEAN Investment Area (AIA), the ASEAN Framework Agreement on Services (AFAS), and the Framework Agreement on Intellectual Property Rights (Thanadsillapakul 2001: 14).

Asia-Pacific Economic Co-operation (APEC) (1989)

APEC was chiefly an Australian–Japanese trade initiative (Cooper *et al.* 1993: 92), and now comprises members from four continents. APEC links a number of free trade areas together, including AFTA, NAFTA and the Australia–New Zealand Closer Economic Relations (CERTA) customs union. APEC's membership extends to Latin America (Chile and Peru), as well as the former Cold War 'socialist bloc' of Russia, China and Vietnam. Taiwan and Papua New Guinea are also included.

Box 9.3 Membership of East Asian regional organizations

ASEAN (1967)	APEC (1989)	EAEC Proposal (1990)	ARF (1994)	ASEM (1996)	ASEAN Plus Three (1997)
Brunei	Australia	ASEAN	ASEAN	China	ASEAN
Indonesia	Brunei Darussalam	China	Australia	South Korea	China
Malaysia	Canada	Taiwan	China	Japan	Japan
Myanmar	Chile	Japan	Canada	ASEAN	South Korea
Philippines	China	South Korea	European Union	Austria	
Singapore	Hong Kong (China)	Vietnam	Japan	Belgium	
Thailand	Indonesia	Hong Kong	New Zealand	Denmark	
Vietnam	Japan		South Korea	Finland	
Cambodia	South Korea		Russia	France	
Laos	Malaysia		North Korea	Germany	
	Mexico		India	Greece	
	New Zealand		Papua New Guinea	Ireland	
	Papua New Guinea		United States	Italy	
	Peru		Mongolia	Luxembourg	
	Philippines			Netherlands	
	Russia			Portugal	
	Singapore			Spain	
	Chinese Taipei (Taiwan)			Sweden	
	Thailand			United Kingdom	
	United States				
	Vietnam				

A key feature of the APEC agenda is 'open regionalism'. In stating this, APEC members commit themselves to non-discriminatory trade and investment policies in accordance with the WTO's MFN principle. As such, APEC differs considerably from PTAs such as NAFTA and the EU. Unlike many of the East Asian intra-regional dialogues, APEC has the rudiments of an institutional structure, with a secretariat based in Singapore and annual meetings. In this respect, it has developed consistency as an international forum. Keohane and Nye (2001: 2) describe APEC as 'mullti-continental interdependence'.

The high-tide mark of APEC was the Bogor Declaration (1993), which committed member states to the elimination of trade barriers by 2010 for developed economies and 2020 for developing countries. Following the summit, President Clinton described the Declaration as an exemplar of 'open regionalism'. However, it was clear that by the 1996 Manila APEC summit that the 1995 Kyoto Action Plan targets would not be met, and Japan, China and South Korea openly declared that agriculture would not be on the free trade agenda. Trade tensions between APEC partners were worsened by the US's policy of 'aggressive unilateralism', which saw the USTR target Japan, South Korea and Taiwan for alleged use of non-tariff barriers (NTBs) in traded goods sectors, such as automotive parts, imaging products and agriculture, as well as intellectual property (product patent piracy). While US demands were largely met in the face of threats of trade retaliation, the APEC process was disrupted to the extent that its agenda became derailed. Moreover, APEC's in-principle commitment to external liberalization through open regionalism obscured the fact that APEC itself was dealing with complex regional liberalization issues of its own. This was demonstrated by APEC's decision at the 1997 Vancouver summit to abandon consensus decision making and to focus on individual action plans (IAPs) to achieve Bogor's goals. Effectively, this means APEC members may offer unilateral trade concessions; however, there is no commitment to reciprocity, which means there are few incentives for members to grant concessions when there are no guarantees of reciprocity. The 1997 Asian economic crisis derailed any prospect of ASEAN or South Korea implementing IAPs, beyond insignificant tariff concessions.

Recent literature argues that APEC has largely failed to gain momentum, following initial support for the Bogor initiatives. Aside from the IAPs, APEC has lost political support from key players, including Australia, the US and ASEAN. Australia has pursued an FTA with the US, while the US itself has become more inwardly focused upon NAFTA and a North/South American trade agreement, as well as the war on terror. Since 1997, ASEAN has also become much less enthusiastic about open regionalism, evidenced by its cautiousness in pursuing the radical liberalization agendas of APEC and AFTA.

The East Asian Economic Caucus (EAEC) proposal (1990)

The EAEC was proposed by Malaysian Prime Minister, Dr Mahathir Mohammad, as a counter to the newly formed APEC grouping. Mahathir envisaged an eleven-member trade bloc, with the controversial inclusion of both China and Taiwan. Equally controversial was Malaysia's exclusion of Australia and New Zealand (Davison 1991: 56). A senior Malaysian government official said that Mahathir had deliberately excluded Australia and New Zealand because '[they] cannot make up their minds whether they are part of the West or Asia' (*The Age* 1990: 1). Mahathir envisaged a form of 'closed' regionalism, which would protect East Asian states until they had achieved a sufficient stage of industrial development. The US government strongly opposed the EAEC initiative, and exercised substantial diplomatic pressure to prevent Japanese participation in the proposal. The Mahathir proposal saw opinion divided within the ASEAN camp and made the US government suspicious of Malaysian pan-Asian regional proposals. However, the failure of the EAEC initiative was not total, as many commentators view the promulgation of ASEAN Plus Three (APT) as an indirect consequence of the original EAEC proposals.

The ASEAN Free Trade Agreement (AFTA) (1992)

In 1992, AFTA envisaged a functional ASEAN free trade area by 2002 for the original ASEAN six, with the FTA schedules to be incorporated by Vietnam in 2006, Laos and Myanmar by 2008, and Cambodia by 2010. AFTA itself was a reaction to the development of APEC's open regionalism, in the absence of which, Bello (2000) argues, AFTA's preferential trade agreements would have been 'irrelevant'. While ASEAN states feared the development of 'closed regionalism' in NAFTA and the EU, they nevertheless opted to give preferential tariffs to ASEAN members, under the Common Effective Preferential Tariff (CEPT). This encourages intra-ASEAN trade, as members gradually reduce their tariffs on an MFN basis. As this results in a larger regional market for third-country investors and traders, AFTA subscribes to the principle of 'open regionalism'. Nevertheless, the same argument may be applied to the EU and NAFTA, which also apply similar, discriminatory tariff regimes.

AFTA has broadly supported the principle of open regionalism, although there are exceptions. Despite moves by individual AFTA members, such as Indonesia and the Philippines, to unilaterally extend to all of their trading partners on an MFN basis in 1996, unilateral liberalization is unlikely to cover key sectors, such as TFC and agriculture (Bergsten 1997). The 1997 economic crisis meant that the incentives for further unilateral liberalization were few. AFTA missed its 2002 deadline for the implementation of the FTA, with outstanding issues including Malaysian auto tariffs (extended to 2005) which, in turn, encouraged other members to extend the deadline for the implementation schedule. In 2000, Bello argued that creeping protectionism made it increasingly likely that AFTA would postpone its deadline until 2010; his prediction was mostly accurate: the 2003 ASEAN summit saw the deferment of AFTA targets to 2020.

Arguably, AFTA has imposed fewer restrictions upon trade and investment since the external imposition of the IMF adjustment programmes. The withdrawal of government support from some public enterprises, increased regional investment co-operation, and reduced influence from 'crony capitalists' and presidential families in the assignation of contracts has been at least an indirect consequence of IMF conditionality. This was evidenced by post-currency crisis initiatives, such as the ASEAN Investment Area (AIA) (1998). Ironically, as closer regional co-operation on investment has developed, FDI scarcity may force AFTA members into closer competition. For example, FDI in ASEAN plummeted from US$27.3 billion in 1997 to US$10.4 billion in 2000 (Wee and Mirza 2001).

ASEAN Plus Three (APT) (1997)

Although the EAEC proposal had failed to gain significant support in the region, the 1999 initiative to form APT represented a major turning point in intra-regional relations between Northeast and Southeast Asia. APT comprises ASEAN, plus the three largest East Asian economies: Japan, China and South Korea. Again, this involves a case of soft regionalism, in the form of dialogue, rather than 'hard' institution-building. While significant in terms of the new linkages it brings to Northeast/Southeast Asian relations, the APT's only major initiative, the AMF, has not been pursued since its proposal in 2000. The APT's importance to Northeast Asian dialogue should not be understated, however, given the traditional economic rivalry which underpins relations between Japan, South Korea and China.

China's growing importance to the region was demonstrated by the considerable leverage Beijing exercised in negotiating the FTA it signed with ASEAN. The 2001 ASEAN–China FTA encompasses 1.7 billion persons and two-way trade totalling US$1.2 trillion (Reuters

2001). The agreement set a target of 2010 for the completion of a free trade area between China and the original ASEAN six, and 2015 for Cambodia, Laos, Myanmar and Vietnam. Tariff reduction talks are scheduled for completion by mid–2004. With access to the Chinese market, ASEAN is likely to make considerable economic gains. However, the FTA will also give Chinese exports a considerable presence in a part of Asia traditionally dominated by Japanese firms and investment.

Intra-regional FTAs such as ASEAN–China demonstrate the importance of the regional balance of economic and political power within the East Asian region. Buffered by a considerable trade surplus in the region, Japanese governments did not pursue regional agreements seriously during the 1990s, preferring to free ride on APEC's promise of open regionalism. In marked contrast with the progressive 2001 ASEAN–China bilaterals, Japan spent the year engaged in a tit-for-tat protectionist dispute with China; refused to include agriculture in a Japan–Singapore bilateral FTA; and damaged relations with its neighbours by backing away from its AMF proposal, opting instead for an IMF fallback position (i.e., that no funds would be disbursed to Asian countries in difficulty, without seeking IMF approval). Slow to react to the ASEAN–China FTA, Japan finally responded in 2002 with Prime Minister Koizumi's Initiative for Japan–ASEAN Comprehensive Economic Partnership. Labelled 'ASEAN Plus Five', Koizumi's cabinet were clearly attempting to block Chinese attempts to establish an ASEAN–China trade area by provocatively including Taiwan, as well as Hong Kong. The Japanese government stated that, 'In the future, the area could be extended to Australia and New Zealand, as well as the United States' (*Japan Times* 2002). As a counter to an ASEAN–China FTA, Japan is likely to offer some type of FTA to ASEAN. Such a move would demonstrate the power of centrifugal, regionalizing forces in East Asia, which are at odds with Japan's traditional alliance with the US. Japanese bilateral agreements (such as Singapore–Japan) are important, but are relatively insignificant to Japan, given the quantitative limits of Singapore's market. In attempting to balance China's growing economic power, Japan will need to tread a delicate path in its relations between ASEAN, China and the US. In terms of the regional co-operation agenda, APT may be the most effective vehicle with which to accomplish this.

Despite the APT, intra-regional disagreements suggest that great power rivalry – principally between Japan and China – can play a major role in determining the shape and outcomes of regional policy; in other words, not only globalization but *inter-state rivalry within the region* has also been responsible for prompting the growth of regional co-operation. Japan's traditional regional economic hegemony faces the dual challenges of ascendant China, and Japan's domestic economic difficulties. The result has been an enhanced role for relatively small, but influential organizations, such as ASEAN, to play a brokering role. Individual ASEAN countries' markets on their own are too insignificant to bring bargaining leverage to negotiations between China or Japan. However, acting in concert, ASEAN represents a market too large to ignore, particularly given ASEAN's highly skilled service sector, a resource base China lacks.

However, intra-APT rivalries tend to mask the fact that the group represents a fallback position for East Asia, should 'blocism' emerge. The APT can also present a co-operative front in trade talks, similar to the common positions adopted by NAFTA and the EU. The sixth APT summit in Phnom Penh in November 2002 demonstrated that APT is not an inconsequential dialogue process, but an increasingly significant regional forum.

The Asian Monetary Fund proposal (1997)

A proposal for an Asian Monetary Fund (AMF), with initial capitalization of US$17 billion, emerged from the Chiang Mai initiative by the APT in 2000. The AMF was clearly the result of ASEAN members' dissatisfaction with the SAPs demanded by the IMF, which involved large-scale structural reform. The AMF initiative envisaged an East Asian system of central banks monitoring and co-ordinating speculative banking activities, such as debt-for-equity swaps. The reasoning was that AMF co-ordination would limit the degree of speculation by international markets and, therefore, serve to stabilize East Asian currency markets. Although the AMF was a Japanese proposal, the US government's strong opposition to its formation – as either a supplement or as an alternative to the IMF – resulted in Japanese abandonment of the idea. There were clear reasons for Japanese support for, and US opposition to, the AMF concept. Firstly, despite its economic problems, Japan remains the world's largest creditor nation; Japanese financial institutions made credit widely available to East Asian countries affected by the 1997 crisis, giving Japanese lenders a distinct competitive advantage over US and European capital in the East Asian market. Japanese banks also held almost 50 per cent of Thai foreign debt and 40 per cent of Indonesia's, suggesting protection of the Japanese banking sector was in reality the key objective (Higgott 1999: 268–9). Secondly, Japanese financial institutions made loans available without imposing the harsh conditionality inherent in the IMF's SAPs. Thirdly, the Japanese government argued that any AMF role would be subordinate to that of the IMF, which meant that, in effect, the IMF remained the 'lender of last resort', and would, therefore, carry the largest part of the risk.

The proposal revealed a serious deterioration in relations between the APT and the IMF. However, some parts of the AMF agenda have been implemented in a number of bilateral agreements within the APT, which exemplifies the importance of 'soft' regionalism in East Asia, particularly when dealing with sensitive areas of national economic sovereignty, such as central bank independence. However, the Chiang Mai initiative did lead to concrete developments, such as the ASEAN Swap Arrangement (ASA), a currency stabilization programme which dates from 1997. Chiang Mai pointed to the growing dependence of the ASEAN states' financial systems upon their Northeast Asian partners, exemplified by China's two bilateral currency swap agreements with Malaysia and Thailand. Moreover, as Beeson (2003) argues, APT may well exemplify 'reactionary regionalism' to the extent that it corresponds with an economic and cultural rejection of US-led market liberalism.

Conclusion: globalization *v.* regionalism?

A major theme in this chapter is that accelerating globalization has served to prompt increased regionalization, as individual states demonstrate a decreasing ability to deal with the diverse range of problems presented by globalization by implementing state-centric policies. In this respect, intra-regional and inter-regional initiatives, such as AFTA, APEC, APT and ASEM, are responses to complex policy dilemmas which states are unable to resolve individually. Regional initiatives also 'bring the state back in' by giving national governments a key role in regional agenda-setting and policy making. Globalization may force the state to confront new and difficult challenges to their policy making autonomy but, as Hirst and Thompson (1996) argue, the state has been far from passive or defenceless in the face of globalization.

References

Age, The (1990) 'Asian trade plan snubs Australia', 18 December, p. 1.

Asia-Pacific Economic Co-operation (APEC) (1995) *Achieving the APEC Vision: Free and Open Trade in the Asia-Pacific*, Second Report of the Eminent Persons' Group, Singapore: APEC Secretariat.

Asian Development Bank (ADB) (2003) *About the ADB: Funding and Lending*, Manila: ADB.

Beeson, M. (2003) 'ASEAN Plus Three and the rise of reactionary regionalism', *Contemporary Southeast Asia*, 25: 251–68.

Bello, W. (2000) 'The Association of Southeast Asian Nations: a preliminary autopsy'. Online. Available HTTP:<http://www.focusweb.org/publications/2000/The_Association_ of_Southeast_ Asian_Nations.htm> (accessed 3 February 2003).

Bergsten, C. F. (1997) 'Open regionalism', Institute for International Economics Working Paper No. 97–3, Washington, DC: IIE.

Boediono (2002) 'The International Monetary Fund support program in Indonesia: comparing implementation under three presidents', *Bulletin of Indonesian Economic Studies*, 38: 385–91.

Butler, F. (1997) 'Regionalism and integration,' in J. Baylis and S. Smith (eds) *The Globalization of World Politics*, Oxford: Oxford University Press, pp. 409–28.

Cho, L.-J. and Katz, S. (2001) 'A Northeast Asian Development Bank?', *NIRA Review*, Winter. Online. Available HTTP: <http://www.nira.go.jp/publ/review/2001winter/choandkatz.pdf> (accessed 3 February 2003).

Cooper, A., Higgott, R. and Nossal, K. (1993) *Relocating Middle Powers*, Vancouver: University of British Columbia Press.

Cox, R. W. (1996) 'A perspective on globalization', in J. H. Mittelman (ed.) *Globalization: Critical Reflections*, Boulder, CO: Lynne Rienner.

Davison, R. (1991) 'Between Europe and Asia: Australia's options in the world economy of the 1990s', *Melbourne Journal of Politics*, 20: 40–67.

Evans, P. B. (1987) 'Class, state and dependence in East Asia: lessons for Latin Americanists', in F. C. Deyo (ed.) *The Political Economy of the New Asian Industrialism*, Ithaca, NY: Cornell University Press, pp. 203–26.

Fukuyama, F. (1992) *The End of History and the Last Man*, New York: The Free Press.

GATT Secretariat (1947) *General Agreement on Tariffs and Trade*, Geneva: GATT Secretariat.

Gill, S. (1990) *American Hegemony and the Trilateral Commission*, Cambridge: Cambridge University Press.

Gordon, P. H. (2002) 'It's time for a trans-Atlantic summit', *International Herald Tribune*, 13 March.

Haas, E. (1989) *The Asian Way to Peace: The Story of Regional Co-operation*, New York: Praeger.

Haggard, S. and Cheng, T.-J. (1987) 'State and foreign capital in the East Asian NICs', in F. C. Deyo (ed.) *The Political Economy of the New Asian Industrialism*, Ithaca, NY: Cornell University Press, pp. 84–129.

Higgott, R. (1999) 'The international relations of the Asian economic crisis: a study in the politics of resentment', in R. Robison, M. Beeson, K. Jayasuriya and H.-R. Sim (eds) *Politics and Markets in the Wake of the Asian Crisis*, London: Routledge, pp. 261–82.

Hirst, P. and Thompson, G. (1996) *Globalization in Question*, Cambridge: Cambridge University Press.

Huntington, S. P. (1996) *The Clash of Civilizations*, New York: Simon & Schuster.

Hurrell, A. (1995) *Regionalism in World Politics: Regional Organization and International Order*, Oxford: Oxford University Press.

Japan Times (2002) 'Japan considering creation of East Asia Free-Trade Area before 2010', 14 April.

Keohane, R. and Nye, J. (1977) *Power and Interdependence: World Politics in Transition*, Boston, MA: Little, Brown.

Keohane, R. and Nye, J. (2001) 'Introduction', in J. Nye and J. D. Donahue (eds) *Governance in a Globalizing World*, Washington, DC: Brookings Institution Press, pp. 1–41.

Korea Times (2000) 'Korea, Japan to hike co-operation in info tech investments', 3 November.

Krugman, P. (1998) 'Fire-sale FDI', Online. Available HTTP: <http://web.mit.edu/krugman/www/ FIRESALE.htm> (accessed 19 January 2003).

Lampert, D. (1989) 'Patterns of transregional relations', in W. Feld and G. Boyd (eds) *Comparative Regional Systems*, Oxford: Pergamon Press, pp. 429–72.

Lutz, M. (2001) 'Globalization, convergence and the case for openness in developing countries: what do we learn from open economy growth theory and empirics?' CSGR Working Paper No. 72/01, May.

Mahathir, M. (2001) 'The future of Asia in a globalized and deregulated world', speech delivered at The Future of Asia conference, Tokyo, 8 June 2001.

Nye, J., Biedenkopf, B. and Shiina, M. (1991) *Global Co-operation after the Cold War: A Reassessment of Trilateralism*, New York: Trilateral Commission.

Ohmae, K. (1990) *The Borderless World: Power and Strategy in the Interlinked Economy*, London: Fontana.

Ohmae, K. (1995) *The Evolving Global Economy: Making Sense of the New World Order*, Boston, MA: Harvard Business School Press.

Ohmae, K. (1996) *The End of the Nation State: The Rise of Regional Economies*, New York: The Free Press.

Reuters (2001) 'Southeast Asia, China create world's biggest free trade area', 4 November.

Rodrik, A. (1998) 'Globalization, social conflict and economic growth', *The World Economy*, 21: 143–58.

Scholte, J. A. (1997) 'Global capitalism and the state', *International Affairs*, 73: 427–52.

Thanadsillapakul, L. (2001) 'Open regionalism and deeper integration: the implementation of ASEAN Investment Area (AIA) and ASEAN Free Trade Area (AFTA)', *CEPMLP On-line Journal*, 6, 16. Online. Available HTTP: <http://www.dundee.ac.uk/cepmlp/journal/vol6–16.html> (accessed 3 February 2003).

Wallerstein, I. (1979) *The Capitalist World Economy*, Cambridge: Cambridge University Press.

Wee, K. H. and Mirza, H. (2001) 'ASEAN investment co-operation: retrospect, developments and prospects', in *Globalization and Poverty*. Online. Available HTTP: <http://www.gapresearch.org/finance/ASEAN%20Investment%20Co-operation.pdf> (accessed 19 January 2003).

Wei, S. and Frankel, J. A. (1998) 'Open regionalism in a world of continental trade blocs', *IMF Staff Papers*, 45: 440–53.

Wolf, M. (2002) 'Doing more harm than good', *Financial Times*, 8 May.

Woods, N. (2001) 'Prague – a failed opportunity', *Prospect*, December.

Yoshihara, K. (1988) *The Rise of Ersatz Capitalism in Southeast Asia*, Oxford: Oxford University Press.

Zoellick, R. (2002) 'Unleashing the trade winds', *The Economist*, 7 December.

10 The Asian economic miracle and its unmaking

Michael K. Connors

Before the Asian economic crisis of 1997 a rash of books on the 'Asian miracle' appeared that praised Confucian culture, the strong development state, and the region's export-oriented industrialization strategy. Asian difference was lauded. Most commentators predicted smooth and spiralling economic growth into the future. When the region nose-dived after the currency crises of 1997 praise turned to derision, with book titles such as *The Tigers Tamed* and *The Asian Eclipse: The Dark Side of Asia* typifying much popular writing on Asia's economic malaise. Asian difference was now a liability: Asian states were said to be too interventionist, Asian culture was endemically corrupt, and Asian education failed to spark entrepreneurship. In this chapter the 'Asian economic miracle' and the subsequent economic crash is used to introduce some key themes in international political economy. The main concern is to show that both the causes of the Asian economic miracle and the subsequent crash are heavily contested. The first section describes the Asian economic miracle. Secondly, competing explanations for the 'miracle' are explored. Thirdly, the economic crisis that besieged the region in 1997–98 is described, and is then followed by an examination of competing explanations of the crisis and its consequences.

The Asian economic 'miracle'

As economists surveyed the wastelands of East Asia after the Second World War, few expected an economic miracle. Consider for instance that in the decades after the war South Korea was plunged into a war with North Korea, Taiwan was in the hands of the unproven Kuomintang, Hong Kong was a centre for fleeing Chinese refugees, Indonesia was subject to Sukarnoism, and in China the dogma-driven programmes of the cultural revolution and the Great Leap Forward suggested imminent catastrophe (Rowen 1998: 1–2). However, by the 1980s the region was described as having performed an economic miracle. One author notes that, 'The various macroeconomic statistics on Japan, Taiwan, and Korea have become boringly familiar even to those who are not specialists on the region' (Pempel 1999: 147).

The 'miracle' is that a number of countries in East and Southeast Asia are said to have achieved rapid economic growth with equity. In its famous report *The East Asian Miracle: Economic Growth and Public Policy* (1993), the World Bank listed Japan as leading the high performing Asian economies (HPAEs) of Hong Kong, Singapore, South Korea (the four tigers, or the first-tier newly industrializing countries, or NICs) and Indonesia, Malaysia and Thailand (the second tier of the newly industrializing countries). These countries taken together experienced higher growth rates than anywhere else in the world between 1965 and 1990, averaging 4.6 per cent per annum, compared with 0.2 per cent for sub-Saharan Africa,

1.8 per cent the Middle East and Latin America, 1.9 per cent South Asia and the high income economies of the West at 2.4 per cent. At the same time, most of them experienced growing equal distribution of income relative to other economies. Some statistics help us understand how growth was related to equity. In 1960 life expectancy in the eight HPAEs was 56 years. By 1990 it was 71. Each country experienced dramatic declines in the levels of absolute poverty (World Bank 1993). If we include China in our survey we get an even more striking picture:

> Prior to the Asian Financial Crisis in 1997, East Asian region as a whole exported $1,392 billion to rest of the world, accounting for 25.6% of the total world export. Compared to the 14.29% share of total world export in 1978, the relative importance of the East Asian region in the world economy has increased substantially.
>
> (Bark 2000: 1–2)

Let us look more specifically at a few countries. Japan stands in the vanguard. There are many stark claims about Japan's rebound after its surrender to the Allied Powers in 1945, perhaps none as astonishing as the fact that between 1948 and 1960 Japanese industrial production increased eight-fold (Garran 1998: 24). The pace of gains barely halted until the 1990s:

> Between 1965 and 1990 Japan's Industrial production increased fivefold whereas it only doubled in the United States and leading economies of Western Europe. By 1980, the Japanese economy represented 44% of the US economy; by 1990 the proportion had risen to 62%.
>
> (Camilleri 2000: 68)

Despite the fact that Japan suffered economic stagnation throughout the 1990s it still retains a massive trade surplus with the rest of the world. Furthermore, Japan had by the mid-1980s become the world's largest creditor nation and provider of foreign aid; it was also the largest exporter of foreign direct investment. Japan is clearly a leader of the industrialized world. Its success is often attributed to the 'iron triangle', a unique pattern of relations between business, politicians and bureaucrats, who worked closely to plan economic development.

No less spectacular has been the growth of other East Asian economies, especially the 'tigers' South Korea, Taiwan, Hong Kong and Singapore normally described as newly industrializing economies (NIEs). There are various definitions of NIEs, the one favoured by the Organization for Economic Co-operation and Development (OECD) defines newly industrializing economies as having

1   fast growth in both the absolute level of industrial employment and the share of industrial employment in total employment;
2   a rising share of the world exports of manufactures;
3   fast growth in real per capita GDP such that the country was successful in narrowing the gap with the advanced industrialized countries (Chowdhury and Islam 1993: 3).

All the tigers possessed these three attributes in the 1960s and 1970s, while the second-tier NIEs underwent similar processes in the last two decades. Combining the experience of Japan with the NIEs, it is no wonder that observers were enthralled. It was commonplace to assume that the 'miracle' flowed from an emulation of Japanese-style development by the

NIEs. Strong states with the ability to implement plans seemed to be the key to the miracle and this assumption led to the rather grandiose notion of 'Asian capitalism'. Yet these countries, on examination, have significantly different state and society structures sufficient to bring into question the idea of an 'Asian form of capitalism'. Speaking of the different forms of economic governance in East Asia for instance, Kim (1999: 99) notes that it is possible to distinguish between *chaebol* capitalism in South Korea where there is a dominance of large-scale conglomerates with a high degree of concentration and vertical integration, family capitalism in Taiwan characterized by small-to-medium medium enterprises' reliance on patrimonial networks, and alliance capitalism in Japan where small and large businesses form networks and institutional linkages through subcontracting.

If the dominant economic actors are different, so too are the institutional arrangements for economic governance. Pempel (1999) points to the differentiation of the countries in terms of four factors: politics, financial and business structures, and state strategy. Politically the countries are different, with Japan having sustained a form of democracy for all of the post-war period, while power in Taiwan and South Korea, until the late 1980s, was held by militaristic cliques or autocrats. In terms of financial structure the three states differ significantly. In Japan, most banks are private and often linked to industrial groups, but the keystone of the system, the Bank of Japan, is controlled by the government's Ministry of Finance, while the public postal saving system is a key component of the entire system. In South Korea foreign capital inflows were limited, but considerable capital was raised abroad. Most banking was privatized, yet government oversight was critical in directing capital to desired sectors. In Taiwan, the ruling party was in charge; capital control by local Taiwanese was minimized in favour of mainlander control, and finance and industry were kept as quite different spheres. Pempel goes on to list other differences regarding business structures and state strategy. What becomes clear is that the idea of a development state or Asian capitalism is far too general inasmuch as it suggests massive similarities between states (Pempel 1999). Furthermore, the experience of the second tier of NIEs differs from the first. These economies were less likely to have strong states with the capacity to implement plans. They were also more open than Japan and the first-tier NIEs to high levels of FDI. The point here is that HPAEs do not display commensurable structure or experience. Indeed, as MacIntyre (1994: 16) notes, there are significant difficulties in any attempt to generalize East Asian development because the 'differences in the patterns of business–government interaction *among* the Southeast Asian countries or the Northeast Asian countries are as notable as the differences *between* the two sub regions . . .'.

None the less, in commentary on the region the idea of a specifically Asian form of capitalism has been consistently present. This idea is generally related to the notion of the capitalist development state (CDS). The idea of the CDS is most famously attached to the work of Chalmers Johnson (1985; 1999) who studied the role of the Japanese Ministry of International Trade and Industry (1982). The CDS, as Johnson described it in terms of the Japanese state, encompassed a number of features including a state bureaucracy closely associated with economic planning, state allocation of credit, state-led industrial policy and specifically planned for growth outcomes. The state's various machinations induced Japanese business to take a particular course of action that conformed not only to business profit requirements, but which conformed to national objectives set down by the state in the name of the 'national interest'. This, Johnson described as a plan-rational political economy, in contrast to the regulatory state of Western capitalism and the centralist state of communism. Johnson (1985) has argued that in some senses the key economies of the region (Japan, Taiwan and South Korea), can be identified as capitalist development states.

Thus far we have suggested that the seeming success of HPAEs had something to do with the nature of the state in the region. This issue leads us to more theoretical concerns and an outline of the basic approaches to political economy.

Approaches to political economy

The different schools of thought in international political economy may be broadly classed as realist, liberal and radical, or neo-Marxist. It must be said at the outset that these schools are characteristically broad and that writers within each school do not necessarily agree on most things. While political economy studies the relationship between economic and political processes, each school differs on the nature of this relationship. For liberals, economic activity should be largely free of political interference. Political institutions need to be constrained so as not to interfere in the market. A state should provide no more than the necessary legal regulatory framework for capitalism and the basic infrastructure such as education and roads. Should this be the case, the market can lead to economic growth that benefits all. For realists, the international system requires the prevalence of politics over economics. In the rush to self-reliance, and facing ever diversifying security dilemmas, the state must ensure the economic underpinnings of military capacity. Economic developments are, in this stream of thought, largely explicable by looking at political motives related to national power and interest. For radicals, the fundamental division seen by liberals between economics and politics is an illusion. Furthermore, political institutions are understood as serving the interests of the social classes that prevail at any one moment, not the national interest as posited by realists. Economic developments are not neutral, from this perspective, but reflect an ongoing struggle between classes, both domestically and transnationally. At the same time, different fractions (conceived by economic sector and nationally) of the capitalist class are recognized as being in contestation, so reference is also made to intra-class conflict in the radical perspective. The different perspectives are not just neutral positions but represent different underlying political values about the nature of the good society. By extension, what is at stake in the debate about Asian economic growth and crisis is not just 'facts' – that is, what variables allowed economic growth to proceed at a rate higher than the rest of the world – but normative positions about how states should be structured, how civil society and business should interact with the state, and how countries should relate to the international economy.

Explaining the growth: liberal perspectives

Liberalism purports to treat the individual as the key unit of analysis. This stream of thought claims that individuals, conceived as maximizers of their own interests, know what they want best, and they will seek this in a freely interacting market place. The market, seemingly responsive to individual demands, is seen as the best driver of growth and the most efficient means of resource allocation. Liberals support the expansion of trade at the international level, arguing that greater competition will lead to more efficient production outcomes. This would be an optimal outcome for all, especially the citizen who is conceived as a consumer. Liberals perceive the growing international economic interdependencies as beneficial to all, or as positive sum. Because trade furthers economic growth, countries are seen as having an interest in pursuing international co-operation. Furthermore, as economies become increasingly interdependent, and as institutions arise to regulate economic and other interactions, states are increasingly compelled to work together to maintain an international order that benefits all. In summary, the liberal approach is one that embraces free trade in the belief that market efficiencies will deliver better outcomes to consumers; further, that the intensification of economic interdependencies between national economies will tie states into co-operative and reciprocal relations with each other, diminishing the prospect of a world of warring states.

In explaining the Asian 'miracle' liberals will first point to the general structural factors sustaining Asian economic growth. The first is the existence of international trading and monetary regimes, known as the Bretton Woods system, established after the Second World War and composed of institutions such as the World Bank, the International Monetary Fund, the General Agreement on Tariffs and Trade, and a system of relatively fixed exchange rates. These institutions, sustained by the mutual interdependence of different states and economies, provided the rules, procedures and norms for the conduct of trade and commerce. More specifically, in the early years of East Asia's rapid economic growth, there was a temptation to see the success of the tiger economies, and indeed of Japan, as reflective of a broad embrace of market economics. Some commentators spoke of 'market economy superstars', and as recently as 1998 Palma described Korea as an example of 'virtual free trade' (cited in Raffer and Singer 2001: 139). Liberals also speak of nations possessing a 'comparative advantage', meaning what a country is able to produce more efficiently than another country. Should countries develop this comparative advantage they would be able to compete in the world market and earn foreign exchange with which to purchase goods from other countries and upgrade their own productive capacity. For liberals, the long history of international trade is seen as a positive process entailing liberalization and the breaking down of national borders. The key actors in this are multinational corporations (MNCs), liberally oriented states, and international governmental organizations that are charged with regulating the international economy. Liberals note that the East Asian economies were adept at promoting their comparative advantage (cheap labour and an educated workforce) in order to climb up the developmental ladder, at the same time as reducing tariffs and opening up to the world market. Having initially looked towards import-substitution strategies, the HPAEs all turned towards export-oriented industrialization, the first-tier NICs in the 1960s and the second-tier NICs in the 1980s.

As the 1980s progressed it became apparent that the 'market' could not totally account for the growth sustained by the HPAEs. For one, an increasingly frustrated United States, facing chronic balance of payments deficits and high levels of foreign debt, began to critique the trade practices and state interventions in East Asia, especially Japan and South Korea, as market deforming. This led to the revisionist attack on Japan (see Chapter 3). However, liberals were not incapable of countenancing a role for the state in economic development. Indeed, throughout the 1990s there emerged a greater appreciation of the state. While liberals give priority to market freedom, the state is recognized as providing the regulatory framework necessary for the operation of a free market. It provides guarantees for property, it provides the policy framework for economic matters, and it enforces rules and laws. Liberals could see well enough that if markets were to function, institutions were required. This 'institutional political economy' became increasingly influential, and from the early 1990s onwards the World Bank and the International Monetary Fund began to call for 'good governance' (transparency, participation and efficiency) as part of the necessary institutional ingredients of sustainable economic growth in East Asia.

This shift from market fundamentalism to recognition of the role of institutions in providing the necessary security for market exchanges and the reproduction of society at large was reflected in the World Bank's attempt to explain the East Asian miracle in a 1993 report

(World Bank 1993; Rodan *et al.* 2001: 17–20). The World Bank's appraisal of the role of the state in the HPAEs was ambiguous. The report praised the market-facilitating behaviour of states, such as the provision of the regulatory framework for markets in commodities and labour, and the provision of sound macroeconomic management of the economy. However, it also sounded a warning in regard to behaviour which was at variance to the desired level playing field of the free market. Such variances included subsidies of infant industries, excessive protection and strict management of resources by the state. Perhaps seeing these actions as undesirable but understandable, the report argued that in the era of the global economy such interventions should be avoided (World Bank 1993), suggesting that countries should conform more to market-facilitating strategies. Eager to attribute East Asia's success to market-oriented economies, liberals tended to gloss over the significant role played by the state.

Explaining the growth: realist perspectives

In the economic arena, realist perspectives are often described as realist–mercantilist. This approach to international political economy focuses on the state and its role in advancing the interests of a national economy against other states. Seeing interaction in the international economy as zero-sum, realists advise the pursuit of economic strategies that maximize national interests at the expense of rival states. From the realist perspective the kind of interdependency valued by liberals invites danger, particularly if there is asymmetrical inter-dependency on another state for key factors of production. Thus, in the realist perspective, states should attempt to establish and maintain strategic industries that provide the national economy with a degree of self-sufficiency, and to manage international economic relations in a manner that does not augment the power of rival states. As Gill and Law (1988: 28) explain, the concept of 'strategic industries' relates to

> the constellation of industries which can create the optimum conditions for a high degree of national autonomy and economic sovereignty. . . . This also entails the ability to exert power within the inter-state system. . . . Such strategic industries might there-fore include arms and related industries, capital goods more generally, and sometimes agriculture.

More specifically related to East Asia, we have already noted the importance of 'develop mental states'. A realist would extend this argument further and argue that the East Asian states pursued a strategy of neo-mercantilism, as part of the more general quest for security, national power and prestige. At a concrete level mercantilism describes a political economy of national growth based on limiting imports and encouraging exports, while maintaining a positive balance of payments. Profoundly nationalist in orientation, Japan is said to pursue a Mercantilist strategy. Japanese economic planners were greatly influenced by European mercantilist thought which had informed Bismarck's strategy of industrialization in late nineteenth-century Germany (Deans 1999: 78). Unlike the liberal approach which posits mutual benefit from growth in trade, mercantilism proposes opportunistic behaviour at the expense of rivals. This approach suggests that fundamentally, no matter what international engagements, regimes and treaties a state submits to, the state stands perennially poised against other states; it remains concerned with relative gain over absolute gain (Gilpin 2001: 33). The developmental states may be seen as having taken advantage of the international trading regime to bolster their own national wealth, not that of the global community at large. Japan is often described as having a contemporary mercantilist orientation. For example, in classic mercantilist fashion, it has limited foreign investment. Speaking of the early 2000s, one Japanese institute reports that, 'FDI inflow is equivalent to 1.2% of GDP, far less than the near 20% averaged in other major industrialized countries' (Japan External Trade Organization 2002: 22). Likewise, Japan has robustly resisted import penetration by the major industrialized nations, securing for itself massive trade surpluses (Heginbotham and Samuels 1998).

In summary, in the realist–mercantilist approach the state is a central actor. Further, there is an implicit assumption that this actor is unified and rational in pursuit of its mercantilist objectives defined as national interest. Clearly the stress on the centrality of the state is a far cry from the World Bank's notion of a market-enhancing role for the state. The two interpretations stand opposed.

Before we move on to the third perspective it is worth noting that an attempt was made to synthesize liberal and realist approaches to explain the international economic order after the Second World War. For a number of realists and liberals the Bretton Woods system, which provided the international context for export-led growth for East Asia, was secured by the continuing leadership and dominance of the US, which was seen as having an interest in maintaining and leading the system for its own economic benefit. This explanation of US leadership has become known as the 'hegemonic stability thesis', an approach that conflates liberal and realist premises. It consists of a number of propositions. Given the premise of fundamental anarchy that realists invoke as an attribute of the international system, it follows that authority is required to bring some semblance of order to militate against the pull of anarchy. A dominant power is seen as the only entity able to establish order and enforce relevant rules. By leading and sustaining the system of liberal trade and stable currency exchange rates, and by the provision of international security through military projection and threat, the US effectively functioned as a hegemonic power that stabilized the international system. As Gilpin noted, being a hegemon was not merely about providing so-called public goods (security, trade regime), there was a good deal of self-interest going on: 'The United States has assumed leadership responsibilities because it has been in its economic, political and even ideological interests to do so, or at least it has believed this to be the case' (Gilpin 1987: 88). Whilst realists would expect a hegemonic power's interests to prevail in any international order that it controls, liberals see the possibility of that system transforming into an order that benefits an increasingly interdependent world of states.

Explaining the growth: radical perspectives

There are competing radical interpretations of economic growth in East Asia. Here we will look briefly at dependency thought and Marxist thought. The dependency school of thought was concerned with developing a political economy focused on the power asymmetry between the developed and developing countries. The benign interdependency envisioned by liberals was seen as ideological obfuscation by dependency theorists. In short, dependency theorists posited that a fundamental condition of dependence characterized developing countries (the Global South) and tied them to the economic fortunes of the industrialized capitalist countries (the Global North). This relationship entailed the extraction of the South's surplus by the North and the reproduction of exploitative relations between the two. Furthermore, in some instances it was argued that the exploitation of the South by the North led to a condition of systematic underdevelopment (Frank 1967). This suggested that the nature of global trade functioned to actively construct underdevelopment in the Global South.

In the light of East Asian economic growth the merit of these ideas came under question. Observable growth suggested that the premise of dependence and underdevelopment was wrong (Harris 1986). However, those sympathetic to dependency currents of thought argue that East Asian growth occurred because the various CDSs acted in a manner that partially broke through power asymmetries. Indeed their mercantilist strategies, which were implemented in order to catch up with the industrialized North, were said to have been inspired by Paul Presbisch, an economist who considerably influenced the dependency school (Raffer and Singer 2001: 141). However, while many held that growth in the first tier of NIEs was real, there were criticisms of Southeast Asian growth as externally driven, and therefore dependent growth. Kunio Yoshihara (1988), writing in the late 1980s, argued that Southeast Asian capitalism was ersatz capitalism, by which he meant a form of capitalism that was an inferior imitation of developed industrial capitalism. Yoshihara recognized that the role of foreign capital in the ASEAN economies was declining and that some gains in economic development were evident (especially in the tertiary sector). However, the appellation 'ersatz' indicated a level of dependency on foreign capital in relation to large export-oriented industrial enterprises. The result of this dependence was the emergence of 'technologyless capitalism' and the rise of 'technologically dependent capitalists as comprador capitalists . . . [which has] . . . allowed foreign capital to come in, in order to generate new exports' (Yoshihara 1988: 132). This kind of capitalism was also noted for its lack of a productive domestic and indigenous capitalist class that focused on long-term economic growth and productive investment. Instead the economic arena was said to be animated by all sorts of 'deviant' speculative capitalists focused on short-term gains who pursued market-distorting strategies to enhance their own wealth, including rent-seeking activities such as 'protection from foreign capital . . . concessions, licences, monopoly rights and government subsidies . . .' (Yoshihara 1988: 3). Another feature of ersatz capitalism militating against industrial growth was the historically precarious position of Chinese capitalists within Southeast Asia. Yoshihara's solution to these 'intractable' problems and the problem of dependency (1988: 118–20) was to preach a strategy of national economy development that weaned Southeast Asian nations off their need for foreign capital and for the state to take a greater role in research and development. Dependency theory, in its various forms, is often attacked from those on the left who argue that it is too focused on the national issue of dependence, when the defining feature of political economy is not the struggle between nations but between classes in the international political economy. (Rodan *et al.* 2001: 23–5). This brings us to Marxist political economy.

If individuals and states are the driving force of economics in the liberal and mercantilist perspective respectively, Marxist political economy focuses on the role of classes in the construction of world order. For Marxists the state system is dominated by capitalist interests, it is a system which expands the capitalist mode of production in the interests of capitalists. To understand this system Robert Cox (1981), an influential Marxist political economist, calls for a critical theory that throws light on the way in which the existing structures of power, accumulation of capital and exploitation have emerged and how they are maintained through practices of hegemony. In line with its radical posture, Marxist political economy also attends to the question of which social forces might be in a position to transform existing world orders. Regarding East Asian economic growth a Marxist perspective would first map out the general system into which East Asia was integrated. This may be seen as the world capitalist system, reconstructed after the Second World War and facilitated through the instruments of discipline created by the dominant powers such as the IMF and the World Bank. Yet integration into the international capitalism was uneven, and was shaped by historical and political differences.

In order to place East Asian growth into a system level of analysis that relates to class and conflict, Marxists deploy the concept of hegemony. As described by Cox, hegemony

> means dominance of a particular kind where the dominant state creates an order based ideologically on a broad measure of consent, functioning according to general principles that in fact ensure the continuing supremacy of the leading state or states and leading social classes but at the same time offer some measure or prospect of satisfaction to the less powerful.
>
> (1986: 7)

For Cox and others, at the end of the Second World War the United States emerged as the hegemonic power and established Pax Americana, through which it regenerated the industrialized states of Europe and Japan, in order to construct an open world economy. Furthermore, it linked developing countries into this project. These states were not compelled by means of force into a US-led system, but rather elites could see benefits for their own countries by submitting to a US-led order. These benefits included stability and relations with an international trading regime through which economic growth could be pursued. In this new world order, production was to be increasingly linked to the world economy. Cox argues that to further this liberal order elites in the hegemonic state had to forge alliances with other states and elites, drawing them into its hegemonic bind, in order to sustain a project of liberal trade and capitalist development (1986: 211). At the core of the liberal world system, Western industrialized states were generally liberal in orientation. At the periphery of the system, in developing countries, the hegemonic power sustained authoritarian developmentalist regimes in order to achieve the suppression of communism in the periphery, to undertake restructuring necessary for integration into the world market, and generally to keep the peripheral economies on the side of the 'free world' (Cox 1986: 231–44). The United States poured aid for economic development into developmentalist regimes, especially Taiwan and South Korea. Such inputs, and they were dispersed throughout East and Southeast Asia, provided the necessary capital injection that eventually transformed the region (So and Chiu 1995).

In this approach the intimate connection between economics and politics is paramount: the hegemonic project of the United States to isolate the communist sphere led to a strategy that enhanced the prospects for economic growth. Furthermore, geopolitical concerns may be said to have led the US administration to accept forms of capitalism not in tune with liberal dictates. In this context the developmental states of East Asia were in a position to benefit from economic inputs by the United States and also to have access to the liberal trading regime, without being subject to its rules and regulations. This is necessarily a simplified story, but it indicates that Marxist political economy attempts a complex reckoning of East Asian growth.

We have reviewed at a basic level three competing interpretations of East Asian economic growth. All agree that the existence of an international trading regime was fundamental to Asia's growth and all, significantly, point to the importance of a hegemonic power in at least establishing a world order to which capitalist East Asia, as an economic entity, could direct its productive activities.

The unmaking of the miracle

The Asian economic crisis is commonly understood as beginning in 1997 when currency speculators launched an attack on the Thai baht. However, it is probably useful to recognize that before the dramatic events that unfolded in 1997, the Asian economic miracle was under strain in the core economy of Japan.

The bare facts of this are commonly known. In 1985, in an agreement known as the Plaza Accord, the central banks of the major industrialized economies moved to depreciate the dollar. This was related to the US's ongoing quest to reassert its economic position that had been eroded by the rise of Japan since the 1970s, whose currency it viewed to be deliberately undervalued. In Japan, the Plaza Accord led to an appreciation of the yen, and resulted in a mild recession. In response the government promoted economic stimulus measures such as loosening monetary policy, which led to a greater supply of credit. In effect the government partially liberalized capital markets, and began to undo the close relationship between banks and industry that had characterized the economy. Furthermore, the Bank of Japan embarked on an expansionary programme to return the economy to growth. With excessive credit in the system, much was lent to various projects, many in real estate, leading to a massive rise in land prices and a property boom. At the height of the boom, for instance, it was said that the Imperial Palace Grounds alone were of greater market value than Canada! (Murphy 2000: 37). On average, commercial properties quadrupled in value between 1985 and 1991, while residential and industrial properties 'were a comparatively modest 250% above their earlier value.' (Alexander 1997: 7). Effectively Japan had become a bubble economy in which price rises in assets (such as land and stocks) were unrelated to economic fundamentals (incomes, GDP, productivity), but based on the expectation of rising prices driven by demand. Stocks also tripled in value between 1989 and 1995 (Alexander 1997: 4–5).

Several factors led to an end to the bubble. The Basle Accord of 1988, which stipulated certain conditions relating to minimal capital requirements for banks, eventually forced Japanese banks to impose stringent criteria on loans, leading to a drying up of credit. The government itself imposed new taxes on retail sales, land and capital gains, in order to slow the bubble (Reynolds 2002). These factors led to a downturn in the economy. Many banks had loaned money based on land as collateral. That land was heavily overpriced, and throughout the 1990s experienced successive annual declines in value. This left banks saddled with non-performing loans running into trillions of dollars. Since the 1990s the country's growth rate has barely jumped above 1 per cent. Although still the world's net creditor, the country is none the less in the grip of an economic malaise which throws a shadow across the region. In the West, Japan's economic problems have led to attacks on its unique political economy and calls for profound reform.

If the Plaza Accord of 1985 may be said to have triggered a series of events leading to the bubble and its burst in Japan, in some senses the same may be said for Southeast Asia. As a result of the revaluation of the yen in the years after the Plaza Accord, the region experienced rising foreign direct investment from Japan. By the late 1980s Japanese FDI began to tail off, but credit was now also readily available from European and United States sources eager to tap into the region's boom and extract quick profits.

The funds that entered Asia, fuelling the bubble, were made possible by significant changes in the world economy. Under the Bretton Woods system it was assumed that capital flows between nations would largely relate to trade matters and investment: capital would be productively invested in order to produce goods or services for the market, or would be transferred in order to pay for imports. It was also expected that capital flows would take the form of loans for productive investment. With the collapse of the system in 1971, when the US ended its fixed exchange rate, this expectation proved increasingly irrelevant. Encouraged by new communications technologies, international capital has flowed along largely divergent paths, rarely related to what actually gets traded or produced in the economy. Since the 1960s international finance has largely been 'decoupled' from production and has taken on a life of its own. Vast flows of money are sent in search of profits though short-term portfolio investments, currency speculation and high-risk loans and so on. The scale of financial movement compared to trade is obvious if one considers that in 1990 the value of world trade was estimated at US$5.2 trillion while daily foreign exchange transactions stood at US$1 trillion (Maswood 2000: 86). This increase in capital mobility was felt in developing countries. Before the end of the 1960s government loans to developing countries accounted for the bulk of foreign finance. Steadily, the proportion of private capital flowing to developing countries mounted, so that between 1996 and 1997 some US$300 billion was invested by private investors; this compared with the US$300 billion provided by the World Bank over its fifty years of operation (Winters 1999: 36).

The increasingly deregulated flow of capital placed significant pressure on states. In the Western capitalist countries, the 1980s had been marked by increasing deregulation of all economic sectors, privatization and reduced taxation, as different states competed with each other in order to attract capital. In the developing world, various forms of state intervention related to late industrialization strategies, such as high tariffs, industrial policies, limits to foreign ownership and capital controls, had been retained. Increasingly economic liberals, both domestically and internationally, were seeking the end of these obstacles to foreign entry. According to Bello from the early 1990s onwards a number of states, especially South Korea, Thailand and Indonesia, in various ways responded to the demands for liberalization and devised strategies to attract the much desired foreign capital. This included:

- Financial liberalization: this might involve removal of restrictions on foreign exchange or other capital controls that limit the inflow and outflow of foreign capital; allowing foreign banks and other financial institutions greater entry into domestic markets; opening the stock exchange to foreign portfolio investors.
- The maintenance of high interest rates relative to interest rates in other countries in order to attract foreign capital.
- Providing exchange rate stability, by pegging the currency, in order to provide peace of mind to investors who converted their money into local currency and wanted a guarantee that the local currency would not suddenly devalue. (Bello 1998: 11)

Once provided with these basic conditions, capital quickly flowed into the countries, fuelling speculation in property and stock markets in the region. Then the crash happened. The details are too haphazard and country specific to give in this chapter. Giving a brief account of the Thai experience provides some taste, however, of what South Korea and Indonesia experienced.

Thailand's fall from grace in 1997 was as quick as it was devastating. One Thai minister spoke of his country as being caught up in a 'beauty syndrome':

> One thing in life, you never want to become [is] a beauty queen. When you become a beauty queen you have so many suitors, and they all come asking for love, for this, and for that and offering you everything. The temptations can be so great you can lose

yourself in the process. But when you are dethroned and you are no longer the beauty queen, nobody comes to offer you anything . . .

(Cited in Garran 1998: 74)

Under the conditions of capital deregulation described earlier, Thailand sucked in massive amounts of foreign loans. However, when Thai exports began to dry up in the mid-1990s, capital markets began to get jittery. After all, it appeared that Thailand had borrowed too much in short-term capital markets and this at a time when it was facing decreased export income. In this context, investors holding Thai baht began to panic. Reading Thailand's economic situation as unsustainable, currency speculators began to offload their baht currency holdings in droves. They felt that the baht's value was unsustainable and sooner or later it would have to come down. This placed great stress on the government's pegged rate of 25 baht to the dollar. Although Thai business was largely opposed to devaluation because much of its debt was dollar denominated, in July 1997 Thailand surrendered and floated the baht. In the following weeks its value dropped by 50 per cent. Firms and financial institutions which had debts denominated in dollars now found the value of their debts doubled in relation to the baht. Thailand crashed, and its economy came to a standstill. Millions lost their jobs, and thousands of businesses went bankrupt.

Similar love affairs with foreign capital had been experienced in Indonesia, Malaysia, the Philippines and South Korea, where, for example, foreign debt relative to GNP in 1996 was 64, 52, 51 and 51 respectively. What was more worrying was that much of this debt, as in Thailand, was short-term foreign debt, requiring repayment just at the time that the economies became embroiled in uncertainty, especially in the regional crisis triggered by Thailand's collapse. In response to their fears that the region's growth was not only unsustainable, but that the economies would collapse like a pack of cards, there was a massive outward flow of capital, with tens of billion of dollars departing in 1997 (Winters 1999: 38). The impact of capital withdrawal and the drying up of credit for investment was massive. For instance, in 1998 Indonesia, Korea, Malaysia and Thailand experienced a 13.0 per cent, 6.7 per cent, 7.4 per cent and 10.2 per cent decline in real GDP respectively. Evidence of the crisis is no more obvious than the import statistics which declined exponentially: Indonesia (36.3 per cent), Korea (38.0 per cent), Malaysia (25.0 per cent), and Thailand (40.4 per cent) (Greene 2002: 4–7).

Faced with the credit tap being turned off, massive depreciation of currencies, contracting markets, and with the bailiff at the door, the afflicted countries turned to the International Monetary Fund in order to seek temporary funds to keep the economies afloat. The IMF injected over US$120 billion into Indonesia, South Korea and Thailand. However, in agreeing to render assistance, the IMF imposed a series of conditions on loans, which recipient countries were required to follow. Among these measures were:

- temporary budgetary cuts;
- 'structural reforms to remove features of the economy that had become impediments to growth (such as monopolies, trade barriers, and nontransparent corporate practices) and to improve the efficiency of financial intermediation and the future soundness of financial systems';
- the closure of unviable financial institutions, with the associated write-down of shareholders' capital;
- increased potential for foreign participation in domestic financial systems (IMF 1999).

Explaining the crisis

The most pervasive explanation of the Asian economic crisis has been developed from a broadly liberal perspective that views the demise of the Asian economies as indicative of the crisis of the development state and, more colloquially, the consequences of 'crony capitalism', a catch-all term that captures the prevalence of corruption and collusion between political, business and bureaucratic elites. Having once hailed the region's HPAEs as exemplars of growth, liberals now turned to attacking the governance structures in each country as corrupt and incapable of proper market regulation.

The leading liberal critique came from the IMF, which argued that the crisis

> stemmed from weaknesses in financial systems and, to a lesser extent, governance. A combination of inadequate financial sector supervision, poor assessment and management of financial risk, and the maintenance of relatively fixed exchange rates led banks and corporations to borrow large amounts of international capital, much of it short-term, denominated in foreign currency, and unhedged. . . . Although private sector expenditure and financing decisions led to the crisis, it was made worse by governance issues, notably government involvement in the private sector and lack of transparency in corporate and fiscal accounting and the provision of financial and economic data.
>
> (IMF 1999)

Liberals argued that with high levels of political intervention and corruption in the Asian economies, the market effectively malfunctioned. Robison *et al.* (2002: 18) explain the liberal position succinctly: 'Market discipline . . . was simply not strong enough in these economies, and the task of recovery had to centre on establishing this discipline'. More generally, liberals hailed the crisis in Asia, and Japan's own crisis, as signalling the demise of alternative approaches to capitalist organization and the convergence of economic models around neoliberalism. While the state may have had a significant role to play during the catch-up phase, the developmental state was seen as being unable to perform a credible governance function in the 'transition towards a market-embracing economy' (Kim 1999: 101). Perhaps most emphatic was the estimation of Chung In Moon and Sang Young Rhyu that the 'coming end of East Asian capitalism signals the triumph of Anglo-American capitalism' (1999: 97).

From a realist or state-centred perspective, the Asian economic crisis proves one of the basic points about the centrality of politics over economics, of the state over markets and the importance of power capability in the international system (see Acharya 1999). Against the idea that globalization is an ineluctable force, realists will likely point to its limits, and the centrality of home-based MNCs and the role of the state in shaping economic institutions both at home and abroad (Waltz 1999). In this perspective, the United States remains the dominant power, and indeed has assumed greater power given the disappearance of the Soviet Union. Given the premise of realism, that states pursue their interests defined as power, in the current situation of unipolarity, the predominant state is likely to advance its own interests and manipulate economic circumstances to its own benefit. And further, 'More than any other state, the United States makes the rules and maintains the institutions that shape the international political economy.' (Waltz 1999). Given these premises, a realist perspective focuses on how the crisis has been used to advance US interests in the region, and in particular to push forward its opening of trade and capital markets in the region. In this respect the US might be seen as advancing its own cause against the interests of its regional competitor, the Japanese state, most obviously in its opposition to an Asian Monetary Fund. For decades the United States attempted to open up the region to US corporations. APEC, structural adjustment programmes, the protection of intellectual property, and various GATT discussions all indicate the extent of US designs on the region. Given Japan's perilous economic position, the US may be seen as having used the crisis to advance its liberalization agenda further. Certainly, this is how the issue is often perceived among East Asian elites (Higgott 1998). Thus the crisis has allowed Western states, led by the US, to dismantle key aspects of mercantilist strategies. It is just one more episode in the battle of relative benefit. Realists find further vindication of their perspective in the fact that the regional institutions such as ASEAN did little to mitigate the crisis – suggesting that their significance had been overstated by liberal institutionalists.

Neo-dependency observers see the crisis and the intervention of the international financial institutions as evidence of further attempts to downgrade the gains made by the NIEs in the 1970s and 1980s leading to new ties of dependency as well as further integration into a Northern-dominated economy. The crisis is seen as limiting the capacity of Southeast Asian countries to resist fast-track liberalization sought by IFIs and the US (Bello 1998: 12). The crisis is also said to vindicate the thesis of dependency, that the South is dependent on Western capital and agencies in the determination of its economic future. The Asian Miracle, especially in Southeast Asia, is retrospectively described as Western capital driven, having led the region into a debt crisis and further delimiting its capacity to resist Northern penetration. If the IMF intervention is to be understood as anything it is simply a battering ram for advanced capitalist interests in the region. The words of Larry Summers, US Treasury Chair, are often cited as evidence of this. Summers, speaking in 1994 on the structural adjustment programmes in Argentina, positively crowed about the results:

> Today, fully 50 per cent of the banking sector, 70 per cent of private banks, in Argentina are foreign controlled, up from 30 per cent in 1994. The result is a deeper, more efficient financial market, and external investors with a greater stake in staying put.
>
> (Cited in Bello 1999)

From the dependency perspective, there is no reason not to think that the US hopes to make the same gains in Asia through the restructuring forced on the economies as part of their IMF loans.

If the dependency thesis sees Pax Americana alive and well in the events of the Asian economic crisis, the more classically oriented Marxist account suggests that the crisis reflects a new era of capitalism in which transnational classes, through international agencies and through the alliances of various state institutions, work together in order to advance the interests of capitalism in general. According to this perspective, from the 1970s onwards the increasing internationalization of production by MNCs and the creation of global financial markets set the scene for a fundamental shift in the nature of national capitalisms, as states became hostage to market discipline and the structural power of capital. Especially in the 1980s states were required to pursue policies that made them attractive sites for investors, thus creating policy convergence across much of the Western world. The 1990s may be read as the attempt to extend this process to developing countries. Robert Cox has argued that increasingly there is loosely ordered global governance centred on what he calls a *'nebuleuse'* or 'a loose elite network of influentials and agencies, sharing a common set of ideas that collectively perform the governance function' (1997: 60). Constituting the *nebuleuse* are organizations such as the World Bank, the OECD, the IMF and the World Economic

Forum. These organizations function to bring together global elites who hammer out a consensus on the requirements for a flourishing and viable capitalism. By this process and through these institutions, a common economic ideology emerges and is dispersed through intergovernmental agencies, texts and networks. This leads to national policy that is largely in conformity with the hegemonic ideology of economic liberalism. Related to the Asian economic crisis, the IMF intervention is seen as furthering the advance of 'disciplinary neoliberalism' at the expense of the poor. According to Stephen Gill, the neoliberal perspective as it manifests itself in various international financial institutions (IFIs) privileges 'investors'. States are ever cautious to please investors in order to attract capital; the result is a mind-set that believes

> economic growth depends on the need to maintain investor confidence and thus governments are driven to sustain their credibility in the eyes of investors by attempting to provide an appropriate business environment. This is a form of the structural power of capital.
>
> (Gill 2000: 4)

The strictures of the IMF and of economic commentators close to the IFIs have always been about the creation of market-friendly environments. Thus the crisis is read, in this radical account, as having furthered the cause of market opening in the interests of capital, and as having fundamentally altered the configuration of power in the region. In imposing conditions on the loans, largely at the behest of the United States, there has been significant progress in bringing the states in the region into line with the dominant liberal orthodoxy.

Conclusion

The consequences of the crisis for the political economy of the Asia-Pacific are an ongoing issue and the direction remains unclear. Those supportive of the IMF role are eager to point out that after an initial negative growth in the affected economies, by 1999 onwards modest economic growth has been achieved. In some countries such as South Korea growth has been at high levels. This is despite the legacy of bad debt, much of which was largely nationalized through government-established asset management companies in an effort to restructure the financial sector. However, while the programme of debt restructuring in South Korea and Malaysia is generally described as successful, in Thailand it is seen as moving too slowly because of the influence of bureaucrats and business in the determination of restructuring. In Indonesia the government asset management company is considered to have effectively been captured by vested interests who have used it to minimize debt restructuring (Cochrane and Larmer 2003: 28). Another feature of the crisis has been the growing levels of foreign ownership of banking and other sectors of the economy. After the crisis the IMF negotiated lifting the ceiling on foreign ownership in a number of sectors. The result has been expanded foreign ownership (see Hewison 2001).

Yet despite inroads into the Asian economies it is clear that there are limits to the neoliberal agenda. In considering the impact of the crisis on Southeast Asia it has been suggested that

> the triumph of the neo-liberal regulatory state has been ambiguous and inconclusive. Even where the path of the crisis was most destructive, attempts to reorganise banks and financial regimes, to transform systems of corporate governance and to replace

systems of money politics with representative forms of political democracy has been bitterly contested . . .

(Robison *et al.* 2002: 3)

Indeed, careful country case studies, unable to be undertaken here, suggest that despite the ambitious programme of liberalization, domestic coalitions have formed to limit the impact of the post-crisis reform agenda. From Singapore to Indonesia to Thailand, different strategies are being deployed to maintain a degree of national control over the economy (Weiss and Hobson 1999). Moreover, the general nature of state–business relations still fails to conform to that sought by the IFIs. Even in Thailand, once considered the star pupil of the IMF in that it moved to implement IMF reforms in the 1997–99 period, the pace of reform has slowed in order to give domestic capitalist groupings a 'breathing space' to compete with foreigners (Robison *et al.* 2002). Given these qualifications to the advance of the neoliberal project, the idea of 'convergence' is looking every bit as slippery as the idea of the 'End of History' pronounced by Francis Fukuyama after the end of the Cold War.

What should become clear from this brief survey of Asian economic growth and crisis is that faced with the same phenomena political economists will interpret events in fundamentally different ways. Depending on where you stand the Asian crisis may be seen as a 'blessing in disguise', paradoxically advancing the cause of economic liberalization; it may be seen as just a bleep in the endless quest of power that constantly animates the international system; or most bleakly, it may mark the further advance of a particular brand of capitalism that places the logic of the market above human need. The 'logic of the market' in the radical perspective, of course, is nothing but the veiled interests of capitalist elites.

References

Acharya, A. (1999) 'Realism, institutionalism, and the Asian economic crisis', *Contemporary Southeast Asia*, 21: 1–17.

Alexander, A. (1997) 'Asset prices in Japan: the bubble and its breaking', *Japan Economic Institute Report*, 36, September.

Bark, T. (2000) 'Trade patterns of East Asia: before and after the currency crisis', *Journal of International and Area Studies*, 7: 1–14.

Bello, W. (1998) 'The end of the miracle: speculation, foreign capital domination and the collapse of the Southeast Asian economies', *Multinational Monitor*, 19, 1 & 2.

Bello, W. (1999) 'Deconstructing Harry: what the new man at Treasury has in store for Asia', *The Nation* (Bangkok), 28 July. Online. Available HTTP: <http://www.tni.org/archives/bello/larry.htm> (accessed 19 January 2003).

Camilleri, J. A. (2000) *States, Markets and Civil Society in Asia-Pacific*, Cheltenham: Edward Elgar.

Chowdhury, A. and Islam, I. (1993) *The Newly Industrialising Economies of East Asia*, London: Routledge.

Cochrane, J. and Larmer, B. (2003) 'The cronies return', *Newsweek*, February, p. 28.

Cox, R. W. (1981) 'Social forces, states and world orders: beyond international relations theory', *Millennium: Journal of International Studies*, 10: 126–55.

Cox, R. W. (1986) *Production, Power, and World Order*, Vol. 1, New York: Columbia University Press.

Cox, R. W. (1997) 'Democracy in hard times', in A. McGrew (ed.) *The Transformation of Democracy*, Cambridge: Polity Press.

Deans, P. (1999) 'The capitalist developmental state in East Asia', in R. Palan and J. Abbott, with P. Deans (eds) *State Strategies in the Global Political Economy*, rev. edn, London Pinter Pty Ltd pp. 78–102.

Frank, A. G. (1967) *Capitalism and Underdevelopment in Latin America: Historical Studies of Chile and Brazil*, New York: Monthly Review Press.

Garran, R. (1998) *Tigers Tamed: The End of the Asian Miracle*, St Leonards: Allen & Unwin.

Gill, S. (2000) 'The constitution of global capitalism', paper presented at International Studies Association Annual Convention, Los Angeles.

Gill, S. and Law, D. (1988) *The Global Political Economy: Perspectives, Problems, and Policies*, Baltimore, MD: Johns Hopkins University Press.

Gilpin, R. (1987) *The Political Economy of International Relations*, Princeton, NJ: Princeton University Press.

Gilpin, R. (2001) *Global Political Economy: Understanding the International Economic Order*, Princeton, NJ: Princeton University Press.

Greene, J. E. (2002) 'The output decline in Asian crisis countries: investment aspects', IMF Working Paper No. 02/25.

Harris, N. (1986) *The End of the Third World*, London: Tauris.

Heginbotham, E. and Samuels, R. J. (1998) 'Mercantile realism and Japanese foreign policy', *International Security*, 22: 171–203.

Hewison, K. (2001) 'Pathways to recovery: bankers, business and nationalism in Thailand', Working Paper No. 1, Southeast Asian Research Centre, City University, Hong Kong.

Higgott, R. (1998) 'The Asian economic crisis: a study in the politics of resentment', *New Political Economy*, 3: 333–6.

International Monetary Fund (1999) 'The IMF's response to the Asian crisis: a factsheet'. Online. Available HTTP: <http://www.imf.org/external/np/exr/facts/asia.htm> (accessed 19 July 2000).

Japan External Trade Organization (2002) *2002 White Paper on International Trade and Investment (Summary)*. Online. Available HTTP: <http://www.jetro.go.jp/it/e/pub/whitepaper/2002.pdf> (accessed 27 November 2003).

Johnson, C. (1982) *MITI and the Japanese miracle*, Stanford, CA: Stanford University Press.

Johnson, C. (1985) 'Political institutions and economic performance: the government–business relationship in Japan, South Korea and Taiwan', in R. Scalapino, S. Sato and J. Wanandi (eds) *Asian Economic Development: Present and Future*, Berkeley, CA: Institute of East Asian Studies, University of California.

Johnson, C. (1999) 'The development state: odyssey of a concept', in M. Woo-Cumings (ed.) *The Development State*, Ithaca, NY: Cornell University Press, pp. 32–60.

Kim, H. (1999) 'Fragility or continuity? Economic governance of East Asian capitalism', in R. Robison, K. Jayasuriya, M. Beeson and R. H. Kim (eds) *Politics and Markets in the Wake of the Asian Crisis*, London: Routledge, pp. 99–115.

MacIntyre, A. (1994) 'Business, government and development; Northeast and Southeast Asian comparisons', in A. MacIntyre (ed.) *Business and Government in Industrializing Asia*, St Leonards: Allen & Unwin, pp. 1–28.

Maswood, J. (2000) *International Political Economy and Globalization*, Singapore: World Scientific.

Moon, C. I. and Rhyu, S. Y. (1999) 'The state, structural rigidity, and the end of Asian capitalism', in R. Robison, K. Jayasuriya, M. Beeson and R. H. Kim (eds) *Politics and Markets in the Wake of the Asian Crisis*, London: Routledge, pp. 77–98.

Murphy, R. T. (2000) 'Japan's economic crisis', *New Left Review* (New Series), 1: 25–53.

Pempel, T. J. (1999) 'The developmental regime in a changing world economy', in M. Woo-Cumings (ed.) *The Development State*, Ithaca, NY: Cornell University Press.

Raffer, K. and Singer, H. W. (2001) *The Economic North–South Divide: Six Decades of Unequal Development*, Cheltenham: Edward Elgar.

Reynolds, A. (2002) 'Economic distinction', *The Washington Times*, 13 October.

Robison, R., Rodan, G. and Hewison, K. (2002) 'Transplanting the regulatory state: a pathology of rejection', Working Paper Series No. 33, September, Southeast Asian Research Centre, City University, Hong Kong.

Rodan, G., Hewison, K. and Robison, R. (2001) *The Political Economy of South-East Asia*, 2nd edn, Melbourne: Oxford University Press.

Rowen, H. S. (ed.) (1998) *Behind East Asian Growth: the Political and Social Foundations of Prosperity*, London: Routledge.

So, A. Y. and Chiu, S. W. K. (1995) *East Asia and the World Economy*, Thousand Oaks, CA: Sage.

Waltz, K. (1999) 'Globalization and governance', *PS Online*, December. Online. Available HTTP: <http://www.mtholyoke.edu/acad/intrel/walglob.htm> (accessed 15 January 2003).

Weiss, L. and Hobson, J. (1999) 'State power and economic strength revisited: what's so special about the Asian crisis?', in R. Robison, K. Jayasuriya, M. Beeson and R. H. Kim (eds) *Politics and Markets in the Wake of the Asian Crisis*, London: Routledge, pp. 53–74.

Winters, J. A. (1999) 'The financial crisis in Southeast Asia', in R. Robison, K. Jayasuriya, M. Beeson and R. H. Kim (eds) *Politics and Markets in the Wake of the Asian Crisis*, London: Routledge, pp. 34–52.

World Bank (1993) *The East Asian Miracle: Economic Growth and Public Policy*, Washington, DC: World Bank.

Yoshihara, K. (1988) *The Rise of Ersatz Capitalism in South-East Asia*, New York: Oxford University Press.

11 Transnational actors in the Asia-Pacific

Rémy Davison

Introduction: defining transnational actors

A key issue in this chapter is the extent to which transnational actors (TNAs) have challenged the centrality of the state as the most important actor in international relations. Realists, such as Mearsheimer (1995: 9–11), argue that TNAs and intergovernmental organizations (IGOs) are second-order actors; they are merely 'intervening variables in their ability to change state behaviour'. Conversely, some liberal and radical analyses assert that TNAs are an integral part of the structure of international politics, advancing interests as diverse as transnational capital, secessionist movements, women, children and the environment. In this respect, TNAs can redefine the boundaries of political community.

In this chapter, international institutions are largely excluded from the discussion, as they are essentially IGOs and, thus, state-based actors. Although some non-state actors have representation or observer status at certain IGOs, membership and voting is generally restricted to states. As some TNAs perceive IGOs as essentially state-centric, they have frequently directed their discontent at IGOs, such as the IMF, World Bank and WTO. Conversely, other non-state actors, such as transnational corporations, have strongly supported IGOs dealing with international trade and finance, while often opposing issues on the global agenda raised by environmental NGOs, such as the Kyoto Protocol. Nevertheless, non-state actors view the infiltration of IGOs as crucial to the promotion of their policy agendas. Major transnational NGOs are affiliated with the UN's Economic and Social Committee (ECOSOC), which does not give them similar power and influence to states within the UN, but it does accord them a legitimate place in international diplomacy.

TNAs can play a significant role in international politics, particularly in terms of their influence upon negotiations and the policy-making process. TNAs may be defined as contributors to these processes, but they are not parties to actual decisions, which remain in the hands of states or IGOs. Many TNAs, such as transnational corporations (TNCs), do not have a local basis in a state; they may merely be 'hosted'. Depending upon the issue area and their relative resources, TNAs' influence varies considerably. TNAs can also operate not only across a number of states, but also at the subnational level in order to promote their agendas and interests. 'International relations' describes intercourse *between* states, whereas 'transnational relations' describes interactions *across* state boundaries.

The term 'transnational actor' describes an exceptionally broad range of activities and organizations including labour unions, industrial groups, the media or environmental lobbyists. TNAs also include non-state actors such as private citizens living in different states connected through private, rather than governmental, channels. Examples include transnational business enterprises, religious groups and terrorist organizations. It is notable that although TNAs may interact frequently with the state, they are not state-based actors. However, Higgott *et al.* (2000) argue that TNAs are increasingly important contributors to the process of globalization, as their networks form important transnational linkages across a range of issue areas. Moravcsik's (1993) 'two-level' perspective asserts that domestic as well as international actors affect and constrain policy making, although TNAs are largely excluded from the two-level framework. Conversely, Ataman (2002) suggests that international relations theory overlooks the significance of TNAs, and that the domestic–international nexus, together with the influence of TNAs, effectively forms a 'three-level game'. According to Ataman (2002: 2), this means that TNAs have become 'significant determinants of foreign policy orientation and behaviour of nation-states'.

TNAs operate across national borders, rather than globally, although some are global in their composition and reach. Such is the diversity and extent of TNAs that Castells (1999) has argued we live in a 'network society'. Risse-Kappen (1995) defines the transnational as interactions across national borders involving at least one non-state actor. Liberal critiques of TNAs go further, asserting that INGOs are instrumental to the formation of global civil society. However, realists argue that INGOs and other TNAs remain constrained by the state, and that shared norms and values among some TNAs are not sufficient to overcome competition and often differing objectives between actors (Cooley and Ron 2002). Conversely, Bello (2002) takes a more radical perspective, arguing that:

> The days when technocrats, politicians, and industrial elites monopolized decision making when it came to regional coordination are over. Whatever one thinks about civil society groups or NGOs, they are on the rise and they will make tremendous demands for inclusion in decision making in this decade.

TNAs are frequently regionally based, due to their links with a particular geographic part of the world. Relatively few, such as the largest firms, are truly global actors. Conversely, nationally based actors tend to be limited to particular countries, with their agendas and impact restricted to individual states. In this respect, TNAs differ markedly from their state-based counterparts in that they often break down the barriers between countries by establishing frequently sophisticated networks which transcend national boundaries. While some, such as manufacturing or trade organizations, operate in tandem with governments, others, for example environmental groups (Greenpeace), human rights organizations (Amnesty) and wilderness/animal rights groups (the Humane Society), may be at odds with national governments in a wide range of issue areas.

Transnational firms have been arguably the most influential TNAs, although IGOs have also developed critical policy relevance, particularly after the 1997 currency crisis. Organizations such as the IMF and World Bank, together with the Asian Development Bank, have gained increasing responsibility for policy formulation and development in the region. To a certain extent, this has resulted in the loss of some aspects of economic sovereignty in states such as Malaysia, Thailand, Indonesia, South Korea and the Philippines.

Domestic firms have also been powerful locomotives of regional economic integration in the Asia-Pacific, evidenced by the interdependence between Hong Kong, Taiwan and mainland China, as well as Japan's development of intra-firm and intra-industry linkages throughout the ASEAN region. National business associations in certain industry sectors (automotive products; oil; steel) have also expanded within the region, resulting in more cohesive lobbying by industry associations of governments at both the local level, and in various regional and international forums. These transnational networks and linkages at the firm level mean government and business throughout the region have become increasingly interdependent; for example, it is more difficult for Japanese governments to countenance tariffs or other barriers to Taiwanese imports when major Japanese corporations, such as NEC and Sony, are heavily reliant upon Taiwanese manufacturing for their consumer electronics industries.

Transnational activism has also increased exponentially, partly as a result of, and partly as a response to, the accelerating pace of globalization. Domestic NGOs frequently develop links with other domestically based NGOs, resulting in regionally based, transborder networks. For instance, human rights groups have been responsible for monitoring and publicizing human rights violations (Burma; PRC) or development projects which affect traditional inhabitants (Yangtze; Tumen River Delta). Ghils (1992) argues that activist NGOs form the basis for a transnational civil society. NGOs themselves have become so proliferate across a range of issue areas that they are given specific acronyms, such as religious international NGOs (RINGOs); business international NGOs (BINGOs); and environmental NGOs (ENGOs) (Stephenson 2000: 270).

Transnational cultural networks are also highly visible within the Asia-Pacific region, and these often extend globally. Connections between individuals, social groups, family members and cultural organizations transcend borders and provide for continuous interaction across an extremely broad range of issue areas. Some contacts may be between business and government elites, such as the Australia–China Business Council; however, groups such as this partly reflect their expatriate Chinese citizenship, and the family, business and regional connections that arise from this. As Chapter 4 notes, the Chinese diaspora represents a significant transnational investor in the PRC (Arrighi 2002).

Analysts frequently emphasize the role of the capitalist-development state in promoting not only export-led growth, but also the labour conditions which make the state attractive to transnational capital. According to Deyo *et al.* (1987), the demands of foreign actors (TNCs) and international market pressures condition East Asian domestic labour regimes to some extent. This has meant that NGOs concerned with labour conditions in the region face opposition from both states and firms. Although it is a UN organization, the ILO has had a limited effect upon the development and maintenance of labour standards and working conditions in East Asia. However, some TNCs, such as Nike and Mattel, have been forced to abide by the ILO Code of Conduct due to pressure from NGOs in their home countries, which had widely publicized these firms' labour exploitation in East Asia (ILO 2003). This is due partly to the fact that it is widely regarded as a 'Western' organization, but also partly because government and international business in the Asia-Pacific view the ILO's role as interventionist, regulatory and likely to impose considerable costs upon business. However, this has not prevented human rights NGOs in East Asia from networking and formulating harmonized strategies for dealing with the protection of workers across the region. For example, the Asia-Pacific Centre of Education for International Understanding (ACEIU), which is sponsored by UNESCO, has NGO worker-representatives from Cambodia, India, Indonesia, Japan, Korea, Malaysia, Mongolia, Nepal, Pakistan, Philippines, Singapore, Sri Lanka, Taiwan, Vietnam, People's Republic of China, Bangladesh, Hong Kong, Papua New Guinea and Thailand. Through advertising, research, training and education, NGOs, such as ACEIU, maintain pressure on governments, as well as attempting, where possible, to elicit international support for transnational human rights issues (Human Rights Osaka 2000).

The plethora of TNAs demands a wide-ranging discussion, particularly as TNAs' influence varies considerably in different states and issue areas. The following section considers the issue of the relative autonomy of 'insularity' of 'strong' and 'weak' states in the East Asian region from rent-seeking TNAs. The third section discusses the power and influence of the TNC and transnational capital. The fourth section examines the proliferation of transnational NGOs and assesses their influence upon national policy making.

The influence of TNAs: the 'strong state' versus 'weak state' conundrum

The 'strong state/weak state' thesis argues that the more susceptible states are to infiltration by rent-seekers, such as domestic interests, transnational firms, NGOs and other TNAs, the weaker they are. This hypothesis is particularly applicable to Southeast Asia. The degree to which rent-seekers and transnational actors can gain access to national political systems is often governed by their level of openness. In both democratic and non-democratic political systems, coalitions of domestic and TNAs can frequently influence policy making. Risse-Kappen argues that differences in domestic structures determine the variation in the policy impact of TNAs (Risse-Kappen 1995).

In Johnson's (1982) conception of the capitalist development state, Japan is characterized as a 'strong state' as it was able to organize and implement its administrative guidance model via the *keiretsu* networks. In China, the Communist Party under Deng in the 1980s radically shifted the economy to export-led growth and market-based capitalism. In South Korea, the Park government from the early 1960s forcibly compelled industrialists to merge firms into giant *chaebols* – massive industrial conglomerates which would drive South Korean export growth. In Taiwan, the governing KMT developed strategies such as 'guerilla capitalism', which encouraged the development of small firms specializing in particular products, such as electronic components. Thus, there is a general consensus that Northeast Asian economic development has been largely based around the existence of the 'strong' state, relatively untainted by excessive business infiltration. China, for example, limits TNC ownership of productive assets, while Japan accomplished this successfully for decades. However, even the 'strong' Japanese state has become more susceptible to rent-seeking by its own TNCs. There are other exceptions to the 'strong state' rule: pre-1997 Hong Kong was an exceptional economic success which was notable for the *absence* of the strong, guiding (or deadening) hand of the state. However, Hong Kong's system of governance was not heavily affected by rent-seeking or corruption either. In critiquing this 'strong state' hypothesis, Arts (2000: 525) argues that 'any "weak" agent is able to mobilise (at least some) countervailing power *vis-à-vis* any "strong" agent'.

The experience of Southeast Asia has been utterly different from the North, with the exception of Singapore. In its drive to survive as a small, independent state, Singapore is notable for its commitment to public investment, infrastructure development and compulsory pension fund schemes. Conversely, Indonesia, Malaysia, the Philippines and Thailand have traditionally been viewed as exponents of 'crony capitalism', exemplified by the influence of 'presidential families' (Indonesia, the Philippines), and party-political cronyism (Malaysia, Thailand). Weak states are also characterized by a 'captive bureaucracy', which is driven by the policy agendas of rent-seekers, rather than efficiency and the implementation of national policy objectives. This has resulted in 'weak' Southeast Asian states, easily permeable by influential non-state actors, such as firms, which limit the state's relative autonomy.

Box 11.1 Strong states v. weak states

1   Extent of financial control over the economy.
2   Extent of control over labour relations.
3   The degree of autonomy of the economic bureaucracy.
4   The degree to which the state has been captured by its main economic clients.
5   The balance between incentive and command in economic guidance.
6   Special private sector organizations (e.g., *chaebols* (ROK) and *caifa* (Taiwan)).
7   The role of foreign capital.

Source: Johnson (1987)

In effect, weak states often provide the antithesis of national policy autonomy; more accurately, policy beneficiaries are rent-seeking firms and individuals (associates of presidential families; members of political parties; interest groups; and domestic and foreign TNCs). The key problem is that 'weak' states are unlikely to achieve optimal policy outcomes in terms of their technical, dynamic or allocative efficiency, due to penetration by both domestic and TNAs, particularly firms. The environment wrought by the Asian economic crisis demonstrated the extent to which 'weak' states of Southeast Asia – as well as some 'strong' states, such as South Korea – were susceptible not only to the vagaries of transnational capital, but also to the influence of international institutions (IMF, World Bank). Transnational NGOs also exploited states' relative weakness; the pressure placed upon Indonesia to hold an autonomy/independence ballot in East Timor demonstrated how NGOs could affect the national policies of weak states, particularly when supported by other actors, such as the UN, the US and Australia. However, although strong states are less vulnerable to the influence of TNAs than weak states, the diversity, resources and networks developed by TNAs suggest that no state can claim complete autonomy in policy making.

Transnational corporations

Also known as international or multinational corporations (MNCs), TNCs have developed considerable politico-economic influence. The TNC dates from at least the nineteenth century, and possibly even earlier. During the 1970s, TNCs were the subject of widespread criticism for their activities, which some viewed as antithetical to the social, economic and environmental goals of developing countries. Wilson (1990: 163) argues that TNCs may be viewed as 'companies without governments'. Although the OECD has developed a number of guidelines governing the behaviour of TNCs in member countries, most East Asian states are not party to conventions governing workers' conditions, such as the International Labour Organization's (ILO) Fundamental Conventions. Thus, TNCs' behaviour is more likely to be regulated by pressure from either their parent country or transnational NGOs, rather than the host state.

Realists, such as Gilpin (1975), Waltz (1970) and Krasner (1978), argue that TNCs frequently operate as adjuncts of the state, increasing the state's international diplomatic leverage and projecting its economic and market power. It is difficult to dissociate GM, Ford, IBM and Microsoft from the US, just as it is hard to conceive of Toyota, Mitsubishi and Sony as anything but 'Japanese' corporations. For Waltz (1970: 218), TNCs are not international corporations; they are 'national corporations operating abroad'. As Stopford and Strange (1991) note, firms are not autonomous actors; they rely heavily upon states to provide public goods, as well as a stable market environment. Both states and firms engage in competition for markets. States' revenues and market power are enhanced by a strong economy, giving them the opportunity to project their power and influence the policies of others. However, Gilpin (2001: 17) argues that 'realism should acknowledge the importance of such non-state actors as transnational firms, international institutions and NGOs in the determination of international affairs'. This point is taken up by Nye, who argues that

> the realist assumption is that security is the dominant concern, force is the major instrument, and governments more or less maintain their coherence as they interact with each other. In complex interdependence, security is less dominant as a concern, force is less useful as an instrument, you have many TNAs that are going to and fro across borders, making coalitions that are not always well described by national labels . . .
>
> (Institute of International Studies 1998)

The world's largest corporations are US-based, and 90 per cent of the world's 200 biggest TNCs are based in America, Japan, Germany, Britain and France. Approximately 150–160 of the world's largest corporations by revenue listed in the *Fortune 500* are US-based, while 130–140 are from Japan, 40 each from France and Germany and 35 from Britain. Very few of the top 500 are from developing countries, with the notable exception of China, which has three entries. Two developing countries had their first entries in 1995: South Korea (Daewoo) and Venezuela (Venezuela Oil). However, the net foreign assets of TNCs headquartered in the 'big five' in 2002 (US, Japan, UK, France and Germany) dwarfs those of any other state's TNCs, totalling around US$3 trillion. In 2002, the world's largest corporation, Wal-Mart, had almost US$220 billion in turnover. GM frequently tops the list, trailed by Ford, the world's third-biggest corporation. Only around twenty countries have a GDP larger than the five largest TNCs. To place this in context, Toyota is 'bigger' than any ASEAN country, while Ford is larger than Saudi Arabia and South Africa. In 1968, there were 7,276 firms operating globally, with the number rising to 35,000 in 1990. By 2000, there were approximately 45,000 global firms operating 280,000 subsidiaries internationally, accounting for one-third of the world's products (Aventis Triangle Forum 2003). TNCs are also heavily dependent upon revenues from their foreign operations. On average, the 100-largest US-based TNCs derive 40 per cent of their income from overseas, while for Coca-Cola, Palmolive, IBM and Exxon the figure is 60 per cent (Forbes 2003; Fortune 2003).

TNCs may often control more assets than a state; however, these assets do not include the state's monopoly over the means of coercion, in the form of police, courts, bureaucracy and the military. Moreover, sales and assets do not necessarily provide an adequate picture of a firm; in 1992, GM was dangerously close to bankruptcy. Thus, while TNCs can wield considerable politico-economic influence, like states, they are susceptible to market forces and corruption. In 2002, Enron, the world's sixth-largest firm, collapsed, while Amoco, Compaq, Chrysler and DEC have disappeared, having been acquired by, or merged with, larger corporations.

Although Microsoft is the world's largest technology firm in terms of market capitalization, IBM's sales revenues are considerably higher than Microsoft's. However, due to Microsoft's overwhelming dominance in PC operating systems and business software markets, it has considerable economic and political leverage both in the US and internationally. In an attempt to reduce its dependence upon Western high-technology TNCs and costly licensing the Chinese government in 2003 announced it would develop its own audiovisual (AV) standards and supercomputers. Ironically, however, the Chinese government was compelled to invite Microsoft, IBM and Philips to form a consortium to help develop the AV standard (c|net Asia 2003). Another example is the Business Software Alliance (BSA), whose members include the world's three largest software publishers – Microsoft, Adobe and Apple – which has successfully lobbied both the US and Asian governments, leading to crackdowns on software piracy in China, Japan, Taiwan, Hong Kong and South Korea. In the mid-1990s, GM, Ford and Chrysler charged that Japanese protectionism and dumping were behind US automotive trade deficits, leading to threats of retaliation from the US Trade Representative (USTR). The Japanese government capitulated, encouraging similar lobbying from Eastman-Kodak against allegedly protectionist Japanese and South Korean trade practices. Again, the USTR intervened, in this case to protect US film and camera makers. In summary, the considerable resources available to TNCs, as well as business–government networks, can translate into significant influence upon national policy formation.

Commentators frequently compare the revenues and assets of giant TNCs with states' GDPs, but the comparison is not particularly helpful. Although TNCs can exercise considerable policy leverage in states where there is relative investment scarcity (for example, Toyota's FDI in Myanmar, Vietnam and the Philippines), individual firms have little influence in highly competitive investment climates, even in developing countries. The technological prowess and vast capital of Japanese firms such as Toyota and Nissan was of little consequence to the Chinese government as it sought to enter the global automotive industry in the early 1990s. Given Japanese dominance of the auto industry at the time, it would have appeared rational for China to adopt the best technology and production processes available. However, three key factors influenced the Chinese government to form joint ventures with European and American firms, such as VW, Daimler-Benz, Fiat, Chrysler and GM. Firstly, anti-Japanese sentiment still runs deep in China; secondly, Japanese corporate culture is resistant to non-Japanese financial or management control, which posed difficulties, as the Chinese were proposing 50 : 50 joint ventures; and, thirdly, China's model of capitalist economic development was heavily based upon Japan's post-war experience, which had largely kept foreign ownership and firms out of the Japanese market. Between 1980 and 1994, Japanese FDI in China actually *decreased* from 10.7 per cent to 8.0 per cent of net FDI in the PRC (Dobson and Yue 1997). China's selective FDI policy demonstrates the difficulty even TNCs can face in attempting to penetrate 'strong' states.

At the height of East Asia's extraordinary growth cycle of the mid–1990s, the number of Asian TNCs among the world's 200 largest grew rapidly. Japan accounted for the largest proportion, while South Korean *chaebols*, such as Samsung, Hyundai and Daewoo, emerged as global corporations of considerable importance. However, the post–1997 period saw GM acquire most of Daewoo's assets, while other South Korean TNCs struggled to accommodate the dual problems of debt and softer global export markets. Even China, which escaped much of the damage wrought by the 1997 crisis, has begun to develop a growing dependence upon TNCs for FDI, technology transfer and joint ventures. Two thousand TNCs were operating in Hong Kong before the PRC resumed sovereignty in 1997, while around 400 of the world's 500-largest firms have a presence in China (Sheng 1997; *Asia Times* 2000).

Japan has not been immune to the growing domestic influence of foreign TNCs either.

Japanese firms began to suffer catastrophic liquidity shortages as early as 1990, leading to the *hansei* recession, from which the country only emerged very slowly late in the decade. When in the mid-1990s, Ford acquired 25 per cent of Toyo Kogyo (Mazda) and assumed effective control, one MITI official said in amazement, 'How could an inefficient American corporation take over a Japanese firm?' Japanese corporate collapses persisted throughout the 1990s, including Daiwa, the world's third-largest bank. In line with new banking policies, Japanese governments began to refuse to guarantee bank deposits or rescue financial institutions from debt, as they had in the past. The impact was regional; as Asian currencies crumbled in 1997, the Japanese government floated the idea of an Asian Monetary Fund (AMF; see Chapter 9), which was conceptually similar to the IMF. Japan was motivated less by altruism than by the need to protect its financial sector, which faced a heavy debt exposure in Southeast Asia. Although the AMF proposal was not adopted due to US opposition, its proposition demonstrated the strong nexus between the Japanese government and its TNCs. As a consequence, Japan has shifted from using its TNCs as engines of growth and vehicles of international expansion, to being driven largely by the policy demands of its TNCs.

Transnational investment in the Asia-Pacific

Foreign investment has two classifications: foreign direct investment (FDI) through direct equity in firms or plant; and foreign portfolio investment (FPI), which denotes private or corporate investment in stocks, bonds or other financial instruments, such as derivatives. During the 1980s, FDI was increasingly directed towards mergers and acquisitions (M&A) as firms sought to buy out competitors or to strategically enhance their ability to compete on global markets. Although during the 1950s and 1960s, MITI had forced firms such as Nissan and Prince to merge in order to *reduce* domestic competition, US firms in Asia, conversely, sought 'greenfields' investment, where they established service-sector and manufacturing subsidiaries. These included American Express (region-wide), GM (Philippines) and Ford (Malaysia). By 1997, M&A activity had increased for the ninth consecutive year, with Chinese M&A accounting for US$4.5 billion in the first half of 1997. Three of the four largest M&A activists in the Chinese market were from East Asia: Japan, Singapore and Hong Kong. In 1997, South Korean outward FDI (US$4.8 billion) exceeded that of Japan (US$4.4 billion) for the first time, including Daewoo's US$1.4 billion merger with Kazaktelekom (Kazakhstan) (KPMG 1997).

The extraordinary growth of FDI/FPI flows to the East Asian region from the mid 1980s until 1997 illustrates the importance of the region to TNCs. In the mid–1990s, East Asia was the destination of over half the world's FDI and FPI directed towards developing countries, accounting for some 15 per cent of total investment in the region. In 1993, total global investment in China exceeded foreign investment in the US (World Bank 1999b). As Chapter 10 suggests, the East Asian economies developed a dangerous degree of dependence upon, and vulnerability to, shocks in the international financial system. In this context, East Asian governments (Japan excepted), with few policy tools with which to deal with monetary policy changes in the 'big five', were highly susceptible to abrupt changes in the FDI climate.

Liberals argue that all states exhibit considerable vulnerability to the withdrawal of FDI. Throughout 1990–91, Japanese financial institutions withdrew some US$500 billion from the US economy. In the first six months of 1990, Japanese TNCs repatriated US$2 billion in direct investment from Australia. The timing was critical; despite the disparity in size between the US and Australian economies, the cause and effect were the same: Japanese parent firms in desperate need of liquidity repatriated capital within a very short space of time, contributing to the onset of recession in Australia and the US in 1990–91 (Davison 1991: 56).

Throughout the 1990s, TNCs demonstrated an increasing preference for subcontracting manufacturing. In sectors such as textiles, footwear and clothing, US retailing giants, such as Wal-Mart and Target, looked to East Asia as their manufacturing base. Similarly, PC manufacturers, including Hewlett-Packard, Dell and Apple, subcontracted the majority of their output to medium-sized Taiwanese firms. By the late 1990s, China and Malaysia developed niches in computer peripherals markets, such as printers and input devices, while South Korean manufacturers, including LG and Samsung, gained strong positions in display technology. However, although Japanese, US and European firms continued to direct their FDI towards East Asian manufacturing investments, they retained the high value-added service sector positions in their 'home' economies. For example, while large volumes of circuit boards are manufactured in Taiwan, processor and circuit board design and technology remain largely in the hands of the transnational parent, such as Intel, Apple or IBM.

Particularly in knowledge-based sectors, TNCs remain powerful and influential actors, as developing countries are keen to obtain not only investment, but also technology transfers. Intellectual property – governed much more stringently by the WTO since 1994 – is frequently a corporation's most valuable asset. Northern firms invest significant proportions of their revenue in R&D, whereas business in the East Asian NICs invest in plant in order to manufacture TNCs' products. Although NICs' firms are eager to obtain technology transfers, TNCs are naturally cautious about product piracy, reverse engineering or design theft. Hatch and Yamamura note that Japanese firms tend to dissuade local manufacturers from developing or supplying components, preferring to encourage Japanese components makers to establish themselves in Southeast Asia. Local executives of Japanese TNCs also lack the autonomy to make decisions concerning suppliers. Domestic manufacturers interested in supplying Sanyo's VCR plant in Indonesia were told they would need to express their interest through the firm's Tokyo headquarters: 'The drawings and designs are all made in Japan. You have to sell to Sanyo in Japan' (Hatch and Yamamura 1997: 171). Effectively, this has resulted in mature technologies and some elaborately transformed manufactures (ETMs) being relocated to the first- and second-tier NICs, such as Taiwan, Indonesia and Malaysia. Even Singapore, which has invested heavily in high-technology manufacturing and a knowledge-based economy, has begun to feel the heat of competition from Taiwan and its ASEAN neighbours, largely due to the other NICs 'leap-frogging' the technology gap through technology transfers and investment by TNCs.

Northern TNCs continue to exercise a considerable monopoly over key factors of production in East Asia, such as capital and high technology. Despite the brief success of the first- and second-tier NICs during the 1980s and 1990s, East Asian countries, with the notable exception of Japan, remain 'host' countries to transnational capital, supplying low-cost manufacturing and labour at the expense of their own development. Apart from Japan and, to a lesser extent, Singapore, East Asian states tend to remain FDI recipients, rather than originators, which suggests a considerable degree of dependence upon foreign capital. Of more concern to East Asian governments is the fact that their countries are the source of few technological innovations. Even Japan produces less new scientific knowledge *in toto* than Australia annually. BMW chief Erbhardt von Kuenheim in the late 1980s predicted – accurately – that Japan, despite its economic ascendancy and burgeoning trade surpluses, was vulnerable because its strengths were concentrated in very few products: cars and consumer electronics. However, as Japanese TNCs sought to remain competitive in the 1990s, the strong yen meant Japanese FDI was directed increasingly towards Southeast Asia,

and production moved to the second-tier NICs. Although Southeast Asian countries benefited from FDI, industrial development and a higher rate of employed labour, Japan experienced a phase of deindustrialization, which led not only to the 1990s *hansei* recession, but
also to structural unemployment, giving Japan a Western unemployment rate of over 5 per
cent, a condition brought about largely by Japan's own TNCs.

By the late 1980s, Japanese TNCs had voted with their feet and moved significant proportions of their capital and production to less costly regions of Asia in order to avoid the high
wages and real estate costs associated with manufacturing in Japan. In this respect, TNCs
have demonstrated the dependence of the Japanese economy upon firms' strategies.
Although Japanese governments had exercised considerable control over most domestic
firms via *keiretsu* networks, much of this influence disappeared during the 1980s, as corporations began to behave more independently of the 'administrative guidance' model MITI
had established in the 1920s. From 1993, Japanese governments were forced into a radical
restructuring of the economy, due partly to the policy preferences of their TNCs, and partly
to exogenous pressures from the US and the WTO.

Dobson and Yue (1997) argue that East Asian integration has been largely driven by the
TNC, particularly as Japanese firms have spread their wings across Asia (the 'flying geese'
thesis). Dobson and Yue assert that in China, Hong Kong, Indonesia, Malaysia, the
Philippines, Singapore, Taiwan and Thailand, intra-firm, inter-firm, inter-industry and
intra-industry trade has been largely responsible for economic growth. They also note that
foreign firms – especially from Japan and the US – are central economic actors in the first-
and second-tier NICs. However, they conclude that East Asia's heavy reliance upon transnational networks of foreign firms introduces a strong element of risk and weakness (Dobson
and Yue 1997). Although this network of TNCs supplies FDI, which acts as an employment
multiplier, Dobson (2001: 2) notes that at the time of the 1997 crisis, '[t]hese activities
increased the openness and integration of economies but also increased vulnerability to
external shocks'.

The emergence of the TNC as a transnational actor has profound implications. Economic liberals assert that TNCs can contribute positively to growth, development, employment, infrastructure, technology transfer, trade and training. However, non-liberals argue
that TNCs in East Asia, particularly before the economic crisis, acted as catalysts of the
collapse, engaging in speculative foreign exchange deals and short-term investment. The
implications of dependence upon FDI are clear enough: decisions made by firms in Tokyo,
London and New York have ultimately forced East Asian governments to engage in serious
structural reform, significant micro- and macroeconomic policy change, and increased
trade liberalization. In the absence of a recovery in domestic investment, transnational
capital has arguably become more important in East Asia, with foreign investment as a
proportion of gross domestic investment (GDI) increasing in South Korea, Malaysia and
Thailand in 1997–99.

TNCs have had a significant impact upon the relative autonomy, living standards and type
of industrial development experienced by East Asian states. The region's NICs are hosts to
Western capital, drawn predominantly from the US, Japan and the EU. In a world of capital
scarcity, governments and indigenous firms are forced to compete for FDI. As investment is
the engine of growth, East Asian governments are, to some extent, compelled to orient
policy to accommodate TNCs. Affected policy areas may include taxation, environmental
regulations or labour relations. For example, in return for a US$375 million investment,
Toyota demanded – and received – a single union agreement from the Australian government, the first in its automotive industry history. Since 1997, the US-dominated IMF has

required East Asian governments to address sector-specific issues, including state revenues via asset sales, corporate governance and market-determined prices. Labour may be particularly subject to exploitation by TNCs in the absence of strong unions or government regulation, as well as the need for employment growth in highly competitive labour markets. The 2000 Asia-Pacific NGO Symposium attributed the vulnerability of low-paid workers largely to globalization and TNCs:

> This vulnerability stems from the myriad effects of capital mobility, re-structuring of production systems and increased exploitation of labour, including child labour brought about by economic globalization. Some of these forms of economic related violence against women include sexual exploitation in prostitution and trafficking, slavery-like labour conditions facing certain migrant workers, trans-border smuggling of humans and human organs, occupation-related accidents and ailments among cheaply paid women workers in overseas factories of transnational corporations.
>
> (Asia-Pacific NGO Symposium 2000)

If East Asian states remain heavily dependent upon TNCs as the major source of capital and technology in the longer term, this may validate some neo-Marxist theories which have long asserted that transnational forces, such as firms, and ownership or control of the means of production, lead, ultimately, to a state of *dependency* (Frank 1975; Yoshihara 1988). Nevertheless, some neo-Marxists, such as Wallerstein, viewed the 1997 economic crisis as temporary, arguing that 'the so-called East Asian financial crisis is a minor, temporary event of limited importance, which will probably change nothing of the underlying rise of Japan or Japan/China or Japan/East Asia' (Wallerstein 1998). Other neo-Marxists, notably Yoshihara (1988), disagree, arguing that the Southeast Asian NICs in particular are structurally dependent upon TNCs and transnational capital. Conversely, economic liberals assert that the forces of globalization will impose necessary adjustments upon East Asian states, compelling them to abandon 'crony capitalism' and state-led economic intervention, resulting in economic stabilization, while Dobson and Yue (1997) argue that Japanese and US firms will remain the key TNAs driving growth within the region. Regardless of which explanation proves correct, it is virtually certain that the TNC will remain an entrenched TNA within the region.

Transnational NGOs/civil society actors

The number of non-governmental organizations (NGOs) operating internationally increased from 1,899 in 1968 to 4,646 in 1990. The number doubled between 1990 and 2000. In 1999, there were an estimated 42,100 domestic and transnational NGOs (*Yearbook of International Organizations* 1999: 549). Transnational NGOs may be defined as cross-border interactions between civil society actors, a process Falk (1999: 130) describes as 'globalization from below'. Transnational NGOs have almost developed into a distinct field of study, as analysts determine the extent of NGOs' influence and significance in national policy-making processes.

Keck and Sikkink (1998: 12) describe NGOs operating across borders as 'transnational advocacy networks', arguing that even domestic NGOs 'bypass their state and directly search out international allies to try to bring pressure on their states from outside'. Conversely, some analyses do not characterize NGOs as 'networks'; rather, they categorize NGOs by identifying essential NGO attributes. According to Salamon and Anheier (1994), all NGOs have characteristics in common. These include non-governmental and non-profit-making status; and possessing a solid and continuing form.

The importance of NGOs is exemplified by the fact that the US government now prefers to direct the largest proportion of its aid budget through NGOs, rather than UN agencies. The impact of NGOs upon significant areas of national policy can also be critical. For example, the International Committee of the Red Cross (ICRC), in coalition with five other NGOs, launched the International Campaign to Ban Landmines (ICBL) in 1987. More than 1,000 NGOs joined the campaign, which resulted in most states signing the Ottawa Landmine Convention in 1999 (Vines and Thompson 1999). However, despite a campaign which persuaded many states to ban the production and deployment of landmines, the largest producers and consumers of landmines (China, Russia, India, Pakistan, Iraq and the US) refused to sign the Convention.

Transnational NGOs in the Asia-Pacific region

Although many NGOs remain independent of government, they are frequently co-opted by governments as policy operatives. One reason for this is that NGOs are often heavily dependent upon government funding. For example, Japan's Ministry of Foreign Affairs (MFA) directly funds a large number of nominally independent NGOs, such as the Overseas Economic Co-operation Fund (OECF). However, managers at the OECF are predominantly private-sector professionals, seconded from the Japanese engineering, manufacturing

Table 11.1 The diversity of NGOs operating in the Asia-Pacific

Base	NGO/grouping	Issue area	Affiliation (if any)
Cambodia	Women's Media Centre of Cambodia	Development	USAID Office of Women in Development
Cambodia	Women for Prosperity	Development	USAID Office of Women in Development
China	China Youth Development Foundation	Development	
China	Network of Foundations and Non-profit Organizations	Reference	
Hong Kong	Asian Human Rights Commission	Human rights	UNHCR
Hong Kong	Greenpeace: Hong Kong	Environment	
Indonesia	Watch Indonesia	Human rights	
Indonesia/UK	Tapol	Human rights	
Malaysia	Aliran	Human rights	UN ECOSOC
Philippines	Philippine NGO Beijing Score Board	Human rights	
Singapore	Institute of Southeast Asian Studies	Development	ASEAN
EU–UN	EC/UNFPA Initiative for Reproductive Health in Asia	Women	EU/UNFPA
Transnational	Médecins sans Frontières	Medical health	
Transnational*	Green Empowerment	Environment	
Transnational	Asian and Pacific Development Centre	Development	
Transnational	Southeast Asia Watch	Human rights	

* Involves NGOs based in Malaysia, Indonesia, Nepal, Papua New Guinea, India and the Philippines.

Source: *Yearbook of International Organizations (2001/2002)*, Edition 38, pp. 1529–32; various.

and securities industries (Hatch and Yamamura 1997: 125–8). OECF managers evaluate aid projects in Southeast Asia, and report on their feasibility and desirability. In turn, the OECF reports to another NGO, the Overseas Development Agency (ODA), which then determines whether the project will be funded from Japan's aid budget. In this respect, there is a powerful nexus between the Japanese government, business and NGOs, which serves to increase the politico-economic influence of the MFA, as well as Japanese TNCs' leverage in the region.

Despite this, many commentators argue that the government–NGO relationship also works to strengthen global civil society. Both TNCs and NGOs assist governments by relieving them of growing domestic and international welfare demands. States generally do not and cannot use their military forces to distribute aid and run medical facilities. However, UN agencies, such as the World Food Programme (WFP) and the World Health Organization (WHO) depend heavily upon NGOs in the South to co-ordinate and distribute food, provide medical treatment and help develop industries, such as agriculture. TNCs are also frequently involved in such programmes. Partly because TNCs generally wish to be viewed as 'good international citizens', and partly because work with NGOs can provide practical experience for their professionals, corporations have increasingly sought to co-ordinate their charitable activities with NGOs. There is also a strong commercial incentive; in some emerging national markets, it makes sense for firms, such as McDonald's, Microsoft and Toyota, to develop and promote their brands through good corporate citizenship.

The relative power and influence of TNCs and NGOs governs the extent to which they can influence national decision making. TNCs' access to capital, and their importance to economic development, assures firms an influential role in the policy-making process. As Risse-Kappen (1995) notes, the governmental structure of the state can be a key factor in determining the level of influence exerted by TNAs. As firms' and NGOs' policy objectives are frequently diametrically opposed (for example, ocean and land-mining firms versus Greenpeace), the case for economic development often takes precedence over environmental concerns. However, this is not always the case. In 1993, Greenpeace gained Japanese support against Russian nuclear waste dumping in the Sea of Japan. Japan obtained East Asian and EU support for a UN resolution banning the practice, although China abstained (Ringius 1997: 84).

NGOs and transnational economic policy making

The restructuring package developed by the IMF and World Bank following the Asian economic crisis caused protest among a number of transnational NGOs, which viewed the strict conditionality associated with loans as excessively stringent. As a result, the World Bank sought to integrate NGOs into its decision-making processes. As the Bank itself acknowledged:

> There is widespread scepticism in the NGO community concerning what they call 'the World Bank's development/growth paradigm'. In East Asia, some NGOs felt that the World Bank was part of the problem rather than part of the solution. They felt that the World Bank needed 'to be made accountable for the crisis' . . . NGOs still need to be convinced that the World Bank talk of participation is more than a 'marketing trick' . . .
>
> (World Bank 1998: 4)

In order to encourage NGO participation in the World Bank's Asia programme, the Bank organized an East Asia-Pacific Regional Working Group. The group's Steering Committee is chaired by, and involves, a number of NGOs, including ANGOC (Indonesia), NGO-Cord (Thailand), Bina Swadaya (Indonesia), NGO Forum of Cambodia, Oxfam UK (Vietnam office), Consortium Laos, and Freedom from Debt Coalition (Philippines). Of the twenty-six Steering Committee members, ten are drawn from NGOs across the Asian region (World Bank 1999a). The first meeting was held in the Philippines in 1999 and was attended by representatives of five Southeast Asian NGOs from Indonesia, the Philippines, Cambodia, Thailand and Vietnam. The meeting established a secretariat and initiated plans for convening a regional assembly of NGO representatives (World Bank 1998: 4–12).

Similarly, civil society actors were prominent in the protests at the Seattle WTO meeting in 2000, which saw highly organized protests of 40,000 to 60,000 people, initiated largely by transnational and domestic NGOs, mobilizing against the WTO's free trade agenda. Despite US offers to extend bilateral aid to developing countries in an attempt to salvage the Seattle WTO meeting, it was insufficient to prevent a unified effort by African, Caribbean and Latin American countries to abandon the trade talks (Vidal 1999). Although most Southeast Asian governments and South Korea, dependent upon the US-controlled IMF and World Bank for assistance, supported the US position, many of their NGOs did not. Asian NGOs' organized protests persisted well beyond the Seattle WTO meeting, with the Asian Third World Network (Malaysia), Focus on the Global South, the Transnational Institute, and the International Society for Ecology and Culture pledging to continue their opposition to the trade round. NGO anti-WTO activity continued beyond the Doha WTO ministerial. In summary, the 1990s saw a transformation in the tactical, organizational and communications efficiency of NGOs, partly as a result of technologies such as the internet. Transnational NGOs, far from being mere lobby groups or aid agencies, are arguably part of a broader social movement which seeks to challenge the neoliberal orthodoxy which dominates the global trade system.

The gulf between the policy objectives of intergovernmental organizations, such as the WTO, and transnational NGOs is ironic, given that many IGOs rely heavily upon transnational and domestic NGOs' expertise to implement projects, as well as research. Transnational groups, such as Médecins sans Frontières, contribute to the WTO's TRIPS negotiations, particularly in the area of public health. Transnational NGOs, such as Oxfam, represent the interface between UN agencies, such as the World Health Organization, and impoverished people in the global south (ICTSD 2001).

International investment regulation has been one area where transnational NGOs have had notable success. The OECD's proposed Multilateral Agreement on Investment (MAI) in 1995 was the subject of an exceptionally vigorous campaign which lobbied national governments to refrain from signing the agreement. The MAI was generally viewed by transnational NGOs as particularly disadvantageous to countries of the global south. States such as Indonesia, the Philippines, Malaysia, Thailand and Vietnam, which compete for a share of global FDI in a world of investment scarcity, would have been forced to accept investment on terms heavily biased in favour of TNCs under the MAI.

NGOs and transnational environmental activism

Environmental NGOs also have a notable presence in the East Asian region. The first conference of Asia-Pacific ENGOs was held in Bangkok in 1991. They developed co-ordinated and influential strategies which gained the support of a number of major powers for the Kyoto Declaration (1994) (Asia-Pacific NGOs' Environmental Conference 1994). The Declaration established the Asia-Pacific NGO Environmental Council and Secretariat (based in Seoul), which was instrumental in developing the framework for the UN-sponsored Kyoto Protocol (1996). Asia-Pacific ENGOs have since developed strong links with research centres and development NGOs. The Kyoto Protocol proposals have been succeeded by more ambitious Asia-Pacific ENGO plans, detailed in the Singapore (1998), Agra (2000) and Kaohsiung (2002) Declarations (Asia-Pacific NGOs' Environmental Conference 2002). Wapner argues that ENGOs have been particularly effective as TNAs, especially in Asia where high levels of pollution, generated by 'smoke-stack' industries, have been exported largely from developed Northern economies. Wapner (1995: 311–40) asserts that ENGOs 'disseminate an ecological sensibility'. However, he also argues that the 'influence' TNAs have upon state behaviour is less important than 'manipulating governing structures of global civil society'. Nevertheless, lack of state ratification of the Kyoto Protocol has meant it has not entered into international environmental law, which suggests ENGOs have had a relatively limited impact on states' policies, at least in relation to carbon emissions.

The relative influence of transnational NGOs needs to be qualified and contextualized. Although both East Asian and other ENGOs were instrumental in assisting in the establishment of the framework for the 1996 Kyoto Protocol, ratification and implementation was left to states. The US's refusal to ratify Kyoto meant that the world's largest producer of carbon dioxide, a key factor in ozone depletion, remained uncommitted to pollution reduction targets adopted by a large proportion of states.

NGOs and labour conditions

NGO influence in the East Asian region is particularly apparent in the area of labour conditions. The ILO and a number of NGOs were responsible for widely publicizing Nike's use of child labour in Indonesian factories, which drew much media attention. As a result, firms – particularly Western firms operating in Asia – have been forced to adhere more closely to international labour standards, even if the country in which they operate is not a party to the relevant ILO conventions. Most East Asian countries have yet to ratify all eight of the ILO's fundamental conventions, adopted in 1998. These include freedom of association and the right to collective bargaining; the elimination of forced labour; abolition of child labour; and abolition of discrimination at work (ILO 1998). Moreover, the right to strike is not part of the ILO's conventions. Consequently, NGOs' and INGOs' influence upon workers' rights in East Asia is generally very limited. One reason for this is that exploitation, such as child labour, is often done behind closed doors, or within the confines of a family enterprise.

In this context, a link can be made between the influence of TNAs, such as TNCs, East Asia's export-oriented industrialization and labour conditions in the region. Park argues that in South Korea, TNCs 'accept traditional attitudes towards women where they justify giving women lower wages . . . and expect greater deference to authority and conscientiousness at work from them'. A representative of a US TNC has noted, 'It is in our own selfish interest to have a strong government that controls . . . labour so everything will blossom and we can continue to make profits' (Park 1993: 127–46).

In Taiwan, girls and boys under ten years of age are permitted to work in textile and related industries. Child labour is extremely common, and children are often injured when using factory machinery, due to poor occupational safety. Workers are usually fired when injured; as a result, girls who are laid off and unable to work often turn to prostitution.

Although the ILO requires member states which have not ratified ILO Conventions 138 and 182 to abolish child labour, the ILO and NGOs monitoring abuse are forced to rely heavily upon the co-operation of governments and police. In this respect, the East Asian state's emphasis upon industrial development means labour standards run a poor second to productivity and economic growth.

Conclusions

Detailed empirical studies of the level of influence exercised by TNAs are lacking; thus, it is difficult to evaluate the extent of their impact upon states' national policy decisions. As Uhlin *et al.* (2002) note, 'The routine work of networking (across geographical and organizational boundaries as well as between issue areas), planning campaigns, seeking funding, collecting information, producing documents and other everyday activities of transnational activists is a highly under-researched topic'. Despite the attention paid to the power and policies of TNCs, the level of influence exercised by firms remains a strongly contested area. Realists assert that the TNC remains a subordinate actor to the state, while non-realists argue that the largest firms have become more significant actors than many states. Equally, proponents of global civil society point to the Kyoto Protocol, East Timorese independence and democracy in the Philippines as evidence of the influence exerted by NGOs on the state. However, Betsill and Corell (2001: 65) point out that 'there is a surprising lack of specification about what is meant by "influence" and how to identify NGO influence in any given arena'.

As the ACEIU reports, divisions between Asia-Pacific NGOs on a wide range of policy issues dilutes their effectiveness as TNAs: 'There are many divisions among them [Asia-Pacific NGOs]. Much of their time is consumed by fighting each other rather than developing a common stand' (Human Rights Osaka 2000). Critics of the liberal view of NGOs also argue that:

> this view [liberalism] does not adequately address the organizational insecurity, competitive pressures, and fiscal uncertainty that characterize the transnational sector. Powerful institutional imperatives can subvert IO and INGO efforts, prolong inappropriate aid projects, or promote destructive competition among well-meaning transnational actors.
>
> (Cooley and Ron 2002: 6)

The disparity in the relative power and resources of TNAs is also demonstrated by the financial dependence many NGOs have upon UN agencies or national governments, while TNCs have their own resources and, frequently, privileged access to government. Conversely, NGOs may have limited resources, flexibility or detailed knowledge in given issue areas, which can reduce their effectiveness. As Betsill and Corell (2001: 81–2) note, only more systematic studies of the conditions under which NGOs and other TNAs are more or less likely to influence states and international negotiations, will determine the extent of their centrality to domestic and international politics in the Asia-Pacific region.

References

Arrighi, G. (2002) 'The rise of East Asia and the withering away of the interstate system', Fernand Braudel Research Centre. Online. Available HTTP: <http://fbc.binghamton.edu/gaasa95.htm> (accessed 20 February 2003).

Arts, B. (2000) 'Regimes, non-state actors and the state system: a "structurational" regime model', *European Journal of International Relations*, 6: 515–44.

Asia-Pacific NGOs' Environmental Conference (1994) 'Kyoto Declaration towards co-operation among environmental NGOs and sharing of its outcomes in the Asia-Pacific region', press release, Kyoto, 19 November.

Asia-Pacific NGOs' Environmental Conference (2002) 'Kaohsiung Declaration', press release, Kaohsiung, 3 November.

Asia-Pacific NGO Symposium (2000) *Final Report of the Asia-Pacific NGO Symposium, Asia-Pacific Women 2000: Gender Equality, Development and Peace*, Part B. Online. Available HTTP: <http://www.aworc.org/bpfa/ngo/bangkok99/reports/partb.html> (accessed 10 March 2003).

Asia Times (2000) 'China a magnet for multinationals', 7 December.

Ataman, M. (2002) 'Three-level games or ignored actors of world politics? Transnational factors', paper presented at Middle East Technical University Conference on International Relations, Ankara, Turkey, 3–5 July 2002. Online. Available HTTP: <http://www.ir.metu.edu.tr/conf2002/papers/ataman.pdf> (accessed 15 February 2003).

Aventis Triangle Forum (2003) *Future Societies*, Ch. 3. Online. Available HTTP: <http://www.aventis-foundation.org/> (accessed 30 March 2003).

Bello, W. (2002) 'East Asia's future strategic economic co-operation or marginalisation?', Asia Europe Crosspoints, Transnational Institute, September. Online. Available HTTP: <http://www.tni.org/reports/asia/crosspoints/paper6.htm> (accessed 15 February 2003).

Betsill, M. and Corell, E. (2001) 'NGO influence in international environmental negotiations: a framework for analysis', *Global Environmental Politics*, 1: 65–85.

Castells, M. (1999) *The Rise of the Network Society*, Cambridge, MA: Blackwell.

c|net Asia (2003) 'China to snub MPEG standard for own format', 1 August. Online. Available HTTP: <http://asia.cnet.com/newstech/applications/0,39001094,39144293,00.htm> (accessed 1 August 2003).

Cooley, A. and Ron, J. (2002) 'The NGO scramble: organizational insecurity and the political economy of transnational action', *International Security*, 27: 5–39.

Davison, R. (1991) 'Between Europe and Asia: Australia's options in the world economy of the 1990s', *Melbourne Journal of Politics*, 20: 40–67.

Deyo, F. C., Haggard, S. and Koo, H. (1987) 'Labour in the political economy of East Asian industrialization', *Bulletin of Concerned Asian Scholars*, April: 42–53.

Dobson, W. (2001) 'Deeper integration in East Asia: implications for the international economic system', ADB Working Papers, Asian Development Bank, Tokyo.

Dobson, W. and Yue, C. S. (eds) (1997) *Multinationals and East Asian Integration*, Ottawa: IDRC.

Falk, R. (1999) *Predatory Globalization – A Critique*, Cambridge: Polity Press.

Forbes (2003) 'Global 500'. Online. Available HTTP: <http://www.forbes.com/lists> (accessed 22 March 2003).

Fortune (2003) 'Global 500'. Online. Available HTTP: <http://www.fortune.com/fortune/global500> (accessed 22 March 2003).

Frank, A. G. (1975) *On Capitalist Underdevelopment*, Oxford: Oxford University Press.

Ghils, P. (1992) 'International civil society: international nongovernmental organisations in the international system', *International Strategic Studies Journal*, 133: 417–31.

Gilpin, R. (1975) *US Power and the Multinational Corporation*, New York: Basic Books.

Gilpin, R. (2001) *Global Political Economy*, Princeton, NJ: Princeton University Press.

Hatch, W. and Yamamura, K. (1997) *Asia in Japan's Embrace: Building a Regional Production Alliance*, Cambridge: Cambridge University Press.

Higgott, R., Underhill, G. and Bieler, A. (eds) (2000) *Non-State Actors and Authority in the Global System*, London: Routledge.

Human Rights Osaka (2000) 'Human rights NGOs in Asia and the Pacific', *Focus Asia-Pacific News*, 22.

Institute of International Studies, University of California, Berkeley (1998) 'Harry Kreisler interviews Joseph S. Nye on theory and practice in international relations' for Conversations with History.

Online. Available HTTP: <http://globetrotter.berkeley.edu/conversations/Nye/1> (accessed 15 February 2003).

International Centre for Trade and Sustainable Development (ICTSD) (2001) 'NGOs pursue new avenues to get their voice to the table', *ICTSD Weekly*, 5, 39, 15 November.

International Labour Organization (ILO) (1998) *Declaration of the Fundamental Principles and Rights at Work*, New York: ILO.

International Labour Organization (ILO) (2003) *Codes of Conduct for Multinationals*, Bureau for Workers' Activities. Online. Available HTTP: <http://www.itcilo.it/english/actrav/telearn/global/ilo/guide/main.htm> (accessed 30 March 2003).

Johnson, C. (1982) *MITI and the Japanese Miracle: The Growth of Industrial Policy, 1925–1975*, Stanford, CA: Stanford University Press.

Johnson, C. (1987) 'Political institutions and economic performance: the government–business relationship in Japan, South Korea and Taiwan', in F. C. Deyo (ed.) *The Political Economy of the New Asian Industrialism*, Ithaca, NY: Cornell University Press, pp. 136–64.

Keck, M. E. and Sikkink, K. (1998) *Activists Beyond Borders: Advocacy Networks in International Politics*, Ithaca, NY: Cornell University Press.

KPMG (1997) *Annual Survey of Global Takeover Activity*, Melbourne: KPMG.

Krasner, S. D. (1978) *Defending the National Interest: Raw Materials Investments and US Foreign Policy*, Princeton, NJ: Princeton University Press.

Mearsheimer, J. (1995) 'The false promise of international institutions', *International Security*, 19: 5–49.

Moravcsik, A. (1993) 'Introduction: integrating international and domestic theories of international bargaining', in P. B. Evans, H. K. Jacobson and R. D. Putnam (eds) *Double-Edged Diplomacy: International Bargaining and Domestic Politics*, Berkeley, CA: University of California Press, pp. 3–42.

Park, K. A. (1993) 'Women and development: the case of South Korea', *Comparative Politics*, 25: 127–46.

Ringius, L. (1997) 'Environmental NGOs and regime change: the case of ocean dumping of radioactive waste,' *European Journal of International Relations*, 3: 61–104.

Risse-Kappen, T. (1995) 'Bringing transnational relations back in: introduction and structures of governance and transnational relations: what have we learned?', in T. Risse-Kappen (ed.) *Bringing Transnational Relations Back In: Non-State Actors, Domestic Structures, and International Institutions*, Cambridge: Cambridge University Press.

Salamon, L. M. and Anheier, H. K. (1994) *Emerging Sector: The Nonprofit Sector in Comparative Perspective – An Overview*, Baltimore, MD: Johns Hopkins University Institute for Policy Studies.

Sheng, A. (1997) 'Hong Kong and Japan in East Asian finance', keynote address delivered to the 'Hong Kong after the handover' seminar, Nikko Research Centre, Hong Kong, 11 April.

Stephenson, C. M. (2000) 'NGOs and the principal organs of the United Nations', in P. Taylor and R. J. Groom (eds) *The United Nations at the Millennium*, London: Continuum, pp. 270–94.

Stopford, J. and Strange, S. (1991) *Rival States, Rival Firms: Competition for World Market Shares*, Cambridge: Cambridge University Press.

Uhlin, A., Piper, N. and Lindquist, J. (2002) 'Everyday forms of transnational activism: networks in and beyond Southeast Asia', Department of Sociology, Stockholm University. Online. Available HTTP: <http://www.soc.lu.se/soc/distans/global/uhlin.pdf> (accessed 15 February 2003).

United Nations Conference on Trade and Development (UNCTAD) (various years) *World Investment Report*. Online. Available HTTP: <http://r0.unctad.org/wir/> (accessed 16 May 2003).

Vidal, J. (1999) 'The WTO in Seattle: why the talks collapsed', *The Observer*, 5 December.

Vines, A. and Thompson, H. (1999) *Beyond the Landmine Ban: Eradicating a Lethal Legacy*, London: Research Institute for the Study of Conflict and Terrorism.

Wallerstein, I. (1998) 'The so-called Asian crisis: geopolitics in the Longue Durée', paper presented at International Studies Association meeting, Minneapolis, 17–21 March.

Waltz, K. (1970) 'The myth of national interdependence', in C. P. Kindleberger (ed.) *The International Corporation*, Cambridge, MA: MIT Press, pp. 205–23.

Wapner, M. (1995) 'Politics beyond the state: environmental activism and world civic politics', *World Politics*, 47: 311–40.

Wilson, G. K. (1990) *Business and Politics: A Comparative Introduction*, Basingstoke: Macmillan.

World Bank (1998) *Summary of the Fourth Meeting of the World Bank/NGO Asia-Pacific Committee*, Washington, DC: World Bank.

World Bank (1999a) 'East-Asia-Pacific Regional NGO Working Group in the World Bank: a briefer', press release, 29 April.

World Bank (1999b) *Managing Capital Flows in East Asia*, Washington, DC: World Bank.

Yearbook of International Organizations 1998–1999 (35th edn 1999) 4 vols, London: K. G. Saur Verlag.

Yoshihara, K. (1988) *The Rise of Ersatz Capitalism in South-East Asia*, Oxford: Oxford University Press.

12 Culture and politics in the Asia-Pacific

Asian values and human rights

Michael K. Connors

In the 1990s an international debate emerged involving academics, prominent politicians, and even the Tibetan Dalai Lama on whether Asian culture somehow sanctioned non-liberal forms of democracy and social organization. This chapter offers a brief outline of the debate, a discussion of the emergence of an international human rights regime and a critical examination of the claims made in the name of 'Asian values'.

The 'Asian values' debate

The debate partly had its origins in response to the promotion of human rights and democracy by Western agencies in the context of post-Cold War international relations. Furthermore, in the 1980s a number of authoritarian regimes within Asia were facing growing domestic movements for democracy. Fearing that the political and economic structures of their states were under threat, prominent Asian leaders argued against calls for greater freedoms and political democracy, claiming that such calls endangered national security and development. To counter-attack an emerging political liberalism within Asia, such leaders claimed that the region's economic growth and relative political stability were due to the specificity of Asian cultural values. Mahathir Mohammad, then prime minister of Malaysia, made it clear that he thought the West's attack on Asian values was selfishly motivated by 'fear that Asian success might lead to Asian self-assertion' (Mahathir 1996a).

The debate was not simply between the West and Asia. In the 1980s, Taiwan, South Korea, Thailand and the Philippines all made significant advances towards more liberal and representative forms of government. There were many Asian advocates of liberal democracy – and indeed many had been imprisoned or died fighting for that very cause. This Asian liberalism was not merely an echo of Western political thinking. Rather, a reappraisal of Asian philosophies and religions led some to conclude that there were indigenous traditions of liberalism within Asia that could be mobilized for the promotion of human rights and democracy. The Dalai Lama, for one, suggested that 'not only are Buddhism and democracy compatible, they are rooted in a common understanding of the equality and potential of every individual' (1999: 4). Kim Dae-jung who would later become president of South Korea, argued that 'there are no ideas more fundamental to democracy than the teachings of Confucianism . . .' (1994: 191). Drawing on the historical experience of the South Korean movement for democracy which had invoked Confucian ideas against military dictatorship in the 1980s, Kim also noted that Confucian scholars 'were taught that remonstration against an erring monarch was a paramount duty' (1994: 192). Despite possible indigenous foundations for an 'Asian liberalism', Asian values proponents further asserted that modernization did not equate to 'Westernization' and that

Asia's social and political organization need not mimic that of the West, as liberal triumphalists such as Francis Fukuyama (1992) had suggested in his infamous book *The End of History*. Since the economic crisis of 1997 some have suggested that the debate has gone into hiding. However, the possibilities of Asian regionalism, the persistence of 'illiberal' democratic governments in Asia, and the increasing focus on security after September 11 2001 ensures that the issue remains firmly outside the dustbin of history and worthy of exploration.

An issue of especial relevance to students of international relations is that this debate, or 'clash of civilizations' as Huntington (1993) would categorize it, occurs in a world in which an emergent international human rights regime regularly and necessarily finds itself in tension with an international system structured around the principle of state sovereignty. Thus, while international agencies of Western liberalism increasingly challenge the nature of domestic political forms around the world, those states subject to criticism invoke the principle of non-intervention in order to safeguard their right to domestic cultural interpretations of democracy and human rights. Certainly, during the Cold War, Western powers were not particularly eager to push forward a rights or democratic agenda, despite frequent rhetorical affirmations and selective action. Outright dictatorships were key allies of the West, including Pak Chung Hee in South Korea and Ferdinand Marcos in the Philippines. During this period, national security and national interest trumped liberal visions of a world of democratic states. However, in the post-Cold War period liberalism has gained ground, with the US, Europe and middle powers such as Australia and Canada increasingly providing aid to further democratic development, in line with liberal interpretations concerning good international citizenship. Liberal and realist world-views thus came into conflict, not only between states, but within them as different foreign policy lobbies pursue particular objectives.

This brief summary highlights that the Asian values debate is located at the intersection of many roads in international politics, of states bent on realist sovereignty, of liberal crusaders pushing markets and democracy, of globalizing tendencies in relation to political forms, and of potential regional projects to resist perceived Western imperialism. The debate, it must be said, is also the site of multiple hypocrisy. For while it is often Asia that is painted as deficient and dictatorial, the West is let off the hook. It is useful then, to recall the West's own shortcomings. Henry Rosemont nicely balances the issue with the following observation, which may well apply to many modern democracies:

> . . . how can Americans justify insisting – by diplomatic, military, economic, or other means – that every other society adopt the moral and political vocabulary of rights? . . . The questions become painful to contemplate when we face the reality that the United States is the wealthiest society in the world, yet after over two hundred years of human-rights talk, many of its citizens have no shelter, a fifth of them have no access to health care, a fourth of its children are growing up in poverty, and the richest two per cent of its peoples own and control over fifty per cent of its wealth . . .
>
> (Cited in Dallmayr 2002: 183)

Within Asia itself, the missionary zeal with which some Westerners promote liberalism as a universal value system provokes severe and often withering criticisms:

> It is, after all, a West that launched two world wars, supported racism and colonialism, perpetrated the Holocaust and the Great Purge, and now suffers from serious social and

economic difficulties. It . . . [is] all too prone to blame others for its own failings, and apparently exhausted of everything except pretensions of special virtue . . .

(Bilahari Kausikan, cited in Wright-Neville 1995: 5)

The human rights regime and democracy

In the West over the last several decades an elite consensus has emerged which defines democracy and human rights in a liberal manner. It is this particular interpretation that is invoked when there is talk about the promotion of democracy and human rights as aspects of Western foreign policy. It is also against such a liberal interpretation that the proponents of Asian values position themselves. By using the term 'liberal', reference is being made to a longstanding interpretation of the so-called 'Western experience' in which political philosophers and historians posit that Western thought, dating back to the ancient Greeks, has long been concerned with elaborating a philosophy of the individual, and the conditions necessary for that individual's freedom. Relatedly, Western history is often presented as the struggle by concrete individuals to carve out a free space for the pursuit of individual lives. A necessary condition of this pursuit has been the limiting of the power of the state and of collectivities that might inhibit the freedom of the individual. Fred Dallmayr speaks of one particular discourse of rights in the rest from 'from the assertion of baronial rights against kings in the Magna Carta to the proclamation of citizen rights against feudal absolutism in the French Revolution to the demand for social and economic rights in the era of industrial capitalism' (2002: 173). He also notes how rights can be a double-edged sword that are used as 'weapons of aggression and domination in the hands of the powerful' (Dallmayr 2002: 173). The contradictory nature of rights is evident, for example, in the fact that rights to citizenship are used to exclude foreigners, and property rights can be used to maintain the luxurious lifestyles of the rich and to justify the poverty of the poor.

Germane to liberal conceptions of rights are two key elements, extracted from a particular reading of 'Western tradition'. Firstly, human beings are said, by virtue of their humanity, to possess various rights: to life, to property, to liberty, to freedom of expression and so on. These rights are taken as absolute. This means that they are held to be inalienable and under no condition may they be violated. This understanding of rights is known as the natural law position because it posits that the intrinsic nature of human beings requires that certain conditions be met for the fulfilment of each person's humanity. Rights flow from the natural state of being human and the limitation of these rights is deemed acceptable only so far as to protect the rights of others. Liberals argue that such rights are necessary for the fulfilment of each individual's potential as a rational agent. Generally speaking, these rights have been articulated to ideas about proper forms of government, which is to say that they have acquired a political dimension known as democracy, encapsulated in the notion of right to representation. This coupling of rights and representation is generally described as liberal democracy. Legitimate government must function so as to protect the exercise of these rights by ensuring that all individuals have the opportunity to live full lives. The state positively protects freedoms by providing things such as education, health and equal opportunity. It is also the function of government, from a liberal perspective, to ensure that no nefarious institution emerge (tyranny, a cumbersome welfare state, oligarchy, communism, absolutism or corruption) that would impinge on such rights. By circumscribing its own role, and that of other actors, the state negatively protects freedoms – it limits, for example, taxation which is seen as a threat to individuals' property rights. Liberals are best described as a house divided, for they differ greatly on the role of the state in terms of providing for positive or negative freedoms. The history of Western governments in the twentieth century is often the history of tension between these competing modes of liberalism.

In the aftermath of the Second World War and the formation of the United Nations, this broad liberal vision has come to inform international practice related to human rights. The 1945 UN Charter declared 'respect for human rights and fundamental freedoms' as one of the organization's prime objectives. Notably the Charter also committed itself to the sovereign right of states to domestic jurisdiction; that is, control of subject populations within territorial borders. The tension between these two objectives is easily illustrated: to what extent does a nation's right to sovereignty override the international community's concern with state compliance to acceptable human rights practice? This question increasingly occupies the agenda of international politics, and there is no easy fix.

Nevertheless, since 1945, there has been an observable expansion of the multilateral human rights regime (buffeted also by individual aid initiatives) which has progressively encroached on the right of states to be ultimate arbiters within their respective borders. Such encroachment might be seen as undermining a principal realist premise that states alone are the holders of rights and responsibilities in the international system, for if internationally sanctioned bodies can now scrutinize state practice, sovereignty is diminished. Indeed in the early years after the Second World War there was an agreed consensus on the need to challenge the model of unlimited sovereignty driving the Westphalian model (Dunne and Wheeler 1999: 1). The early UN system and its commitment to rights has been interpreted as a promise of cosmopolitan democracy in a world of post-sovereign states (Booth 1999: 65), or, put differently, a world where place of birth could not detract from each person's fundamental rights and freedoms. Certainly the first few years after the Second World War inspired such visions. For the first time in history an 'international bill of rights' came into being. The phrase names a body of international agreements that have emerged over the last four decades, but which are rooted in the primary document, the Universal Declaration of Human Rights (UDHR) passed by the Western-dominated UN in 1948. This is basically the ideational infrastructure of the international human rights regime. The organizations, institutions and actors that make it function and bring it into operation are the material infrastructure of the international human rights regime.

Subsequent conventions and covenants have built upon the generalized UNDR including the International Convention on the Elimination of Racial Discrimination (1965), the International Covenant on Civil and Political Rights (1966), the International Covenant on Economic, Social and Cultural Rights (1966), the Convention on the Elimination of All Forms of Discrimination Against Women (1979), the Convention Against Torture and Other Cruel, Inhuman or Degrading Treatment (1984), and the Convention on the Rights of the Child (1989).

It must be noted, however, that the early promise of cosmopolitanism gave way to the logic of the Cold War and states' own restriction of the scope of the regime and their limited goal to merely set normative standards. As Jack Donnelly writes,

> Work on a covenant to give greater legal force and specificity to the rights enumerated in the Universal Declaration became bogged down ... This reflected a more general return of human rights to the fringes of international relations. The rise of the Cold War ... explains part of this recession. No less important, though, was the fact that most states were satisfied with an international human rights regime that included little more than a strong statement of norms.
>
> (Donnelly 1999: 73)

Despite this limitation, over time human rights re-emerged on the international relations agenda. There was a gradual expansion of the role of international agencies in monitoring and promoting rights. More recently, the role of Western governments in explicit democracy promotion projects seemingly echoes the earlier cosmopolitan promise. Drawing from Donnelly's periodization, this expansion can be traced through four key phases.

Abeyance: 1950s to 1960s

As the Cold War hotted up, human rights virtually disappeared from states' foreign policies. Instead, the terms of international discourse, or conflict, in relation to politics and social organization were democracy, freedom, communism, imperialism, neo-colonialism etc. These terms indicated high-level ideological conflict. If a state was on the side of the United States, and more generally the West, then it was declared as being part of the free world, whatever its regime form might be. In such a world where state power was dominantly structured by great power rivalry, the possibility of human rights protection was marginal. The instruments for protection in any case were very weak. After all, in 1947 the UN Commission on Human Rights had agreed that it held no power to 'take any action in regard to any complaints concerning human rights' (Donnelly 1999: 73).

Political codification: early 1960s to early 1970s

In this period, the post-colonial states of Asia and Africa inspired a new round of human rights activism, especially around the Convention on the Elimination of All Forms of Racial Discrimination (1965). Further codification came with the passing of the ICCPR and the ICESCR in 1966. These two instruments reflected the ideological split in the United Nations between the liberal capitalist democracies and their stress on political and civil rights (reflected in the ICCPR) and the ideological commitment of communist states and the practical development orientation of many Third World countries (reflected in the ICESCR). Indicating the slowness with which the human rights regime emerged, it took nearly a decade before the two covenants secured the thirty-five ratifications required to enter into force. It is worth noting too, that even when ratified, states were simply required to provide reports to the UN. As Donnelly puts it, 'Human rights norms had become fully internationalized. Implementation and enforcement, however, remained almost completely national' (1999: 75).

Revival and extension: 1970s to 1980s

Donnelly suggests that three major events triggered a revival in the lagging fortunes of the international human rights regime. Firstly, there was the 1973 *coup d'état* against President Allende in Chile. The atrocious human rights abuses that followed led to the creation of a specific working group on human rights in Chile. Secondly, the Covenants of 1966 came into force in 1976 and a monitoring forum was established in the Human Rights Committee. Finally, the election of Jimmy Carter as President of the United States in 1977 led to human rights becoming a central, if uneven, component of US foreign policy. These developments are said to have heralded a new era of human rights activism in the UN, with smaller states taking an active role in pushing new treaties and supporting higher levels of scrutiny (following the Chilean precedent). The expansion of non-governmental organizations related to human rights promotion and protection throughout further entrenched the importance of human rights in international politics. By the 1980s human rights had become common currency in international relations dialogue. It is in this period too that the United States government began to prefer limited democratic forms of government over the perennial civil wars waged between leftist guerillas and right-wing dictatorships. Accordingly, it began to selectively support efforts towards political democracy, where its interests were not threatened. However, in the Philippines, where it had important strategic military bases, the US maintained support for the notorious Filipino dictator Ferdinand Marcos until the 'people's power' movement overthrew him in 1986.

Post-Cold War: deepening of the international human rights regime

Freed from the politics of the Cold War, the UN has increasingly been able to address questions of human rights, within limits that states, protective of domestic sovereignty, will allow. The scope for intervention has widened however, and it is notable that in the 1990s there has been international support for interventions on humanitarian grounds where gross violations were judged as overriding a state's legitimate sovereign right to non-intervention. This shift occurred for several reasons: including the freeing of the UN system from the Cold War veto, and the increasing growth of the legitimacy of human rights discourse through the proliferation of struggles and organizations. It does well to remember that in the 1970s the international community fully condemned Tanzania's invasion of Uganda and Vietnam's invasion of Cambodia, despite those invasions ending the murderous rule of Idi Amin and Pol Pot respectively. As Hedley Bull put it:

> The reluctance evident in the international community even to experiment with the conception of a right of humanitarian intervention reflects not only an unwillingness to jeopardize the rules of sovereignty and non-intervention by conceding such a right to individual states, but also the lack of any agreed doctrine as to what human rights are . . .

> (Cited in Dunne *et al.* 2001: 98)

The 1990s, however, have seen UN peacekeeping operations carried out with reference to human rights in countries as varied as Namibia, Bosnia, Mozambique, Cambodia and Guatemala. Further, interventions or UN-endorsed interventions in, on humanitarian grounds, in Iraq, Liberia, Somalia, Rwanda and East Timor have extended the horizon of when it is permissible to take action against states. All of these interventions, as well as interventions outside the UN system, have brought into focus the steadily eroding legitimacy of the absoluteness of the principle of non-intervention. This is not to say that rights have trumped states at this point in time; the UN and states remain cautious in implementing intervention strategies. In many cases where intervention could be justified on humanitarian grounds states are protected by abidance to the principles of sovereignty and non-intervention, and calculations by other states that it would not be in their interest to intervene. It arguably remains the case that the majority of foreign policy practitioners within states hold to a certain agnosticism about the efficacy of international promotion and protection of human rights and have a keener regard for sovereignty as the key principle of international order.

Context and contest

Within Asia the principle of non-intervention has been jealously, if unevenly, guarded, especially by the post-colonial states that comprise ASEAN (see Chapter 5). Not surprisingly, the liberalism that has lain behind the extension of the human rights regime has not found itself particularly welcome in states where there are different cultural and political 'traditions' and imperatives that differ greatly from the Western experience. What may be said here, by way of shorthand, is that the Western promotion of human rights, and democracy, cautious as it was, nevertheless aroused the concern of Asian elites for whom state sovereignty was an absolute principle and furthermore who were not supportive of liberalism in general. The extent to which the human rights regime in Asia is underdeveloped is grasped if it is noted that Asia alone, among regions in the world, does not have a governmental regional human rights mechanism.

There is a long subscription in East Asia and Southeast Asia to the idea that Asian or country specificity effectively sanctions different forms of social and political life that differ from the West. Furthermore, this specificity is seen as having sustained economic growth and social order. The Japanese had attempted to bring this idea into imperial realization during its efforts to construct an East Asian Co-Prosperity Sphere. After the Second World War, the South Korean military dictatorship (Thompson 1999: 21) emphasized a social order predicated on Confucian values that elevated the collective over the individual, emphasized the value of social hierarchy in furthering national objectives, and the right of leaders to rule without participation from subject populations. Similar positions (without the Confucian tag) were developed in the Philippines under President Marcos, Sarit in Thailand, and Suharto in Indonesia. What was articulated in each of these instances was national ideology that stressed national unity and order, above the liberal regard for the individual, for the sake of economic development. In contrast to these nationally focused ideologies, the Asian values debate witnessed the emergence of a pan-Asian position that attempted to articulate cross-national values that could unite non-liberal democratic countries in Asia to resist the pressure of liberalization that was being felt both domestically and from external forces (Wright-Neville 1995).

In the 1990s, the Asian values position became identified with two relatively small Southeast Asian states – Singapore and Malaysia – and it was within these states that the pan-Asian position became pronounced. As Kenneth Christie writes:

> Both countries share the reputation of being the champions of the 'Asian way'. . . .
> Their respective statesmen, Dr Mohammed Mahathir and Lee Kuan Yew . . . have
> become self-appointed spokesmen for East Asian values in general, regularly appearing
> at international conferences, meetings and in the media to denounce Western interfer-
> ence, Western value systems, liberal versions of democracy and human rights . . .
>
> (Christie and Denny 2001: 31)

In both of these states modernizing elites had seized state power and were able to rule with relative immunity from popular pressure. While each country's political system resembled democracy, the internal operations of the system militated against the system's proper functioning. It would be useful to briefly consider the nature of the political systems in both these states.

In Singapore, a small island state with one of the highest standards of living in the world, the People's Action Party (PAP) has ruled since 1965, being returned to office in five-yearly elections. The system is formally based on the Westminster system, reflecting the country's past colonial association with Britain. Between 1965 and 1981 the PAP held all parliamentary seats. Subsequently, the political opposition has managed only a handful of seats, despite gaining the support of 30–40 per cent of the votes (Eldridge 2002: 44–5). The success of the PAP partly lies in its capacity to unite different sections of the bureaucracy and capitalist classes, and in delivering spectacular growth. However, it remains the case that the hold on power remains tied to an elaborate system of repressive measures, including political use of the judiciary. The attitude towards political opposition in Singapore is severe, with opposition figures regularly attacked in the press, and charged with criminal offences. Attempts to form non-parliamentary-based political opposition meets equal resistance. The existence of an Internal Security Act (a legacy of British colonialism!), provides the government with easy measures to remove opposition. As Thompson illustrates:

> The internal security law was invoked in 1987 to arrest Catholic Church activists supposedly engaged in a Marxist conspiracy, an action meant to destroy the country's nascent NGO movement. Shortly thereafter, when the president of the law society criticized curbs on the press, he was blocked from re-election, arrested, and – after a brief stint in an opposition party – forced into exile.
>
> (1999: 11)

Malaysia shares with Singapore a British colonial legacy in that it too has a parliamentary system largely akin to the Westminster one, with federal modifications. The country gained independence in 1957, taking its present form in 1965 when Singapore withdrew from the Malaysian federation. Malays account for 55 per cent of the population, Chinese 30 per cent, and Indians 9 per cent. The early years of the country were marked by racial tension between the Chinese and ethnic Malays, which resulted in rioting in the late 1960s. Parliament was suspended and a national emergency was declared. In 1971, when parliament reconvened, the emergency laws were not withdrawn. Since 1957 the ethnic-based United Malay National Organization has dominated national politics, often in coalition with minor parties. In 1971 the government launched the New Economic Programme in order to increase indigenous Malay control over an economic system that was dominated by the Chinese. Additionally, quota systems give preference to Malays in education and government service. In the 1990s the New Economic Policy was superseded by a more racially inclusive policy aiming at making Malaysia a modern industrialized and commercial country. Nevertheless, the polity remains ethnicized, with significant Chinese and Indian business groupings trading political power for economic concessions within the framework of Malay dominance (Eldridge 2002: 91). Under the leadership of Mahathir, from 1981 to the end of 2003, the politicized Malay elite has managed to maintain substantial control over the political system and has used the Internal Security Act to quash political opposition. Further restrictions exist in the form of the 1971 Sedition Act that prohibits public discussion on Malay rights and the citizenship rights of non-Malays among other things. Effectively this means that criticism of Malay access to employment and education is prohibited. Malaysia's judiciary has been subject to constant political and bureaucratic interference, although it has at times struck an independent note. The rights of defendants are also heavily curtailed by virtue of procedural rules relating to court cases in which the prosecutor has licence to introduce new charges and witnesses during a trial (Edwards, cited in Eldridge 2002: 94).

It is perhaps worth highlighting that both of these states, along with Brunei, Indonesia, Laos and Myanmar, have not ratified the ICCPR or the ICESCR. Cambodia's ratification of the treaties reflects the dominance of the UN in reconstructing the state during the early 1990s, but practice hardly reflects commitment to the Covenants. North Korea's ratification of the ICCPR of course also demonstrates that membership and nominal participation in a regime does not necessarily mean anything; conversely, non-ratification does not necessarily entail active abuse of human rights. However, it must be said that despite recognition of liberal rights in both Malaysia's and Singapore's constitutions, the list of legislation that qualifies these rights is staggering, and all too often invoked. Journalists and academics are extremely cautious in their work in order to avoid state sanctions. Politicians fearful of politically motivated trials keep quiet.

Malaysian and Singaporean leaders became increasingly concerned that the legitimacy of their regimes was being called into question by international observers and domestic opposition. Within Singapore and Malaysia liberal political oppositions were gathering strength and demanding greater political space for the exercise of rights and freedoms congruent with liberalism in general – however, their impact has been limited because of successful state repression and management. Furthermore, in East and Southeast Asia, a number of democratic transitions were taking place that undermined the legitimacy of the soft-authoritarian regimes. In South Korea, Taiwan, Thailand and the Philippines erstwhile dictatorships had given way to emergent democracies. The causes of these transitions were complex and contradictory. Taiwan, South Korea and Thailand had each undergone substantial economic growth that had spawned a middle class which some authors see as pro-democratic in consciousness. Others saw democracy as offering these countries the best solution to perennial conflict among political and economic elites. Democracy offered the possibility of turning that conflict into regularized and manageable conflict through the use of parties and parliaments. Democratic transitions, then, were seen as offering political solutions to increasingly modernizing societies in which there was a plurality of power (as opposed to the centralization of power under authoritarianism). Furthermore, the transitions were said to be liberal in that they attempted to entrench a separation between the political and the economic spheres. While political power was now open to contestation, the nature of capitalism and the right to property ownership were untouched.

Another factor in the transitions was a more receptive international environment from the 1980s, reflected best in US attempts to more vigorously promote democracies. In the early 1980s the US set up important organizations, especially the National Endowment for Democracy, through which it sponsored democratic education throughout the world, and dispersal of technical knowledge about judicial, legislative and party processes. USAID also played a role in sponsoring democratic development (Robinson 1996). Liberals in democratizing countries were thus buttressed by both domestic constituencies seeking more open political environments, and the world's hegemonic power sanctioning such a process, as long as it did not threaten US economic interests. Indeed, the new democracies proved themselves to also be more liberal in economic policy, opening themselves to the inflow of foreign capital.

Furthermore, as the US increasingly felt its economic system being threatened by the rise of the Asian economies, it moved to criticize their political and social organizations. This has been linked to domestic capitalist lobbies within the West, especially in the US, who wanted to link trade rights to the observance of human rights. It was thought that many Asian countries had an absolute advantage in production because of the poor state of human and labour rights. Better human rights would effectively increase the cost of the products of such countries, making them less competitive *vis-à-vis* the US. Given that the lobby for linkage of trade with rights threatened the economic gains of East Asia, Mahathir argued that the West was attempting to thwart the rise of Asia. That the US had blocked Malaysia's East

Asian Economic Caucus proposal fuelled this argument further. For those committed to the Asian development model, the US was seen as trying to fix the rules of the game in trade to its own advantage. Talk of minimum labour standards in developing countries, by Western countries, was seen as an attempt to weaken those countries' comparative advantage. The position for linkage of trade with human rights in general gained momentum under the Clinton Administration, but was dropped very early into the administration's tenure, when China's most favoured nation status was delinked from the question of human rights in 1994.

The Asian values position

It is now time to turn to the substance of the Asian values position. It has been shown that both Mahathir and Lee presided over societies in which there was substantial tension related to order and economic growth and the question of democracy. Each moved towards a system of one-party dominance (in effect), and each has justified this as assisting the respective countries to reach new economic goals. In articulating a pan-Asianism, both leaders began to find common cause against Western liberalism and political opposition, despite the tensions between their respective states. They, along with many others, may be seen as arguing for a distinctive notion of Asian values related to the commonality of Asian societies. These values are given prominence in their explanations of Asian economic growth and political stability. Rather than simply arguing that growth flowed from well-thought-out development policies, culture was aggressively invoked by Asian values proponents as an attributing factor. In a sense, this might be understood as expressing no more than a pragmatic need to shroud economic success in cultural terms, to give it a kind of spiritual and nationalist meaning: an ideology for domestic consumption. However, it was also part of the articulation of Asian regionalism – part of the attempt to construct Asian identity. Asian values then might be seen as an assertion of confidence that while modernizing the newly industrializing countries were not Westernizing, and indeed were resistant to Western culture. In that sense Asian values were a culturalist assertion that stamped economic growth with an endogenous rationale and a programme for the protection and promotion of values that could sustain growth and social order (Kahn 1997). Furthermore, against the West, the Asian values position cohered into a discrete position. Bruun and Jacobsen suggest that four key claims are made concerning Asian values: the cultural specificity of rights; communitarianism; the role of discipline for the common good; and the organic nature of the state (Jacobsen and Bruun 2000: 3).

Firstly, a claim is made that human rights are contextual and culturally specific, emergent in specific historical, political and economic settings. This clearly goes against the grain of the abstract individual endowed with natural rights that figures in liberal theory. In the famous Bangkok Declaration of 1993, issued by Asian governments in preparation for the Vienna World Conference on Human Rights (1993), the universality of rights was recognized, but their particular meanings and the methods of implementation were to be interpreted through a cultural prism:

> While human rights are universal in nature they must be considered in the context of a dynamic and evolving process of international norm-setting, bearing in mind the significance of national and regional particularities and various historical, cultural and religious backgrounds . . .

(Cited in Christie and Denny 2001: 10)

Secondly, a claim is made that Asian values orbit around a communitarian world-view, where the individual is obliged to the family and the community. Thus Asian culture is seen as eschewing individualism. Individual rights are seen as undermining social order and distracting individuals from the fulfilment of social roles. Lee Kuan Yew, for instance, speaks of communities having precedence over individuals in Asia: 'Whether in periods of golden prosperity or in the depths of disorder, Asia has never valued the individual over society. . . . The society has always been more important than the individual' (cited in Christie and Denny 2001: 69).

The communitarian perspective is one in which a social order is conceived as being held together by shared common values that bring people into a sense of togetherness and common identity. In this view, individuals are typically understood as emerging out of cultural contexts and dependent on them; the community is reckoned as prior to the individual, while in the liberal perspective the individual is reckoned as prior to society and born with a bundle of rights that have precedence over society.

One consequence of this communitarian interpretation is that the Western stress on the rights of individual as universally valid, is perceived to flow from Western conceit, produced by the decadent individuals of Western capitalist and consumer societies. Again, Lee explains:

> The expansion of the right of the individual to behave or misbehave as he pleases has come at the expense of orderly society. In the East the main object is to have a well-ordered society so that everybody can have maximum enjoyment of his freedoms. This freedom can only exist in an ordered state and not in a natural state of contention and anarchy.
>
> (Cited in Zakaria 1994: 111)

Thirdly, a claim is made that, on the whole, Asians are predisposed to 'discipline' in order to serve the greater social good. Thus the political rights of the individual are secondary to the rights of the community and nation to development. Development will deliver well-being, which is seen as a more concrete outcome than compliance to the abstract rights of individuals. As one official from the Ministry of Foreign Affairs in Singapore has noted:

> Asian societies are now searching for their own distinctive configurations of market, state, and society. . . . The real debate is not about values of any particular geographic area, but about values per se; it is about which values, in what degree and in what proportion, are necessary for sustained development, the maintenance of social cohesion . . .
>
> (Kausikan 1998: 24–5)

Finally, a claim is made that the state is able to rule for the common good. It is assumed that state elites, endowed with national vision, are able to determine policies without the conflictive nature of public policy processes and interest groups. This is essentially an argument for the organic nature of state and society, which is to say that state and society are fused as if a single body, and act in unison as do the brain and body. In effect, the state is imagined as a benevolent patriarch, overseeing the interests of the common family, the nation. This position involves a critique of Western democracy and its perceived state of perennial conflict, excessive individualism and predatory interest group politics. The distaste for pluralist democracy in which conflict and adversarial politics abound is palpable in the Asian values position, as Mahathir sarcastically puts it: 'Having multi-parties and holding elections are not enough. To be truly democratic we must change Governments with each election, endure civil strifes and frequent disruptive demos and generally verge on anarchy' (Mahathir 1996b).

Against this caricatured image of democracy Mahathir argues that:

> Once a government has been elected, we believe it should be allowed to govern and to formulate and implement policies . . . we believe that strong, stable governments . . . are a prerequisite for economic development. . . . When citizens understand that their right to choose also involves limits and responsibilities, democracy doesn't deteriorate into an excess of freedom . . .
>
> (Mahathir 1995: 82)

It should be noted that in the above quotations there is an implicit attack on liberal understanding of the state as a neutral mechanism through which the competing interests of society are articulated and given policy form. Contra the liberal view of the state, a strong leader, in Asian democracy, functions to repress the play of pluralism and institute national visions and goals that benefit all collectively. A government's legitimacy in this vision of democracy comes not from the consent of the people as such, although there are concessions in regard to elections, but flows from effective government and economic development. While the proponents of Asian values do not necessarily dispense with the forms of democratic rule, they clearly interpret the nature of democracy in an authoritarian or illiberal manner (Bell and Jayasuriya 1995). Moreover, rather than rights being stressed, obligations and duties of citizens to the state are put to the forefront.

Furthermore, as indicated earlier, the organic conception of the state implicit in the Asian values position 'has implications for foreign policy: the organic argument is expanded into an unyielding policy of state sovereignty and international non-interference, denying foreign governments and NGOs the right to monitor domestic human rights' (Jacobsen and Bruun 2000: 3). In this vein, in 1993 Asian governments also issued a condemnation of the linkage of aid to human rights and asserted state sovereignty. And to point to their own concerns with democracy, they called for reform of the UN system to make it more representative (Hurrell 1999: 296).

Critiques of the Asian values position

The Asian values position has attracted an enormous response from academics, and in the following section three basic critiques are discussed. The first critique focuses on the extent to which the Asian values position resonates with Western conservatism. Just as Western conservative ideas in the eighteenth and nineteenth centuries were a defensive response to rapid economic, social and cultural change, Asian values express, in the face of destabilizing tendencies brought on by profound economic transformation, a desire for cultural continuity, so that the social order has some sense of unity. Hewison and Rodan (1996) argue, for example, that the themes of Western conservatism are reprised in the Asian context. Some of these themes include: the evils of human nature and the need for discipline and a strong state to repress individual vice; the importance of hierarchical order and authority to ensure social order in the face of impending social chaos; the role of traditional values in promoting social solidarity and unity of purpose. In identifying the commonality of Asian values and Western conservatism it becomes possible to think of the Asian values position as being not so much about the expression of a separate civilizational identity, but rather a contingent, in time and geography, expression of modernizing elites seeking to advance economic development and change while maintaining selected traditional values.

A second critique focuses on the instrumental use of Asian values by elites. The defence of hierarchy, social order and social harmony essentially serves the consolidation of state power, in its economic development projects, enabling it to marginalize dissent and resistance (Robison 1996). A strong state is able to repress labour 'strife' and alternative economic or social visions. In essence the constant promotion of Asian values serves to place a smoke-screen around the government's real intent – which is largely to maintain its authority against other claimants.

A final, constructivist, critique rests on a critical reading of the politics of identity. Those who take this position are interested in the way that particular identities are articulated in international relations and the consequences of such identities. In the long history of Western global ascendancy, from the seventeenth century onwards, Western intellectuals began to sketch out civilizational and racial stereotypes. One particular sketching was that of the Orient. In his book *Orientalism*, Edward Said (1978) notes how 'Orientalism', or the positing of certain attributes about Orientals, functioned to provide the 'West' with a foil against which it could sketch its own identity. Travel books, poetry, novels and political tracts of the nineteenth century, for example, present an image of the typical 'Oriental' man who was irrational, lazy, undisciplined and feminine, while the typical Western man was seen as rational, masculine, disciplined and, consequently, able to rule and guide the natives. In effect, representations of the Oriental strengthened European identity, and this strengthening of identity provided spiritual sustenance for projects of domination over non-Western parts of the world.

Given this background to the politics of identity, it would seem unfortunate that some Asian leaders have seemingly appropriated the polarizing logic of civilizational identity and seem to fall into the trap of assuming an 'Asian' and 'Western' identity. Of course these leaders do not subscribe to historical images of the Orient, but positively revalue Asian identity and contrast it to the West. However, as Callahan (1996: 3) notes, this reconstruction of Asian identity is 'not for the progressive project of dismantling dominance, but to try and beat imperialism at its own game by scripting a discourse of domination in terms of democracy: *Asian* democracy'.

Conclusion

In sum, it becomes clear that the arguments made for Asian values represent a distinctive claim not necessarily about the absoluteness of Asian values, but about their appropriateness given the circumstances in which Asian societies exist. This is an important point because much ink has been spilt on an endless debate about the universality of liberally interpreted rights, as if it were possible to ground notions of the rights in the abstract individual that liberals invoke. The liberal vision, it should also be noted, is contested within Western societies. Instead of granting either liberalism or the Asian values position status as 'right' or 'wrong', it might be more useful to think of them as particular projects promoting particular ways of being (Dallmayr 2002). At the same time, these projects cannot be seen to exist in a vacuum: the actors and states that promote them have particular interests related to their position in terms of state and economy and the global order. Both of the positions are elite ones propagated by people and agencies in power. Secondly, it is possible to also suggest that far from being a civilizational clash, the Asian values debate may be taken as a precursor to a more general debate about the kind of political and social forms relevant to the globalizing age. Taking the debate outside of its geographic confines, Hewison and Rodan (1996) have suggested that the debate points to a global convergence among national elites around particular political positions: defined essentially as liberal and conservative. Thus, one will find exponents of liberalism in Asia, just as one will find exponents of ideas similar to Asian values in the West. In a world still feeling the dominance of security imperatives in state policy after September 11, this notion of convergence is particularly apposite. In the 'war on terror', the West's own commitment to liberalism is now coming into question.

References

Bell, D. A. and Jayasuriya, K. (1995) 'Understanding illiberal democracy', in D. A. Bell, D. Brown, K. Jayasuriya and D. Jones (eds) *Towards Illiberal Democracy in Pacific Asia*, New York: St Martin's Press, pp. 1–16.

Booth, K. (1999) 'Three tyrannies', in T. Dunne and N. J. Wheeler (eds) *Human Rights in Global Politics*, New York: Cambridge University Press, pp. 31–70.

Callahan, W. (1996) 'Rescripting East/West relations, rethinking Asian democracy', *Pacifica Review*, 8: 1–25.

Christie, K. and Denny, R. (2001) *Politics of Human Rights in East Asia*, London: Pluto Press.

Dalai Lama, His Holiness the (1999) 'Buddhism, Asian values, and democracy', *Journal of Democracy*, 10: 3–7.

Dallmayr, F. (2002) 'Asian values and global human rights', *Philosophy East and West*, 52: 173–89.

Donnelly, J. (1999) 'The social construction of human rights', in T. Dunne and N. J. Wheeler (eds) *Human Rights in Global Politics*, New York: Cambridge University Press, pp. 71–102.

Dunne, T. and Wheeler, N. J. (1999) 'Introduction: human rights and the fifty years' crisis', in T. Dunne and N. J. Wheeler (eds) *Human Rights in Global Politics*, New York: Cambridge University Press, pp. 1–28.

Dunne, T., Hill, C. and Hanson, M. (2001) 'The new humanitarian interventionism', in M. Hanson and W. T. Tow (eds) *International Relations in the New Century: An Australian Perspective*, South Melbourne: Oxford University Press, pp. 93–116.

Eldridge, P. J. (2002) *The Politics of Human Rights in Southeast Asia*, London: Routledge.

Fukuyama, F. (1992) *The End of History and the Last Man*, New York: The Free Press.

Hewison, K. and Rodan, G. (1996) 'A "clash of cultures" or the convergence of political ideology?', in R. Robison (ed.) *Pathways to Asia*, St Leonards: Allen & Unwin, pp. 29–55.

Huntington, S. (1993) 'The clash of civilisations', *Foreign Affairs*, 72: 22–49.

Hurrell, A. (1999) 'Power principles and prudence: protecting human rights in a deeply divided world', in T. Dunne and N. J. Wheeler (eds) *Human Rights in Global Politics*, New York: Cambridge University Press, pp. 277–302.

Jacobsen, M. and Bruun, O. (2000) *Human Rights and Asian Values: Contesting National Identities and Cultural Representations in Asia*, Richmond: Curzon.

Kahn, J. (1997) 'Malaysian modern or anti-anti-Asian values', *Thesis Eleven*, 50: 15–34.

Kausikan, B. (1998) 'The Asian values debate', in L. Diamond and M. Plattner (eds) *Democracy in East Asia*, Baltimore, MD: Johns Hopkins University Press, pp. 17–27.

Kim Dae-jung (1994) 'Is culture destiny?', *Foreign Affairs*, 73: 189–94.

Mahathir Mohamad (1995) 'Western modernism vs. Eastern thought', in M. Mohamad and S. Ishihara (eds) *The Voice of Asia*, Tokyo: Kodansha International. (Paper to be presented at the ECPR Joint Sessions of Workshops.)

Mahathir Mohamad (1996a) 'Speech' presented at the 29th International General Meeting of the Pacific Basin Council, 21 May. Online. Available HTTP: <http://www.smpke.jpm.my/gn-data/ucapan.pm/1996/960521.htm> (accessed 12 February 2000).

Mahathir Mohamad (1996b) 'Speech' presented at the Third Pacific Dialogue, Hotel Istana, Kuala Lumpur, 21 November. Online. Available HTTP: <http://www.smpke.jpm.my/gn-data/ucapan.pm/1996/961121.htm> (accessed 12 February 2000).

Robinson, W. (1996) *Promoting Polyarchy: Globalization, US Intervention, and Hegemony*, Cambridge: Cambridge University Press.

Robison, R. (1996) 'The politics of "Asian values" ', *The Pacific Review*, 9: 309–27.

Said, E. W. (1978) *Orientalism*, London: Routledge & Kegan Paul.

Thompson, M. R. (1999) 'Asian values as Zivilisationskritik?', paper presented at Workshop No. 4: Conservative Politics and the Nature of Consensus in the 1990s, Mannheim, 26–31 March.

Wright-Neville, D. (1995) 'The politics of pan Asianism: culture, capitalism and diplomacy in East Asia', *Pacifica Review*, 7: 1–26.

Zakaria, F. (1994) 'Culture is destiny: a conversation with Lee Kuan Yew', *Foreign Affairs*, 73: 109–26.

Index